National Socialism and German Discourse

W J Dodd

National Socialism and German Discourse

Unquiet Voices

palgrave
macmillan

W J Dodd
Department of Modern Languages
University of Birmingham
Birmingham, UK

ISBN 978-3-319-74659-3 ISBN 978-3-319-74660-9 (eBook)
https://doi.org/10.1007/978-3-319-74660-9

Library of Congress Control Number: 2018935569

Cover credit: Walter Zerla/Getty Images

Printed on acid-free paper

This Palgrave Macmillan imprint is published by Springer Nature
The registered company is Springer International Publishing AG
The registered company address is: Gewerbestrasse 11, 6330 Cham, Switzerland

In memory of
Peter von Polenz

Note on the Front Cover Image

The inscription "DEM DEUTSCHEN VOLKE" ("for the German 'Volk'") on the architrave of the REICHSTAG building, was inscribed in 1916 after two decades of debate using the winning font design by Peter Behrens and Anna Simons. The letters were created by melting down two canons captured in the Napoleonic 'War of Liberation' (1813–1815). This work was carried out by the Loevy foundry (a Jewish firm). The font is an Uncial Blackletter (Broken) Bastarda, a modernized Gothic script ('deutsche Schrift') distinguished by rounded letter shapes replacing traditional angular designs. For a fuller account, see Chap. 3.

In 2000, following the relocation of the BUNDESTAG to the refurbished REICHSTAG building, Hans Haacke's art installation "DER BEVÖLKERUNG" ("for the population") was installed in the north inner courtyard. The wording of the inscription, agreed by the Bundestag, takes up Bertolt Brecht's words in 1934: "Wer in unserer Zeit statt *Volk Bevölkerung* und statt *Boden Landbesitz* sagt, unterstützt schon viele Lügen nicht. Er nimmt den Wörtern ihre faule Mystik". ("Whoever in our time says *population* instead of *Volk*, and *land ownership* instead of *soil*, has already ceased to support many lies. He deprives the words of their foul mysticism.") For a fuller account, see Chap. 4.

Preface

This study is intended for a wide range of readers, including those who have little or no expertise in German. English translations are given for German terms and texts. I have incurred many debts in researching and writing it. The first and greatest of these is to my wife Kath for her understanding and support, especially since my 'retirement', when work on the book intensified. The long gestation of the book was made possible by a Leverhulme Trust Major Research Fellowship, grants by the British Academy and the University of Birmingham, and a Senior Fellowship of the Alfried Krupp Wissenschaftskolleg, Greifswald.

I would like to acknowledge a particular debt of gratitude to the late Professor Peter von Polenz, who gave generously of his time to discuss my research and his own life and work. His influence and that of the many other scholars on whose work I have drawn will be evident throughout. As always, any shortcomings are entirely those of the author. I would like to thank Professor Jürgen Schiewe and Professor John Klapper for reading and commenting on the manuscript; and Caroline Cabarth, Professor Günther Gillessen, Sybil Oldfield, Professor Ritchie Robertson and Professor Wolfgang Teubert for reading and commenting on individual chapters. I am indebted to Dr Heidrun Ehrke-Rotermund and Professor Erwin Rotermund for generously sharing their knowledge of the discourses and politics of German 'inner emigration', to the late Professor Klaus Landfried and the Dolf Sternberger Gesellschaft for permission to publish from Sternberger's papers, and to Insel Verlag for permission to reproduce texts by Sternberger. Mr Neal Cobourne, Professor Heidrun Kämper, Dr Dorit Krusche, Professor Matthias Lorenz, Dr Friedrich Pfäfflin, Professor Hartmut Schmidt, Dr Gerd Simon, Professor Edward Timms, Dr Sabine Werner and Dr Tara Windsor have provided invaluable support and suggestions on various aspects of the book. I would like to thank the staff of the Staatsbibliothek in Berlin, the Institut für deutsche Sprache in Mannheim, the University Library in Mannheim, and the Deutsches Literaturarchiv, Marbach am Neckar, for their professionalism in aiding my researches, and the Manuscript Section of the Deutsches Literaturarchiv for permission to quote from an unpublished manuscript of Mechtilde Lichnowsky.

Birmingham, UK W J Dodd

Contents

1 Introduction: Towards a Discourse History of National Socialism 1

2 The Emergence of National Socialist Discourse 13

3 The National Socialist Discourse "Community": Norms and Contradictions 45

4 Voices from Abroad: Thomas Mann, Karl Kraus, Ernst Bloch, Bertolt Brecht, Irmgard Keun, Heinz Paechter 71

5 Voices at Home (I): Private Notes for Posterity 113

6 Voices at Home (II): From Resistance to 'Resistenz' in the Printed Word 155

7 Voices at Home (III): The Case of the *Frankfurter Zeitung* 187

8 Aftermath: Entnazifizierung 227

9 Legacy: Vergangenheitsbewältigung 253

10 Conclusion 291

Appendix 301

Discourse-Relevant Expressions 311

Bibliography 319

Index 339

1

Introduction: Towards a Discourse History of National Socialism

The three focal points of this study are National Socialism, discourse, and language criticism. Language is conceived here as language-in-use, as discourse. From this perspective, 'the German language' is understood not so much in terms of the combinatorial rules of grammar and vocabulary, but rather in terms of the uses to which they are and have been put by German speakers in their social interactions. The 'power of language' is a common axiom in many of the commentaries reviewed in this study, and it is possible to overstate this power. The National Socialists did not acquire and hold on to power solely by means of rhetoric, nor were they defeated by an opposing discourse, but—in both cases—by dint of physical force. But this does not mean that 'language' can be pushed to the margins in a discussion of National Socialism, as "only words". As Michael Townson (1992, p. 135) observes, "the brutalisation through language was a necessary prerequisite for the physical brutality which was to follow" in the 'Third Reich'.

The discourse practices of National Socialism are at the centre of this study, but so, too, are the testimonies of contemporary German speakers who found themselves in a kind of exile from their speech community, even while remaining in Germany. The experiences, observations and

W J Dodd, *National Socialism and German Discourse*,
https://doi.org/10.1007/978-3-319-74660-9_1

commentaries of these 'unquiet voices', the mental and linguistic resilience of their private and public counter-discourses, occupy the central chapters of this study. Finally, building on the strengths but also on the shortcomings of these first critics of 'Nazi language', this book traces the development of a peculiarly German academic tradition of political discourse analysis, informed as perhaps in no other country by the urgent need to understand a nation's shame by asking how National Socialism could acquire not just political power but the active or passive support of millions of Germans.

Discourse and Discourse History

There are many definitions of discourse, perhaps the most influential in the socio-political field being those centred on the works of Michel Foucault, Pierre Bourdieu, and Antonio Gramsci. All of these are relevant in various ways to the present study, but they will not be explicitly referenced. Instead, a very basic linguistic model of discourse is adopted, as a kind of social conversation about a given topic—sport, food, the weather; gender, ethnicity, the nation. Discourses (fundamentally in the plural) can merge and overlap: a discourse on the state of the language can feed into and be part of a larger discourse on national identity, which can in turn feed into a discourse on ethnicity and migration, or into a discourse on empire. On one view, discourses 'transport' knowledge; on another, they actually create and validate what members of the discourse community regard as knowledge, and truth. Discourses have a historical as well as a synchronic dimension, indeed the power of a discourse at a given point in time may be difficult to understand without appreciating the historical impetus of the discourse traditions—grand narratives—on which it draws in shaping and maintaining a system of attitudes, beliefs and values—an ideology. Such discourses thrive on metaphor and stereotypes, shape and confirm identity by creating in- and out-groups, function as affective (emotional) as well as intellectual rallying points and recruiting sergeants and, perhaps most crucially, are fluid and constantly evolving.

The diverse theoretical orientations and practical applications of discourse studies are reflected in recent collections of essays (e.g. Wetherell et al. 2001; Angermuller et al. 2014). The concept of discourse and the principles of analysis and commentary underlying the present study are broadly those set out in the "Bozen Manifesto" (Lanthaler et al. 2003), the main points of which are encapsulated in the following statement by Jürgen Schiewe and Martin Wengeler:

> Sprachkritik ist streng genommen nur als Sprachgebrauchskritik, Wortkritik nur als Wortgebrauchskritik möglich. Es sind die Kontexte, die über die Bedeutung von Wörtern entscheiden, es sind die Diskurse, in denen Wörter ihre semantische Prägung erhalten. | In sprachlichen Diskursen, in der Ordnung der Zeichen und Texte, eignen wir uns psychisch Wirklichkeit an. Eine Kritik der Diskurse, innerhalb derer die Kritik des Wortgebrauchs einen wichtigen Teil ausmacht, vermag aufzuzeigen, dass wir die Wirklichkeit prinzipiell auch anders sehen, erfassen, kategorisieren können. Der Sprachkritik geht es letztlich um die Frage, welche Sicht der Wirklichkeit von wem aus welchen Gründen konstituiert worden ist. (Schiewe and Wengeler 2005, p. 7)

> Language criticism, strictly speaking, is possible only as criticism of the use of language, lexical criticism only as the criticism of the use of words. It is the contexts which decide the meaning of a word, it is in discourses that words receive their semantic imprint. | In linguistic discourses, in the arrangement of signs and texts, we acquire reality psychologically. A critique of the discourses, within which the critique of word use plays an important part, has the ability to reveal that in principle we are capable of seeing, comprehending and categorizing reality differently. | Language criticism is in the final analysis concerned with the question of what view of reality has been constructed, by whom, and for what purposes.

Language-as-discourse, then, implies the study of the *use* of language (*parole*) as opposed to the language system (*langue*) as traditionally codified in dictionaries and grammars. This is not to deny the influence of the language system on the way speakers conceptualize the world. Syntax and semantics, for example, already provide cognitive frameworks within which 'reality' is organized, in the latter case by establishing an inventory of lexicalized concepts. Nevertheless, it is discourse which is held to be ultimately constitutive of our psychological reality: linguistic meaning is fully unfolded not at the level of the word (lexical semantics), or the clause or sentence, or the paragraph, or even the complete text, but at the level of discourse. Schiewe and Wengeler argue that 'Sprachkritik' in the sense of a description of or commentary on discourse should not itself seek to be normative, but to uncover the often conflicting norms encapsulated in particular discourse practices and make them available for rational discussion. This view of 'Sprachkritik' emphasizes its role as an arbitrator in language disputes, and as a potential corrective to the power of hegemonic discourses. A slightly different stance is taken by Teubert (2014, pp. 108, 113), who has argued that whilst traditional 'Sprachkritik' has the potential to contribute to the ideal of a "deliberative democracy" of discursively empowered citizens, it also operates within the discourse community it addresses, and like all such contributions to the discourse, seeks to present a particular view of reality and normality, typically in opposition to powerful established discourses.

As Schiewe and Wengeler point out, a critique of individual lexical items (phrases as well as words) can play an important role in the study of discourse. The present study follows the majority of language commentators reviewed in this book in seeking to access discourses through their keywords. It is not, however, a lexicographical study and makes no claims to be encyclopaedic. More comprehensive lists and categorizations of words and expressions associated with the 'language of Nazism' can be found, for example, in Keller (1978, pp. 603–607, 609–621), Wells (1985, pp. 407–420), the Wikipedia "Glossary of Nazi Germany", and in Brackmann and Birkenhauer (1988). The concept of the keyword adopted here is much broader than that of the (high) cultural keyword analyzed by Raymond Williams (1983). It extends to everyday expressions which have the force of the 'Schlagwort' (literally, 'hit word'), for which the closest English equivalent is the slogan. One of the most trenchant observations on the 'Schlagwort' was given by Karl Jaspers in *Von der Wahrheit* (1947, On Truth), a work conceived in inner exile from National Socialism, when Jaspers and his Jewish wife narrowly avoided 'deportation' to a death camp:

> Worte sind allzu leicht Schlagworte. Wenn ich an Worten hafte, so verlasse ich die Bewegung aus der Offenheit für Bedeutungen und gebe das eigene Wesen preis an eine versimpelnde Starrheit. | So können Worte relativ gleichgültig werden vermöge des Zusammenhangs der Sätze, in denen im Ganzen erst der Sinn aufleuchtet. Andererseits können Worte hinreißen als diese Worte. | Dann werden Worte zu etwas wie Fahne und Symbol. Die Worte sind es, auf die schon ohne Satz der Mensch mit seiner ganzen Leidenschaft reagiert, in ihnen Wahrheit und Falschheit wie weiß und schwarz unterschieden sieht. (Jaspers 1947, p. 409)

> Words all too readily become slogans. When I attach myself to such words I take leave of the possibilities inherent in an openness for meanings und betray my own being to a simplifying rigidity. | Words can be relatively imprecise in meaning due to the context of sentences in which the meaning first lights up as a whole. But in the other case, words as single words can infatuate. | Then words become something like a flag and a symbol. It is to such words that a person reacts with their utmost passion even before they are put in a sentence, seeing truth and falsehood distinguished in them as clear as black and white.

German linguists have developed a range of terms for the ideologically-primed 'Schlagwort' depending on its pragmatic use in a battle for and with words (Klein 1989), some of which are referenced in this study: the 'Fahnenwort' (banner word) acts as a rallying point for supporters, the 'Stigmawort' (stigma word) attacks the integrity of opponents' keywords, the 'Hochwertwort' (prestige word) proclaims a shared value of high importance to the believers, the 'Schimpfwort' (cuss word) and 'Schmähwort' (smear word) hurl insults and slurs. In these metaphors of battle we see the traditional approach to meaning as (lexical) semantics translated into a model of language-in-action, pragmatics. 'Pragmatized' semantics, a theme in the academic debate on language since the 1960s, is the logical correlative of seeing language in socio-pragmatic terms, as discourse. The popularly understood concept of (positive and negative) connotation is clearly relevant here, and it is only a short step from connotation to contestation—the need to define, claim, or defend one's territory against alternative value systems—as the essence of political and ideological discourse. The existence of contestation in a discourse community might be taken as evidence of democratic health, its absence as evidence either of a utopia or of a fully realized regime of terror. Even in Nazi Germany, battles for and with words were not completely suppressed.

The first task of a discourse analysis is to identify the discourse by describing its defining features. Only then does it become available for discussion. This is no simple task, however, since there is no one-to-one relationship between discourses on the one hand, and individual lexical items and texts on the other. A single text can contain features of several and disparate discourses on a topic, indeed this kind of textual hybridity is key to the texts discussed in Chaps. 6 and 7. Conversely, individual lexical expressions are not necessarily the exclusive 'property' of a particular discourse, indeed the same word can acquire very different meanings in different discourses: in National Socialist discourse 'Volk' encapsulates a biological view of nationhood, in Marxist discourse a class-based vision of society. This last example is an illustration of the not uncommon phenomenon of ideological polysemy (Dieckmann 1969, pp. 70–75; Klein 1989).

Discourses are constructed using the linguistic resources of the 'rule-governed' language system (lexis, grammar) and conventions of style (the free choices of speakers to deploy lexis and grammar in an individualized way). Visual and aural factors may also play a role: the conventions of use of 'Gothic' and 'Roman' typefaces in printed texts; the vocal range and tone of the spoken address. As systems of 'knowledge' and 'truth', discourses are also characterized by argumentation strategies used to validate their 'truths', often by seeking to invalidate counter-discourses. In the present study, for example, we find the 'double indemnity' logic of apparently contradictory positions being held to be true, so that the negation of one serves to validate the other ("the 'Aryans' are the natural master-race, but their supremacy is threatened by 'inferior' peoples"). We also find examples of coercive persuasion ("if you said/did/believe A, you have to say/do/believe B"), and of trivializing arguments designed to disarm criticism, as in the 'toothbrush fallacy' encountered in Chap. 9 ("the Nazis used toothbrushes but no one is suggesting that we should ban toothbrushes today"). Such argumentation strategies, patently illogical to outsiders, play an important role in bolstering the emotional and intellectual solidarity of those who subscribe to the value system.

A discourse history has the advantage that it presents words, phrases, and other linguistic items in a dynamic, socio-pragmatic framework, displaying the different ideological networks defining their respective definitions. Amongst the potential disadvantages is the problem of evidence and representativeness. Outside of specific instances of use, the problem lies in generalizing statements about how typical the identified phenomena are or were of a more general usage. To some extent, this can be addressed by modern techniques in corpus linguistics which allow the researcher to study the first appearance, frequency, and collocational environment of lexical items in large digitized text collections. To this end readers with a knowledge of German are recommended to conduct their own explorations in the on-line resource of the Digitales Wörterbuch der deutschen Sprache (dwds.de), and especially the chronological corpus of the Twentieth Century ('Kerncorpus 20'), which is referenced at various points in this study. A related issue is the tension between the general and the particular: a history of discourses can appear as a kind of aggregated abstraction in which individual speaking subjects are marginalized in favour of a generalized characterization of language use. The present study attempts to redress this imbalance by focusing on particular historical subjects, notably the 'unquiet voices' of those rejecting Nazism.

'Unquiet Voices' and Exile

The 'Third Reich' offers a particularly instructive case study of a near-monopolized ('hegemonic') public discourse under dictatorship, and of linguistic and other modes of response to hegemony. The regime's attempts to manage public discourse have their corollary in the language critiques of its beleaguered opponents reviewed in this study—a form of mental opposition, if not of active resistance. These commentaries on 'Nazi language' are grouped in three broad categories reflecting the different circumstances of text production and propagation under the Nazi dictatorship: (a) territorial exile; and inner exile in its (b) private and (c) public manifestations. The existential situations reflected in these categories importantly shape what is experienced, what can be said, and how it can be said. For the categories of inner exile, in particular, the limits of the (safely) sayable are an ever-present consideration.

The concept of inner exile, particularly important in the middle sections of this study, needs some introductory explanation at this point. An instructive text on the existential situation of inner exile is Bertolt Brecht's

"Maßnahmen gegen die Gewalt" (1932, Measures against violence, *Werke*, Bd. 18, p. 13f.), in the figure of Herr Egge, who in his own apartment is made to be the servant of the agent of 'Gewalt' (power, violence). Although Herr Egge serves his powerful master as he is told to, he repeatedly answers the agent's question "Will you serve me?" with silence before finally, after the agent's death, removing his body and uttering the single word "No". The story of Herr Egge is told by another of Brecht's figures, Herr Keuner, to explain his own apparent hypocrisy when confronted by deadly power. In a sense, Brecht's parable captures the extreme point at which, to paraphrase Erving Goffman, it is not a matter of human beings and the situations they create, but of situations and the human beings they create (cf. Goffman 2005, p. 3). Acknowledging Goffman's point about the ethnography of speaking highlights a radical feature of the German discourse community under Nazism, but as Gerhard Bauer (1988, p. 13) observes, it does not absolve individuals of responsibility for their linguistic and non-linguistic actions in such a situation. Nevertheless, the moral ambiguities of such a situation will be apparent, and have understandably dogged the reception of 'inner emigrant' discourse on Nazism in post-1945 Germany. Like Herr Egge, some of the 'unquiet voices' in inner exile discussed in the present study had little choice but to withhold their public "No" until the dictatorship fell. Others went further than Herr Egge and Herr Keuner, venturing into the public arena, subjecting their discourse to the constraints of hegemony whilst probing the limits of the sayable. One of the themes of this book is the perhaps surprising amount of coded public dissent in German print media during the 'Third Reich' and the picture of the National Socialist discourse community as a battlefield ("Kampfplatz") on which, as Bauer (1988, p. 10) observes, "battles were fought with grossly unequal and frequently changing methods, but unceasingly" ("mit äußerst ungleichen, vielfach wechselnden Mitteln, aber unaufhörlich gekämpft wurde").

Overview

The book begins by reviewing the ensemble of precursor discourses on nationhood, language and culture, ethnicity, and empire in the long nineteenth century from which the ideology of National Socialism emerged after the First World War (Chap. 2). Chapter 3 describes life in the 'co-ordinated' discourse environment of the 'Third Reich' from the perspective of Germans who felt alienated from it. This chapter outlines the 'new normality' imposed by the now near-hegemonic discourse of National Socialism, but also its paradoxes and contradictions. The next four chapters introduce some of the 'unquiet voices' articulating opposition to National Socialism from abroad (Chap. 4) and from positions of inner exile within the 'Reich', in unpublished (Chap. 5) and published critiques of language (Chaps. 6 and 7, the latter devoted to the discourse on language in the *Frankfurter Zeitung* between 1933 and 1943). Chapter 8 reviews the debates on (the language of) National Socialism and 'Nazi language' between 1945 and 1949 under the auspices of a "denazification of the language" sponsored by the Allies and supported by many of these 'unquiet voices'. Chapter 9 reviews the continuing legacy of these debates in two phases, from 1949 to 1989, and in the unified Federal Republic from 1990 to the present day. The retrospective discourse on National Socialism and language reviewed in Chaps. 8 and 9 is characterized by contestations of 'tainted' language, opportunistic instrumentalizations of Nazi comparisons for political advantage, and intense academic debate, particularly in West Germany, surrounding the notion of a 'Nazi language' and the principles for a rigorous analysis of Nazism and its linguistic manifestations. Chapter 9 also briefly considers the question of taboos in contemporary usage which are traceable to the legacy of Nazism, and the discourse practices of resurgent nationalist politics in the unified Germany. A brief Conclusion draws together the main strands of this discourse history as a historical, a retrospective, but also a continuing discourse with contemporary relevance, identifying the principal features of a linguistically informed political language criticism and reflecting on the relevance of these findings for present and future engagement with political discourses. The book is completed by an appendix of texts and text extracts (identified by an asterisk in the body of the book), and an alphabetical index of discourse-relevant expressions identified in the course of this study. Unless otherwise indicated, all translations into English are my own.

A Note on Terms and Typographical Conventions

German terms commonly used in English (such as Reich, Führer, Wehrmacht, Bundestag, Reichstag, Wirtschaftswunder) are not marked in the running text. SMALL CAPITALS indicate that an expression is being viewed as a constituent element of the discourse under investigation. Often, this reflects the analyses of commentators discussed in this study, but in some cases it reflects my own judgment, which of course is open to question. English renditions of expressions relevant to the German discourse are generally enclosed in brackets without further marking. Italics are used for book titles, to indicate emphasis either in an original quotation or added by a commentator, and for expressions derived from a third language, such as *langue*, *parole*, *ad hominem*. Double quotation marks are used for essay titles and for direct quotation of passages or individual expressions extracted from a cited text. Single quotation marks are used (a) to indicate authorial distance from the implications of an expression, as in 'Third Reich' (a legal entity in its time, but with dubious deeper meanings and implications); (b) to render German terms (such as 'Entnazifizierung' (denazification)) which may not be familiar to most speakers of English; (c) to render certain German concepts which play a key role in the discussion and are difficult to translate and cumbersome to paraphrase. The following in particular should be noted:

'Fremdwort': The 'foreign word' is a long-established concept in popular and academic descriptions of German lexical borrowing from other languages. Its coherence and relevance as a descriptive category is increasingly questioned in academic linguistic discourse today.

'Gleichschaltung'/'gleichgeschaltet': The German term, often translated as 'co-ordination'/'co-ordinated', is a metaphor derived from the mechanical switch-gear. By throwing the switch, different sources of energy are made to flow in the same direction.

'Imitat': The German term denotes a text or expression used in ironic imitation of a text or expression belonging to the criticized discourse.

'Resistenz'/'resistent': In German medical discourse, the term (stressed on the final syllable) denotes the body's immunity from/ resistance to/rejection of infection. As a political metaphor, it denotes forms of immunity from, and rejection of, Nazi values in linguistic and non-linguistic behaviour short of overt political resistance ('Widerstand'). The distinction between resistance and 'Resistenz' is central to this study.

'sprachlos'/'Sprachlosigkeit': The political metaphor of being 'speechless' means 'being without a voice'. On rare occasions this may include literally not speaking, but usually the situation so described is one in which there are social constraints on what a speaker can say and how s/he can speak (cf. Bauer 1988).

'Unmensch': Often translated as 'monster', this term designates a real or imagined person embodying the polar opposite of the qualities encapsulated in the term 'Mensch' (human being) and its derivations 'menschlich' (human/humane) and 'Menschlichkeit' (humaneness). The contrast here is between human beings and animals.

'Volk': The word carries a wide range of meanings, including the connotationally neutral 'nation' or 'people', and the socialist/Marxist sense of 'working class'. In National Socialist discourse, however, the term carries biological racial inflections.

'völkisch': carries an endorsement of the concept of the racially superior 'Aryan' 'Volk' which is not captured in the English 'folkic'.

'volkhaft': Strictly much closer to 'folkic' in designating attributes of folk or national culture in a non-evaluative way, this word also begins to acquire some of the evaluative meanings of 'völkisch' in the period of Nazi hegemony.

Finally, it should be noted that the word race should ideally be marked as 'race' or RACE throughout as a reminder that it designates a socially constructed, not a scientific concept. The National Socialist discourse on VOLK is predicated on RACE.

Bibliography

Angermuller, Johannes, Dominique Maingueneau, and Ruth Wodak, eds. 2014. *The Discourse Studies Reader. Main Currents in Theory and Analysis*. Amsterdam: John Benjamins.

Bauer, Gerhard. 1988. *Sprache und Sprachlosigkeit im "Dritten Reich"*. Köln: Bund-Verlag.

Brackmann, Karl-Heinz, and Renate Birkenhauer. 1988. *Nazi-Deutsch. "Selbstverständliche" Begriffe und Schlagwörter aus der Zeit des Nationalsozialismus*. Straelen: Straelener Manuskripte Verlag.

Dieckmann, Walther. 1969. *Sprache in der Politik. Einführung in die Pragmatik und Semantik der politischen Sprache*. Heidelberg: Carl Winter.

Goffman, Erving. 2005. *Interaction Ritual: Essays in Face to Face Behavior*. With a New Introduction by Joel Best. New Brunswick, London: Albine Transactions.

Jaspers, Karl. 1947. *Von der Wahrheit (Philosophische Logik, erster Band)*. Verlag, München: R. Piper & Co.

Keller, R.E. 1978. *The German Language*. London: Faber.

Klein, Josef. 1989. Wortschatz, Wortkampf, Wortfelder. In *Politische Semantik. Beiträge zur politischen Sprachverwendung*, Hg. J. Klein, 3–50. Opladen: Westdeutscher Verlag.

Lanthaler, Franz, Hanspeter Ortner, Jürgen Schiewe, Richard Schrodt, and Horst Sitta. 2003. Was ist der Gegenstand der Sprachbetrachtung?. *Sprachreport* 2/2003, Mannheim: Institut für Deutsche Sprache, 2–5. ("Bozener Manifest").

Schiewe, Jürgen, and Martin Wengeler. 2005. Einführung der Herausgeber zum ersten Heft. *Aptum. Zeitschrift für Sprachkritik und Sprachkultur* 01 (05): 1–13.

Teubert, Wolfgang. 2014. Die Bedeutung von Sprachkritik für die Demokratie. *Aptum. Zeitschrift für Sprachkritik und Sprachkultur* 02 (14): 98–114.

Townson, Michael. 1992. *Mother-Tongue and Fatherland: Language and Politics in German*. Manchester: Manchester University Press.

Wells, C.J. 1985. *German: A Linguistic History to 1945*. Oxford: Clarendon.

Wetherell, Margaret, Stephanie Taylor, and Simeon J. Yates, eds. 2001. *Discourse Theory and Practice. A Reader*. London, Thousand Oaks, New Delhi: Sage.

Williams, Raymond. 1983. *Keywords. A Vocabulary of Culture and Society*. Rev. ed. London: Fontana.

2

The Emergence of National Socialist Discourse

Whilst the year 1933 marks a clear caesura in German political history, the same cannot be said in relation to German discourse history.[1] The discourse practices of National Socialism, a fringe political faction in the German polity of the 1920s, were an amalgam of historical discourses which had gained currency in the long nineteenth century, were reinvigorated in 1914, and intensified after the defeat of 1918. Peter von Polenz describes an intensification of these precursor political discourses after the birth of the German nation state:

> Bald nach der Reichsgründung von 1871 radikalisierte sich politischer Sprachgebrauch in Deutschland und Österreich in verschiedenen konservativen und nationalistischen Gruppen zum Nationalchauvinismus, Imperialismus und Antisemitismus. Dadurch wurde die Entwicklung der Rede- und Schreibweisen der politischen Intoleranz, Menschenverfolgung und Kriegsbegeisterung, über den Ersten Weltkrieg und die Weimarer Zeit bis zur nationalsozialistischen Diktatur, zum Zweiten Weltkrieg und zum Holocaust, zu einem historischen Kontinuum. (von Polenz 1999, p. 523)

> Soon after the founding of the Reich in 1871, political language use became radicalized in Germany and Austria in various nationalist and conservative groups towards national chauvinism, imperialism, and anti-semitism. As a

W J Dodd, *National Socialism and German Discourse*,
https://doi.org/10.1007/978-3-319-74660-9_2

> result, the modes of expression, in speech and writing, of political intolerance, persecution, and enthusiasm for war formed a historical continuum through the First World War and the Weimar period into the National Socialist dictatorship, the Second World War, and the Holocaust.

The Weimar Republic would carry the blame for humiliated national pride, focused on the terms of the Treaty of Versailles, which fed a revanchist 'Conservative Revolution' against the 'un-German' constitutional parliamentary democracy of Weimar and the narrative of German guilt (and military defeat). These right-wing narratives of Germanness fed on discourses on nationhood, race (specifically the 'Jewish question') and culture which had antecedents in seventeenth-, eighteenth-, and especially early nineteenth-century debates on language, culture, and identity. With the founding of a German nation state in 1871 by dint of (Prussian) militarism, a discourse on empire was added to this ensemble, its main components being the assertion of German commercial and military prowess in competition with France and Britain.

Von Polenz makes an important three-way distinction between the language *of* National Socialism, language *in* National Socialism, and language *leading to* National Socialism ("zum Nationalsozialismus hin", von Polenz 1999, p. 547), and has written a compelling contribution to this last category.[2] From the time of the French occupation of German territories in the early 1800s, extreme anti-French sentiments are found in major writers and thinkers like Kleist and Fichte, whose "An die teutsche Nation", a key tract on language, nationhood and race, was delivered in French-occupied Berlin in 1808. Tellingly, a disproportionately large place is occupied in this discourse history by minor propagandists like Ernst Moritz ("Vater") Arndt (1769–1860) and Friedrich Ludwig ("Turnvater", Father of Gymnastics) Jahn (1778–1852), "marginal men" (Berger 2004, p. 13) who would be commemorated into the twentieth century in the nationalistic pantheon. Jahn was the founder of paramilitary nationalistic gymnastics in the cause of building 'national character', an influential figure in the development of patriotic student fraternities ('Burschenschaften'), and an anti-Semite. His belligerent nationalism and anti-Jewish sentiment converged in a metaphysics of generalized hatred for and denigration of other nations and races: THE (generic)

French, Danes, Slavs, and Jews, as 'Germanness' was elevated to an ersatz religion, often supported by explicit or implicit reference to Tacitus's account of the allegedly autochthonous (ethnically intact) ancient German tribes. HUMANITÄT and KOSMOPOLITISMUS, VERNUNFT (reason) and MENSCHHEIT, the ideals of a tolerant 'Kulturnation' and of Weimar Classicism, were rejected as if they were forms of treason, and often ascribed to Jews ("jener allweltliche Judensinn", cf. Schulz 1983, p. 3).[3]

These negatively-inflected 'cosmopolitan' values were opposed by positively-inflected terms of the new religion: NATION, VOLKSTUM, DEUTSCHHEIT. Napoleon's defeat was celebrated in pseudo-religious terms as the AUFERSTEHUNG (resurrection) of a German VOLKSGEIST (national spirit) and its HEILIGE LANDMARKEN (holy marches[4])—the antiquated geographical and topographical vocabulary making an emotional appeal to a past which was still 'authentically' German. The keywords DEUTSCH and VOLK, however, were not yet bound to right-wing politics or the notion of a nation state. Indeed, von Fallersleben's anthemic "Deutschlandlied" ("Deutschland, Deutschland über alles"), with its appeals to FREIHEIT and BRÜDERLICHKEIT (fraternity), was a rallying cry of the (quickly emasculated) revolutionary movement of 1848/1849 for a 'Nationalversammlung' (National Assembly) in Frankfurt to restrain the power of regional monarchs, princes and dukes. The 'Restauration' period from 1815 to 1848 was marked by political repression, censorship, and, in Austria, by Metternich's secret police state. The nation state founded in 1871 promoted a 'conservative turn' which would later undermine the Weimar Republic. Under Bismarck's chancellorship a defining mood of aggressive nationalism ("Abwehr-Nationalismus", von Polenz 1999, p. 538) variously identified cosmopolitan liberals, socialists, Catholics, Jews, and neighbouring populations in disputed territories such as Alsace as REICHSFEINDE who were also typically described as VATERLANDSLOS, unpatriotic 'citizens of nowhere'. A conservative critique of civilization often went hand in hand with these concepts, in reaction to the effects of industrialization, mass urbanization, and political organization of labour, but also spawning a racialized discourse, frequently using verbs with the prefix ENT- calling for the 'removal' of populations and cultures (ENTPOLONISIEREN, 'de-polonize'), of 'inferior' FREMDVÖLKISCH nations such as the 'flood' or 'hordes' of Slavs (SLAWISCHE FLUT, RUSSISCHE

HORDEN) who needed to be 'removed' from 'German' territories (von Polenz 1999, p. 28). Against these enemies within and without, a binary network of evaluative concepts set 'authentic' DEUTSCHES WESEN (German being) against 'decadent' (ENTARTET) Enlightenment values: GEMEINSCHAFT (community (+)) against GESELLSCHAFT (society (−)), GERMANENTUM (+) against BOURGEOISIE (−), BLUT (+) against GEIST (intellect (−)), INSTINKT (+) against VERNUNFT (reason (−)), (DEUTSCHE) KULTUR (+) against ZIVILISATION (−). The Wilhelmine era also echoed Napoleonic nationalism in its BÜNDISCH youth associations and paramilitary outdoor sport and athletics clubs in the spirit of "Vater Jahn", with Jahn's FÜHRER: GEFOLGSCHAFT (follower) hierarchy, code of TREUE (loyalty) and GEHORSAM (obedience) and antiquated 'authentic' German vocabulary: THING (meeting place), GAU (district), SCHAR (troupe, company) (von Polenz 1999, pp. 467–469). To some extent this BÜNDISCH tradition lent itself to adoption by National Socialism.

The intensified anti-Jewish discourse in the new Reich, a consequence of the emancipation of Jews from their geographical and societal ghettos in the middle of the nineteenth century, readily fell back on ancient narratives of Jews as exploiters and traitors.[5] Like other 'STAATSFEINDE', but with much greater intensity, Jews were the object of a concerted biologized discourse which pre-dated Darwin but gathered momentum with the popular 'social' reception of Darwin's theories, especially the notion of a "struggle for existence" (KAMPF UMS DASEIN) between and within species. In this discourse environment, biological metaphors inevitably imply sanctioned violence, in 'justified self defence', towards human PARASITEN, KREBS (cancer), BAZILLEN, POLYPEN, SCHÄDLINGE (destructive pests), UNGEZIEFER (vermin) who were sucking the life out of (AUSSAUGEN) the German 'body politic' (VOLKSKÖRPER), for the 'health' of which they must be expelled (AUSSCHEIDEN)[6] or exterminated (the verbs used here include VERNICHTEN, AUSMERZEN, AUSROTTEN). Some particularly extreme contributions to this discourse are to be found in the writings of the political philosopher Eugen Dühring (1833–1921)[7]: VERTILGEN (eradicate), DESINFEKTION, ENDGÜLTIG LÖSEN (finally resolve [the 'Jewish question']—a precursor of the infamous ENDLÖSUNG (final solution) of the Wannsee conference in 1942)—and GIFT WIE GIFT BEHANDELN (treat poison as poison), an example of a murderous metaphor waiting to be 'realized'.

Alongside the trope of the outcast 'Wandering Jew' responsible for the murder of Christ (EWIGER JUDE, NOMADE, MÖRDER JESU) and the medieval trope of the usurer (WUCHERER, SCHACHER, supplemented by the modern term PLUTOKRAT), assimilating Jews were marked in terms of their professions (BÜCHER-, HANDELS-, ZEITUNGSJUDE) and confessions (GETAUFTER (baptized) JUDE, REFORMJUDE). The family names which most Jews had been obliged to take on as part of their assimilation (e.g. COHN, ITZIG, and names ending in -STEIN, -HEIM, -BERG, -ELES[8]) also marked them out—*nomen est omen*—from 'authentic' Germans. Whilst the most prominent anti-semitic publicist of the mid-century, Arthur de Gobineau (1816–1882), was French, the discursive outcasting of Jews can be found in leading German artists and thinkers, for example in Richard Wagner's "Das Judenthum in der Musik" (1850) and by historian Heinrich von Treitschke (1834–1896), who popularized the slogan DIE JUDEN SIND UNSER UNGLÜCK (The Jews are our misfortune), destined to be printed on the front page of Julius Streicher's *Der Stürmer* between 1923 and 1945. The most infamous exemplar of the narrative of a Jewish conspiracy to take over gentile nations, the fabricated *Protocols of the Elders of Zion*, originated in Russia in 1903 but played a prominent part in Nazi anti-Jewish propaganda in the 1920s and 1930s, and is referenced in *Mein Kampf* (Hitler 1934, p. 337). The narrative of Jewish 'defilement' of DEUTSCHES BLUT (itself perhaps a variant on medieval horror stories of Jewish blood lust for Christian children) merged easily with turn-of-the-century discourses and political programmes for 'racial hygiene', epitomized in the narrative of the VOLK being reduced to a 'bastardized' VOLKSBREI (racial soup).[9] The term ARIER (Aryan, from the Sanskrit *àrya*: 'noble'), the superordinate concept in this pseudo-scientific discourse on 'race', had entered political discourse in mid-century via the work of comparative (historical) linguists, denoting the 'Indo-Germanic' language family, thought to be traceable to an 'Ursprache' in the Indus Valley. In the discourse of (European, white) racial theorists, it quickly came to denote the allegedly superior (quintessentially Germanic and Nordic) white peoples and cultures of Northern Europe. The power of this concept was so great that in 1933 it provided the unquestioned basis for the ARIERPARAGRAPH, which legislated for the 'Aryanization' of Jewish businesses, property, and of German professional and public life.[10]

It needs to be stressed that, as von Polenz implies, this account is a retrospective and partial reconstruction of political discourse history, shaped by historical hindsight. Many aspects of German discourse history—for example the discursive legacies of Christianity, the Enlightenment, the rise of Socialism and Marxism, the discourses on education and gender, the use of biological metaphors and racial stereotypes in left-wing discourses—are pushed to the margin, or omitted.[11] The compressed account offered above should not be taken in support of the teleological fallacy that Hitler was inevitable or that, in Daniel Goldhagen's thesis, most Germans possessed an "eliminationist mind-set" (Goldhagen 1996, p. 69). A more nuanced analysis is offered by Ritchie Robertson in his study of Jewish emancipation "and its discontents" from the middle of the eighteenth century. Robertson (1999, p. 184f.) points out, for example, that techniques of discursive 'othering' remain largely constant while their targets change: "Herder associated language and creativity; Fichte maintained that the French were debarred from creativity by their superficial language; and Wagner transferred this stigma to the Jews". Anti-semitism was actually not the defining feature of German life before 1933, Robertson finds, it tended rather to be "part, and not necessarily a prominent part, of a wider world-view" or "cultural code", in Shulamit Volkov's phrase, which bundled together diverse fears about the direction and pace of change in an accelerating modernity.[12] Robertson (1999, p. 182) also points out the existence of "a succession of overlapping varieties of anti-semitism: völkisch, racial, and cultural anti-semitism. When one variety becomes untenable, another, more immune to disproof, takes its place". Similarly, one can perhaps identify three main types of political action against Jews: (social) exclusion, (territorial) deportation, and (physical) elimination. These also overlap discursively in a graduated continuum of violence. The contradictions in this narrative on race, and indeed across the whole narrative of German essentialism—'Aryan' Germans are the natural masters of the world, but their culture and existence are under threat—are no impediment to its discursive power, as Robertson observes in respect of arguably the most influential anti-semitic tract at the turn of the century, Houston Stewart Chamberlain's *Die Grundlagen des neunzehnten Jahrhunderts* (1899, *The Foundations of the Nineteenth Century*, 1911), "because events that seem to threaten one part of the fantasy, such as Germany's defeat in 1918, can be taken to support the other part" (Robertson 1999, p. 185).

1914: The Great War as a Discourse Event

In Germany, as in Britain, some welcomed war as an opportunity for spiritual renewal—"like swimmers into cleanness leaping | Glad from a world grown old and cold and weary", in the words of Rupert Brooke's early war poem "Peace".[13] The continuities in German discourse between the nineteenth and twentieth centuries are evident in the German and Austrian imperial proclamations which launched the war, in which an Emperor addresses His people(s) in the capitalized first person to appeal to their sense of PFLICHT (duty), TREUE (loyalty) and EHRE (honour) in defence of the VATERLAND/DEUTSCHLAND against scheming foreigners.[14] With hindsight, invoking past military glories through the trope of taking up the sword (ZUM SCHWERTE GREIFEN) in both documents, and of fighting to the last breath of man and steed ("Mann und Roß") in the German proclamation, betrays a naivety about or cold disregard for the mechanized slaughter about to be unleashed. Undaunted, Emperor Franz Joseph gave a solemn assurance:

> In dieser ernsten Stunde bin Ich Mir der ganzen Tragweite Meines Entschlusses und Meiner Verantwortung bewußt. | Ich habe alles geprüft und erwogen. | Mit ruhigem Gewissen betrete ich den Weg, den die Pflicht Mir weist.
>
> In this momentous hour I am aware of the magnitude of My decision and My responsibility. | I have examined and weighed everything. | With a clear conscience I start out on the path to which duty directs Me.

Franz Joseph blamed the thwarting of his peaceful rule on providence (VORSEHUNG, unusually carrying a negative connotation). Kaiser Wilhelm II, however, was clear about God's allegiance: "Vorwärts mit Gott, der mit uns sein wird, wie er mit den Vätern war" ("Forward with God, who will be with us just as he was with our fathers"). The German document is particularly revealing of industrial and colonial rivalry as an underlying cause of the war: "Aber die Gegner neiden uns den Erfolg unserer Arbeit" ("But our opponents envy us the success of our work"). War, moreover, is viewed in all-or-nothing metaphysical terms as an existential moment in the history of "German being", to be fought "um Sein oder Nichtsein deutscher Macht und deutschen Wesens" ("for the existence or non-existence of German power and German being"). The popular enthusiasm for mobilization saw the internationalism of the Social Democrats in Germany crumble under the sheer weight of the "ideas of 1914", summarized in the slogan GOTT, KAISER, VATERLAND. War was embraced not only by government and military officials, but by whole sections of society, including artists and intellectuals, ninety three of whom signed the "Aufruf an die Kulturwelt!" (Appeal to the Cultural World!) on 4 October.[15] The document is notable for rejecting the (mainly true) accusations with the six-times-repeated phrase "Es ist nicht wahr, daß …" (e.g. "… wir freventlich die Neutralität Belgiens verletzt haben" ("It is not true that … we wantonly violated Belgium's neutrality")). Alongside references to the DASEINSKAMPF (existential struggle) and the SELBSTAUFOPFERUNG (self-sacrifice) of German soldiers, to atrocities committed by RUSSISCHE HORDEN (Russian hordes), the narrative of a long-suffering, peace-loving Germany surrounded by scheming and brutal enemies also enlists racist discourse:

> Sich als Verteidiger europäischer Zivilisation zu gebärden, haben die am wenigsten Recht, die sich mit Russen und Serben verbünden und der Welt das schmachvolle Schauspiel bieten, Mongolen und Neger auf die weiße Rasse zu hetzen.
>
> Those who ally with Serbs and Russians and offer the world the shameful spectacle of setting Mongols and Negroes on the white race, have the least right to present themselves as the defenders of European civilization.

The reference to "Mongols and Negroes" and the WEISSE RASSE presumably reflects encounters on the western front with soldiers from French and British colonies, and on the eastern front with 'Asiatic' Russian troops, revealing a sub-text of colonial envy. Of particular interest here is the importance of KULTUR in this narrative of national identity. The

Allies' claim is not true, the "Appell" states, that the war is with the militaristic, not the cultural Germany, for there is no such distinction: without German military might, German KULTUR would have long since been wiped from the face of the earth ("vom Erdboden getilgt"). The xenophobia in this declaration was even echoed by Thomas Mann, whose "Gedanken im Kriege" (1914, Thoughts in the War) endorsed this view in a convoluted argument which claimed for Germany a spiritually profound KULTUR, in contrast to the shallow ZIVILISATION of France and Britain. For Mann (in 1914 still an instinctively conservative 'unpolitical'), ZIVILISATION was manifest in parliamentary democracy and superficial cultural achievements, whilst German KULTUR embraced the full spectrum of human endeavour from metaphysics and art, to warfare.[16]

1914: "The German Language Will Rule the World"

The first weeks of the war saw a remarkable and previously unremarked meeting of minds between a Jew and an anti-semite.[17] Eduard Engel (1851–1938), former stenographer in the Reichstag, author of histories of German literature, prominent advocate of 'purifying' the German language of foreign expressions, and campaigner for German summer time (introduced in 1916), was a vituperative chronicler of the war, and Jewish. In his '*Kriegstagebuch*' ('War Diary') for 16 September 1914, as the report from the General Staff indicated for the first time that the German forces were engaged in a decisive great battle in which victory may not be guaranteed,[18] Engel voiced his anxieties:

> Das Schicksal der Völker des Erdballs, das Schicksal unseres Vaterlandes hängt von der Entscheidung dieser Riesenschlacht ab; aber, obwohl wir bangen, wie es nur menschlich ist, Furcht ist es nicht, die uns erfüllt, sondern nur das Gefühl des ungeheuren Ernstes dieser Stunden. (Engel 1915, p. 218)[19]

> The fate of the peoples of this earth, the fate of our Fatherland hangs on the outcome of this giant battle. But although we are nervous, as is only human, it is not fear that occupies us, but only the feeling of the enormous seriousness of these hours.

Engel's words brought a comradely response from Houston Stewart Chamberlain (1855–1927), whose *Kriegsaufsätze* (War Essays) contained the essay "Die deutsche Sprache",[20] which we know was begun before 22 September.[21] Published in the form of a "letter to E.E.", it begins:

> Gewiß, Du hast Recht; es wäre frevelhaft, wollte man gerade in diesen Septembertagen, wo die erste große Entscheidung noch schwebt—diejenige, die wahrscheinlich über alle weiteren Entscheidungen 'entscheiden' wird—, es wäre frevelhaft, wollte man sich dem Rausch einer übermütigen Zuversicht hingeben [...]. (1915, p. 24)
>
> Certainly, you are right. It would be wanton, especially in these September days, when the first great decision is still in the balance—the one which will probably 'decide' all future decisions—it would be wanton if one were to give oneself over to the intoxication of an arrogant confidence.

What seems remarkable today about this exchange is that Chamberlain, the English Germanophile (and, since 1907, German national), son-in-law of Richard Wagner, member of his Bayreuth circle, was the most prominent anti-Jewish publicist of the day,[22] a future favourite of Adolf Hitler and leading Nazis, who demonstratively attended his funeral in 1927. Engel, however, would die in poverty and isolation in 1938, having been denounced as a Jew, his right to comment on German language and culture denied. Like many Jewish Germans in 1914 (including the co-author of the 1914 "Appell" Ludwig Fulda, who was excluded from public life in 1933 and committed suicide in 1939), Engel regarded himself as German, indeed he was prone to anti-Jewish sentiments. Chamberlain's warm response might suggest that he was unaware of Engel's Jewishness—this remains unclear—but it is important to note that Chamberlain engaged actively and respectfully with Jewish intellectuals of his day, including Karl Kraus, Walther Rathenau, Maximilian Harden, Otto Weininger und Martin Buber.[23]

At the head of his essay, Chamberlain cites Schiller's line celebrating the depth and extent of German as a burgeoning 'Kultursprache' at the end of the eighteenth century: "Die deutsche Sprache wird die Welt beherrschen"[24]—as Engel would do on the frontispiece of *Sprich Deutsch!* (1917). In Chamberlain's mystical account, the HEILIGE DEUTSCHE SPRACHE (1915, p. 35) has a direct line to God, "geeignet, einem Göttlichen zum Gefäß zu dienen" ("suited to serve as a vessel for the divine", 1915, p. 28), "ein Segen, der unmittelbar aus Gottes Hand ins Herz sich schenkt" ("a blessing which bestows itself directly from God's hand into the heart"). The reason for this is German's allegedly autochthonous state, unlike French and English with their "catastrophic" high proportion of FREMDE WURZELN (foreign roots)—mainly Latin and Greek, and since Latin itself was dependent on Greek borrowings, French, derived from Latin, was doubly removed from the mystical union of word and world. Fichte and Chamberlain's own father-in-law are quoted approvingly:

> "jene Völker haben", sagt Fichte mit Recht, "genau genommen eine Muttersprache gar nicht", eine Tatsache, für welche Richard Wagner den schlagenden Ausdruck fand: "Ihre Sprache spricht für sie, nicht aber sprechen sie selbst in ihrer Sprache". (1915, p. 26f.)
>
> "These peoples", Fichte says quite correctly, "strictly speaking do not have a native language at all", a fact for which Richard Wagner found the telling words: "Their language speaks for them, but they do not speak in their own language".

The relatively 'autochthonous' German and Scandinavian languages occupy a privileged position in Chamberlain's mythical hierarchy, in marked opposition to English and French, whose linguistic 'impurity' is seen to be reflected in a morally degenerate national CHARAKTER, as evidenced in the British conduct of the war. Accordingly, Germany is said to have a moral duty to bring its language and culture to the world, by military force if necessary. Here, we clearly see the interconnectedness of the discourses on language, national identity, and empire in justification of the war.[25] German military might, her sea power, will secure German's destiny to supplant English as the WELTSPRACHE and "rule the world"—albeit not quite as Schiller intended.

Engel, the most prominent campaigner for 'pure' German, produced a series of popular works before, during and after the war: *Deutsche Stilkunst* (1911 [1922]), *Sprich Deutsch!* (1917), and *Entwelschung*, subtitled a *Verdeutschungsbuch* (1918 [1929]).[26] For Engel, too, this was a war "ums deutsche Dasein" ("for German existence", Engel 1917, p. 5). Language and 'Volk' are programmatically equated in statements which claim legitimacy by implicitly invoking Wilhelm von Humboldt: "Sprache ist Volk,

Volk ist Sprache", "Eine Sprache ist eine Weltansicht" ("A language is a worldview", Engel 1922, p. 282). However, Germans have sullied their language with foreign borrowings, especially since Renaissance Humanism ("Humanistenzeit"), producing a defiled variant of it, a MENGSELSPRACHE (mongrel language). Engel's wrath is directed at the enemies within, the WELSCHER UND FÄLSCHER (foreignizers and counterfeiters) who are the agents of this AUSLÄNDISCHE SPRACHSUDELEI (foreign defilement of the language). Engel warns of an imminent "sprachliche Entvolkung" ("linguistic dilution of the German 'Volk'", Engel 1917, p. 11) which will hand Germany to her enemies without the need for military action. Especially after 1918, he condemns the continued use of 'Fremdwörter' as "geistiger Landesverrat" ("intellectual/spiritual treason", Engel 1929, p. 24). The Germans are in danger, he writes, of throwing away a prize which even "die niedrigsten unserer vielfärbigen Feinde" ("the lowest of our multi-coloured enemies" Engel 1917, p. 10), know how to value: the integrity of their language. (Once again, one suspects the racist remark refers to the soldiers from French and British colonies fighting on the western front.) Engel's discourse is driven by organicizing metaphors drawn from biology, botany and zoology, especially in the prophecies of impending doom if Germans don't mend their ways. The 'Fremdwort' is "eine bis ins Mark, bis ins Herz der deutschen Sprache vorgedrungene krankhafte Entartung" ("a pathological degeneration which has penetrated to the marrow and the heart of the German language", Engel 1917, p. 16). Like a SCHIMMELPILZ (fungus), it works to destroy the German ecosystem ("wirkt zerstörend", Engel 1917, p. 286) and "plants itself" (Engel 1917, p. 282) in the place of the German word. Germans have lost contact with their MUTTERSPRACHE "durch lebenslange Verbildung und Entwöhnung" ("through life-long deformed growth and desisting use", Engel 1929, p. 5). (Note the persistence of the biological metaphor in the use of ENTWÖHNUNG—"weaning" the baby off the mother's milk.)

The organicist and elemental metaphors running through this popular discourse on language (and culture) may appeal to nationalist sentiment, but are rebutted by linguistic science. It makes no sense to talk of THE ENGLISH LANGUAGE, for example, 'invading' or 'killing off' THE GERMAN LANGUAGE like a cancer or a weed where cultures come into contact. As Weinrich (1985, p. 7) points out:

> Languages do not grow like trees. They do not function like machines. They are finely-attuned social structures which are situated in the minds of many speakers and which are constantly changing according to the changing consciousness of these speakers.[27]

Engel also presents the linguistic 'foreign invasion' using the water-borne imagery of the flood typical of migration discourses (FLUT, ÜBERFLUTUNG, cf. Jung et al. 1997). A religious discourse construing the language as a holy shrine (HÖCHSTE DEUTSCHE HEILIGKEIT, Engel 1917, p. 8) is enforced by declamatory biblical rhetoric: "Sie haben Augen und sehen nicht; sie haben Ohren und hören nicht" (cf. Mark 8:18). These pronouncements on the language, most of them formulated during the war, were supplemented and intensified in the extended editions and new titles published by Engel after the defeat. Indeed, after 1918 the German language is referred to as "unser einziges Vaterland" ("Our one and only Vaterland", Engel 1922, p. 284).

1918 and the Legacy of Defeat

A common picture of the Weimar Republic is the teleological view (from 1933) of a doomed democratic experiment undermined by events and by the polarization of its politics between authoritarian nationalism and Communism, in which the centre ground collapsed and the Republic never had enough republicans.[28] Attitudes towards the lost war illustrate this dichotomy most clearly, in the clash between pacifist sentiments (Remarque's *Im Westen nichts Neues* (1929, *All Quiet on the Western Front*)) and militaristic hero discourse valorizing the trench experiences (Ernst Jünger's *In Stahlgewittern* (1920, *In Storms of Steel*)). From its inception, its right-wing opponents insisted that defeat had been inflicted on a proud unbeaten military as a DOLCHSTOSS (stab in the back) by liberals and Jews at home,[29] that the founding of the Republic in November 1919 (after the army had obliged the Kaiser to abdicate) was a criminal act by NOVEMBERVERBRECHER. The most prominent of these reviled figures, the distinguished Jewish Foreign Minister Walther Rathenau, was murdered in 1922. The Social Democratic government suffered from being seen to implement the humiliating terms of the Treaty of Versailles, and from the disastrous economic situation which ensued. Talk of a DRITTES REICH entered right-wing political discourse in 1923 through Arthur Moeller van den Bruck.[30] The preceding Reichs were evidently the Holy Roman Empire of the German Nation and the 'unified' Reich of 1871, but the term was political and mystical at the same time, as Moeller made clear in his Introduction: "Der Gedanke des Dritten Reiches ist ein Weltanschauungsgedanke, der über die Wirklichkeit hinaushebt" ("The idea of a Third Reich is an idea of Weltanschauung which transcends reality").[31] The Republic was disparaged on the right as an artificial SYSTEM devoid of organic life. Grand narratives further undermining the democratic ethos of the Republic included Oswald Spengler's *Der Untergang des Abendlandes* (*The Decline of the West*, 1918/1923) Alfred Rosenberg's *Der Mythus des zwanzigsten Jahrhunderts* (*Myth of the Twentieth Century*, 1930), and Chamberlain's *Foundations of the Nineteenth Century*. However, the 'Conservative Revolution' was not a monolith, it ranged across monarchists, advocates of a 'Ständestaat' (corporative state), and other proponents of authoritarian national conservatism, some of whom were scandalized by the racism and street fighting of the Nazis.[32] It is important to note how many of these 'Conservative Revolutionaries' would later oppose or withhold support from the Nazis: Ernst Jünger declined to represent the NSDAP in the 1933 Reichstag, Rudolf Pechel was imprisoned in 1941, and Edgar Julius Jung was murdered in the "Night of the Long Knives" on 30 June 1934.

A common cliché presents the cultural life of this period in terms of the contrast between a flourishing liberal culture and an increasingly intolerant political environment, in which the nationalist right was opposed to all forms of modernism in literature (e.g. expressionist poetry, montage in the novel), art (e.g. abstract painting), architecture (e.g. the Bauhaus) and music (e.g. Schoenberg's atonal system). This may be generally true of Hitler, a failed artist who had strong views on these subjects, especially when Jews like Schoenberg could be accused of 'defiling' German culture, but it overlooks continuities between revolutionary art and political extremism on the right as well as the left. Goebbels, for example, was an admirer of literary expressionism, and modernist techniques are evident in Ernst Jünger's writings. Whilst some in the middle classes may have been swayed by right-wing attacks using MODERNE as a "semantic weapon", one should not forget that the 'Conservative Revolution' had its own modernist aesthetics, and that the Nazis proved particularly adept at aestheticizing fascism.[33]

The conservative backlash was also directed at the 'New Woman' who had begun to emerge before the First World War. Until 1908 women were forbidden by law to engage in organized political activity, but in 1919 women over twenty-one had gained the vote. Nazism was not unique in insisting that this trend be reversed and women be returned to the confines of KINDER, KÜCHE, KIRCHE (children, kitchen, church) while men got on with politics. An example of the conservative backlash is the coining of the term DOPPELVERDIENER (double earner/s) in the mid-1920s to arouse jealousy and resentment in the unemployed and the poorly paid. This anti-feminist programme did not have to wait for Hitler's appointment as Chancellor: the Brüning government passed a law facilitating the dismissal of married women from the civil service in May 1932. Politically organized women in the Weimar Republic who played a prominent role in defending not only women's rights but fledgling democratic values against an increasingly belligerent 'Conservative Revolution' included Käthe Kollwitz, Constanze Hallgarten, Erika Mann, Emmy Ender (of the 'Bund deutscher Frauen' (League of German Women)), and Lida Gustava Heymann, who in January 1933 stood guard at the door of the 'Internationale Frauenliga für Frieden und Freiheit' (IFFF, International Women's League for Peace and Freedom) in the Hofbräukeller in Munich to face down the SA who sought to disrupt the meeting. An IFFF leaflet warned German women, just days before 30 January, against falling for Hitler's words:

> Hitler bedeutet Krieg, schützt Eure Kinder, laßt Euch nicht von diesen Phrasen bluffen; hinter diesen Phrasen steht die brutalste Gewaltpolitik, die ihr alle am Leib zu spüren bekommt. Gebt keine Stimme für Hitler, der der Handlanger Eurer Ausbeuter, Euer Feind ist! Schließt Euch zusammen, organisiert Euch für Frieden und Freiheit! (cf. Oldfield 1986, p. 83f.; Ley n.d.)

> Hitler means war, protect your children, don't let yourselves be fooled by these phrases. Behind these phrases lies the most brutal politics of violence which you will all come to witness on your own flesh. Don't vote for Hitler, who is the lackey of your exploiters, your enemy! Come together, organize for peace and freedom!

Such warnings from mothers, widows, sisters and daughters of men and boys slaughtered in the First War marked these women activists out for concerted and sometimes brutal treatment by the new regime, and did not prevent many women from voting for National Socialism.

The "Language of National Socialism": Key Features

The political programme of National Socialism was set out in two key texts: the NSDAP's twenty five point programme (1920), and Hitler's personal political biography and prospectus, *Mein Kampf* (1925, 1926). In the 1920s, these were merely features of a party-internal discourse, but they would come to shape the Nazi state from 1933, and indeed in the final years of the Republic. In the 1920 Party Programme, authored by Hitler, Anton Drexler, Gottfried Feder and Dietrich Eckart, we find the concepts GROSSDEUTSCHLAND, VOLKSGENOSSE ('Aryan' German), DEUTSCHES BLUT, VERBRECHEN AM VOLKE (crime against the 'Volk'), VOLKSGESUNDHEIT (health of the 'Volk'), KÖRPERLICHE ERTÜCHTIGUNG (physical hardening), MATERIALISTISCHE WELTORDNUNG (materialist world order), KAMPF GEGEN DIE BEWUSSTE POLITISCHE LÜGE (struggle against the deliberate political lie [of the liberal press]), ZERSETZENDER EINFLUSS (degenerate influence), SITTLICHKEITS- UND MORALGEFÜHL DER GERMANISCHEN RASSE (sense of decency and morality of the Germanic race), JÜDISCHMATERIALISTISCHER GEIST (Jewish materialist spirit). Point 3 contains the demand for "Land und Boden (Kolonien) zur Ernährung unseres Volkes und Ansiedlung unseres Bevölkerungsüberschusses" ("land and soil (colonies) for feeding our 'Volk' and settling our population overflow"). The Programme is also notable for its discursive creation of out-groups against whom the Party will take action: NICHT-DEUTSCHE and

NICHT-STAATSBÜRGER, whose right to stay in the Reich is curtailed. The threat to Jewish Germans is articulated both implicitly, in the threat of the death penalty for WUCHERER (money lenders) and SCHIEBER (black marketeers), and explicitly, in the measures to be taken against large retail stores (Points 16, 17, 25) and in the racial redefinition of citizenship in Point 4: "Staatsbürger kann nur sein, wer Volksgenosse ist. Volksgenosse kann nur sein, wer deutschen Blutes ist, ohne Rücksichtnahme auf Konfession. Kein Jude kann daher Volksgenosse sein" ("Only a VOLKSGENOSSE can be a citizen of the state. Only those OF GERMAN BLOOD, irrespective of religious denomination, can be a VOLKSGENOSSE. No Jew, therefore, can be a VOLKSGENOSSE"). Point 6 rejects the principle of allocating parliamentary seats by party without regard to CHARAKTER (a nebulous term which, in context, carries arbitrary racial and political inflections). The rhetoric is one of "merciless struggle" (RÜCKSICHTSLOSER KAMPF) against opponents.

The Party Programme is curiously absent from *Mein Kampf*, in which Hitler reiterates and supplements the cornerstones of his political ideology. The NSDAP is not a party but a movement (BEWEGUNG) grounded in a WELTANSCHAUUNG (literally, way of looking at the world). A WELTANSCHAUUNG, Hitler explains, is intolerant ("unduldsam") of and bent on eliminating other views of the world. Unlike political parties in bourgeois democracies, which acknowledge political opponents, 'Weltanschauungen' proclaim their "infallibility" ("Unfehlbarkeit", p. 507).[34] The main organizational principle of this movement is that of FÜHRERAUTORITÄT (p. 378) whereby power is distributed top-down and implemented by a loyal GEFOLGSCHAFT (collective of followers) in the racially defined VOLKSGEMEINSCHAFT, for which the FÜHRER ultimately carries sole responsibility. The ideal characteristics of this racial community include TREUE UND GEHORSAM (loyalty and obedience), OPFERWILLIGKEIT/ OPFERBEREITSCHAFT (willingness to self-sacrifice), VERSCHWIEGENHEIT (secrecy), WILLENS- UND ENTSCHLUSSKRAFT (strength of will and decisiveness), and the prioritization of KÖRPERLICHE ERTÜCHTIGUNG (physical hardening) over intellectual skills in the education of the youth. The duty (PFLICHT) of all members of the 'Volk' community is productive work; there is a clear calculation of the individual's utility value (VERWERTBARKEIT) for the 'Volk'. The central element of this WELTANSCHAUUNG is its VÖLKISCH commitment to combative racial awareness in the struggle for survival (Kampf ums Dasein) and supremacy (p. 419). These attributes contribute to the positively connoted construct of the ideal völkisch Charakter. Germans and Nordic nations, it is asserted, are the most racially 'pure' of the Arier, although their racial integrity is threatened by Nichtarier living amongst them, mainly, but not exclusively, Jews, who through sexual contact with Germans, denounced as Rassenschande (racial defilement), have been responsible for a racially mixed society for which wildly derogatory metaphors such as Missgeburt (misshapen freak) and Rassenbrei (race soup) are reserved. On the relationship between language and race, Hitler is quite clear. He views Jewish Germans' relation to Deutschtum as resting solely on language—more precisely, on their ability to radebrechen (speak broken German). Whilst repeating the standard prejudices about Jewish Germans' relationship to German, however, Hitler was clear that language is not a characteristic of race:

> Die Rasse aber liegt nicht in der Sprache, sondern ausschließlich im Blute, etwas, das niemand besser weiß als der Jude, der gerade auf die Erhaltung seiner Sprache nur sehr wenig Wert legt, hingegen allen Wert auf die Reinhaltung seines Blutes. Ein Mensch kann ohne weiteres die Sprache ändern, d.h. er kann sich einer anderen bedienen; allein er wird dann in seiner neuen Sprache die alten Gedanken ausdrücken; sein inneres Wesen wird nicht verändert. (p. 342, cf. p. 337, p. 428f.)
>
> Race does not lie in language, however, but in blood alone, something that no one knows better than the Jew, who notably places little value on the retention of his language, and everything on keeping the purity of his blood. A human being can change his language quite easily, i.e he can make use of another language. But then he will express the old ideas in the new language: his inner being is not changed.

Of particular interest to students of political discourse are Hitler's prescriptions for an effective Propaganda:

> Jede Propaganda hat volkstümlich zu sein und ihr geistiges Niveau einzustellen nach der Aufnahmefähigkeit der Beschränktesten unter denen, an die sie sich zu richten gedenkt. Damit wird ihre rein geistige Höhe um

> so tiefer zu stellen sein, je größer die zu erfassende Masse der Menschen sein soll. Handelt es sich aber, wie bei der Propaganda für die Durchhaltung eines Krieges, darum, ein ganzes Volk in ihren Wirkungsbereich zu ziehen, so kann die Vorsicht bei der Vermeidung zu hoher geistiger Voraussetzungen gar nicht groß genug sein. (p. 197)

> All propaganda must be vernacular and set its intellectual level by the ability of the most limited of those it is aimed at to understand it. It follows that its purely intellectual level will have to be set lower, the greater the numbers that have to be reached. But when, as in the case of propaganda for enduring a war, an entire people is to be drawn into its influence, the caution needed to avoid intellectual assumptions which are too high, can never be great enough.

"Volkstümlich" propaganda is populist by design, countering the masses' low attention span by focusing on a small number of points and hammering them home in "Schlagwort" (political keyword) fashion until the slowest member of the target group has understood what is intended ("und diese schlagwortartig so lange zu verwerten, bis auch bestimmt der letzte unter einem solchen Worte das Gewollte sich vorzustellen vermag"). Interestingly, because the term was expressly discouraged in 1937, Hitler in 1924 also uses the term (POLITISCHE) REKLAME (p. 200) as a synonym of PROPAGANDA:

> Jede Reklame, mag sie auf dem Gebiet des Geschäftes oder der Politik liegen, trägt den Erfolg in der Dauer und gleichmäßigen Einheitlichkeit ihrer Anwendung. (p. 203)

> Every advertisement, be it in commerce or in politics, finds success in the duration and never-changing uniformity of its use.

This concept of propaganda maximizes emotional impact by cutting out the elaborated discourses of the intellectual classes, found in the essay and other genres of the written language. The written word is largely removed from the logical constraints of a syntactic frame and made to serve the visual image in declamatory headlines and 'Schlagwörter'. Hitler's preference for the live spoken word, especially to a live audience, is a logical correlate which also privileges radio and newsreel over print media as the chosen media of impact. An early example of this understanding of political discourse can be found in the campaign against Bernhard Weiss (1880–1951), Deputy Chief of Police in Berlin and a political opponent of Goebbels after the latter's appointment as Berlin Gauleiter in 1926.[35]

"That Is the Language of Fascism!": Oppositional Voices

The fascist tendencies in German political discourse in the latter half of the 1920s were described and critiqued in cultural-political journals which took a stand against Nazism, often inspired by Karl Kraus's *ad hominem* language-critical method in *Die Fackel* (The Torch). Perhaps the best-known today is *Die Weltbühne* in Berlin (Kurt Tucholsky, Carl von Ossietzky).[36] Other publications included *Der Brenner* in Innsbruck (Theodor Haecker), *Fanal* in Munich (Erich Mühsam),[37] and the Frankfurt journal *Deutsche Republik*, founded in 1926 by former Reich Chancellor Joseph Wirth, its contributors including centre-leftist Catholic writers such as Walter Dirks (1901–1991) and the nominally Lutheran Dolf Sternberger (1907–1989).[38] There, in September 1932, Sternberger's "Wörterbuch der Regierung von Papen in Auszügen" (Lexicon of the von Papen Government in Extracts) delivered a counter-factual "translation" of these politicians' use of words into the ordinary language of the people, declaring "Das ist die Sprache des Faschismus!". In a classic description of the 'weasel word', Sternberger observes that those who govern us conceal their intentions in "abnormally normal language", until their actions reveal that their words were hollow shells, to be filled later with surprising content.[39] Based on a close reading of Papen's government declaration of 4 July, Sternberger's critical Lexicon glosses Papen's use of twelve words and phrases[40]—FRESSENDES GIFT (corrosive poison[41]), GOTTGEWOLLT (god-ordained), HEIMATKRÄFTE (homeland forces), LEBENSWILLE (will to life), LIEBE, MARK (bone, marrow), ORGANISCH, SITTLICHE GRUNDLAGEN (moral foundations), SCHICKSAL (fate), SOHN, STÄNDE (social estates in a corporative state), WIEDERGEBURT (rebirth)—tracing (1) a rhetoric of concealment, (2) the use of mythical and mystifying language to conceal material interests,

(3) lurking biological metaphors and profane misuse of religious terms. Once opponents are constructed as FRESSENDES GIFT, Sternberger remarks, like poisonous snakes, all that remains is their extermination ("Vernichtung") in order to defend the 'body' politic, a metaphorical conceit signifying "alles, was die Interessen der Herrschenden stützt,—der Rest ist Gift" ("everything that supports the interests of the powerful—the rest is poison").[42] Sternberger warns Germans against letting these organicist metaphors pass without comment:

> "*Organisch*": (-e Regelung, -er Umbau der Wirtschaft. Überall zu hören und zu lesen!) Gleichnisse über Gleichnisse! Körper, Mark, Kräfte, Lebenswille, und jetzt organischer Aufbau usw.! Das ist die Sprache des Faschismus! Jeder hüte sich, diese Worte unbesehen und harmlos durchgehen zu lassen! (cf. Sternberger 1991, p. 31)
>
> "*Organic*": (o. management, o. reconstruction of the economy. Can be read and heard everywhere!). Metaphor upon metaphor! Body, bone marrow, forces, will to life and now organic reconstruction etc.! That is the language of fascism! Let everyone be on their guard against letting these words pass unexamined and harmlessly!

This was one of the last critiques to appear before the Nazi accession to power. A sequel, on the public pronouncements of Schleicher, Papen, Hindenburg and Hitler, apparently prompted by the formation of the Schleicher/Papen government on 3 December 1932 and the advance of Hitler towards power, was prepared for *Deutsche Republik* but never appeared.[43] This second Lexicon exposes, inter alia, Schleicher's 'confessional' first-person discourse (ICH)[44] as a deflective argumentation strategy. It is introduced by a quotation from the "unsurpassable" ("unübertrefflich") Hitler (whose own first-person discourse was, Kurt Tucholsky observed,[45] "borrowed from the Kaiser"):

> Immer vermögen die materiellen Interessen der Menschen solange am besten zu gedeihen, als sie im Schatten heldischer Tugenden bleiben.
>
> The material interests of people are always best able to prosper when they remain in the shadow of heroic virtues.

Not so, says Sternberger: the rhetoric of heroism and virtue is a veneer concealing the promotion of very specific material interests. Hitler and Schleicher are effectively called liars. Sternberger "translates" Schleicher's condescending references in his speech on 26 July 1932 to unnamed ÄNGSTLICHE GEMÜTER (anxious spirits) in industry concerned at the militarization of the economy, and those who worry that an expanded Wehrmacht is being politicized for domestic purposes. These doubters arouse Schleicher's EHRLICHES ERSTAUNEN (honest amazement), his ÄRGER (anger), and his BETRÜBNIS UND BESCHÄMUNG (despondency and shame) at finding his opponents' words being cited by the French. Rather than answer these questions, the politician parades his injured personal feelings. Papen's radio address to America in July 1932 is exposed as a thinly disguised appeal to American capital to invest in Germany as the bulwark against Soviet Communism. These material interests lie concealed beneath Papen's clichéd depiction of the economic and political reliability of the German CHARAKTER, its KLASSISCH (classic) values of OPFERBEREITSCHAFT in a nation so disciplined that vast areas can be policed by a single GENDARM (for Sternberger the symbol of the perfected police state). Beneath Papen's lauding of Christian values of SELBSTÜBERWINDUNG (self-overcoming) Sternberger finds a crude attempt to persuade American capital to overcome its nervousness and re-invest in Germany. The last entry in this Lexicon, STÄHLUNG (steeling)[46] comments on Hindenburg's decree of 15 September 1932 establishing a Reich Supervisory Body for JUGENDERTÜCHTIGUNG (physical training of the youth). Recent history, Sternberger insists, shows how these young bodies will be shattered by the machines of war. Interestingly, especially in light of the coded turn his journalistic practice would take in the 'Third Reich', the telling keyword of the counter-discourse is left implicit: the "steeling" of German youth (to make them HART WIE KRUPPSTAHL, hard as Krupp steel) is in reality preparing them for a destiny as cannon fodder (KANONENFUTTER).

Conclusion

This chapter has traced discourse traditions which contributed to the "language *of* National Socialism". These precursor discourses were formed substantially at the beginning of the nineteenth century and the period of "teutsche Romantik", as Victor Klemperer would remark in his diary on 17 August 1942, shaped importantly by the French occupation in the 1800s, and inflected even then with anti-Jewish narratives. Alongside these ran a complementary discourse on the 'integrity' of the German language and its destiny as a world language to rival English and French. These historical discourses received new impulses in moments of national euphoria, in 1871 (when the new nation state also promoted a discourse on empire and colonies) and 1914, but also in the national calamity of 1918, informing different strands of 'Conservative Revolution' undermining the Weimar Republic. The final years of the Weimar Republic saw some exemplary critiques of fascist discourse, not only that of the Nazi party and its supporters, but more tellingly, in the public language of governing conservatives, including von Papen, Schleicher, and Hindenburg. The acuity of these analyses stands in stark contrast, however, to their political efficacy.

The focus on Sternberger's oppositional Weimar Lexicons serves to uncover a telling feature of the unfolding anti-Nazi discourse. The Weimar critiques are forthright, solidly *parole*-based, and *ad hominem*. As we will see, this critical tradition begins to metamorphose as Sternberger and others go into 'inner exile' (and self-censorship was a factor even before January 1933), whilst it is broadly continued by those who leave Germany for territorial exile. A comparison of Sternberger's "Lexicon of the 'Unmensch'" (1945) and his Weimar Lexicons reveals the extent to which the habitus of political language criticism had been affected by the experience of living *in* National Socialism. The following chapters trace the evolution of these strands of discursive encounter with German fascism, and the Nazis' ultimate dismissal of the notion that the German language was, like Blood and Soil, an essential constituent of Germanness.

Notes

1. Cf. Sauer 1989, p. 114; "Sprachlich gesehen gab es keine Wende" ("As far as language is concerned, there was no 'turn'").
2. The following section is indebted to von Polenz 1999, pp. 522–547.
3. A recurrent feature of this discourse, however, which persisted into the Nazi era, is the attempt to claim Goethe and Schiller, and other 'greats', as emblematic members of the racial 'Volk'. Cf. Zeller et al. 1983.

4. MARK and GAU are terms for administrative areas, resuscitated also by German Romanticism in this period in the attempt to construct an 'authentic' world of experience located in an idyllic past.
5. Cf. von Polenz 1999, pp. 541–544. For a detailed study of anti-semitism in German literature and culture, see Robertson 1999, especially pp. 151–232.
6. Used transitively, AUSSCHEIDEN can mean 'excrete'.
7. For example in "Die Judenfrage als Frage der Racenschaedlichkeit" (1881). Cf. Dühring 1997, p. 228.
8. As Karl Kraus would later point out (see Chap. 4), this includes GOBBELES.
9. 'Racial hygiene' and the need to eliminate 'non-viable' forms of life were not specifically German at the turn of the twentieth century, they were widespread in Europe and North America. The term EUGENICS was coined by Francis Galton, Charles Darwin's cousin, who founded the *Eugenics Review* in 1909. Cf. Gillham 2001.
10. On this topic, see especially Römer 1989, Hutton 1999, Lerchenmüller and Simon 1997. Several of the keywords in this section, and their relation to the 'language *of* National Socialism', are analyzed in Schmitz-Berning 2000.
11. 'Racial hygiene', for example, was not exclusive to the political right. Cf. Burleigh and Wippermann 1991, p. 36.
12. Robertson 1999, p. 182f., citing Volkov 1978.
13. Brooke's words remind us that British public discourse also had its 'ideas of 1914'. German suspicion and hostility were fully reciprocated. For example, William Le Queux's prototypical spy novel *The Invasion of 1910* (1906), serialized in Lord Northcliffe's *Daily Mail* (along with publicity events such as actors in German uniform walking down Regent Street), fed on and intensified the already widespread fear of an 'aggressively competitive' Germany and its challenge to 'legitimate' British imperial interests. Le Queux's earlier attempt at the genre, *The Great War in England in 1897* (1894) had fed upon similar fears of France and (as did Conrad's *The Secret Agent* (1907)) of Russia, but it was the anti-German novel of 1906 that proved the runaway best-seller, to be followed in 1909 by the non-fictional *Spies of the Kaiser*. The genre of 'invasion literature' in Britain, and specifically German invasion, goes back, significantly, to 1871 and George Tomkyns Chesney's *The Battle of Dorking*. 1915 saw the publication of John Buchan's *The Thirty-Nine*

Steps, and widespread anti-German riots following the sinking of the Lusitania. Popular hostility to all things German was presumably one of the motivations (alongside the Russian Revolution) for George V's proclamation in 1917 changing the name of the British royal family from Saxe-Coburg-Gotha to Windsor.

14. "Aufruf Wilhelms II., 'An das deutsche Volk'", 6.8.1914. Deutsches Historisches Museum (Stand 05.08.2014.): [https://www.dhm.de/lemo/bestand/objekt/schmuckblatt-mit-der-rede-wilhelms-ii-zum-kriegsbeginn-1914.html] (18.2.2017). Franz Joseph, "An meine Völker!", 28.7.1914 [http://www.uibk.ac.at/zeitgeschichte/zis/library/rauchensteiner.html] (18.2.2017). Von Polenz (1999, p. 525, following Schmidt 1998) points to the discursive continuities between these first-person declarations of 1914 and a series of proclamations from 1813, 1849, 1861, 1866, 1871 and 1888 in which rulers address their subjects.
15. http://www.nernst.de/kulturwelt.htm (1.4.2017). For a critical study see Ungern-Sternberg 1996.
16. Mann 1914. For a fuller treatment of this aspect of Mann's position, see Reed 1996, p. 186ff.
17. For a fuller account of this relationship, see Dodd 2015a.
18. Presumably the first Battle of the Aisne, 13–28 September, which followed the Battle of the Marne, 5–12 September, generally considered to have gone in the Allies' favour.
19. The book was published in instalments. The passage quoted here is from the "Fourth Book", which closes on 23 September 1914.
20. References to this essay are to Chamberlain 1915, pp. 24–35. Some of these essays were first published in journals. The book sold 160,000 copies in the first six months (Field 1981, p. 390) and earned an enthusiastic response from the Kaiser (Urbach and Buchner 2004, p. 132f.). An English translation with an ironic Introduction appeared in 1915 under the title *The Ravings of a Renegade*.
21. Urbach and Buchner 2004, p. 142. The preface to the book is dated 28 October 1914. Beyond the evidence of this exchange, the precise details of the relationship between Engel and Chamberlain remain unclear.
22. For a summary account, cf. Robertson 1999, pp. 169–171.
23. See Brömsel 2015. On Chamberlain's anti-Jewish discourse, see Lobenstein-Reichmann 2005, 2008. Chamberlain's *Foundations* had been accorded a brief, and unfavourable mention in Engel 1906, p. 2503.
24. Friedrich Schiller, "Deutsche Größe", cf. Schiller 2004, p. 737.

25. On colonialism in German discourse in the nineteenth and twentieth centuries, cf. Rash 2011, 2012, 2017; Horan et al. 2013.
26. These are the dates of the first editions. They were constantly expanded in subsequent editions. *Deutsche Stilkunst* reached its thirty-first edition in 1931, *Sprich Deutsch!* its fortieth in 1923, *Entwelschung* its fifth in 1929. These works constitute a significant corpus of the discourse on language in the 1920s.
27. For further discussion on this point with reference to the present day, see the debate between Jürgen Schiewe and Thomas Paulwitz, reported in Dodd 2015b.
28. For surveys in English, see Gay 1969, Kaes et al. 1994, Peukert 1992, Williams 2011. Recent discourse-historical studies in German include Eitz and Engelhardt 2015 and Kämper et al. 2014.
29. The process of undermining the historical role of German Jews in the war effort dates back to the decision in 1916, supported by the Kaiser, to carry out a census (JUDENZÄHLUNG) to establish how many German Jews were fighting at the front as the war was perceived to be going badly. Cf. Angress 1978.
30. van den Bruck 1923. He was also chief editor of the Piper Verlag "Complete Works" of Dostoevsky which introduced the Russian author as a pan-Slavist to German readers during the First World War. Cf. Dmitri Mereschkowski's Introduction to the *Politsche Schriften* (Dostojewski 1917). Cf. also Dodd 1992, pp. 20–23.
31. van den Bruck 1923, p. ix. On the history of the term, see Berning 1964, p. 55; Schmitz-Berning 2000, pp. 156–160; Eitz and Stötzel 2007, pp. 135–141.
32. For a detailed study, see Woods 1997, pp. 111–134.
33. For a discussion of this thesis, see Hung 2016 (p. 452 on the "semantic weapon"). The most prominent contemporary commentator on Nazi aesthetics was Walter Benjamin, cf. Benjamin 1936.
34. References in this section are to Hitler 1934. A useful overview is Zentner 1974. For studies in English of rhetoric and metaphor in *Mein Kampf*, see Mieder 1997, Rash 2006.
35. Cf. von Polenz 1999, p. 545; Bering 1991. In a campaign carrying many characteristics of what has recently been called 'post-truth' discourse, Goebbels habitually referred to Weiss as ISIDOR, reducing him to a racial stereotype which was gleefully received by National Socialists, anti-semites, and the criminal classes of Berlin, for whom the taunt served as

a rallying call. Weiss's protestations simply increased their shared enjoyment at his discomfiture. In pointing out that his name was not Isidor, Weiss drew renewed attention to his Jewishness. On the 'fate' of names, see Bering 1987. The political discourse of the 2016 presidential election in the USA would throw up an even more radical variation on this theme, in the widespread speculations about Barack Obama's nationality and possible Muslim identity.

36. Tucholsky left Germany in 1929, settling in Sweden, where he committed suicide in 1935. Ossietzky, like Mühsam, was arrested in February 1933. He was awarded the Nobel Peace Prize in 1935, and died in 1938 from the effects of incarceration in Esterwegen concentration camp.
37. Mühsam was imprisoned in 1920 as a member of the failed Munich Workers' Republic, released in 1924 under the same amnesty that released Hitler, arrested in February 1933, and murdered in Oranienburg concentration camp in 1934. His story "Die Affenschande" (1923, The Ape Scandal) satirized Nazi racial theories.
38. The majority of contributions in this journal are anonymous or pseudonymous. Identifiable authors of anti-Nazi articles include Sternberger, Günter Dallmann, F. M. Reifferscheidt and Werner Thorman. Cf. Dodd 2007, p. 130f; Prümm 1982.
39. Equivalent German terms include 'Leerformel' (Topitsch 1960; von Polenz 1999, p. 63) and 'Vexierwort' (Teubert 1989).
40. For a detailed analysis, see Dodd 2007, pp. 134–139.
41. 'Corrosive' here does not capture the literal meaning of 'fressen', which denotes animals eating. The image invoked is of a poisonous creature eating away at the body.
42. Cf. Gift wie Gift behandeln (Dühring), discussed above.
43. For a detailed analysis, see Dodd 2007, pp. 139–145, 303–308.
44. Terms appearing in small capitals here are headwords in this "Lexicon".
45. Tucholsky 1975, Bd. 9, p. 182. The analysis of proprietary style in nineteenth and twentieth-century monarchical addresses proposed by von Polenz (1999, p. 525) could clearly be extended beyond 1914.
46. Again, comparison of the texts on which Sternberger drew confirms the topicality of this attack. See Dodd 2007, pp. 139–148.

Bibliography

Angress, Werner T. 1978. The German Army's 'Judenzählung' of 1916. Genesis – Consequences – Significance. *Leo Baeck Institute Yearbook* 23: 117–137.

Benjamin, Walter. 1936. Das Kunstwerk im Zeitalter seiner technischen Reproduzierbarkeit. In *Gesammelte Schriften*, Unter Mitwirkung von Theodor W. Adorno und Gershom Scholem, Hg. von Rolf Tiedemann und Hermann Schweppenhäuser, Bd. 1/2 (1972), 471–508. Frankfurt/Main: Suhrkamp.

Berger, Stefan. 2004. *Inventing the Nation: Germany*. London: Arnold.

Bering, Dietz. 1987. *Der Name als Stigma. Antisemistismus im deutschen Alltag 1812–1933*. Stuttgart: Klett-Cotta.

———. 1991. *Kampf um Namen. Bernhard Weiss gegen Joseph Goebbels*. Stuttgart: Klett-Cotta.

Berning, Claudia. 1964. *Vom 'Abstammungsnachweis' zum 'Zuchtwart'. Vokabular des Nationalsozialismus*. Berlin: de Gruyter.

Brömsel, Sven. 2015. *Exzentrik und Bürgertum. Houston Stewart Chamberlain im Kreis jüdischer Intellektueller*. Berlin: Ripperger & Kremers.

van den Bruck, Moeller. 1923. *Das Dritte Reich*. Dritte Auflage, bearbeitet von Hans Schwarz. 11. bis 15. Tausend. Hamburg, Berlin, Leipzig: Hanseatische Verlagsanstalt.

Burleigh, Michael, and Wolfgang Wippermann. 1991. *The Racial State: Germany 1933–1945*. Cambridge: Cambridge University Press.

Chamberlain, Houston Stewart. 1899. *Die Grundlagen des neunzehnten Jahrhunderts*. München: F. Bruckmann.

———. 1911. *The Foundations of the Nineteenth Century*. London, New York: John Lane.

———. 1915. *Kriegsaufsätze*. München: F. Bruckmann.

Dodd, William J. 2007. *Jedes Wort wandelt die Welt. Dolf Sternbergers politische Sprachkritik*. Göttingen: Wallstein.

———. 2015a. 'Die deutsche Sprache wird die Welt beherrschen': Randbemerkungen zu einem deutschen Sprachdiskurs vor hundert Jahren. *Aptum. Zeitschrift für Sprachkritik und Sprachkultur* 01 (10): 226–239.

———. 2015b. Under Pressure? The Anglicisms Debate in Contemporary Germany as a Barometer of German National Identity Today. *German Politics and Society* 33 (1&2): 58–68.

Dostojewski, F.M. 1917. *Politische Schriften. Sämtliche Werke I/13. Unter Mitarbeiterschaft Dmitri Merschkowskis*. Herausgegeben von Moeller van den Bruck. Zweite Auflage. München: Piper.

Dühring, Eugen. 1997. *Eugen Dühring on the Jews*. Brighton: Nineteen Eighty Four Press.

Eitz, Thorsten, and Isabelle Engelhardt. 2015. *Diskursgeschichte der Weimarer Republik*. 2 Bde. Hildesheim: Olms Weidmann.

Eitz, Thorsten, and Georg Stötzel. 2007. *Wörterbuch der 'Vergangenheitsbewältigung'. Die NS-Vergangenheit im öffentlichen Sprachgebrauch*. Hildesheim, Zürich, New York: Olms.

Engel, Eduard. 1906. *Geschichte der deutschen Literatur*. 2. Band. Wien, Leipzig: Tempsky und Freytag.

———. 1915. *Ein Tagebuch. Mit Urkunden, Bildnissen, Karten*. Bd. 1: *1914. Vom Ausbruch des Krieges bis zur Einnahme von Antwerpen*. Berlin: Westermann.

———. 1917. *Sprich Deutsch! Ein Buch zur Entwelschung*. 2. Aufl. Leipzig: Hesse & Becker.

———. 1922. *Deutsche Stilkunst*. Dreißigste, umgearbeitete und vermehrte Auflage. 47. bis 57. Tausend. Leipzig, Wien: Hesse & Becker.

———. 1929. *Verdeutschungsbuch. Ein Handweiser zur Entwelschung für Amt, Schule, Haus, Leben*. Fünfte durchgesehene und stark vermehrte Auflage, 41–45. Tausend. Leipzig, Wien: Hesse & Becker.

Field, Geoffrey G. 1981. *Evangelist of Race: The Germanic Vision of Houston Stewart Chamberlain*. New York: Columbia University Press.

Gay, Peter. 1969. *Weimar Culture: The Outsider as Insider*. London: Secker & Warburg.

Gillham, Nicholas Wright. 2001. *A Life of Sir Francis Galton: From African Exploration to the Birth of Eugenics*. Oxford: Oxford University Press.

Goldhagen, Daniel. 1996. *Hitler's Willing Executioners: Ordinary Germans and the Holocaust*. London: Little, Brown & Co.

Hitler, Adolf. 1934. *Mein Kampf. Zwei Bände in einem Band*. Ungekürzte Ausgabe. 97–101. Auflage. München: Franz Eher Nachfolger.

Horan, Geraldine, Felicity Rash, and Daniel Wildmann, eds. 2013. *English and German Nationalist and Anti-semitic Discourse, 1871–1945*. Bern, Oxford: Peter Lang.

Hung, Jochen. 2016. 'Bad' Politics and 'Good' Culture: New Approaches to the History of the Weimar Republic. *Central European History* 49: 441–453.

Hutton, Christopher. 1999. *Linguistics and the Third Reich: Mother Tongue Fascism, Race and the Science of Language*. London: Routledge.

Jung, Matthias, Martin Wengeler, and Karin Böke, Hgg. 1997. *Die Sprache des Migrationsdiskurses. Das Reden über "Ausländer" in Medien, Politik und Alltag*. Wiesbaden: Westdeutscher Verlag.

Kaes, Anton, Martin Jay, and Edward Dimendberg, eds. 1994. *The Weimar Republic Sourcebook*. Los Angeles: University of California Press.

Kämper, Heidrun, Peter Haslinger, and Thomas Raithel, Hgg. 2014. *Demokratiegeschichte als Zäsurgeschichte: Diskurse der frühen Weimarer Republik*. Berlin: de Gruyter.

Lerchenmüller, Joachim, and Gerd Simon. 1997. *Im Vorfeld des Massenmords. Germanistik und Nachbarfächer im 2. Weltkrieg: eine Übersicht*. Dritte Auflage ed. Tübingen: Gesellschaft für interdisziplinäre Forschung.

Ley, Anna. n.d. *Geschichte der deutschen Sektion der Internationalen Frauenliga für Frieden und Freiheit*. wipf.de. Accessed 19 March 2017.

Lobenstein-Reichmann, Anja. 2005. Sprache und Rasse bei Houston Stewart Chamberlain. In *Brisante Semantik. Neuere Konzepte und Forschungsergebnisse einer kulturwissenschaftlichen Linguistik,* Hg. Dietrich Busse, Thomas Niehr, and Martin Wengeler, 87–208. Tübingen: Niemeyer.

———. 2008. *Houston Stewart Chamberlain: Zur textlichen Konstruktion einer Weltanschauung. Eine sprach-, diskurs- und ideologiegeschichtliche Analyse*. Berlin, New York: de Gruyter.

Mann, Thomas. 1914. Gedanken im Kriege. *Die Neue Rundschau* 25: 1471–1484.

Mieder, Wolfgang. 1997. '… as if I Were Master of the Situation'. Proverbial Manipulation in Adolf Hitler's *Mein Kampf*. In *The Politics of Proverbs. From Traditional Wisdom to Proverbial Stereotypes*, ed. Wolfgang Mieder. Madison: University of Wisconsin Press.

Oldfield, Sybil. 1986. German Women in the Resistance to Hitler. In *Women, State and Revolution*, ed. Sian Reynolds. Wheatsheaf: Brighton.

Peukert, Detlev. 1992. *The Weimar Republic: The Crisis of Classical Modernity*. Translated by Richard Deveson. New York: Hill and Wang.

von Polenz, Peter. 1999. *Deutsche Sprachgeschichte vom Spätmittelalter bis zur Gegenwart*. Bd 3: *19. und 20. Jahrhundert*. Berlin, New York: de Gruyter.

Prümm, Karl. 1982. Antifaschistische Mission ohne Adressaten. Zeitkritik und Prognostik in der Wochenzeitschrift *Deutsche Republik* 1929–1933. In *Weimars Ende. Prognosen und Diagnosen in der deutschen Literatur und politischen Publizistik 1930–1933*, Hg. Thomas Koebner, 103–142. Frankfurt/Main: Suhrkamp.

Rash, Felicity. 2006. *The Language of Violence. Adolf Hitler's 'Mein Kampf'*. New York, Washington: Peter Lang.

———. 2011. German Nationalist and Colonial Discourse: An Introduction. *Patterns of Prejudice* 45 (5): 377–379.

———. 2012. *German Images of the Self and the Other: Nationalist, Colonialist and Anti-semitic Discourse 1871–1918*. Basingstoke: Palgrave Macmillan.

———. 2017. *The Discourse Strategies of Imperialist Writing. The German Colonial Idea and Africa 1848–1945*. London: Routledge.

Reed, T.J. 1996. *Thomas Mann: The Uses of Tradition*. Oxford: Clarendon.

Robertson, Ritchie. 1999. *The 'Jewish Question' in German Literature 1749–1939: Emancipation and Its Discontents*. Oxford: Oxford University Press.

Römer, Ruth. 1989. *Sprachwissenschaft und Rassenideologie in Deutschland*. München: Wilhelm Fink.

Sauer, Wolfgang Werner. 1989. Der *Duden* im 'Dritten Reich'. In *Sprache im Faschismus*, Hg. Konrad Ehlich, 104–119. Frankfurt/Main: Suhrkamp.

Schiller, Friedrich. 2004. *Werke und Briefe in zwölf Bänden*. Bd. 1: *Sämtliche Gedichte*. Hg. von Georg Kurscheidt. Frankfurt/Main: Suhrkamp.

Schmidt, Hartmut. 1998. 'An mein Volk'. Sprachliche Mittel monarchischer Appelle. In *Sprache und bürgerliche Nation. Beiträge zur deutschen und europäischen Sprachgeschichte des 19. Jahrhunderts*, Hg. Dieter Cherubim et al., 167–196. Berlin, New York: de Gruyter.

Schmitz-Berning, Cornelia. 2000. *Vokabular des Nationalsozialismus*. Berlin, New York: de Gruyter.

Schulz, Gerhard. 1983. *Die deutsche Literatur zwischen Revolution und Restauration 1806–1830. Geschichte der deutschen Literatur*, Hg. Helmut De Boor and Richard Newald, Bd. VII/2. München: Beck.

Sternberger, Dolf. 1991. *Sprache und Politik, (Schriften XI)*. Frankfurt/Main: Insel.

Sternberger, Dolf, Gerhard Storz, and Wilhelm E. Süskind. 1945–1948. Aus dem Wörterbuch des Unmenschen. *Die Wandlung* 1/1–3/3.

Teubert, Wolfgang. 1989. Politische Vexierwörter. In *Politische Semantik. Bedeutungsanalytische und sprachkritische Beiträge zur politischen Sprachverwendung*, Hg. Josef Klein, 51–68. Opladen: Westdeutscher Verlag.

Topitsch, Ernst. 1960. Über Leerformeln. Zur Pragmatik des Sprachgebrauches in Philosophie und politischer Theorie. In *Probleme der Wissenschaftstheorie. Festschrift für Viktor Kraft*, Hg. Ernst Topitsch, 233–264. Wien: Springer.

Tucholsky, Kurt. 1975. *Gesammelte Werke*. Herausgegeben von Mary Gerold-Tucholsky, Fritz J. Raddatz. Reinbek: Rowohlt.

von Ungern-Sternberg, Jürgen. 1996. *Der Aufruf "An die Kulturwelt!": das Manifest der 93 und die Anfänge der Kriegspropaganda im Ersten Weltkrieg*. Mit einer Dokumentation. Stuttgart: F. Steiner.

Urbach, Karina, and Bernd Buchner. 2004. Prinz Max von Baden und Houston Stewart Chamberlain. Aus dem Briefwechsel 1909–1919. *Vierteljahrshefte für Zeitgeschichte* 52 (1): 121–177.

Volkov, Shulamit. 1978. Antisemitism as a Cultural Code. Reflections on the History and Historiography of Antisemitism in Imperial Germany. *Leo Baeck Institute Yearbook* 23: 25–46.

Weinrich, Harald. 1985. *Wege der Sprachkultur*. Stuttgart: Deutsche Verlags-Anstalt.

Williams, John, ed. 2011. *Weimar Culture Revisited*. Basingstoke: Palgrave Macmillan.

Woods, Roger. 1997. *The Conservative Revolution in the Weimar Republic*. Basingstoke: Palgrave Macmillan.

Zeller, Bernhard, Friederike Brüggemann, and Albrecht Bergold, Hgg. 1983. *Klassiker in finsteren Zeiten, 1933–1945: eine Ausstellung des Deutschen Literaturarchivs im Schiller-Nationalmuseum*. Marbach am Neckar: Deutsche Schillergesellschaft.

Zentner, Christian. 1974. *Adolf Hitlers 'Mein Kampf'. Eine kommentierte Auswahl*. München: Paul List.

3

The National Socialist Discourse "Community": Norms and Contradictions

This chapter reviews the norms of public discourse after 30 January 1933. It is necessary to do so in order to understand the practices against which the 'unquiet voices' discussed in the following chapters reacted. These norms were primarily imposed through intimidation, through actual and threatened acts of extreme violence against opponents and enemies. The oppressive discourse environment inducing and enforcing a pervasive 'Sprachlosigkeit' is characterized by Bauer as follows:

> Die Befehle und der Druck dahinter, das begeisterte 'Gemeinschaftsgefühl', die 'selbstverständliche' Norm, der Opportunismus des Mitlaufens und Mitbrüllens, der Widerwille, das Erlahmen, der Ekel und das Entsetzen bildeten zusammen die höchst komplexe Redewelt des 'Dritten Reiches'. (Bauer 1988, p. 117)

> The orders and the pressure behind them, the enthusiastic 'community feeling', the 'self-evident' norm, the opportunism of going along and shouting along with the others, the aversion, attrition, revulsion and horror all combined to make up the highly complex discourse world of the 'Third Reich'.

W J Dodd, *National Socialism and German Discourse*,
https://doi.org/10.1007/978-3-319-74660-9_3

The first section of this chapter reviews this programme of terror and Gleichschaltung ((enforced) co-ordination) and seeks to capture the strident and radicalized public discourse which accompanied and underpinned it, from the perspective of those who were alienated and excluded from the public arena and sensitized to the coarseness and violence of its language. The second section focuses on the regime's attempts to regulate ('co-ordinate') the public discourse and impose its ideological norms by overt and covert means—through (self-)censorship, secret 'Sprachregelungen' (instructions on usage) issued to the media, and re-codification of the meaning of words in dictionaries and other reference books, as evidenced by the case of the *Duden* dictionary. The third section of this chapter focuses on the question of the ideological status of the German language as a 'third force' of racial ideology (alongside Blut and Boden) and reveals how after much confusion this particular 'language question' was emphatically resolved by Hitler personally. The chapter concludes with observations on the reach of mother-tongue fascism under National Socialism, despite the regime's rebuttal of linguistic purism.

Terror and 'Gleichschaltung'

The Nazis' own myth of a total Gleichschaltung, together with post-1945 discourse on totalitarianism, needs to be challenged at the outset of this section. The hegemonic discourse which the regime sought to impose was both incomplete in its reach and characterized by inner contradictions, a consequence in part of the chaotic organization of the state apparatus and of responsibility for interpreting Nazi ideology under the Führerprinzip.[1] Such internal contradictions created ambiguous spaces within which oppositional discourses could be articulated, albeit cautiously, in the public arena. To do so required a degree of ingenuity, a calculation of the possible consequences, and a measure of civil courage.

After the formation of the Hitler-Papen government on 30 January, the regime quickly consolidated its power, and free speech was severely curtailed. The main tool was terror, fronted in some cases by laws and decrees. Book burnings, organized by Nazi student organisations with the encouragement of the regime, were symbolic of the new order, as were political murders, for example the murder of the Jewish philosopher and cultural critic Theodor Lessing (1872–1933) on 30 August 1933, in exile in Marienbad. Free speech retreated in the face of denunciations, real and imagined Gestapo *agents provocateurs*, (rumours of) postal censorship and 'Spitzel' (spies, informers). Newsreels openly reported on the first KZs ('Konzentrationslager'), notably the one opened on 20 March at Dachau near Munich. In the course of 1933, some seventy KZs were established, complemented by some thirty institutions cynically designated as places of SCHUTZHAFT (protective custody)—these in addition to the sixty or so detention centres run independently by the SA, SS, and Gestapo.[2] A few telling statistics provided by Claudia Koonz (1987, p. 315) may help us to grasp the scale of repression: within a year, half of the Communist Party's 300,000 members were in prisons, camps, or dead; 18,000 alone were rounded up after the Reichstag fire on 27 February 1933. Communists and Socialists constituted most of the two hundred "political enemies" killed in the following months in the "battle against terrorism"; three million Germans were arrested for questioning in 1933; and some 150,000 "politicals" were incarcerated at any given time between 1933 and 1939, during which period about one million Germans served jail sentences. These numbers escalated from 1939, to include some seven million Europeans 'transported' (TRANSPORTIERT) or 'evacuated' (EVAKUIERT) to concentration camps and to extermination camps in the occupied eastern territories. By 1945, some 92,000 women from the Reich and occupied territories had died at the largest women's concentration camp alone—Ravensbruck, just north of Berlin (Koonz 1987, p. 334).

A framework of 'legal' texts gave a spurious impression of a state still governed by the rule of law.[3] These included the Reichstag Fire Decree (February 28); the 'emergency measures' "for the protection of 'Volk' and state", an Enabling Act effectively suspending the Reichstag (March 24); the law for the "restoration of the professional civil service" (April 7); the law against founding new political parties (July 14); and in September the establishment of a Chamber of Culture ('Reichskulturkammer') with constituent chambers for literature, music, theatre, radio, film, fine art and the press, which began registering and regulating those engaged in cultural life. All of these measures were designed to exclude discriminated groups (mainly 'non-Aryans' and political opponents) from public engagement and deprive them of the right to earn a living from their profession. Other laws created new crimes and expanded the number of offences incurring the death penalty—on one calculation from three to forty six (Oldfield 1986, p. 93). One such measure was the ordinance for the "defence against malicious attacks on the government of national uprising" (23 March), commonly referred to as HEIMTÜCKEGESETZ (law against malice), which penalized unauthorized wearing of party insignia and uniform, and disrespectful talk about and attitudes toward the regime. The special courts (SONDERGERICHTE) set up under this ordinance were the forerunner, under its 1934 revision, of "treason" cases tried by Roland Freisler's infamous "court-martial of the home front", the VOLKSGERICHT. Some eleven thousand Germans would be executed under this legislation by 1945. Equally ominous was the legislation based on race theory. Long before the Nuremberg Laws of September 1935 laid down a foundation for racial persecution of NICHTARIER, the 'Gesetz zur Verhütung erbkranken Nachwuchses' (14 July 1933, Law for the prevention of offspring with hereditary diseases) targeted the 'Aryan' population with a programme of 'racial hygiene', providing the legal foundation for programmes of voluntary and involuntary sterilization, and for the killing of 'inferior' exemplars of the master race which reached its zenith with Hitler's secret instruction of 1 September 1939 for the killing of LEBENSUNWERTES LEBEN (life unworthy of life), a concept not limited to the 'Aryan' population and specifically including all gypsies.

It is not difficult to imagine the impact of this programme of semi-legalized terror and murder on those who did not support the regime and could not or would not emigrate. The vast majority lived in enforced 'Sprachlosigkeit'. Of course, people could hardly avoid speaking in the course of their everyday lives, at work, in the social spaces, as well as in their private spaces. But even the private space was no longer safe, given people's widespread and justified fear of informers, including their own children.[4] Most of the general population had learned to keep their heads down long before the political elite learned the hard way in the 'Night of the Long Knives' (30 June–2 July 1934). Its first victim, Edgar Julius Jung (1894–1934), a national conservative and political advisor to the former Reich Chancellor and current Vice Chancellor Franz von Papen, was the author of von Papen's 'Marburg Speech' of 17 June 1934 which finally voiced concern about his political bedfellows. Papen's voice was not heard outside the hall. Copies of the text were seized, newspapers warned not to print or report it, the politician was eventually banished as ambassador to Austria (and then Turkey), whilst the speech-writer was murdered. An elitist intellectual of 'Conservative Revolution', Jung had, as Magub (2017, p. 229) remarks, "seriously underestimated the brutality of the Nazi regime and overestimated the protection he would receive from Papen and Hindenburg".

Radicalization of the Public Discourse: The New Normal

In the Nazi state, the language *of* National Socialism reviewed in the previous chapter became the prescribed language of public discourse *in* National Socialism, the new normal in all but the most trusted private spaces. As we shall see, Germans who did not subscribe—although millions did—to the euphoric narrative of the resurgent chosen 'Volk' viewed these developments almost as outsiders estranged from their own language. They were struck by the strident, bullying, self-congratulatory tone of pronouncements; by their hyperbolic excesses—the relentlessly emphatic, repetitive, and inflated phraseology, and by the 'us and them' friend/foe dichotomies which glorified conflict and excluded many Germans from a common German identity. To many it seemed that, as Theodor Haecker wrote in 1933 (see Chap. 6), familiar words no longer meant what they used to mean, and that ugly new expressions and meanings were sprouting all around them. Some were suspicious of the mystical Romanticism in the revival of ancient and medieval Germanic words and runes, and appalled at the appropriation of religious language to glorify the 'Volk', the Party, and particularly the FÜHRER. More detailed lists of the changes in the meaning and use of lexical and phraseological items can be found in Keller (1978, pp. 603–607, 609–621) and Wells (1985, pp. 407–420). At this point, a brief survey of the new discourse norms must suffice, in anticipation of the commentaries reviewed in the following chapters.

Whilst much can be gleaned from words on a page, we can only really begin to comprehend how intimidating this discourse environment must have been with the help of audio and video recordings—of Nuremberg rallies, for example, or a Hitler speech, or a 'Volksgericht' trial. But to understand the full gamut of menace we might view Willi Schaefer's cabaret performance, preserved on video in 1936, in which the wit elaborates a musical metaphor on what should happen to the QUERPFEIFER (fife players, also: those playing a different tune)[5]:

> … und vielleicht auch mal solche, die gerne mal wieder die Zentrummel rühren mechten, sogenannte Devisenmusikanten, nich wahr, och, da machen wir wenig Federlesen. Die kommen zu ihrer weiteren Ausbildung in ein Konzertlager, wo man ihnen dann so lange die Flötentöne beibringt, bis sie sich an eine taktvolle Mitarbeit gewöhnt haben.
>
> … and perhaps also those who would like to mix it up a bit, the so-called speculators with notes, oh we'll deal with them. They'll be put for their further education in a concert camp, where they'll be taught the flute for as long as it takes until they have grown accustomed to playing along in time.[6]

It would be wrong to categorize KONZERTLAGER here as a euphemism, if we understand euphemism as a device for concealing reality. Like SCHUTZHAFT and many terms in the language of National Socialism, even arguably words such as such as EVAKUIEREN, the word does not, and is not meant to, conceal the reality it designates. On the contrary, this is verbal terrorism laced with anti-semitism. Schaefer's words are chilling enough, but their menace lies even more in the 'witty', smiling delivery with its playful, mocking intonation.

Metaphors give perhaps the greatest insight into the internal organization and subliminal power of the discourse. The two most important grand metaphors serve to militarize and racialize everyday discourse. Metaphors from sport (football, boxing) run alongside military metaphors, presided over by the overarching ideologeme of KAMPF. The racial inflection of VOLK and ART (manner, kind, species) colours hundreds of derived terms such as VOLKSGENOSSE (fellow member of the 'Volk'), and ARTFREMD (alien to the race). The result is that a surprising amount of vocabulary, when compounded terms are included, becomes laden with new ideological colouring. The multiplying effect is the result of the productivity of morphological derivations (ART > ARTFREMD) but also of shifts in semantic fields. MISCHEHE (mixed marriage), for example, moves from the ecclesiastical domain to become a term in the discourse on race and especially on 'inter-racial' sexual relations ('miscegenation').[7] The ideology of KAMPF also normalizes brutality in the sheer frequency and positive connotation of attributes like BRUTAL, RÜCKSICHTSLOS (without regard) and ERBARMUNGSLOS (merciless). A similar phenomenon can be observed in adjectives and adverbs like GANZ, GÄNZLICH, and TOTAL, reflecting the fashion for hyperbole and an 'all or nothing' mentality. Already in the apparently casual use of such secondary word classes (i.e. not nouns or verbs) we can see the ubiquity of norms reflecting and endorsing the unforgiving 'new normal' philosophy of brutality from which no one was exempt. All individual life, even that of 'Aryans', was of value only as MENSCHENMATERIAL with its biological ERBWERT (genetic value), or economic VERWERTBARKEIT (utility value) for the good of the 'Volk'. Outside the chosen VOLK, the value of an UNTERMENSCH is encapsulated in a word like the compound adjective JUDENFREI, which asserts the 'normality' of an area or country 'cleansed' (GESÄUBERT) of Jews. Warfare added numerous terms to this discourse of hatred and struggle, such as the triumphant COVENTRIEREN (to reduce a city to rubble) following the devastating bombing attack of 14 November 1940[8]; the infantile designation of the Allies as GANGSTER once German cities suffered similar attacks, and the continuation of this narrative of grievance in Goebbels's designation of V1 and V2 missiles as weapons of "vengeance" (VERGELTUNG).

The 'Co-ordinated' Public Voice of Women

One of the most striking changes in 1933 concerned the construction of femininity in the public discourse. The 'New Woman' of the Weimar period was largely to disappear (with notable exceptions, such as the test pilot Hannah Reitsch, a rare exemplar of the Nazi modern woman warrior), to be replaced by the official voice and image represented by the 'Nationalsozialistische Frauenschaft' (NSF, National Socialist Women's

Organisation) and its REICHSFRAUENFÜHRERIN, Hitler's "perfect woman" Gertrud Scholtz-Klink. Images of Nazi womanhood were propagated in magazines and newspaper supplements ('Frauenbeilagen') aimed specifically at women, a "Politikon ersten Ranges" ("politicum of the first order") for the Nazification of society, propagating "germanisch-nordisches Empfinden" ("Germanic-Nordic sensibility") and the motto GEMEINNUTZ VOR EIGENNUTZ (the common good over individual interest).[9]

It would be wrong, however, to assume that women were entirely confined to the clichéd roles of KINDER, KÜCHE, KIRCHE. The ideal Nazi woman was also hardened for battle and sacrifice with her male companion. The NSF provided the guards for the only women's KZ to be opened in 1933 (Moringen in Lower Saxony), ninety percent of whose inmates were Jehovah's Witnesses (Koonz 1987, p. 334), and in the late 1930s, as women became increasingly visible in the war economy, Scholtz-Klink (from 1936 also Head of the 'Frauenbüro' of the German Labour Front ('Deutsche Arbeitsfront', DAF)) voiced their "selbstverständliche[n] innere[n] Gehorsam" ("natural inner obedience") to the Führer (Schneider 2001, p. 96; Koonz 1987, p. 338). Recent studies, including those by Geraldine Horan, Claudia Koonz, and Jill Stephenson, have painted a more detailed picture of women's position and experiences in Nazi society than can be given here. Whatever the nuances of this picture, there can be little doubt that what power women possessed was largely separate from, and subordinate to, male power. Horan (2003, p. 122) notes, for example, that "women in National Socialism were primarily concerned with organising and appealing to other women". Women also appear to have been disproportionately targeted by implementation of the race laws, more likely than men to be accused of RASSENSCHANDE, and denounced as ARTVERGESSEN ('race-forgotten') whores (Koonz 1987, pp. 177–219).

Attempted Regulation of the Media

Control of radio (incorporated into the Propaganda Ministry) and the new medium of film (through state-controlled production companies) was relatively easy, but the arts and the print media, with their diverse outlets and established traditions, presented a much greater challenge.

GLEICHSCHALTUNG was never fully achieved in these spheres (Toepser-Ziegert 1984, p. 23f.). In journalism, a law regulating the activities of newspaper editors ('Schriftleitergesetz') established professional courts to dispense punishments, including suspension from the profession. Regulation of the public discourse in the print media began with regular Press Conferences ('Pressekonferenzen') at the Propaganda Ministry, to which representatives of newspapers were invited, to be told what was expected from them in terms of what stories were (or were not) to be covered, how prominently, and which words and expressions were to be preferred, or avoided. These instructions to the press were to be kept secret from the public: each correspondent was required to attest in writing that any notes and records from these meetings had been destroyed. The sanctions against those who disobeyed this order included the death penalty, and there is at least one record of a journalist being sentenced to life imprisonment for breaching this stricture.[10] The rising number of these 'Presseanweisungen' (instructions to the press) reveal the increasing reach of the Propaganda Ministry: 1933: 300; 1934: 1000; 1938: 3750; 1939: 4620.[11] We know this because two men in particular disobeyed the order to destroy their records: Fritz Sänger (1901–1984) of the *Frankfurter Zeitung*, and Karl Brammer (1891–1964) of the National Daily Newspaper Service (DINATAG).[12] In addition, from 1 November 1940 the Reich Press Chief Otto Dietrich distributed daily instructions ('Tagesparolen'), which were to be passed on verbatim to the editorial offices. By the outbreak of war in 1939, it has been calculated, 15,000 secret instructions had been issued, rising to somewhere between 65,000 and 80,000 by the end of the war (Sänger 1975, p. 74–77; Toepser-Ziegert 1984, p. 24). Press control operated on a number of levels: institutional, economic, and at the level of content (Toepser-Ziegert 1984, p. 23f.). At the institutional level, the employment, training, and activities of journalists were regulated by a byzantine system of statutes and regulatory bodies which, inter alia, excluded Jews and Marxists from the profession. The 'Schriftleitergesetz' regulated entry to the profession, and journalists further had to be members of the Reich Press Chamber ('Reichspressekammer'). Once admitted to the list of approved journalists, they were enrolled in the Reich Association of the German Press ('Reichsverband der Deutschen Presse'), a kind of professional association which also set up special courts for settling professional disputes. Economic control was exercised through threats of closure in an overcrowded market, by a programme of 'Aryanizing' titles in Jewish ownership and (more or less compulsory) purchase by the NSDAP's own publishing enterprise, the Franz-Eher-Verlag under the directorship of Max Amann, president of the Reich Press Chamber. At the level of content, stories were sourced through a single news agency, the German News Bureau ('Deutsches Nachrichtenbüro', DNB, sarcastically known as DARF NICHTS BRINGEN: "not allowed to report anything"), and the secret directives which soon began to issue from the Propaganda Ministry.

The Imperfect Control of the Print Media

The system of censorship and control of the print media was far from uniform, and far from perfect. Journals and periodicals were in general subject to pre-publication censorship. There are cases (see Chap. 6) of individual issues of a journal being delayed or withdrawn because of an offending article. The vast majority of book publications, on the other hand, were subject to a rather lax post-publication censorship. What this meant in practice was a system of self-censorship by authors (who had to be registered with the appropriate chamber of the 'Kulturkammer') and publishing houses. There is, to the surprise of those not familiar with the field, quite a rich non-conformist, coded literature (see Chap. 6) which could be considered oppositional. Many of these books escaped censure, some were even positively reviewed, and those that did attract the attention of the Propaganda Ministry or one of the many agencies for monitoring literary output, such as the 'Amt Rosenberg' or the SS journal *Das schwarze Korps*, were already on the market and received a warning that their non-conformity had been noted, in itself an uncomfortable experience.

Control of the press was equally complex, and it needs to be remembered that in 1933 Goebbels chose to allow independent titles to continue, calculating that they could be useful to the regime's image abroad and for reaching those who were resistant to 'gleichgeschaltet' titles. Here too, self-censorship and fear of repercussions was a powerful means of control, but in addition there were the thousands of 'Presseanweisungen' and 'Tagesparolen'. Those issued from 1933 to 1939 have now been published. Many, perhaps surprisingly, were formulated as suggestions and invitations, leaving editors discretion, which they then exploited. Much more telling are the instructions to silence, and even here not all were complied with. Thus, "the implausibility of the prosecution witnesses" in the Reichstag fire trial prompted a request that reporting of the day's proceedings "be kept to a minimum". This did not deter the *Hamburger Nachrichten* from printing a headline mentioning "untrustworthy witnesses" the following morning (17.11.1933).[13] The degree of control could be intense, however, as in the diktat that von Papen's (and Jung's) Marburg speech of 17 June 1934 "darf in der Presse nicht gebracht werden" (18.6.1934, "must not be published in the press"). The reporting of the murders of 30 June 1934 was also strictly controlled. Death announcements by the victims' families needed clearance by the Ministry (4.7.1934). The death announcement for Erich Klausener, Director of the 'Katholische Aktion' in Berlin, led to a publication ban for the Catholic *Germania*. The *Neue Züricher Zeitung*, which reported the Vatican's rejection of the official version that he had committed suicide, received a two-week import ban. Reproduction of the pastoral letter of the German bishops, on 4 July 1934, was forbidden. On the other hand, American news reports of Schleicher's contacts with France were to be reported prominently (5.7.1934). Toepser-Ziegert (Bohrmann/Toepser-Ziegert Bd. 2, p. 35) observes that, contrary to popular belief, the 'Night of the Long Knives' was a tightly managed media non-event, in which all independent reporting and commentary was forbidden: "the events were played down and presented as an unpleasant but necessary duty which Hitler had to perform in the interests of Germany. The newspapers presented a fake impression of daily normality, and the press instructions show why". The tens of thousands of secret instructions to the press demonstrate just how important the control of information was to the regime. This vast expenditure of effort was directed not only at regulating knowledge of events by determining what stories appeared (and did not appear) in the press, with what degree of prominence, and from what point of view, but also at surreptitiously altering the usage, and therefore the meaning, of words and expressions—a covert exercise in semantic manipulation.

Rewriting the Lexicon I: Covert Instructions

"Dieses Wort existiert nicht mehr" ("This word no longer exists"). This statement is found in a 'Presseanweisung' of 13 February 1937 concerning the word 'Völkerbund' (League of Nations). Henceforth, the German press must refer to the 'GENFER ENTENTE' (Geneva Entente). Examples of attempted manipulation of public language by hundreds of secret 'Sprachregelungen' include a direction to replace the word 'antisemitisch' with ANTIJÜDISCH in order not to alienate other semitic peoples (22.8.1935); to restrict MISCHEHE to 'inter-racial' marriages (19.12.1935); and to proscribe the use of RASSE in the sense 'kind of/make of/brand of' ("Rasse der formvollendeten Modehüte", make of shapely fashionable hats). RASSE was to be used only in racial contexts (14.1.1937). PROPAGANDA was declared a legally protected term ("gewissermaßen ein gesetzlich geschützter Begriff") to be used positively about official German propaganda (28.7.1937). For hostile propaganda, a term such as GREUELHETZE (not 'Greuelpropaganda') should be used. In 1939 the title FÜHRER UND REICHSKANZLER is abandoned; in future Hitler was to be described simply as FÜHRER (14.1.1939). A similar decision directs that the term DRITTES REICH "is no longer to be used". The compulsory designation is now GROSSDEUTSCHES REICH (22.6.1939). Sometimes these instructions contain politically sensitive information about the aims of the regime. After the incorporation of Austria into the Reich, a "strictly confidential" instruction advises on the use of the terms GROSSDEUTSCH and VOLKSDEUTSCH, explaining that GROSSDEUTSCH can still be used to draw a distinction with KLEINDEUTSCH (the German part of the Reich), but must not give the impression that Germany has no more territorial claims beyond Austria (21.3.1938). With surprising candour, the directive explains that other territories "naturally" belong to the GROSSDEUTSCHES REICH, "which we will lay claim to in due course". On the other hand, the term VOLKSDEUTSCHES REICH must be avoided, as this might imply designs on German-speaking territories "in south-eastern Europe" which is "of course not our intention".

Such instructions were implemented with varying degrees of rigour, and it is a moot point to what extent this hidden manipulation of words and their uses succeeded in changing public perceptions and attitudes (Glunk

1966–1971). A case in point, to which we will return in Chap. 6, is PROPAGANDA, where attempts to school the population in the Party's usage largely failed. Such cases highlight the limits of GLEICHSCHALTUNG and serve as a warning not to subscribe uncritically to its 'totalitarian' myth.

Rewriting the Lexicon II: The Example of the 'Duden' Dictionary

Norms of language behaviour are usually subconscious, formed and endorsed by habitual usage (the target of the 'Sprachregelungen'). Where norms become problematic, for example in disputes about 'what words mean', we often turn to the formal codifications of the language in authoritative reference works. Perusing German dictionaries and encyclopedias published between 1933 and 1945 is an exercise in historical political semantics, for which a brief consideration of the *Duden* dictionary, the subject of a fascinating study by Wolfgang Werner Sauer (1989) must suffice here. In 1933 the editor of the previous (1929) edition, Theodor Matthias, was replaced by the National Socialist Otto Basler, whose 1934 edition contains radical changes reflecting the new ideology. Headwords making a first appearance include those designating concrete institutions of the new political order (such as SA, SS, and FRAUENSCHAFT), but also those carrying Nazi racial ideologemes such as AUFNORDEN (to 'nordify', i.e. increase the 'nordic'/germanic stock), AUFARTEN (similar to AUFNORDEN), ERBGESUND (free from hereditary disease) and FREMDRASSIG (belonging to an alien race); political ones such as MACHTERGREIFUNG (seizure of power); and pseudo-legal ones such as SIPPENHAFT (arrest of family members). Compounded expressions containing or deriving from key ideologemes such as REICH (REICHSERBHOFGESETZ, State Hereditary Farm Law) contributed to the quantitative normalization of ideological vocabulary. KONZENTRATIONSLAGER, another new entry in 1934, is glossed as "Sammellager für Zivilgefangene, Volksschädlinge" ("collection camp for civil internees, elements harmful to the 'Volk'"), thus also normalizing the concept VOLKSSCHÄDLING. The 1934 edition was prepared in co-operation with the Deutscher Sprachverein and the Sprachpflegeamt in Munich, which might explain the introductory reference to the Romantic trope of the German language as “unlösbares Band” (“indissoluble bond”) of the VOLKSGEMEINSCHAFT, the inclusion of WELSCH, defined as speaking UNDEUTSCH by using avoidable (“entbehrliche”) ‘Fremdwörter’; and the differentiation in meaning between REICHSDEUTSCH (i.e. Austrian) and VOLKSDEUTSCH (pertaining to German speaking minorities in third states), reproducing the Pan-Germanic discourse with its roots in the nineteenth century. There were also alterations to or extensions of meaning for headwords contained in the 1929 edition. Thus FEMINISMUS, glossed in 1929 as “women’s emancipation, emphasis of the female principle”, is defined in 1934 as “excessive emphasis of the female principle, dominance of unmanly attitudes”; and the 1934 definition of ARIER, glossed in 1929 as “eastern Indogermanic ‘Volk’”, distinguishes between “sprachlich”: “member of a ‘Volk’ with Indogermanic language”, and “rassenpolitisch”: “im Gegensatz bes. zum jüd. Volk gebraucht: Deutschblütiger; Angehöriger einer europäischen Hauptrasse” (“used in contradistinction especially to the Jewish ‘Volk’: person of German blood, member of a major European ‘Volk’”). These speedy accommodations in the 1934 edition were possible, Sauer observes, not only because of Basler’s editorship, but also because these expressions and meanings had been common currency in the years before 1933. The ‘new normal’ had not appeared from nowhere in 1933. It is worth noting that even the 1929 edition had normalized ideological vocabulary of the far right, including SCHMACHFRIEDEN (shameful peace, i.e. the Versailles Treaty), ENTJUDUNG (‘dejewification’) and FREMDVÖLKISCH (pertaining to an alien ‘Volk’).

The German Language and the ‘Volksgeist’

German language purists believed that the regime would embrace their vision of the language as a ‘holy’ manifestation of the ‘Volk’, and their long-standing campaign to ‘cleanse’ (SÄUBERN) German of foreign elements. They were mistaken, although the fact that it took the regime some seven years to make this clear might explain the persistence of the purists’ naivety. Initially the regime was probably happy to enjoy the support of this fervently nationalistic constituency in the early months and years of its rule. Indeed, there was some support for purist attitudes in the Nazi hierarchy before the key players, notably Goebbels, won the argument. Finally, by 1940 the war had rendered arcane arguments about the 'völkisch' credentials of the German language peripheral. A pragmatic view of language prevailed. The anticipated victory (ENDSIEG), with its prospect of a NEUORDNUNG (re-ordering) of Europe under German hegemony, prompted ever more practical thinking about what kind of German would best serve as the language of administration in the conquered territories. A German which was Gothic in its printed form and deprived of lexical internationalisms would clearly make this task much more difficult. The *coup de grâce* was delivered in two decrees from the Führer, jettisoning any vestige of ideological allegiance to Gothic script and to linguistic purism, both of which, to the general astonishment of the population, were declared to be Jewish in inspiration.

The Demise of Linguistic Purism

The campaign against the "un-German" 'Fremdwort', the hobby horse of the Deutscher Sprachverein (German Language Association) since its founding in 1885 by Hermann Riegel, was finally swatted aside by Hitler's pronouncement of 19 November 1940.

> Der Führer wünscht nicht derartige gewaltsame Eindeutschungen und billigt nicht die künstliche Ersetzung längst ins Deutsche eingebürgerter Fremdworte durch nicht aus dem Geist der deutschen Sprache geborene und den Sinn der Fremdworte meist nur unvollkommen wiedergebende Wörter.[14]
>
> The Führer does not wish to see this kind of forced Germanizing of foreign words and does not approve of artificially replacing foreign words which have long since become part of the German language with words which are not born from the spirit of the German language and which frequently render the sense of the loan words only imperfectly.

For half a century the Verein had campaigned against the "degeneration" (ENTARTUNG) caused by lexical borrowing, especially from English, and for the nationalistic and normative cultivation of a 'pure' MUTTERSPRACHE, and so it seemed only natural that it should welcome the new regime. Indeed, the purist agenda had found supporters in some key ministries (Darré, Frick, and Buttmann, who became the Association's new Chairman in May 1933). In 1933, the association's journal *Muttersprache* had promptly announced the aim of being "the SA of our 'Muttersprache'", and contributions were increasingly characterized not only by the usual nationalism and chauvinism, but also by racist 'völkisch' attitudes. However, some of the contributors seriously misjudged their relationship to power, believing they had the right to praise and criticize the language of the regime. Some levelled the familiar argument against loan vocabulary, that it rendered meaning difficult to access for many Germans (which may of course have been the point of its use). Some even took to *ad hominem* criticisms of leading figures in the government, including the Führer himself, compounding the miscalculation by magnanimously excusing him on the grounds that he was too busy to think about these issues.[15] Some contributors sensed the danger and warned against imputing 'un-German' attitudes to every user of a 'Fremdwort'—negating Engel's hardline attitude of 1914. The tension had finally come to a head in 1937 when Goebbels struck the decisive blow in the *Völkischer Beobachter*, attacking the Association's "presumption" to speak on matters linguistic:

> Unsere heutigen deutschtümelnden Sprachakrobaten vergessen meistens, daß die Deutschheit aus dem Wesen unseres Volkes und nicht aus einer erdachten Theorie abgeleitet werden muß.[16]

> Our teutonizing language acrobats today often forget that Germanness must be derived from the essence of our 'Volk' and not from some made-up theory.

Goebbels cited an article in *Muttersprache* (Rehtmeyer 1937) which rejected the right of the Jew Eduard Engel, fervent German nationalist, most prominent campaigner against WELSCHEREI since before the First World War, and the most well-known Honorary Member of the Association, to comment on German culture. The Association promptly retired hurt to a special conclave in Stuttgart at which its General Director Rudolf Buttmann announced: "Wir rücken weit ab von der Fremdwortfrage" ("We will move far away from the 'Fremdwort' question").[17] At the same conclave, however, arch-ideologist Ewald Geißler aggressively pitched for racial awareness to be the guiding principle of their language criticism and cultivation. His programme was to pursue ARTGEGRÜNDETE SPRACHZUCHT (racially grounded cultivation of the language), to create "einen neuen Adel der Sprache" ("a new aristocracy of the language") by means of WORTAUFARTUNG (increasing the racial stock of the lexicon). But the cause was fatally wounded. Engel, its most prominent spokesman for a quarter of a century, died an impoverished pariah in 1938. Linguistic purism was a spent force. On 9 March 1938 a secret 'Presseanweisung' instructed the press that "kein Wort mehr" was to be printed on purist issues, adding that any newspaper not observing this "absolute proscription" would be "held to account" ("belangt werden") by the Propaganda Ministry.

'Antiqua' Replaces 'Fraktur': A Seismographic Shock

"Auf Anordnung des Führers soll nur noch Antiqua verwendet werden" ("By order of the Führer, only 'Antiqua' is to be used henceforth"). The 'Führererlass' of 9 January 1941 represented a fundamental shift in the politics of typeface and written language. To say that this decision came as a shock to the general population would be an understatement. Germans were completely unprepared for it. The printing presses did not have enough 'Antiqua' type to cope with the new diktat. Hitler's decree was not just unexpected, it appeared like an abrupt *volte face* in the German mindset, so natural had the alignment seemed in the early years of the regime between 'völkisch' politics and Gothic DEUTSCHE SCHRIFT (German Script), now to be replaced by DEUTSCHE NORMALSCHRIFT (German Normal Script), the new official term for 'Antiqua' typefaces.

Until this moment there had been a tendency within the polarized discourse on nationhood to associate Roman fonts (commonly known as 'Antiqua'), and especially non-serif fonts, with cosmopolitan (or 'decadent') Weimar democratic values, whilst Gothic (or 'broken') type (known to most Germans as 'Fraktur') was associated with quintessential Germanness. This neat simplification (still common today) belies the complex history of typeface as a political semiotic in German-speaking Europe, as Peter Rück has shown. In the immediate context of the 'Third Reich', Rück finds that the Nazi accession to power led to "a sudden but short-lived increase in 'Fraktur' which was already over before the beginning of the war and was succeeded by a tendency towards an imperial 'world type', which was then sanctioned in the 'Fraktur' ban of 1941" (Rück 1993, p. 251). (Goebbels's high-quality weekly *Das Reich*, launched in May 1940, already used 'Antiqua' typeface.) Rück traces the tensions in the symbolic associations of broken and Latin letters back at least two centuries, during which time Gothic 'black letter' types had taken on elements of a "heraldry" which "raised the sword against Enlightenment and industrialization". With the founding of the Reich in 1871, the typeface battle had taken on heightened symbolic significance in the atmosphere of cultural and political struggle, with broken types becoming associated with anti-French, anti-English, anti-Catholic, anti-classical, and 'völkisch' sentiments, these being "to this day the common stereotypes of the typographic criticism with which the beginning twentieth century regarded the nineteenth" (Rück 1993, p. 243). Thus, the competition between broken and rounded (Roman) types goes back to the late middle ages and became charged with political and racist meanings in the nineteenth century, when, Rück comments, "the attitude towards the Gothic script, the 'Fraktur', can be considered a seismographic device revealing ideological tendencies" (Rück 1993, p. 231). Von Polenz (1999, p. 48f.) compares the 1941 ban to an earthquake in the German public consciousness, the aftershocks of which were felt for a generation and more. The proscription of 'Fraktur', although it could be implemented only gradually due to lack of 'Antiqua' type and typesetters, has been much more radical and enduring in its impact on German public consciousness than the regime's resolution of the 'Fremdwort' question. In some respects, the two issues were related: in 1941, texts set in 'Fraktur' still conventionally set 'Fremdwörter' in 'Antiqua', and not just in purist publications like *Muttersprache*.[18] For many purists, however, typeface was not the key issue. Eduard Engel regarded the type question as "superfluous, even laughable, as long as the form of the language in the majority of what is printed is *welsch*" (Rück 1993, p. 242).

Gothic type had had its political proponents in the Party hierarchy. In 1933, Minister of the Interior Hans Frick stated that the DEUTSCHE SCHRIFT must never be allowed to lose its "absolute superiority" over the Latin scripts, and even ordered that German typewriters should be produced with Gothic letters (Rück 1993, p. 265). The order was never carried out, and Hitler may well have had Frick in mind in 1934 when he attacked the Romantic "Rückwärtse" (backward-lookers) in the movement. Rück finds an increase in the use of broken letter type in editions of collected works of classic authors between 1933 and 1935, and notes that from 1934 new coins and postage stamps used only 'Fraktur'. This may go some way to explain the widespread perception that broken type, the "stamp of the German spirit" (Rück 1993, p. 259), was the natural typographical manifestation of National Socialism. In fact, as Rück (1993, p. 238) points out, the situation was much more nuanced. Over the previous hundred years 'Antiqua' had become the default "Exportschrift" for scientific texts, accompanying the rise of German as a world language of science, and hybrid typefaces, particularly "modernized" versions of broken type, had become increasingly common in the twentieth century. The most familiar example of a modernized 'Fraktur' is the inscription on the façade of the Reichstag, DEM DEUTSCHEN VOLKE, the letters of which are rounded rather than angular. This particular typeface (and wording—earlier suggestions had included DEM DEUTSCHEN REICHE), dating from 1916, was finally accepted by the Kaiser with an eye on national morale in the war, after a fierce debate lasting some twenty years. There were thus many modernized broken typefaces in circulation, some of which had shed the angular sharpness typically associated with the letters found, for example, on the caps of Kriegsmarine sailors. A curious footnote to Hitler's decree is Martin Bormann's internal memo "by order of the Führer" dated 3 January 1941, anticipating the formal announcement, which asserted (without a shred of evidence) that Schwabacher type, the first widespread broken letter font in the late fifteenth century, in which Luther's 1532 Bible translation had appeared, had been found to be a Jewish invention.

Mother-Tongue Fascism

Today it is tempting to see the Sprachverein and the whole of the purist movement as a rather comical footnote in German discourse history, a madcap movement populated by zealous but harmless amateurs. That would be a mistake, even though these two decrees finally rebutted an ideology which viewed the language as the 'third force' of German fascism which would set MUTTERSPRACHE on a par with BLUT and BODEN as a determining characteristic of 'race'. As noted in Chap. 2, Hitler had been consistently clear on this question. But it would be wrong to close this chapter without pointing to the very real impacts of mother-tongue fascism. Two strands of research deserve mention here. The first, represented in the work of Ruth Römer (1989) and Christopher Hutton (1999), documents the origins of 'Aryan' racist ideology in nineteenth-century linguistics—in the concept of an 'Indo-european Ursprache'—, its claims to the legacy of Herder and Wilhelm von Humboldt, and the continuation of this discourse on language and 'Volk' in academic research and lay writing on language in the Nazi period. Kämper-Jensen (1993) examines sixty one publications on language in which lay and professional commentators placed their 'research' at the service of the regime in tracts lauding the language of the Party and the Führer, the 'Volk''s new racial consciousness and its linguistic renewal. About one third of these publications explicitly equate race with language with 'Volk', excluding Jews from the German speech community, attacking any suggestion that they formed a sub-set of the 'Volk' even linguistically, perpetuating a narrative of difference constructed on notions such as MAUSCHELDEUTSCH and MIMIKRY.[19] Hutton's study adds much detail to this history, including famous names in twentieth-century linguistic theory such as Jost Trier and Leo Weisgerber. Together with the editorial staff of the *Duden*, many professional commentators on language in this period do appear to warrant description as "willing helpers" of the regime.

The second strand, represented particularly in the work of Gerd Simon (1979, 1982, 1985, 1989, 2000; Lerchenmüller and Simon 1997) traces the connections between MUTTERPSRACHE ideology and fascism, murder, and genocide. This discourse was also, Simon observes, "eine auf Gewalt angelegte, zeitweise eine gewaltbegleitende oder -auslösende und begründende Aktivität" ("an activity tending to violence, occasionally accompanying or unleashing and justifying violence", Simon 2000, p. vii). For example, professional philologists (including Weisgerber) were seconded to special units of the SS and the AHNENERBE (set up within the SS to safeguard 'Aryan' blood heritage) in occupied territories. Language policy in these territories, and the designation of groups as VOLKSDEUTSCHE (von Polenz 1999, p. 156f.) often decided between life and death—concentration camp for those who persisted in speaking French in the Alsace; selection by language for survival in the Generalgouvernement in Poland. Linguistic politics also meshed with racial persecution in the Reich, as in the case of the 'Comedian Harmonists' music ensemble, pursued originally because of their English name (Simon 2000, p. 1f.). The crimes of National Socialism were in no small part aided and abetted by mother-tongue fascism, a philosophy of language contradicted by common sense long before Chomsky's work on psycholinguistic universals started from the observation that any human child can acquire any human language regardless of ethnicity.

This all too brief survey of the norms and contradictions of the state-sanctioned hegemonic discourse *in* National Socialism, its foundation in violence and intimidation, and its almost total reach, provides the backdrop for the study of the 'unquiet voices' of those persecuted or repelled by the regime and forced into an existence of inner or outer exile. It is to those that we now turn.

Notes

1. A conspicuous example is the resilience shown by those in the Evangelical Church who formed the BEKENNENDE KIRCHE, resisting the pressure to join the 'co-ordinated' DEUTSCHE CHRISTEN.
2. Grüttner 2014, p. 158f. Cf. Benz 2006, p. 119. The precise number of KZs opened in 1933 is a matter of some variation in the literature: Koonz (1987, p. 334) puts it at ninety.
3. See Benz 2006, especially pp. 121–230 and the chronology on pp. xii–xiv.
4. See the discussion of Brecht's *Fear and Misery of the Third Reich* in Chap. 4.

5. Cf. YouTube: https://www.youtube.com/watch?v=N1cSHyk1yb8 (13.5.2017).
6. The English translation struggles to reflect the multiple meanings and insinuations of the original. "Zentrummel rühren" is a blend of 'Zentrum' (drum in a rotating machine) and 'Werbetrommel rühren' (beat the drum for), and may contain an ironic reference to the Catholic Zentrum party. "mechten" is meant as a stylized Jewish pronunciation. "Devisenmusikanten" plays on 'Devisenspekulanten' (foreign currency speculators). "Jemandem die Flötentöne beibringen" is colloquial for 'teach someone who is the boss', and "taktvoll" implies both 'keeping time' and 'tactful'.
7. Cf. my reading of Sternberger's "Blick der Liebenden" in Chap. 7.
8. The heavy bombing of Birmingham five days later was reported in the German press in terms of multiples of a "Coventry". The term appears to be a modern version of "magdeburgisieren", following the devastation of Magdeburg in 1631.
9. Lethmair 1956, pp. 175–199, quoting Ruth Gaensecke and Josef Goebbels respectively (p. 176f.).
10. Walter Schwerdtfeger, of the *Berliner Börsenzeitung*, in 1935, for passing on information to foreign correspondents. See Bohrmann/Toepser-Ziegert Bd. 3/I, p. 38f.
11. Toepser-Ziegert 2007, p. 87. These records (ZSg. 101 and ZSg. 102 respectively) are housed in the Federal Archive in Koblenz. On the extent and degree of success of these measures, cf. Glunk 1966–1971, Hagemann 1970.
12. For the period 1933–1939, 19 volumes of these combined sets of documents have been published. Brammer's collection carries the classification mark ZSg. 101, Sänger's ZSg. 102. Cf. Bohrmann and Toepser-Ziegert 1984–2001.
13. Instructions to the press are referenced here by the date of issue. They can be located (where cited) in the relevant volume of Bohrmann and Toepser-Ziegert 1984, Bergsdorf 1978, pp. 73–102, and Glunk 1966–1971. Readers are directed to these sources for a comprehensive overview.
14. *Deutsche Wissenschaft, Erziehung und Volksbildung*, Amtsblatt. 6, 1940, p. 534. Cf. Bernsmeier 1983, p. 43. This section is indebted to Bernsmeier 1983.
15. E.g. Arthur Hübner, *Muttersprache* 1934, column 110f.

16. *Völkischer Beobachter*, Munich edition, 3.5.1937. Quoted by Bernsmeier 1983, p. 43; cf. von Polenz 1967, p. 135.
17. The following quotations are from the report of this conclave in *Muttersprache* 52 (1937), Heft 6, pp. 252–258.
18. This convention can also be found in publications in 'Fraktur' after 1945.
19. See Robertson 1999, p. 260f. A particularly interesting case of the subservient academic discourse documented by Kämper-Jensen is the *volte-face* of Georg Schmidt-Rohr, one of the outstanding academic linguists of the day. Heavily attacked for his 1933 work *MutterSprache*, in which he discounted language as a determining characteristic of race, and therefore as a basis for excluding Jews from the 'Volk', his subsequent research conforms to the hegemonic racist narrative. Cf. Simon 1986.

Bibliography

Bauer, Gerhard. 1988. *Sprache und Sprachlosigkeit im "Dritten Reich"*. Köln: Bund-Verlag.

Benz, Wolfgang. 2006. *A Concise History of the Third Reich*. Translated by Thomas Dunlap Berkeley. Los Angeles: University of California Press.

Bergsdorf, Wolfgang. 1978. *Politik und Sprache*. München, Wien: Günter Olzog Verlag.

Bernsmeier, Helmut. 1983. Der Deutsche Sprachverein im 'Dritten Reich'. *Muttersprache* 93: 35–58.

Bohrmann, Hans, and Gabriele Toepser-Ziegert, Hgg. 1984–2001. *NS-Presseanweisungen der Vorkriegszeit*. 7 Bände in 19 Teilen. München: K.G. Saur.

Glunk, Rolf. 1966–1971. Erfolg und Misserfolg der nationalsozialistischen Sprachlenkung. *Zeitschrift für deutsche Sprache* 22–27.

Grüttner, Michael. 2014. *Gebhardt Handbuch der deutschen Geschichte*. 10, völlig neu bearbeitete Auflage, Bd. 19, *Das Dritte Reich 1933–1939*. Stuttgart: Klett-Cotta.

Hagemann, Jürgen. 1970. *Die Presselenkung im Dritten Reich*. Bonn: Bouvier.

Horan, Geraldine. 2003. *Mothers, Warriors, Guardians of the Soul. Female Discourse in National Socialism*. Berlin: de Gruyter.

Hutton, Christopher. 1999. *Linguistics and the Third Reich: Mother Tongue Fascism, Race and the Science of Language*. London: Routledge.

Kämper-Jensen, Heidrun. 1993. Spracharbeit im Dienst des NS-Staats 1933 bis 1945. *Zeitschrift für Germanistische Linguistik* 21 (2): 150–183.

Keller, R.E. 1978. *The German Language*. London: Faber.

Koonz, Claudia. 1987. *Mothers in the Fatherland. Women, the Family and Nazi Politics*. New York: St. Martin's Press.

Lerchenmüller, Joachim, and Gerd Simon. 1997. *Im Vorfeld des Massenmords. Germanistik und Nachbarfächer im 2. Weltkrieg: eine Übersicht*. Dritte Auflage ed. Tübingen: Gesellschaft für interdisziplinäre Forschung.

Lethmair, Thea. 1956. *Die Frauenbeilage der 'Frankfurter Zeitung'*. Ihre Struktur – ihre geistigen Grundlagen: Dissertation, Ludwig-Maximilians-Universität München.

Magub, Roshan. 2017. *Edgar Julius Jung, Right-Wing Enemy of the Nazis. A Political Biography*. Rochester, New York: Camden House.

Oldfield, Sybil. 1986. German Women in the Resistance to Hitler. In *Women, State and Revolution*, ed. Sian Reynolds. Wheatsheaf: Brighton.

von Polenz, Peter. 1967. Sprachpurismus und Nationalsozialismus. In *Germanistik—Eine deutsche Wissenschaft*, Hg. Lämmert et al., 111–165. Frankfurt/Main: Suhrkamp.

———. 1999. *Deutsche Sprachgeschichte vom Spätmittelalter bis zur Gegenwart*. Bd 3: *19. und 20. Jahrhundert*. Berlin, New York: de Gruyter.

Rehtmeyer, V. 1937. Fremdwort, Deutschheit und Schrifttumsgeschichte. *Muttersprache* 52, Heft 4, Sp. 141–143.

Robertson, Ritchie. 1999. *The 'Jewish Question' in German Literature 1749–1939: Emancipation and Its Discontents*. Oxford: Oxford University Press.

Römer, Ruth. 1989. *Sprachwissenschaft und Rassenideologie in Deutschland*. München: Wilhelm Fink.

Rück, Peter. 1993. Die Sprache der Schrift. Zur Geschichte des Frakturverbots von 1941. In *Homo scribens. Perspektiven der Schriftlichkeitsforschung*, Hg. Jürgen Baurmann et al., 231–272. Tübingen: Niemeyer.

Sänger, Fritz. 1975. *Politik der Täuschungen. Missbrauch der Presse im Dritten Reich. Weisungen, Informationen, Notizen 1933–1939*. Wien: Europaverlag.

Sauer, Wolfgang Werner. 1989. Der *Duden* im 'Dritten Reich'. In *Sprache im Faschismus*, Hg. Konrad Ehlich, 104–119. Frankfurt/Main: Suhrkamp.

Schneider, Wolfgang. 2001. *Frauen unterm Hakenkreuz*. Hamburg: Hoffmann und Campe.

Simon, Gerd. 1979. *Sprachwissenschaft und politisches Engagement. Zur Problem- und Sozialgeschichte einiger sprachtheoretischer, sprachdidaktischer und sprachpflegerischer Ansätze in der Germanistik des 19. u. 20. Jahrhunderts* (*Pragmalinguisitk* 18). Basel, Weinheim: Beltz.

———. 1982. Zündschnur zum Sprengstoff: Leo Weisgwerbers keltologische Forschungen und seine Tätigkeit als Zensuroffizier in Rennes während des 2. Weltkriegs. *Linguistische Berichte* 79: 30–52.

———. 1985. Sprachwissenschaft im 3. Reich. Ein erster Überblick. In *Politische Sprachwissenschaft*, Hg. Franz Januschek, 375–396. Opladen: Westdeutscher Verlag.

———. 1986. Wissenschaft und Wende 1933. Zum Verhältnis von Wissenschaft und Politik am Beispiel des Sprachwissenschaftlers Georg Schmidt-Rohr. https://homepages.uni-tuebingen.de//gerd.simon/wende1933.pdf. Accessed 1 October 2017.

———. 1989. *Sprachpflege im 'Dritten Reich'.* Hg. Ehlich, pp. 58–86.

———. 2000. *Muttersprache und Menschenverfolgung. Kollektivkritik zwischen Marginalienkult und Gewaltbereitschaft. Homepage Universität Tübingen.* https://homepages.uni-tuebingen.de/gerd.simon/muttersprache.pdf. Accessed 1 October 2017.

Toepser-Ziegert, Gabriele. 1984. *NS-Presseanweisungen der Vorkriegszeit: eine Einführung in ihre Edition.* Hg. Hans Bohrmann and Gabriele Toepser-Ziegert (1984–2001), Bd. 1. München u.a.: Saur.

———. 2007. Die Existenz der Journalisten unter den Bedingungen der Diktatur. In *"Diener des Staates" oder "Widerstand zwischen den Zeilen"?: die Rolle der Presse im "Dritten Reich": (XVIII. Königswinterer Tagung Februar 2005)*, Hg. Christoph Studt, 75–88. Münster: LIT Verlag Münster.

Wells, C.J. 1985. *German: A Linguistic History to 1945*. Oxford: Clarendon.

4

Voices from Abroad: Thomas Mann, Karl Kraus, Ernst Bloch, Bertolt Brecht, Irmgard Keun, Heinz Paechter

In the early months of the regime, critical voices from abroad may have still found an audience in Germany, but censorship, legislation, and fear quickly deprived the vast majority of Germans of access to these voices, certainly in the print media, as Thomas Mann noted in a radio broadcast in October 1940:

> Im Kriege jetzt gibt es für das geschriebene Wort keine Möglichkeit mehr, den Wall zu durchdringen, den die Tyrannei um euch errichtet hat. ("Deutsche Hörer!", Mann 1990, vol XI, p. 986)[1]
>
> In the war now there is no longer any possibility for the written word to penetrate the rampart which tyranny has erected around you.

Mann's personal safety was under threat after his "Deutsche Ansprache. Ein Appell an die Vernunft" (pp. 870–890, German Address. An Appeal to Reason), a speech delivered in October 1930, and interrupted by Nazi youths, in the Beethoven-Saal in Berlin. He left Germany in February 1933 and settled in the USA in 1938. Through the medium of radio, his "warnende Stimme" (warning voice), informing Germans of the atrocities

W J Dodd, *National Socialism and German Discourse*,
https://doi.org/10.1007/978-3-319-74660-9_4

committed in their name, urging them to look to their consciences, and prophesying the victory of democracy, was one of the very few voices from abroad which could reach Germans in the Reich. Fifty six broadcasts, recorded in Los Angeles between October 1940 and May 1945, were transmitted on long wave by the BBC in London so that they could be picked up on the 'Volksempfänger' in every German home by those prepared to risk arrest on a charge of treason (pp. 983–1123 (p. 997)). The following extract, from the address of 27 September 1942, gives a flavour of these speeches:

> Das Ghetto von Warschau, wo fünfhunderttausend Juden aus Polen, Tschechoslowakien und Deutschland in zwei Dutzend elende Straßen zusammangepfercht worden sind, ist nichts als eine Hunger-, Pest- und Todesgrube, aus der Leichengeruch steigt. Fünfundsechzigtausend Menschen sind dort in *einem* Jahr, dem vorigen, gestorben. Nach den Informationen der polnischen Exil-Regierung sind alles in allem bereits siebenhundertausend Juden von der Gestapo gemordet oder zu Tode gequält worden, wovon siebzigtausend allein auf die Region von Minsk in Polen entfallen. Wißt ihr Deutsche das? Und wie findet ihr es? (p. 1052)

> The Warsaw Ghetto, where 500,000 Jews from Poland, Czechoslovakia and Germany have been crammed together into two dozen miserable streets, is nothing but a pit of hunger, pestilence and death with the stench of corpses rising from it. 65,000 persons have died there in *one* year, the last one. All in all, according to the information of the Polish Government in Exile, 700,000 Jews have been murdered or tormented to death by the Gestapo, of whom 70,000 alone were from the Minsk region. Do you know that, Germans? And what do you think about it?

As Mann observed, it was much easier for the regime to police the written word and prevent its dissemination within the Reich. The voices reviewed in this chapter, though they may be as steadfast and often as forthright as Mann's, fall into this category, and remained largely or wholly unheard in Germany until 1945—and some much later.

The five authors discussed in the remainder of this chapter have been chosen for their closeness to the language question and their responses to the problem of gaining a critical purchase on Nazism through the prism of language. Kraus, Bloch and Brecht appear as exponents of the essay, Brecht and Keun as writers of imaginative fiction,[2] and finally (also in the chronology of these works) Paechter as an example of the inventorist. With the partial exception of Karl Kraus, who withheld sections of his work from publication, they exemplify the plain-speaking free voice—as opposed to the 'subaltern' voice in its various guises which we will encounter in the following chapters. Writing in exile, Bertolt Brecht and Irmgard Keun created damningly realistic reconstructions of everyday life in Nazi Germany. Brecht, Kraus, and Ernst Bloch all reflected on the problems of finding an adequate anti-fascist language: Kraus pessimistically, Bloch analytically, and Brecht both analytically and as the author of practical guidance on the critical role of language in resisting and gainsaying the regime. Brecht, putting his theoretical model into practice, represents, with Keun, the voice of confident contradiction and subversion. Whilst Paechter might be seen to prefigure the kind of critical lexicography which began in the 1960s with the work of Schmitz-Berning and others, it is Kraus and Brecht who are arguably the most important models in the history of German political language criticism in the twentieth century. Their legacy would be taken up in various ways by anti-fascist commentators during the Reich and, to a greater extent, in the public discourse on German fascism from 1945.

Karl Kraus

Karl Kraus was one of the most trenchant contemporary critics of the Nazis, yet his voice was not heard in full until 1952, some sixteen years after his death in 1936, with the posthumous publication of *Dritte Walpurgisnacht*, the "third Witches' Sabbath"—the first two being scenes in Goethe's *Faust*. The work references literary representations of human baseness, with many quotations from *Faust*[3] and from Shakespeare, notably *Macbeth* (which begins with yet another Witches' Sabbath). Kraus is still often remembered for his "Schweigen" (falling silent) when faced with Nazism, and he did decide not to publish the full text of *Dritte Walpurgisnacht*, on which he worked intensively from May to September 1933. As an Austrian citizen, Kraus, in 1933 the most celebrated and pugnacious practitioner of *ad hominem* language criticism in the German-speaking world, was technically not in exile from the regime. Nevertheless, his public silence was rooted in part at least in a justified fear of reprisal against a Viennese Jew—despite his (lapsed) Catholicism—and his followers. The political murder of writers was a reality—indeed Kraus mentions the murder of Theodor Lessing (Kraus 1989, p. 106), on whose head the Nazis had put a bounty, in Marienbad on 31 August 1933,[4] and it is likely that this was a factor in the decision not to publish the whole work. Austria's physical separateness from the Reich offered Kraus no protection, to all intents and purposes he may as well have been writing in Munich.

It is important to note, however, that Kraus did not fall completely silent; he announced his public "Schweigen" in minimal but meaningful statements, and in July 1934 he published extracts from the work in *Die Fackel* (The Torch), the journal he single-handedly wrote and edited. This raises the question of whether the chosen extracts represent a watered-down version of the whole, for quite understandable reasons of self-preservation. My impression, however, is that the published passages from the *Walpurgisnacht*, unlike those from Theodor Haecker's diaries in 1940 in the Catholic journal *Hochland* (see Chap. 5), pay only slight heed to such considerations. Unless otherwise indicated, all quotations from the *Walpurgisnacht* in this chapter are from the extracts published in *Die Fackel* in July 1934 in issue 890–905, an issue of over three hundred pages titled "Why *Die Fackel* is not appearing", in which the opening section of the *Dritte Walpurgisnacht*, with its famous first sentence "Mir fällt zu Hitler nichts ein" ("I can think of nothing to say about Hitler") appears on page 197 (cf. 1989, p. 12), prefaced by a sub-heading "Beginning of May to September 1933". Just before this (p. 194), towards the end of what is effectively a long preamble, Kraus counters the readers' anticipated disappointment in the editor, explaining "that his life is dear to him", as are the lives of others near and dear to him. Prior to this, issue 888 had appeared in October 1933, consisting of just four pages and containing the poem "Man frage nicht" ("Let no one ask"):

Man frage nicht, was all die Zeit ich machte.
Ich bleibe stumm;
und sage nicht, warum.

Und Stille gibt es, da die Erde krachte.
Kein Wort, das traf;
man spricht nur aus dem Schlaf.
Und träumt von einer Sonne, welche lachte.
Es geht vorbei;
nachher war's einerlei.
Das Wort entschlief, als jene Welt erwachte.

Let no one ask what I was doing all this time
I am staying silent
And will not say why.
And there is silence since the earth cracked
Not one word that hit home;
We speak only out of our sleep.
And dream of a sun which used to laugh.
It passes;
And afterwards it was all one.
The word fell asleep[5] as that world awoke.

On one interpretation, having "nothing to say" about Hitler is an admission of defeat, of resignation. But this is also the statement of a satirist made redundant by those he ought to be satirizing. Whereas Kraus had needed to give satirical form to the sayings and deeds of the culpable parties in the First World War, in *The Last Days of Mankind*,[6] he found that the Nazis had left him nothing to satirize:

> Es waltet ein geheimnisvolles Einverständnis zwischen den Dingen, die sind, und ihrem Leugner: autarkisch stellen sie die Satire her, und der Stoff hat so völlig die Form, die ich ihm einst ersehen mußte, um ihn überlieferbar, glaubhaft, und wieder unglaubhaft zu machen: daß es meiner nicht mehr bedarf und mir zu ihm nichts mehr einfällt. (p. 27)

> There is a mysterious unison between the things that are, and those who deny them. In autarkic self-sufficiency they manufacture the satire themselves, and the material has such perfect form as I once had to give it in order to make it communicable, credible, and again incredible; so that I was no longer needed and I can think of nothing to say about it.

Of course, this is still satire, but satire which admits to a very profound sense of being left "sprachlos" (p. 13), bereft of a practical purpose, and despairing of finding the right language for even the most straightforward of thoughts such as would "force the animal part of mankind to sympathy: the mankind which does not kill, but is capable of not believing what it has not experienced" (p. 28). Kraus was probably all too aware that the mention of the Nazis' autarkic self-sufficiency in the production of satire, although it ironically references one of their political keywords (AUTARKIE, encapsulating a demand for German economic and cultural independence from foreign influences), only serves to prove his point that satire has met its match.

It is possible here only to give a selective overview of the *Walpurgisnacht*. The most reliable version of Kraus's text, edited by Christian Wagenknecht and including the extracts published, sometimes with minimal amendments from the main text, in 1934 in *Die Fackel*, runs to some three hundred and fifty pages.[7] Like *The Last Days of Mankind*, the *Walpurgisnacht* offers "a diffuse panorama of linguistic fragments and broken voices", in Edward Timms's apt description, impelled by "a documentary technique modified by inter-textuality and montage" (2005, p. 538, cf. p. 492). Kraus's significance for the history of political language criticism in Germany lies in his direct, *ad hominem* critiques of actual language use by named individuals. The index of Wagenknecht's 1989 edition contains some two hundred names, the vast majority of whom were Kraus's contemporaries, and some fifty of whom are members of the regime. Kraus also singles out individuals who have acted and spoken with civil courage, including James Franck, Ernst Stein, Max Planck, Wolfgang Koehler, Max Liebermann and Ricarda Huch (p. 111), but the bulk of his text is directed at the Nazis and their knowing or witless accomplices. Amongst the many individuals quoted and rounded on as apologists of the Nazis are Franz von Papen, Gottfried Benn, Rudolf Binding, Martin Heidegger, and the venerable Gerhart Hauptmann. The 'gleichgeschaltet' language of the bourgeois press, including the *Berliner Tageblatt*, the *Vossiche Zeitung* and the *Frankfurter Zeitung*, is also condemned. The majority of citations are from Nazi publications and politicians, notably Hitler and Goebbels, who are attacked repeatedly. Kraus at one point notes how with the mass recourse to family genealogy, surnames have become the seal of a family's fate in Nazi Germany, caustically remarking that Goebbels and Ley are spared this fate by the narrowest of margins—the lack of, respectively, a vowel (Goebbels > Gobbeles) and a consonant (Ley > Levy) (p. 172f.). The fate of Germans hung on such fine onomastic distinctions.

Kraus often talks about "die Sprache" "(the) language", but what he means by this is invariably the *use* of the language by given individuals or groups in specific contexts. He remains clearly focused on language as *parole*, and insists on the "inseparability" of language and reality (p. 14), an insistence which (perhaps picking up the baton from Schopenhauer's dictum that "the style is the man") hinges on a belief in the power of language to reveal the true character and intentions of the speaker, even if s/he is seeking to conceal or mislead. ("Your language betrays you", Matthew 26:73). Amongst the many memorable formulations of this thesis, we find: "Genügt denn nicht zur Vergewisserung ihres Tuns, was sie reden und was sie leugnen?" (Kraus 1989, p. 108, "Is what they say and what they deny not enough to reveal what they do?"). For example, in an official statement explaining a death in custody, "Es liegt einwandfrei Selbstmord vor" (p. 207, "It is clearly a case of suicide"), Kraus seizes on the word "einwandfrei", which sits oddly in this sentence, having the focal meaning of 'without any possibility of objection'. Here, he catches the regime inadvertently talking like a criminal boasting of the perfect crime ("You'll never prove it!"). Thus Kraus's maxim that the regime "commands everything except language" (p. 13) offers the possibility of using language, *their* language, as a site of unmasking and resistance. He also shows how this heightened sensitivity to language can be turned into a weapon against them, in this case producing the hauntingly meaningful grammatical solecism—also a feature of oppositional discourse—that in such cases the suicides are persons "AN DENEN SELBSTMORD VERÜBT WIRD" (p. 207, "on whom suicide is committed")—which reminds one of the passage in Victor Klemperer's diary on 14 October 1942 that the Jewish community in Dresden commonly talked of their comrades "having been disappeared" (VERSCHWUNDEN WORDEN) once they were transported from the city to a place called Auschwitz. This possibility offered by language and sensitivity to language was, however, crucially dependent on the ability of opponents of the regime and indeed 'ordinary' Germans to read and listen critically, and it is here, in particular, that Kraus despairs. It is not surprising, therefore, that he heaps scorn on the statements of non-Nazis who pull their punches, who, in his own words, "tiptoe around the gruel that will not (allegedly) be so hot when it is eaten" (p. 105)—a reference to the German saying that the food on the plate is never served as hot as it is made in the kitchen ("things never work out that bad").[8]

The ironic reference to autarky in the above passage may easily be missed by today's readers, and there are hundreds of such ironic asides in the *Walpurgisnacht*. It is important, therefore, that modern readers learn to tune in to Kraus's irony, especially where he does not explicitly mark the Nazi expressions in his running text by placing them in quotation marks or after distancing qualifiers like 'so-called'. This technique of ironic mimicry (of 'Imitat') is used extensively in the *Walpurgisnacht*, and Kraus could reasonably expect his readers to recognize every nuanced switch into 'Imitat', as when he uses the word AUTARKISCH above, or UMSTURZ (upheaval, revolution, p. 122), or SÄUBERUNG (cleansing, p. 143) or ARTEIGEN (characteristic of [the 'Aryan'] race, p. 173) unmarked in his running text. He repeatedly slips in and out of Nazi jargon in passages such as the following, which comments on a quotation from a Nazi source describing in convoluted style the processing of those who have been arrested:

> Dann erfolgt entweder die Ablieferung ins Spital oder, wenn sich die Haftfähigkeit herausstellt, in das Lager, wo die Behandlung des Falles im Rahmen der Gemeinschaft vollzogen wird. [...] Die Zuziehung (und in deren Folge Anlegung) des Verbandes geschieht zur Entlastung der politischen Polizei, die vollauf damit beschäftigt ist, falsche Pässe für Mörder, die nach Österreich reisen, auszustellen, die Einreisegebühr, deren Härte beklagt wird, in solchen berücksichtigungswerten Fällen aufzuheben und schließlich die Feststellung durchzuführen, daß es nicht wahr sei. (p. 209)

This is Kraus mimicking the language of Nazi officialdom, and it is difficult to capture the nuances of the 'Imitat' in an English translation. The passage, beginning "Then there takes place either the delivery into a clinic or, if suitability for detention is established, into the camp, where the treatment of the case is conducted within the framework of the community", quotes the Nazi account of how arrested persons are to be "attached to a national association" which then has the task of interrogating them "for the purpose of relief of the political police". Kraus's commentary picks up the clumsy officialese and creates a monstrous imitation of it, playing especially with its preference for nominal style using abstract nouns derived from verbs ("the treatment of the case is conducted within the framework of the community"), a style which also effectively removes the agents of the action (and in this case also the victims) from grammatical prominence. The effect is not merely comical but grotesque, contrasting the ornate syntax of the officialese with the brutal reality underlying this high-faluting style: people are being beaten, tortured, and delivered to camps by 'community-spirited' "associations" (such as the SA), "for the purpose of relief of the political police" (because there are so many detainees, but also to let the political police off the hook).[9] Kraus's readers would also "hear" the sudden break in style in the middle of this grotesque 'Imitat' when he writes that the political police are too busy "issuing false passports for murderers who travel to Austria" and denouncing reports of their actions as lies. In that one line, the voice of plain-speaking truth breaks through the obfuscating veneer of the sanctioned discourse.

The *Walpurgisnacht* is conceived, as Wendelin Schmidt-Dengler observes (2004, p. 118), as "a counterfactual to a present time, setting its language and its complexity against those terrible simplifiers who beat up the language with abbreviations and commands". This observation stands in need of refinement, however. One may be forgiven for taking from it the image of a language pedant lamenting the impoverished language of his contemporaries (and especially the press, which is in Kraus's view the victim of a monster it has helped to create). Indeed, as we shall see, Kraus does furnish evidence to support this view of him as a language elitist, but seeing him in these terms misjudges the seriousness and the depth of his project. His critique is directed, to be precise, at the behaviour (linguistic and otherwise) of the German-language speech community—at instances of criminal callousness and deviousness at one extreme, and of intellectual and moral acquiescence in the "common places" of popular discourse (the "Gemeinplatz" or "Phrase"), with terrible consequences.[10] Kraus approaches the problem of Nazi language and its all-too-easy conquest of German public discourse with an understanding of linguistic meaning not as a matter of semantics, but of pragmatics, that is to say: meaning is not simply inherent in words and expressions, but is the product of their application in contexts of use (their pragmatic *force*). It is this view of language which, as Lothar Kottnig has recently argued (2013, p. 12, cf. Kottnig n.d.), enabled Kraus to mount a penetrating critique not just of Nazism, but of the German speech community as a whole. The acuteness of this critique is nowhere more evident than in Kraus's treatment of metaphor—for example the ubiquitous references to blood in Nazi discourse, the provenance of which is "easier to trace than, through the Office for Racial Affairs, whether Jewish blood is still present":

> Welcher Anblick schlagartiger als der der Worthülse, die sich wieder mit dem Blute füllt, das einst ihr Inhalt war? Beglückend, wenn dies Blut nur metaphorisch wäre: das Blut des Gedankens, der die Echtbürtigkeit[11] des Wortes beglaubigt. Gorgonisch, da es der Ausbruch physischen Blutes ist, das aus der Sprachkruste zu fließen beginnt. (Es ist—im neuen Glauben, doch ohne daß er's noch ahnt—das Wunder der Transsubstantiation.) Wie doch die Erneuerung deutschen Lebens der alten Redensart zu ihrem unseligen Ursprung half—bis sie ihrer Verwendbarkeit im übertragenen Wirkungskreis verlustig wurde! (1989, p. 138)

> What sight more powerful than that of the word husk that is filling once again with the blood that was once its content? How fortunate, if this blood were merely metaphorical: the blood of the thought that sanctions the racial legitimacy of the word. Like the Gorgon, since it is the upsurge of physical blood that begins to flow out of the word husk. (It is, in the new faith, but without them realizing it, the miracle of trans-substantiation.) How the renewal of German life helped the old saying rediscover its unholy origin—until it lost its figurative use!

Here Kraus traces the implications of BLUT as one of the key ideological tropes of Nazism, as an example of how the content of a word or expression can be hollowed out by usage to the point where the word form exists virtually as an empty shell or "husk". Elsewhere he reserves particular scorn for the "Blutleere" (bloodlessness, p. 113) of pronouncements which effectively opt out of social commitment ("I have not personally witnessed any such thing")—discursive manifestations of "looking and listening the other way", as von Polenz puts it ("WEGSEHEN und WEGHÖREN").[12]

Metaphor is a recurring problem for the analyst of political language. 'Realized' metaphor is a concept frequently invoked in oppositional critiques from this time which point to the links between language and action in the Nazi discourse, as Sternberger (1932) had in critiquing the metaphor of poison in von Papen's depictions of political opponents: "That is the language of fascism!". (Perhaps the most prescient dictum in this respect is Heine's observation, in 1821, that once one starts burning books it is only a matter of time before people are thrown on the fire (Heine 1994, p. 16).) Kraus, too, sees that the dormant literal sense in metaphors such as 'pouring salt in the wound' can be—and recently has been—reactivated and re-enacted in an age of brutality (p. 139f.). Tropes of violence in Nazi discourse are for the most part not dead metaphors. Their talk of "beating down" opponents "with all brutality" is not mere rhetoric, but a "revindication of the dormant content of the phrase" which "runs through all expressions in which an originally bloody or pugilistic meaning has long since resolved itself in the sense of a mental offensive" (p. 140). The "revindication" which Kraus identifies here is the resuscitation of the violence lying dormant in everyday usage (in the "Phrase") and assumed by speakers of the language, if they notice it at all, to be a vestige from the pre-history of civilized society. The "revindication" of violence is so thoroughgoing, Kraus remarks, that one is surprised to encounter metaphors of violence which are not being translated by the Nazis literally into deeds. What Kraus brings to this analysis of metaphorical discourse is an awareness that the binary division between 'literal' and 'figurative' meaning (which underlies the concept of *realized* metaphor) is in some respects inadequate to the task, because the point of metaphorical language is that it can speak truth and untruth at the same time. It is this which makes it an effective political weapon:

> Die Lesart freilich, daß "keinem Juden ein Haar gekrümmt wurde", konnte sich behaupten, weil es nachweislich die einzige Form von Behandlung ist, die nicht geübt ward, während bei manchem die Kopfhaut mitging und mancher geschoren wurde, zwecks Einbrennung des Zeichens, in dem die Idee gesiegt hat. (p. 142. Cf. Hitler's speech of 28 March 1933)

> After all, the interpretation that "not one hair on a single Jew's head has been bent" could be asserted so confidently because it is demonstrably the only form of treatment which was not practised, while for many the scalp went as well and many another was shorn for the purpose of branding the head with the sign in which the Idea had been victorious.

—namely a swastika. Here, in Hitler's infamous joke, the metaphor is deployed with cynical calculation, and one can, Kraus assures us, "take them at their word: they keep it".

These insights into the nature of language and the Nazis' use of language are fine examples of a commentary which is effective on many levels: documenting, quoting, naming, and analyzing (cf. Timms 2005, p. 521). However, when Kraus shifts his focus to place (the German) language itself and issues of grammatical correctness at the centre of this commentary (pp. 122–131), the critique loses momentum. One of the slogans at the book burnings in May 1933, Kraus notes, had been "Against the disfigurement of the German language" ("Gegen die Verhunzung der deutschen Sprache!"). Easier said than done, he adds, and he doubts whether many of those who chant "DEUTSCHLAND ERWACHE!" ("Germany awaken!") and "JUDA VERRECKE!" ("Juda die a miserable death!") can see that a comma should be inserted in these expressions, changing "Deutschland" and "Juda" into second-person addressees, and the phrase as a whole into an imperative, instead of an optative (wish-formula) attached to a third person grammatical subject. It is, to say the least, an abstruse point, as is, to a lesser degree, Kraus's lampooning of the inability, in calls by the Party, to construct the correct informal imperative form of irregular verbs. Thus, in "Vergeß nicht, daß du ein Deutscher bist!" ("Don't forget that you are a German!") the form of the verb is wrongly constructed (it is not Standard German), a mix of the singular form "Vergiß" and the plural "Vergeßt". Such confusion is a feature, we may deduce, not of Nazism as such, but of semi-literacy—a conclusion which is made to reflect on the educational level of the typical Nazi. And this in turn reflects on the users' intellectual capacities. For Kraus, it may also reflect on their moral character. This appears to be the point of Kraus's grammatical quibbling, rather than the politically more telling interpretation (implied in a language gloss in the *Frankfurter Zeitung* in 1936) that this particular grammatical failing unwittingly encapsulates the regime's insincerity in its attempts to adopt an informal tone when ordering its citizens about.[13] Kraus's sarcastic comment on this example is that it is "a reminder of an ideal which it negates in school-book fashion, but without the benefit of the school" (p. 123). The lesson of this episode is surely that Kraus the grammarian is a much less effective political commentator.

Kraus traces several developments in language use to the Nazi accession to power, including the increased use of 'Fremdwörter' (such as 'dynamisch') and of contractions (such as 'Gestapo'). The "journalistic and oratorical proclamation of the new thinking" has often taken place, he notes, without recourse to "a single German word form", preferring the use of 'Fremdwörter' (the first-mentioned is 'Nazi') about whose meaning "one can never be clear". However, whilst he shares the purists' suspicion of the use of 'Fremdwörter' to disguise meaning and befuddle the listeners, he is clear that resorting to "racially pure neologisms" ("arteigene[r] Neubildung", p. 126) does nothing to stop "violence clothing itself in norms" (p. 127). The ideological demand for a German which is ARTEIGEN "makes language serve the need of profound dishonesty and the tendency to false deification, the concealment of shameful realities" (p. 126f.). "Hallucinationary" words such as 'Reichsfachschaftsleiter' (Head of a Reich Professional Division, e.g. within the Reich Culture Chamber[14]) may be pure in their Germanic form, but they also serve GLEICHSCHALTUNG—enforced conformity—by camouflaging violence no less than the monstrous MENSCHENMATERIAL (human material) had done in the First World War (p. 129). Obfuscation is also a function, for Kraus, of the contracted form which, whilst already popular in the Weimar Republic, has spread under the regime: Hapag, Wipag, Afeb, Gesiba, Kadewe, Gekawe, Osaf, Gausaf, Fepo and Uschla are listed as examples (along with Gestapo) of an "enrichment" of the language "through abbreviation" as part of the upheaval of the language ("Umsturz der Sprache", the phrase is ambiguous: upheaval in the language; overturning of the language) in order "to save time and gain space" ("Raum", the German word can also mean geographical space, as in LEBENSRAUM). These abbreviations are "forms of the elimination of a language which, when it is not reducible to clear interpretation of its form, leaves ample room for 'Gleichschaltung'". "Now there is SA and SS", Kraus comments in a humorous but strangely prophetic aside, "our only hope is an SOS to USA" (p. 130).

This last comment illustrates once again Kraus's irrepressible wit, but it also raises the question of whether wit is adequate to the task, or indeed appropriate. Against Nazism, the puns and sarcastic asides which once struck their target in a now lost, benign world of merely verbal fisticuffs, seem at best peripheral, and at worst embarrassingly misplaced. A similar criticism can be made, I would suggest, of Kraus's schoolmasterly tone and grammatical pedantry—hunting down grammatical infelicities, the misuse of a word or wrong placement of a comma for example—at least as weapons in a political critique. As we shall see in the following chapters, these aspects of Kraus's work—humorous asides, often aligned with linguistic pedantry—are discernible in the work of disciples such as Dolf Sternberger and Mechtilde Lichnowsky in their attempts to counter the hegemonic discourse of Nazism from a position of 'inner exile'.

Ernst Bloch

Kraus's measured retreat from the public arena dismayed many opponents of Nazism. Bertolt Brecht at first defended him ("Silence stepped up to the judge's bench | removed the cloth from its face | and announced itself as a witness" (*Werke*, Bd. 14, p. 197)) before distancing himself after Kraus condoned the Dollfuß government's suppression of the February 1934 uprising. Ernst Bloch's short essay of 1938, "Der Nazi und das Unsägliche" (The Nazi and the Unspeakable), published in Moscow in the exile journal *Das Wort*, also contains reflections on Kraus, whose "much attacked poem, in which he justified his falling silent in the face of the Nazi hell, is not simply an act of desertion":

> Wenn Kraus von der ihm vorliegenden antifaschistischen Literatur sagt: "Kein Wort, das traf", wenn der Autor der "Letzten Tage der Menschheit" bekunden muß: "Das Wort entschlief, da jene Welt erwachte", so greift das weit über persönlichen Defätismus, über Defätismus im politischen Sinn hinaus. Es will sehr viel heißen, daß der schärfste, der am wenigsten verlegene Satiriker vor Hitler sprachlos wird.

> When Kraus says of the anti-fascist literature known to him: "Not one word that hit home", when the author of *The Last Days of Mankind* is obliged to announce: "The word fell asleep as that world awakened", this goes far beyond personal defeatism, beyond defeatism in a political sense. It says a lot that the sharpest, the least tongue-tied satirist becomes speechless when faced with Hitler.

In sum, when confronted "with Hitler, with the standing coffins[15] and physiognomies of this regime, the nadir of the inexpressible seemed to Kraus to have been reached". Bloch, utopian socialist and an early vociferous opponent of Nazism, living in territorial exile since being deprived of his German citizenship in 1933, wrote this essay in Prague, following sojourns in Zurich and Paris and before his emigration to the United States. 'Unsäglich', the key word in Bloch's title, points up the inadequacy of language in the face of pain, sorrow and horror, the recourse to cliché in the absence of the "right word": "Weil das rechte Wort fehlt, daher ist die antifaschistische Sprache in Gefahr, zum Klischee zu werden" (Bloch 1938, p. 110, "Because the right word cannot be found, anti-fascist language is in danger of becoming a cliché").

The essay reviews the genres in which the word has been and can be put to use against tyrants, including historical fiction, satire, grotesque, and polemic, and finds them inadequate as weapons against the Nazi. The most effective language, Bloch concludes, is the sober language of factual description and documentation, as in the reports from concentration camps: "Above all, a scientific language is better suited than acidic or glowing language, as the *analysis* which investigates the Nazi also has the effect of exposing him" (p. 113). Bloch finds this kind of response in the work of his fellow Marxist Brecht (cf. Wagner 1989, p. 48). This does not prevent Bloch from venting his own anger in a polemical broadside not unlike Kraus's, which perhaps makes Kraus's achievement, in much closer proximity to the Reich, all the more noteworthy. The seediness ("Schäbigkeit") of the Nazis, Bloch writes, was in itself not new; what was new was the "*Größe*" (*sheer extent*) of this seediness, "the thunderous tone of baseness, the calibre of its triumphant perfidy" ("Donnerton aus Erbärmlichkeit, das Format der reüssierenden Niedertracht"). However, what is truly NOCH NIE DA GEWESEN (historically momentous, unmarked in Bloch's text but clearly an 'Imitat'), namely Hitler as 'the greatest German'—this "renders the language we have inherited speechless" (p. 111). Never before had a society been ruled by a class of failures, its *worst* members. Villains have been around for ever and "many a regime was covered in blood, but the Nazi smells of something quite different to blood" (p. 110), namely the mustiness ("Muff") of unaired beds, with a whiff of urine (p. 113). Our language resources are not sufficient or not yet sufficient, he writes, for woodlice that have grown enormous. These emotive words, though self-professedly inadequate, are nevertheless hurled at the regime and offered in solidarity to fellow opponents: seediness, shabbiness, wretchedness, perfidy, woodlice, the booming and blossoming lie. Many of these characterizations point up the banality, as well as the inherent ridiculousness and puniness ("Mickrigkeit"), of the "bourgeois in goose-step", and it is these features, Bloch argues, that frustrate the search for an adequate anti-fascist discourse rooted in moral outrage.

Bloch's view of human language, expressed in Marxist terms, as "of all the elements of the superstructure, the one which changes most slowly" helps to explain the frustration felt by anti-fascists in finding the "right word" in the present, to find a language which "gets close to and gets after" the Nazi crime (p. 110). Language, Bloch writes, "also as satirical, as cursing language, is a historical material reference system, its expressiveness has historical roots, is historically laden. It contains a lot that has been acquired on the way [...]". On the other hand, the Nazis may be new, but they are not that new. There are historical antecedents: Philipp

Melanchthon's attack on Thomas Müntzer in the 1520s was "as defamatory as a Nazi on Communism", the anti-semitism in Germany in the 1870s already contained "all the baseness [...] all the roughness of Nazism". Consequently, there are literary and artistic precedents for describing and opposing them. It is these that Bloch reviews in his attempt to find an adequate form, the nearest approximation to the "right word". The list of authors includes Juvenal, Dante and Shakespeare, Victor Hugo, Schiller and Büchner, and the contemporaries Johannes Becher and Heinrich Mann. George Grosz's visual caricatures and John Heartfield's photo-montages are praised, as are contemporary authors such as Oskar Maria Graf and Leon Feuchtwanger for their exposés of the "kleinbürgerlich" Nazi. The diminishing caricature is certainly a viable weapon, but the language of righteous indignation and moral pathos, whilst justified, falls short of the task because it is directed at the metaphysical category of evil ("das Böse"), rather than the profane and mundane category of the bad ("das Schlechte"). Instead, Bloch calls for objective genres, of description, stock-taking and analysis, to be the literary forms of opposition and overcoming. Accounts of personal suffering are powerful testimonies, he notes, we still experience the horrors of the Thirty Years War when we read *Simplizissimus*. Tragedy and comedy both fall short of this goal, however. Comedy, for example, stops at the border demarcating it from horror: we laugh at Don Quijote, a harmless lone monomaniac, but recoil from the bloodthirsty fanatic with millions of Sancho Pansas behind him. Satirical jokes ("Jewish hawker bites German Alsatian"; "Moldova boat rams German battle cruiser") provide useful ammunition but have to compete with a reality in which arsonists sit in judgment on an innocent Jew charged with their crimes (the Reichstag fire), when—resorting to a common metaphor—the inmates really have taken over the asylum. The grotesque as a genre, using selection, enlargement and distortion of traits to belittle its target and reveal the larger truth "is clearly not enough in the case of the Nazi: speechless head-shaking predominates". The echoes of Kraus are perhaps not coincidental here, and one wonders whether Bloch had read *Die Fackel* issue 890–905. He had, however, certainly read Brecht's contributions, both theoretical and practical, for which he reserved the highest praise. It is to these that we now turn.

Bertolt Brecht

If Kraus can be seen as an exemplar of the crisis experienced by anti-fascist commentators, and Bloch as its reflective analyst and strategist, then Brecht, whose path of exile led him to Santa Monica via Paris, Svendborg, Helsinki, Moscow and Vladivostok, is arguably the most important exponent of confident rebuttal. His essay "Five difficulties in writing the truth" (first published in the *Pariser Tageblatt* in December 1934) is a practical manual in Aesopian discourse, detailing strategies for rewording the discourses of power to expose their bias and potential for subliminal manipulation. Around the same time he produced counter-factuals of speeches by leading Nazis, "translating" their words into the "truth" which the original concealed. Brecht's Marxist orientation (like Bloch's) gave him a confident purchase on Nazism in a way denied to Kraus, who, Bloch had pointed out, had nothing to say about capitalism as the progenitor of Nazism. In "Writers should write the truth" (1934), a preliminary to "Five difficulties", Brecht expounds on this view: many writers write truths of the kind "the rain falls from the sky", they do not find truth that is worth writing, they are like painters who, in good conscience, cover the walls of sinking ships with still life studies and they sell their wares in the market for bemused pessimism. Against this, art that tackles truths worth telling is a matter of attitude ("Gesinnung"), but also of "acquirable knowledge and learnable methods". It is this art that can address the great truth of the time, "that our continent is sinking into barbarism because the property ownership of the means of production is held in place by violence" (Brecht 1988–, Bd. 22, p. 76f.).

Before we come to these important essays in the theory and practice of oppositional language, however, we should briefly refer to Brecht's dramatic works in this period, which had a considerable political impact abroad. In 1934, in Svendborg, Brecht began to collect press and eye-witness reports of daily life in the Reich, and this material was reworked for his "proletarian theatre in exile", notably in *Fear and Misery of the Third Reich* (*Furcht und Elend des Dritten Reichs*). Originally titled *Anxiety* (*Die Angst*), this grew into a montage of some twenty seven scenes (in the Berlin and Frankfurt edition) depicting everyday existence under the

Nazis. Brecht started work on *Fear and Misery* in 1937, adding new scenes in subsequent years.[16] Seven scenes were published separately in 1938 in *Das Wort* (Moscow), and one further scene in each of *Die neue Weltbühne* (Prague and Paris) and Thomas Mann's *Maß und Wort* (Zurich). A version of the play with thirteen scenes was published in Moscow in 1941 (then in English translation in 1942) after plans to publish in London in 1938 and in Prague in 1939 came to nothing. (It is likely that the proofs in Prague were destroyed given the prospect of the imminent annexation of Czechoslovakia following the Munich Agreement in September 1938.) An English-language version for the American stage, *The Private Life of the Master Race*, also appeared in New York in 1944 and 1945. The publication history of the play tells its own story of the diaspora of German exile, as does the history of its performances. The first production, of a version comprising eight scenes, was performed in Paris in 1938 by German cabarettists in exile, with guest performances from Helene Weigel. Individual scenes were played in later years in France, the Soviet Union,[17] and subsequently in the United States following Brecht's arrival there in 1941. Brecht's dream of an anti-fascist 'Volksfront' can be said to have had some success outside Germany, but sadly, his voice and the voices of others in exile were scarcely, if at all, heard inside the Nazi state.

"Der Spitzel" ("The Informer"), completed in August 1937, is a particularly effective piece of didactic theatre ("Lehrstück") on the anatomy of 'Sprachlosigkeit'. The family home of the teacher Herr Furcke and his wife is no longer a private sanctuary, despite Herr Furcke's bravado:

> In meinen vier Wänden kann ich äußern, was mir passt. Ich lasse mir nicht in meinem eigenen Heim das Wort...
>
> *Er wird unterbrochen, das Mädchen kommt mit Kaffeegeschirr herein. Man schweigt, solange sie herinnen ist.*
>
> Müssen wir ein Mädchen haben, dessen Vater Blockwart ist? (p. 392)

> Within my own four walls I can say what I like. In my own house I will not allow myself to...
>
> *He is interrupted, the maid comes in with the coffee cups. They are silent as long as she is in the room.*
>
> Must we have a maid whose father is the 'Blockwart'? (p. 392)

The Furckes have stopped inviting acquaintances round (the distinction between 'Freunde' and 'Bekannte', between friends and acquaintances, has acquired a vital importance), but the scene is memorable for its dramatic depiction of the ubiquitous fear of being betrayed by one's own child, at school or in meetings of the Hitler Youth or, as in this case, its junior organization 'Deutsches Jungvolk', in which their son is a 'Pimpf'. The tension arises from the unnoticed departure of their son as Herr Furcke vents his anger at the newspapers, the Catholic priest trials (of 1937), and the need for the Nazis to clean up their own act (in the local NSDAP headquarters, the "Brown House"). What did the boy hear? Where has he gone? The parents prepare their defence before the dreaded arrival of the Gestapo, getting out Herr Furcke's Iron Cross, deciding not to move the portrait of Hitler to a more prominent place, as that might look like an admission of guilt, and fabricating harmless versions of what the husband said, in the process lapsing into the register of a formal interrogation, as in Herr Furcke's reconstruction of his remarks on the sordid goings-on in the "Brown House":

> Das kann doch nicht als Angriff ausgelegt werden. Nicht alles sauber oder, wie ich abschwächend sagte, nicht alles *ganz* sauber, was schon einen Unterschied macht, und zwar einen beträchtlichen, das ist doch mehr eine spaßhafte Bemerkung volkstümlicher Art, sozusagen in der Umgangssprache, das bedeutet nicht viel mehr, als dass sogar dort wahrscheinlich einiges nicht immer und unter allen Umständen so ist, wie es der Führer will. Den nur wahrscheinlichen Charakter brachte ich übrigens mit voller Absicht dadurch zum Ausdruck, dass ich, wie ich mich deutlich erinnere, formulierte, es "soll" dort ja auch nicht alles ganz—ganz in abschwächendem Sinne gebraucht—sauber sein. Soll sein! Nicht: Ist! Ich kann nicht sagen, dass dort etwas nicht sauber ist. Wo Menschen sind, gibt es Unvollkommenheiten. Mehr habe ich nicht angedeutet, und auch das nur in abgeschwächtester Form. Und überdies hat der Führer selber bei einer gewissen Gelegenheit seine Kritik in dieser Richtung ungleich schärfer formuliert. (p. 395f.)

> That cannot be interpreted as an attack. Not everything is clean or, as I said by way of moderation, not *completely* clean, which already makes a difference, and a considerable one, well that's more of a joking remark of a popular kind [volkstümlicher Art], in everyday language so to speak, that doesn't

> mean much more than that probably not everything there is always and in every respect the way the Führer wants it to be. I deliberately expressed the merely probabilistic character, incidentally, in the formulation, as I quite distinctly remember, that not everything "was said to be" entirely clean—used in a completely moderating sense. Said to be! Not: is! I cannot say that everything there is not clean, I have no evidence at all of that. Wherever there are people there are imperfections. I didn't suggest anything more than that, and even that in its most moderated form. And moreover the Führer himself has formulated his criticism in this respect on a certain occasion much more sharply.[18]

—to which his wife tellingly responds: "I don't understand you. You don't need to talk to me like that." But of course, he is not talking (only) to her. The important point here is not Brecht's mastery of 'Imitat', but that an ability to *perform* 'Imitat', to 'talk the talk', had become a life skill for ordinary Germans. The passage demonstrates that 'Sprachlosigkeit' need not imply silence, it can also manifest itself in disempowered verbiage. Frau Furcke, incidentally, is also not immune to seeking refuge in the safety of the sanctioned discourse. Early in the scene, perhaps sensing that the boy may still be in the flat, she had countered her husband's outburst over the abominations ("Schweinereien") in the treatment of the Catholic Church, with "It is not so bad that they are cleaning up [AUFRÄUMEN]", and then with "But that is after all the proof of the return to health [GESUNDUNG] of our 'Volk'". The irony is that when the boy returns with chocolate bought with the ten pfennigs they gave him (bribery, too, is a motif in this scene), they still do not feel safe. The fear of informers has penetrated the intimate circles of friendship and family, strangling free speech and replacing it with performed versions of the hegemonic discourse rooted in the instinct for survival.

Brecht relies extensively on 'Imitat' in his dramas, which are intended as didactic pieces delivered to an audience who have been taught to listen and watch critically. The theatre is perfectly suited to opposing the regime's power by literally staging the latent violence and intimidation in everyday linguistic exchanges. When it comes to other genres, however, Brecht is aware that different strategies are required if the hegemonic discourse is to be exposed and challenged. These are set out in the essay

"Five difficulties in writing the truth" (1934), an essay which is at once a practical guide to intellectual resistance and a Marxist polemic.[19] The five difficulties are: having the courage to write the truth; the intelligence to recognize it; the skill to turn it into a weapon; the judgment to select those in whose hands it can be mobilized; and the cunning to spread it amongst the many. These challenges are great for those writing under fascist dictatorship, in exile, and in the liberal democracies ("der bürgerlichen Freiheit", p. 74). It does not require much courage to decry the baseness of the world and praise the defiant human spirit in general. Many do so "as if guns are trained on them, when in fact it is only opera glasses" (p. 75). It does take courage "to speak of such lowly and little things as workers' food and lodging in the midst of an almighty din proclaiming that willingness to sacrifice is the important thing" (p. 74). Being clever enough to find the truth means for Brecht being free from dependence on the material interests which govern the country. Here, he repeats much of the argument in "Writers should tell the truth", quoted above, commending the study of dialectical materialism, economics and history as essential for this purpose. Skill is then required to turn insight into an effective weapon. For this one must stop talking about fascism in terms of a natural disaster, as if "fascism is a wave of barbarism which has come down on some countries with the *force of nature*". This is itself "a fascist assertion, a capitulation before fascism" (p. 77). How can a writer say anything true and effective about fascism "when he will not say anything against capitalism, which ushers it in?" (p. 78). (Bloch makes much the same point in his criticism of Kraus.) The truth then needs to find its audience, a matter of judgment. Its real addressees are the oppressed. Writing is always writing *for*, and if the truth about Nazism is to find its proper audience of fellow soldiers ("Mitkämpfer"), it needs to be spoken loudly and in specifics: "Truth has something warlike about it, it fights not only untruth, but those who spread it" (p. 81).

The fifth and longest section of the essay, "The cunning to spread truth among the many", is rightly seen today as a classic introduction to Aesopian discourse, the art of speaking truth under the nose of the tyrant. Addressed to opponents of the regime trapped in the Reich (although it is doubtful whether it reached them), it commends the art of Confucius, who substituted 'murder' for 'kill' in describing the action of a tyrant (p. 82), and names Thomas More, Jonathan Swift, Voltaire and Lenin as modern exponents of the art. It is in this section that Brecht offers his famous examples for resisting the "foul mysticism" of Nazi keywords, replacing Boden (soil) with Landbesitz (land ownership), Disziplin with Gehorsam (obedience), Ehre (honour) with Menschenwürde (human dignity), and Volk with Bevölkerung:

> Wer in unserer Zeit statt *Volk Bevölkerung* und statt *Boden Landbesitz* sagt, unterstützt schon viele Lügen nicht. Er nimmt den Wörtern ihre faule Mystik. (Brecht 1988–, Bd. 22, p. 81)

> Whoever in our time says *population* instead of *Volk*, and *land ownership* instead of *soil*, has already ceased to support many lies. He deprives the words of their foul mysticism.

This sentence would inspire Hans Haacke's art installation der Bevölkerung, created in the north inner courtyard of the refurbished Reichstag building as a deliberate counterpoint to the inscription dem deutschen Volke on the front architrave of the building (Fig. 4.1).

Fig. 4.1 'der Bevölkerung' Inner courtyard of Reichstag building in Berlin, Germany (C) Oleksandr Prykhodko/Alamy Stock Photo

The letters of Haacke's installation, using the same Uncial Blackletter (Broken) Bastarda font from 1916, surrounded by ferns growing from seeds brought by members of the parliament from their constituencies, and illuminated at night, can be seen by visitors to the Bundestag from various vantage points in the building. Brecht explains the 'tainted' value of VOLK as follows:

> Das Wort *Volk* besagt eine gewisse Einheitlichkeit und deutet auf gemeinsame Interessen hin, sollte also nur benutzt werden, wenn von mehreren Völkern die Rede ist, da höchstens dann eine Gemeinsamkeit der Interessen vorstellbar ist. Die Bevölkerung eines Landstriches hat verschiedene, auch einander entgegengesetzte Interessen, und dies ist eine Wahrheit, die unterdrückt wird. (p. 81f.)
>
> The word *Volk* bespeaks a certain unanimity and suggests common interests, and so should be used only when talking about a plurality of peoples, because only then is a commonality of interests imaginable. The population of a stretch of land has various, even contradictory interests, and this is a truth which is being suppressed.

By the same token, Brecht explains, land should be spoken of as material property, not as mystical soil, "for the smell of the soil is unknown in the stock markets. They smell of something else" (p. 82). The rhetoric of honour and duty also needs critical rewording: the rich shower their poor countrymen with honour (EHRE) in times of crisis but will not help them out of poverty; politicians who send the masses to war and destruction "need to avoid people thinking about the government in their misery":

> Sie reden viel vom Schicksal. Dieses, nicht sie, ist am Mangel schuld. Wer nach der Ursache des Mangels forscht, wird verhaftet, bevor er auf die Regierung stößt. Aber es ist möglich, im allgemeinen dem Gerede vom Schicksal entgegenzutreten; man kann zeigen, dass dem Menschen sein Schicksal von Menschen bereitet wird. (p. 87)

> They talk a lot about fate [Schicksal]. It is fate, not they, which is responsible for want. Whoever researches the causes of want is arrested before they get to the government. But it is possible in general to counter talk of fate; you can show that people's fate is caused by people.

Because the state cannot look everywhere at once, ingenuity can ensure that the message is formulated for impact ("eingreifend gestaltet", p. 86). There are many strategies for evading suppression by the suspicious state: using an elegant literary style (Voltaire, Lucretius) or an ostensibly conformist genre such as the detective novel; substituting not words and phrases, but historical and geographical settings, as when Lenin's intended readers understood, correctly, his tract on Japanese exploitation of Korea as a tract on Russian exploitation of Sakhalin (p. 82f.). Whilst the state may censor discourses on working conditions, it is less likely to do so in domains which it considers useful to its existence. Technology and warfare are examples of domains in which ostensibly descriptive writing can depict actual conditions without voicing approval, leaving questions about war implicit (p. 86). Even a descriptive account of something as mundane as a tobacco shop or a farm, Brecht claims, can contain explosive matter invisible to the authorities (p. 87f.). All these subterfuges are "necessary for the truth to be spread" under conditions of tyranny:

> Und alle diese fünf Schwierigkeit müssen wir zu ein- und derselben Zeit lösen, denn wir können die Wahrheit über barbarische Zustände nicht erforschen, ohne an die zu denken, welche darunter leiden, und während wir, immerfort jede Anwandlung von Feigheit abschüttelnd, die wahren Zusammenhänge im Hinblick auf die suchen, die bereit sind, ihre Kenntnis zu benützen, müssen wir auch noch daran denken, ihnen die Wahrheit so zu reichen, dass sie eine Waffe in ihren Händen sein kann, und zugleich so listig, dass diese Überreichung nicht vom Feind entdeckt und verhindert werden kann. (p. 89)

> And we must solve all these five difficulties at one and the same time, for we cannot investigate truth in barbaric circumstances without thinking of those who are suffering under them, and as we search for the true states of

> affairs, always shaking off every variant of cowardice, with an eye on those who are prepared to use their knowledge, we must also be mindful to give them the truth in such a way that it can be a weapon in their hands, and we must do it at the same time with cunning, so that this transfer is not discovered and prevented by the enemy.

Brecht could voice these practical considerations, of course, because he was not in Germany, and although there is no real evidence that his words reached opponents of the regime in the Reich, his deliberations will be highly relevant when we come to consider the 'unquiet voices' in some form of inner exile in the Reich, particularly those that attempted to be heard in the public space. These opponents of Nazism had to work out their strategies for speaking truth without Brecht's guidance, in many cases falling back on the same examples identified by Brecht (and Bloch). The nature of German exile meant that most of these 'unquiet voices' were not Marxist in orientation, but indebted to humanist and Christian traditions.

In "Über die Wiederherstellung der Wahrheit" (On reinstating Truth, 1934/1935),[20] Brecht commends and illustrates the counterfactual as an oppositional genre. Since the counterfactual is a vehicle of direct confrontation, it is a weapon best used at a safe distance from a murderous opponent. (Sternberger's "Dictionary of the Papen Government", published in September 1932, is an example from an earlier, and safer period). The counterfactual uses lexical substitutions and paraphrases to "translate" them into plain language. For Brecht it empowers the thinking person to "set correct sentences against incorrect sentences", knowing "that the context often gives sentences the appearance of rightness" because many correct sentences can follow on an incorrect one. Brecht's practical demonstration of the technique uses speeches by Goering and Hess. The result is a case study and training manual in intellectual resistance and contradiction, as the following extract from Goering's speech of 12 December 1934 illustrates:

Ich lehne es ab, mich nochmals mit den Beschuldigungen, die gegen die Regierung und gegen mich persönlich im Zusammenhang mit dem Reichstagsbrand ausgesprochen wurden, zu befassen, zumals das Reichsgericht	Ich lehne es ab, mich nochmals mit den Anschuldigungen, die gegen die Regierung und gegen mich persönlich im Zusammenhang mit dem Reichstgsbrand ausgesprochen worden sind, zu befassen, zumal das Reichsgericht, dem inzwischen die Behandlung solcher Prozesse entzogen worden ist,
die Vorgänge um den Reichstagsbrand mit peinlicher Genauigkeit geprüft und seine Entscheidung gefällt hat.	die Vorgänge um den Reichstagsbrand herum mit Pein geprüft und seine Entscheidung dahin gefällt hat, dass die von mir angeschuldigten Kommunisten den Reichstag nicht angezündet haben und dass es den Beweis, dass wir selber dies getan haben, nicht erbringen darf. (p. 91)
I refuse to concern myself once more with the accusations which have been voiced against the government and myself personally in connection with the Reichstag fire, since the Reich Court has	I refuse to concern myself once more with the accusations which have been voiced against the government and myself personally in connection with the Reichstag fire, since the Reich Court, from which the consideration of such trials has since been removed, has
examined the events surrounding the Reichstag fire with painstaking exactitude and has reached its decision.	examined the events round about the Reichstag fire with embarrassment
	and has reached its decision to the effect that the communists accused by me did not set fire to the Reichstag and that it is not allowed to furnish the proof that we did it ourselves.

Printing the two versions in facing columns is the formal realisation of Brecht's demand that "lie and truth should confront each other and one should be able to compare them". The full effect is lost somewhat in translation, as semantic reversal is sometimes achieved by subtle formal alterations in the German. Thus "mit peinlicher Genauigkeit" ("with painstaking exactitude") becomes "mit Pein" ("with embarrassment"), and "um den Reichstagbrand" ("about/concerning the Reichstag fire") becomes "um … herum" ("round about"), suggesting the investigation steered a course around rather than directly towards the goal of the inquiry.

Irmgard Keun

Keun started work on the novel which would become *Nach Mitternacht* (*After Midnight*) in Germany in 1935, some months before she left for Belgium (cf. Häntschel 2001). It was serialized in the *Pariser Tageblatt* and published by Querido in Amsterdam in 1937. The Nazi authorities tried unsuccessfully to prevent its publication and to effect her deportation back to Germany from Ostende, where she was one of a small colony of exiled writers including Hermann Kesten, Stefan Zweig, Egon Erwin Kisch, and Joseph Roth, who was to become her lover. Her earlier novels *Gilgi* and *The Artificial Silk Girl* had been well received abroad, but despite her 'Aryan' background they were viewed by the Nazis as ASPHALTLITERATUR (('degenerate') urban writing) with an anti-German message, and she immediately fell foul of the regime. She left Germany for Belgium in 1936 and lived in exile for the next four years. Amazingly, she returned to Germany in 1940 under a false name and lived incognito until the end of the war.

Keun was familiar with the work of Brecht (Häntschel 2001, p. 66) and, very probably, Kraus (she twice visited Vienna in her exile years), though one cannot be sure that she knew their works cited in this chapter. With or without direct knowledge of those works, Keun's depiction of the self-serving opportunism of the little people echoes Brecht's *Fear and Misery of the Third Reich*. Her analysis also concurs with Bloch's in important respects. *Nach Mitternacht* succeeds in bearing witness to the everyday corruption of Nazi society, painting a devastating picture of the little people who go along with Nazism in order to get on in the world, and the culture of denunciation which allows them to settle scores with enemies and rivals. This Germany, Keun wrote in 1947, was:

> [e]in Deutschland der Nationalsozialisten [...] mit braunen SA-Männern, fischäugigen Gestapo-Mördern und schwachsinnig-fanatischen Stürmer-Verkäufern. Ein Deutschland, in dem Kolonialwarenhändler und Feldwebelwitwen Nietzsches Philosophie vollstreckten. Ein Deutschland mit rohen Gesängen und drohenden Rundfunkreden, mit der künstlichen Dauer-Ekstase von Aufmärschen, Partei-Tagen, Heil-Jubeln und Feiern. Ein Deutschland voll berauschter Spießbürger. Berauscht, weil sie gehorchen und Angst haben durften, und berauscht, weil sie Macht bekommen hatten. Genügte nicht ein Gang zur Gestapo, um sämtliche Stammtischgenossen zumindest ein bißchen unter Verfolgung zu setzen? Ein Deutschland zynischer Geschäftemacher, breit behäbiger Gleichgültigkeit und lauer Zufriedenheit mit dem eigenen Wohlergehen. Ein Deutschland verworrener Hoffnungen und zaghafter Zweifel. Und ein Deutschland voll von schmerzlichem Aufzucken und stillem Jammer, müder Resignation, verzweifelter Ratlosigkeit und dumpfem Zorn. Ein armes, zerschlagenes, sehr kleines Deutschland, dieses letzte Deutschland, verweht und verstreut im eigenen Land, verweht und verstreut über fremde Länder. (Irmgard Keun, Schreiben über Deutschland im Exil, 1947 (p. 163))
>
> [a] Germany of National Socialists [...] with brown SA men, fish-eyed Gestapo murderers and feeble-minded fanatical *Stürmer* sellers. A Germany in which grocers and widows of sergeants implemented Nietzsche's philosophy. A Germany with crude songs and threatening radio speeches, with the artificial permanent ecstasy of parades, Party conferences, shouts of "Heil!" and celebrations. A Germany full of intoxicated philistines. Intoxicated, because they were allowed to obey and be afraid, and intoxicated because they had been given power. Was not a trip to the Gestapo enough to at least put every one of your mates down the pub in fear of persecution? A Germany of cynical deal-makers, widespread casual indifference und luke-warm contentment in one's own well-being. A Germany of confused hopes and hesitant doubts. And a Germany full of painful cringing and silent misery, weary resignation, despairing perplexity and dull rage. A poor, smashed, very small Germany, this last Germany, strewn and scattered in its own land, strewn and scattered across foreign lands.

This Germany of opportunists is re-created in little more than a hundred pages in a tightly-constructed plot covering just two days in Frankfurt in 1936 (cf. Häntschel 2001, pp. 77–91). The nineteen year-old orphan Sanna has come to Frankfurt from Cologne to get away from her aunt Adelheid, opportunist Nazi and 'Blockwart', who resented Sanna's love for her son Franz and reported her to the Gestapo for making remarks about a Goering speech. As a result, Sanna had been summoned to the Gestapo presidium, placed in "protective custody", then released. In Frankfurt Sanna lives with her step-brother Algin, a published novelist, and his wife Liska, becomes friends with Gerti, who has a Jewish boyfriend Dieter Aaron, and makes other acquaintances, including Heini, a disaffected former journalist. She receives a letter from Franz saying he is coming to Frankfurt. The friends go into the city and watch Hitler and Goering driving through the Opera Square from the balcony of a café, then go drinking together in one of the few cafés from which Jews are not yet banned (where Jews drink beer to look like the Aryans, and the Aryans have stopped drinking beer). These events are narrated through Sanna, who also recalls people and incidents from her life in the Mosel valley and Cologne, in a gradual political awakening to the reality of Nazism. On the evening of the second day Liska throws a party, at which momentous decisions are taken after midnight. Heini shoots himself, Breslauer is emigrating, and Franz arrives, having throttled the informer Schleimann in Cologne who denounced him to the Gestapo as a Communist in order to stop him setting up a rival tobacco shop with his friend Paul, of whom there is now no trace. Sanna recalls hearing the screams of those about to be executed in Klingelpütz prison in Cologne (p. 122). She and Franz leave on the overnight train to Rotterdam.

The novel depicts the desperate situation of those at odds with National Socialism, and their desperate outcomes: suicide, leaving the country, conforming, or keeping a resigned low profile in the (vain) hope that they will be left alone. Plot and narrative voice are deployed tendentiously by Keun in a concerted assault on every aspect of Nazism. She reserves her greatest scorn for those who join the Party and its organizations (including the 'NS-Frauenschaft'), and those who inform on family, friends, neighbours and colleagues, driven by fear, hatred, jealousy, and social ambition. Sanna witnesses scores of them during her detention in the Gestapo offices in Cologne, where Aunt Adelheid has already denounced her and the slimy Schleimann will denounce Franz and Paul in order to prevent them setting up a rival tobacco shop. The plot delivers a double blow to the ingratiating Herr and Frau Silias, whose triumph in having their young daughter chosen to "break through" the ring of SS guards and present the Führer with flowers is thwarted first when the Führer fails to see her, and then when the child drops dead, presumably as a result of the relentless pressure on her from her parents. The pressure to conform is typified in Algin, who turns his hand to 'Heimat' literature "als müsse er jedes Häufchen Kuhmist an sein Herz drücken" (p. 9, "as if he had to press every little pile of cow dung to his heart") after his first novel is criticized by the authorities and his father removes the framed review from over the sofa and replaces it with the obligatory portrait of the Führer (just as Herr Furcke thinks of doing in Brecht's *Fear and Misery of the Third Reich*). The novel is also noteworthy for its depiction of the discrimination against Jews, although here, too, the picture is a complex one. Dieter Aaron's Jewish father (deserted by his 'Aryan' wife) refuses to condemn the Nazis (he is still allowed to continue his business as it is important for exports) and prefers to be thought of as a NICHT-ARIER (p. 17). Algin's Jewish friend Doctor Breslauer (modelled on Keun's husband Johannes Tralow), about to emigrate to the United States, is lectured by Heini on his good fortune at being a rich Jew. An embarrassed Breslauer is embraced as a soul-mate by a drunken *Stürmer* seller (they have the same star sign) who explains how he can unerringly "divine" the presence of Jews who don't look like Jews.

Much of the incisiveness of *Nach Mitternacht* as an anti-fascist pamphlet derives from the way Keun deploys two very different kinds of narrative voice. In the latter half of the novel the cynicism of Heini, a former journalist (and modelled, perhaps, on Joseph Roth), comes straight at us in direct speech. His is the angry, weary voice of clear-sighted but disenfranchised political opposition in the Reich. (Other such voices intrude repeatedly into Sanna's memory, for example the pub landlord Segebrecht (see below) and Sanna's neighbour in Cologne Frau Grautisch: "dat janze Volk sitzt als im Konzentrationslager, nur die Regierung läuft frei herum" (2003, p. 65: "It's like the whole 'Volk' is in a concentration camp, only the government is running around free")). In contrast, roughly the first half of the novel, containing the truly biting satire, is dominated by the "adeptly staged naivety" (Marchlewitz 1999, p. 162) of Sanna's voice. Her apparently guileless discourse, ranging over the people in her life and their circumstances, lifts the lid on the reality of the 'Third Reich' rather like a small child unwittingly revealing family secrets to strangers. ("Man darf so etwas ja nicht sagen heutzutage wegen der Weltanschauung und der Regierung" (Keun 2003, p. 8, "You just can't say that kind of thing these days because of the 'Weltanschauung' and the government")). Especially in the opening pages, this faux-naive[21] voice, noted already by Klaus Mann in 1937 (Keun 2003, pp. 166–169), unmasks the reality of the new Germany, often repeating key terms of Nazi discourse which, we come to understand, are trotted out (and not just by Sanna) as standard formulas even if they don't appear to make much sense. In the first pages alone, a series of Nazi keywords are subverted in this carefully constructed 'Imitat': SCHOLLE (clod of earth), HEIMAT (homeland), DEUTSCHE FRAU, DEUTSCHE MUTTER, DAS NEUE DEUTSCHLAND, AUFBAUWILLE (will to build a new Germany), BLOCKWART (block warden), SABOTAGE GEGEN DAS WINTERHILFSWERK (sabotage of the Winter Relief programme), SCHUTZHAFT (protective custody), SCHWARZE LISTE (black list), ZERSETZEND (corrosive, subversive), SICH AM AUFBAUWILLEN DES DEUTSCHEN VOLKES VERGEHEN (to offend against the will of the German people to build a new Germany), ARIER/NICHTARIER, HOHEITSZEICHEN (swastika), MISCHLING, VOLKSEMPFINDUNG (natural sensibility of the German 'Volk'), JUDENKNECHT (servant of Jews). Keun tellingly puts occasional malapropisms into Sanna's mouth as she artlessly mis-speaks the official discourse, associating Gerti and Dieter's 'inter-racial' love with ERREGUNG DES VOLKSEMPFINDENS (arousal of the 'Volk''s sensibility), a comic hybrid of two Nazi ideologemes, ERREGUNG ÖFFENTLICHEN ÄRGERNISSES (arousal of public anger, from the wording of the Nuremberg Laws) and GESUNDES VOLKSEMPFINDEN (healthy instinct of the 'Volk'). Her reference to Dieter as a "Mischling of the first or third class" also reveals her imperfect grasp of terminology:

> Der ist so etwas wie ein Mischling erster Klasse oder dritter Klasse—ich kann nicht klug aus diesen Benennungen werden. Jedenfalls kann Gerti nichts mit ihm zu tun haben, weil doch Rassengesetze sind. Und wenn die Gerti nur einfach mit dem Dieter zusammensitzt in der Ecke von einem

Café, und sie drücken sich mal die Hände, dann können sie gleich schwer bestraft werden wegen Erregung des Volksempfindens. (p. 16)

He is something like a Mischling of the first class or third class—I really don't understand these names. Anyway, Gerti can't have anything to do with him, because there are the Race Laws after all! And if Gerti just sits with Dieter in the corner in a café and they just squeeze hands, well they can be really punished straight away on account of arousal of the people's feelings.

The Nuremberg Laws had established degrees ("Grade"), not classes ("Klassen") of hybridity. There were first and third class railway carriages (and first and second class Iron Crosses), but degrees of MISCHLING. Sanna's voice stands in a complex relation to the tropes of Nazi discourse, vacillating between naive reproduction: "er *hatte* viel gelitten und *wurde* darum Antisemit" (p. 11, "He *had* suffered a lot and so he *became* an anti-semite"), child-like incomprehension: "ich kann nicht klug aus diesen Benennungen werden" (p. 16), and political nous: "die alten Fräuleins [...] standen auf, reckten die Arme. Das muss man, weil man nie weiß, wer einen beobachtet und anzeigt. Vielleicht hatten sie voreinander Angst" (p. 22f., "The old spinsters [...] stood up and raised their arms. You have to do it because you never know who is watching you and will report you. Maybe they were afraid of each other"). Where Heini's words provide a resolute and unshifting perspective on Nazi society, Sanna's provide a more problematical, and typical, take on the linguistic habitus, often incorporating those suasive discourse particles in German, such as 'schließlich' and 'natürlich' (below), 'ja' ("Man darf so etwas ja nicht sagen"), and 'doch' ("Der Führer gibt doch schon allein sein ganzes Leben hin, für sein Volk fotografiert zu werden", p. 25: "After all, the Führer gives his entire life to being photographed for his 'Volk'"), which reproduce the insidious normative power of discourse, often resulting in incongruous humour:

Schließlich meinte der Vater, daß man den Führer hochachten müsse und auch die Hoheitszeichen und daß der Gastwirt Segebrecht es sich selbst zuzuschreiben habe, wenn er ins Konzentrationslager gekommen sei. Dieser Segebrecht [...] hat [...] in besoffenem Zustand mal auf den Boden von seinem Klosett ein Hakenkreuz gemalt. Und als ihn in der Gaststube

> der Lamberts Pitter fragte, was das bedeuten sollte, hat er geantwortet, brüllend und laut: "Dat die Arschlöcher sehn, wat sie jewählt haben". So was kann natürlich nicht gutgehen. (p. 14)
>
> Father thought that after all one had to respect the Führer and the national symbols too and that the landlord Segebrecht only had himself to blame if he had landed in a concentration camp. This Segebrecht had [...] in a drunken state painted a swastika on the bowl of his toilet. And when Pitter asked him in the guest room of the Lamberts, what that was supposed to mean, he had yelled loudly in reply: "So the arseholes can see what they voted for". Of course, that sort of thing can't end well.

The satirical force of this passage is actually not so far removed from Kraus's outraged invective in *Dritte Walpurgisnacht*. It is just that where Kraus's examples are real, Keun's are fictionalized and refracted through Sanna's consciousness. Indeed one wonders whether Kraus, as well as Roth, might be apostrophized in Heini's valedictory description of himself as "[e]ine Maus, die durch Piepsen eine Lawine aufhalten will. Die Lawine ist gekommen und hat alles begraben, die Maus hat ausgepiepst" (p. 125f., "a mouse trying to stop an avanalanche with its squeaking. The avalanche has come and buried everything, and the mouse has squeaked its last squeak").

Heinz Paechter

With the help of German exiles, rudimentary dictionaries recording the new German usage were compiled in the 1940s in Britain (by the BBC), and in the USA (Deissler 2004, p. 60f.). In terms of its impact, perhaps the most influential of these was Heinz Paechter's *Nazi-Deutsch: A Glossary of Contemporary German Usage*, published in New York in 1944. A revised and expanded version of his earlier *Dictionary of Nazi Terms* (1942), it focused clearly on the ideological dimensions of word use, whilst also serving as an introduction to the political, military, and economic institutions of National Socialist Germany. It would appear that this work was commissioned for use by military and civilian administrators tasked with eliminating National Socialism from post-war German society. Born in 1907,

Paechter left Germany for Paris in 1933, arriving in the United States in 1940, where he worked at the Institute for Social Research at Columbia University and, evidently, for the Office of Strategic Services (OSS). Henry Pachter, as he was to become known, remained a combative member of New York Jewish émigré society until his death in 1980 (Jay 1981). His 128 page study is based on a corpus of texts from a number of domains including philosophy (Ernst Jaensch and Alfred Rosenberg), race theory (Hans Guenther and L. Clauss), sociology (Oswald Spengler and Ernst Jünger), and propaganda (Adolf Hitler, Joseph Goebbels and Eugen Hadamovski), pointedly excluding "teutonic cranks and professional purifiers of language" (p. 6). Like many commentators on 'Nazi language', Paechter identifies the noun-centred slogan as key to its impact:

> In this evocative and magic language the ideal sentence is the slogan. When thousands in a Sportpalast meeting chant in unison, "Ein Reich, ein Volk, ein Führer", they do not think of any verb or action. A ritual is performed; three nouns, suggesting an order of the world, evoke acceptance of the structure thus laid out. (Paechter 1944, p. 6)

This quotation is from the Introduction, "The Spirit and Structure of Totalitarian Language" (pp. 5–15), prefaced by the statement "Words are Weapons". This is followed by (1) a lexicon of terms and abbreviations (pp. 16–70), and appendices on (2) the German State (pp. 72–86), (3) Political and Military Organisations (pp. 87–96), (4) Economic Organisation (pp. 97–110), (5) Basic Notions of Nazi Philosophy ("Weltanschauung", pp. 110–124), and (6) School and Church (pp. 125–128). An impression of the nature of this work can be gained from the following necessarily brief samples from these sections (ideological keywords, highlighted below in SMALL CAPS, are not set apart typographically in the original):

1. AUSRICHTEN—to align, to co-ordinate, to adjust, to indoctrinate. Ausrichtung—bringing into line, "toeing the line"; "nach dem Führerwillen ausgerichtete Staatsführung"—government in line with the will of the Führer. (p. 19) | HÖRGOI—Aryan who allows a Jew to use his radio (p. 36) | HSSPf—Höhere SS- und Polizeiführer. (p. 68)[22]

2. VOLKSBEFRAGUNG—plebiscite. In the Weimar constitution the Volksentscheid was the last resort of legislation. Now Volksbefragung is used to give the government *pleins pouvoirs* independently of representative bodies. Volksbefragung results however are not considered as binding upon the Führer. Decree 7/14/1933.
3. The SS—SCHUTZSTAFFEL—is divided in ALLGEMEINE SS and WAFFEN SS. Like the SA, the Allgemeine SS is composed of non-professional men. Its function is to be at the disposal of the police. Members are generally in higher income brackets than SA members, and its ideology is more firmly conceived in terms of a racial elite. Its paper "Das Schwarze Korps" shows a ruthless dynamism in the defence of the regime, and often announces future trends of policy. The SS-SICHERHEITSDIENST controls the German police (*App.1C). The Waffen-SS originated from the SS VERFÜGUNGSTRUPPEN and SS-TOTENKOPFVERBÄNDE. The Totenkopfverbände are also called WACHMANNSCHAFTEN, as part of them served as guards in concentration camps. The SS-Verfügungstruppen manned part of Hitler's body guard, the "BEGLEITBATAILLON DES FÜHRERS", whose first commander was Rommel. [...] (p. 90)
4. The GESAMTORGANISATION DER GEWERBLICHEN WIRTSCHAFT (OGW) organizes all industrial and commercial firms by trades (Law 11/2/1934). The functional division (fachliche Gliederung) consists of 7 Reichsgruppen subdivided into 55 WIRTSCHAFTSGRUPPEN (economic groups) and 52 INNUNGSVERBÄNDE (craft guilds) to which must be added 6 VERKEHRSGRUPPEN (groups in the transportation industry). [...] (p. 97)
5. GEMEINSCHAFT—GANZHEIT, GESAMTHEIT, GEFÜGE (cf. GESTALT, BEZOGENHEIT). The theorem of the whole and the parts has been misused by Nazi philosophers like Jaensch ("Wissenschaft und völkische Bewegung") to deny the existence of the parts or their right to exist. Structures favourable to the Nazi outlook are presented as indivisible organic units. Community, hence, is conceived not as a mutual relation between individuals, but as a pre-existing unity of a race or people. VOLKS-: The commonweal of the race, bent on its own perfection or thriving (the usual translation "community of the people" is a misleading adaptation of liberalistic thinking). [...] (p. 115)

6. Party Schools—(a) Talented and "morally qualified" boys of 12 are selected by the HJ [Hitlerjugend, Hitler Youth] for admission to the leader schools: "ADOLF-HITLER-SCHULEN" (*ENDAUSLESELAGER). (b) The minister of education runs "NATIONALPOLITISCHE ERZIEHUNGS-ANSTALTEN" which prepare for civil service careers. (c) The SS runs "HEIMSCHULEN"—community schools. [...] (p. 126)

Although rudimentary in its lexicographical apparatus, the strength of Paechter's study is its clarity about the social embeddedness of language and the potential, especially in "totalitarian" societies, for ideologically schooling the population. Its relative brevity, compared with *Sprachwandel im Dritten Reich* (reviewed in the next chapter), may be explained by its intended function as a manual for Allied administrators in a soon to be occupied Germany. This is particularly apparent in the cross-referencing between the lexicon and the explanatory appendices with their exposition of political structures and their special terminologies.

Conclusion

These voices from abroad varied greatly in their approach to the problem of how to respond to Nazism: Kraus's calculated and strategic falling silent; Bloch's moralizing polemic, against his better judgment, and call for dispassionate genres of documentation and analysis; Brecht's manual of Aesopian discourse strategies, counterfactuals of speeches, and dramatic enactments of the nature and daily reality of Nazism; and Keun's fictionalized depiction of rapacious petit-bourgeois resentments, score-settling, and opportunist parroting of ideological keywords. These voices signal different degrees of engagement with and confidence in the potential of language as a weapon of resistance and opposition. Bloch's appeal for a cool documenting of facts is most closely met, as the end of the war came into sight, by the contextualizing lexicography of Paechter and others. Kraus documents and reveals, quoting named persons and naming their deeds, but he also embroiders his critique with a formal pedantry and a wit which sits uncomfortably in an attack on torturers and murderers.

Here, especially, Kraus himself realized that the attack failed to engage its target. Bloch's recommendations were more adequately realized by Brecht, who translated his theoretical treatise on the power of language and gainsaying into practical form in his counterfactual rewriting of speeches and in his dramatic works; and by Keun, whose critique of little Nazis is filtered through the outspoken voice of Heini (who speaks more like Brecht, Bloch—and Roth) and the faux-naive, implicated voice of Sanna.

Whether in inventory, documentary or fictional mode, the five voices reviewed in this chapter were clearly focused on critiquing language use in specific social settings, and especially in the case of Kraus and Brecht, in challenging named Nazis. Such an explicit, contextualized, *ad hominem* approach to political language criticism was, for obvious reasons, barely possible inside the Reich. Indeed von Polenz (1999, p. 313) argues that Kraus and Brecht represent important milestones in the development of a political language criticism, exemplifying the kind of socio-pragmatic analysis of texts and their discourse contexts which was rediscovered in Germany only after the social upheaval of the 1960s. The freedom of expression afforded by physical distance from Nazi Germany went hand in hand with remoteness, indeed removal, from the intended audience. The converse situation obtained within the Reich, where practical criticism took a different turn: oppositional commentaries were either produced in private—for posterity, should the authors and/or their manuscripts survive the regime—or in the public arena, at the expense of the kind of plain speaking which we find in the authors beyond the reach of the Nazi state. It is to these voices within the Reich, in some form of 'inner exile', that we now turn.

Notes

1. Following quotations are from this volume.
2. Kraus of course also falls into this category, particularly his drama on the First World War, *The Last Days of Mankind*.
3. A full list is given in Kraus 1989, pp. 352–358.
4. Another prominent case, albeit in 1934, was Edgar Julius Jung, von Papen's speechwriter, the first to be killed in the "night of the long knives" of 30 June 1934.

5. "Das Wort entschlief": 'entschlafen' is also elevated register for 'to die'.
6. Two recent English translations are Kraus 2015, 2016.
7. Kraus 1989. Page references in the text are to this edition, and unless otherwise indicated quotations are from the text published in 1934.
8. 'Es wird niemals so heiss gegessen wie es gekocht wird'. On Sternberger's explication of the contemporary use of this saying, see Chap. 7.
9. Somewhat problematically, it seems that Kraus could not resist exploiting the double sense of 'Verband' here as an association and a bandage, to generate an image of a bandage covering a wound ("Die Zuziehung (und [...] Anlegung) des Verbandes").
10. Timms (2005, p. 523f.) sees Kraus attacking "a proliferation of duplicitous discourses" composed of "a convergence of three ideologies: reactionary nationalism, liberal journalism, and visionary Expressionism".
11. ECHTBÜRTIGKEIT, contrasting in Nazi ideology with AUSSENBÜRTIGKEIT, seems to allude here to linguistic purism as a lesser evil, a discourse in which 'mere' words, rather than people, are the target.
12. von Polenz (1999, p. 97) uses the terms in his discussion of non-text media, particularly radio and its role in distracting attention away from social issues.
13. "Vom Ablaut" (10 September 1936). Cf. Dodd 2013, p. 86f.
14. A 'Reichsfachschaft' (RFF) regulated membership and practices of a profession, from artists to midwives. For example, within the Reich Chamber of Film, the Reichsfachschaft Film, headed in 1933 by Carl Auen.
15. STEHSÄRGE. The reference is to the miniscule dark confinement cells in Nazi concentrations camps, cf. the SS man's threat of the "Bunker" in the scene "Moorsoldaten", set in Esterwegen concentration camp, in Brecht's *Fear and Misery of the Third Reich* (*Werke*, Bd. 4, p. 453). Max Abraham's account of internment in Oranienburg (2003, p. 137) refers to cells dug into the earth.
16. I here follow the editors' notes: Brecht 1988–, Bd. 4, pp. 523–544. Page references in the following passage are to this volume.
17. "The Informer" was played at the Moscow Komsomol Theatre in September 1941, to an audience who presumably recognized a transposed dramatization of their own daily reality, substituting 'stukach' for 'Spitzel'.
18. Presumably a reference to the accusations of homosexual corruption of the youth amongst leading SA men (including Ernst Röhm) after the political murders of 30 June 1934.

19. Brecht 1988–, Bd. 22, pp. 74–89. Page numbers in the text follow this edition. For an English translation see Brecht 1948.
20. Brecht 1988–, Bd. 22, pp. 89–96.
21. Häntschel (2001, pp. 78, 84) describes Sanna as "neither stupid nor naïve", possessed of a "pragmatic intelligence, with keen powers of observation", suspicion of the older generation, but also ambition, desire for a better life, and a need to belong. She also finds traits of depression and a "schizoid" mentality in Sanna's discourse.
22. i.e. senior post-holders in the SS and the police (WJD).

Bibliography

Abraham, Max. 2003. Juda verrecke. Ein Rabbiner im Konzentrations-Lager, mit einem Vorwort von K. L. Reiner. In *Konzentrationslager Oranienburg*, Hg. Irene A. Diekmann and Klaus Wettig, 117–167. Potsdam: Gerhart Seger und Max Abraham.

Bloch, Ernst. 1938. Der Nazi und das Unsägliche. *Das Wort*, Heft 9 (Oktober), 110–114. Also in: Bloch, *Politische Messungen, Pestzeit, Vormärz*. Gesamtausgabe der Werke, Bd. 11, 1970, pp. 185–193. Frankfurt/Main: Suhrkamp.

Brecht, Bertolt. 1948. *Writing the Truth: Five Difficulties*. Translated by Richard Winston. *Twice a Year* (New York), Tenth Anniversary Issue.

Brecht, Bertolt. 1988–. *Werke. Große kommentierte Berliner und Frankfurter Ausgabe*. Hg. von Werner Hecht, Jan Knopf, Werner Mittenzwei, and Klaus-Detlev Müller. Berlin, Weimar: Aufbau Verlag. Frankfurt/Main: Suhrkamp.

Deissler, Dirk. 2004. *Die entnazifizierte Sprache*. Frankfurt/Main: Peter Lang.

Dodd, William J., ed. 2013. *"Der Mensch hat das Wort". Der Sprachdiskurs in der Frankfurter Zeitung 1933–1943*. Berlin, Boston: de Gruyter.

Haecker, Theodor. 1989. *Tag- und Nachtbücher 1939–1945. Erste vollständige und kommentierte Ausgabe*. Herausgegeben von Hinrich Siefken, Brenner-Studien, Bd. 9. Innsbruck: Haymon Verlag.

Häntschel, Hiltrud. 2001. *Irmgard Keun*. Reinbek: Rowohlt.

Heine, Heinrich. 1994. *Historisch-kritische Gesamtausgabe der Werke*, Hg. Manfred Windfuhr, Bd. 5. Hamburg: Hoffmann and Campe.

Jay, Martin. 1981. Remembering Henry Pachter. *Salmagundi* 52 (53): 24–29.

Keun, Irmgard. 2003. *Nach Mitternacht*. Mit Materialien, ausgewählt von Michael Graef. Stuttgart, Leipzig: Ernst Klett.

Kottnig, Lothar. 2013. '*Das Phänomen der Revindikation*'. *Metapher und Phrase in der 'Dritten Walpurgisnacht*'. Diplomarbait, Magister der Philosophie, Universität Wien.

———. n.d. Diesmal ohne den Deckmantel. Der sprachliche Befund der *Dritten Walpurgisnacht* zum Nationalsozialismus. http://www.uni-klu.ac.at/germ/downloads/Kottnig.PDF. Accessed 14 October 2015.

Kraus, Karl. 1989. *Dritte Walpurgisnacht*. Herausgegeben von Christian Wagenknecht. Frankfurt/Main: Suhrkamp taschenbuch.

———. 2015. *The Last Days of Mankind. The Complete Text*. Translated by Fred Bridgham and Edward Timms. New Haven: Yale University Press.

———. 2016. *The Last Days of Mankind*. Translated by Patrick Healy. Amsterdam: November Editions.

Mann, Thomas. 1990. *Gesammelte Werke in dreizehn Bänden*. Frankfurt/Main: Fischer Taschenbuch Verlag.

Marchlewitz, Ingrid. 1999. *Irmgard Keun: Leben und Werk*. Würzburg: Königshausen & Neumann.

Paechter, Heinz. 1944. *Nazi-Deutsch. A Glossary of Contemporary German Usage*. New York: Frederick Ungar.

von Polenz, Peter. 1999. *Deutsche Sprachgeschichte vom Spätmittelalter bis zur Gegenwart*. Bd 3: *19. und 20. Jahrhundert*. Berlin, New York: de Gruyter.

Schmidt-Dengler, Wendelin. 2004. Hüben und drüben. Karl Kraus, der Ständestaat und das Deutsche Reich. In *Stachel wider den Zeitgeist. Kabarett, Flüsterwitze, Subversives*, Hg. Robert Kreichbaumer and Oswald Panagl, 113–120. Wien, Köln, Weimar: Böhlau.

Sternberger, Dolf. 1932. 'Fressendes Gift' bis 'Wiedergeburt'. Wörterbuch der Regierung von Papen in Auszügen. *Deutsche Republik* 6 (2): 1398–1401. July 26.

Timms, Edward. 2005. *Karl Kraus. Apocalyptic Satirist. The Post-War Crisis and the Rise of the Swastika*. New Haven, London: Yale University Press.

Wagner, Frank Dietrich. 1989. *Bertolt Brecht: Kritik des Faschismus*. Opladen: Westdeutscher Verlag.

5

Voices at Home (I): Private Notes for Posterity

As Brecht shows in the Informer scene in *Fear and Misery of the Third Reich* and in the fictional Herr Egge's situation (see Chap. 1), once the agent of power has lodged in his home, the concept of a private space immune from the agents of power is far from straightforward. The writings reviewed in this chapter occupy the precarious private space in which fear of denunciation leading to a house search by the Gestapo was very real, and in these circumstances a degree of self-censorship is perhaps natural, if only to protect others. Was it possible to write in such a way as to protect oneself if the document was discovered? Whilst some coded language is found in the diaries, it is not on the whole a dominant feature: the very attempt to create such a private space for critical thought was in itself potentially life-threatening. In the face of this danger, 'private' writing was for some an existential need, as Victor Klemperer recalled in 1947: "Mein Tagebuch war in diesen Jahren immer wieder meine Balancierstange, ohne die ich hundertmal abgestürzt wäre" (Klemperer 1978, p. 15; "Again and again during these years my diary was my balancing pole, without which I would have fallen down a hundred times." (Klemperer 2000, p. 9)). Indeed, the point of creating this

W J Dodd, *National Socialism and German Discourse*,
https://doi.org/10.1007/978-3-319-74660-9_5

private space is to speak out, in plain language, for the sake of one's own integrity and sanity, and to compile testimonies which might be heard in a future one may not live to see. For the most part, these voices are forthright, their testimonies potentially a pre-emptive counter to the mass amnesia of the immediate post-war period.

The diarists reviewed here are Anna Haag, Theodor Haecker, Ursula von Kardorff, Erich Kästner, Victor Klemperer, and Thea Sternheim. These were Germans in various degrees of 'inner exile' in Nazi Germany or, in Sternheim's case, in territorial exile and, from June 1940, in occupied France. Klemperer, whose diary in these years contains hundreds of observations under the now famous rubric L(ingua) T(ertii) I(mperii) (Language of the Third Reich), is probably the only one of these names known outside Germany today. Before coming to the diarists, however, this chapter reviews examples of two other genres: the private criticism of Hitler's rhetoric and character, exemplified by Mechtilde Lichnowsky, and the card-index inventory of contemporary usage, exemplified by the encyclopaedic project of Eugen Seidel and Ingeborg Seidel-Slotty's *Sprachwandel im Dritten Reich* (Language Change in the Third Reich). This couple do not fit easily into our notional categories. Theirs are not strictly "voices at home", but neither do they sit easily with the (published) voices from abroad in the previous chapter. In contrast to those who will be considered in the next two chapters, these private voices entered the public discourse only after the fall of the regime, in some cases long after 1945 and in the case of Anna Haag only in 2015. With the exception of Klemperer, their impact on German public discourse has been at best marginal. That their testimonies survived was a matter of chance. Pages from both Klemperer's and Haecker's diaries eluded the Gestapo when they searched their apartments. It seems very likely that the surviving corpus of such writings represents only a small fragment of what was written in private at the time, and we can only speculate how many other testimonies of this kind have been lost to posterity. Finally, it should be noted that claims to documentary authenticity may need to be treated with caution, and not just because of the inevitable subjectivity of the commentator. We need to distinguish, for example, between Klemperer's diaries and his selective presentation of them in *LTI* (1947), and to be cautious, for reasons explained below, in our reading of

Kardorff's diary ('written up' in 1947), and Seidel and Seidel-Slotty's study (published in 1961).

Hitler's Style as Character: Mechtilde Lichnowsky

Mechtilde Lichnowsky (1879–1958), widow of Prince Karl Max Lichnowsky (German ambassador to London at the outbreak of the First World War) and friend and admirer of Karl Kraus, published occasional glosses on language (some of them in the *Frankfurter Zeitung*).[1] A collection of language glosses, *Worte über Wörter* (Words about Words),[2] prevented from publication in 1939 because of her closeness to the exiled Jewish publisher Gottfried Bermann Fischer, appeared only after 1945 (Lichnowsky 1946, 1949). Having lived in France since 1928, she was placed under house arrest on visiting Germany in 1939, and from 1941 her books were included in the 'Liste des schädlichen und unerwünschten Schrifttums' (List of Harmful and Undesirable Writing) (Pfäfflin and Dambacher 2001; Dodd 2013, p. 259f.) Her essay "Werdegang eines Wirrkopfs" (Lichnowsky 1948, The Career of a Dizzyhead), composed in 1942, is a psychological profile of a 'type': socially insecure, belonging in an asylum, with the characteristics of a robot, a head full of phrases learned from newspapers, and a vengeful and overblown ego ("großgeschriebene[s] Ich", 1948, p. 606). Hitler, clearly identifiable in this portrait, is however not named (Emonts 2012): "So rasselt und klappert es, wie etwa in einem beschädigten Robot, den ein untalentierter Amateur zusammengebastelt hätte, während unser Wirrkopf steif, mit eckigen Armbewegungen daherkommt und einen eisernen Schlitz öffnet, aus welchem das Blech der fremden Meinung fällt" (p. 613, "So it rattles and clatters like a damaged robot put together by an ungifted amateur, as our Dizzyhead approaches with awkward arm movements and opens an iron slit from which falls the rubbish of alien opinion"). The anger and frustration in this rant, echoing Kraus's *ad hominem* assaults, but also Sternberger's coded commentaries (for example on the "stupid and the vain" discussed in Chap. 7), has its origins in Lichnowsky's attempts to critique Hitler's style in *Mein Kampf*, probably in France in 1933.

The unpublished typescript[3] consists of one hundred and thirty four brief extracts from *Mein Kampf*, mostly sentences or parts of sentences, and fifty brief comments.[4] Here, it is often Kraus's grammatical and stylistic pedantry which is echoed: an allegedly wrongly placed reflexive pronoun (actually quite normal in spoken German); wandering metaphors; his preference for BESITZEN (to possess) over the plainer 'haben' (to have). Hitler's phrase "Gelegenheit besitzen" (literally: possess the opportunity), prompts the response: "Gelegenheit macht Diebe, daher gelingt es diesem Wortdieb, die zu besitzen" ("Opportunity makes the thief, that's how this word thief manages to possess them").[5] These criticisms home in on solecisms of (standard) register, exposing an under-educated man's attempts to put on airs. Like other commentators, Lichnowsky picks out Hitler's clumsy preference for noun phrases over verb-centred statements; his tendency to hyperbole, especially in the use of words such as UNENDLICH, GANZ, and GÄNZLICH; and the "Schwulst" (bombast) of his language, revealing him as a "Gernegross" (would-be Big Cheese). Her attacks tend to be on the person rather than the politics; only rarely do we find the kind of hard-bitten comment which might be mistaken for one by Kraus:

> S.21. *In dieser Zeit bildete sich mir ein Weltbild und eine Weltanschauung, die zum graniten Fundament meines derzeitigen Handelns wurden. […] Ich habe zu dem, was ich mir so einst schuf, nur weniges hinzulernen müssen, zu ändern brauchte ich nichts.*
>
> Abgesehen von dem "gebildeten Weltbild" in "dieser Zeit", das zum Fundament seines "derzeitigen" Handelns wurde, ist die Feststellung, dass er wenig hinzuzulernen und nichts zu ändern brauchte, eine Wahnvorstellung. Solche Sätze werden in Irrenanstalten zu Hunderten verfasst, aber sie bleiben in der Anstalt, sie werden weder gedruckt noch gelesen, ausser unter der Rubrik "Krankengeschichten".

> p. 21. *In that time a world picture and worldview formed before me which became the granite foundation of my actions at this time. […] I did not have to learn much new to add to what I had already created, I did not need to change anything.*
>
> Quite apart from the "formed world picture", which became "in this time" the foundation of his actions, the assertion that he had little more to learn and nothing to change is a delusion. Sentences like this are written in

> mental asylums in their hundreds, but they stay in the asylum, they don't get printed or read, except under the heading of "sick people's stories".

The trope of the mental asylum (again) makes the political point, but *ad hominem*, and in order to make it Lichnowsky passes over the opportunity to expose keywords of the political discourse: "formed world picture", WELTANSCHAUUNG and "granite foundation" (GRANITES FUNDAMENT). Some comments reveal all too clearly, admittedly with the benefit of hindsight, a naivety which is a world away from Kraus's *Walpurgisnacht*:

> S.116. ... *Denn das mögen sich alle schriftstellenden Ritter und Gecken von heute gesagt sein lassen: die grössten Umwälzungen auf dieser Welt sind nie durch einen Gänsekeil geleitet worden.*
>
> H. benützt wohl eine Füllfeder; Ihm sei besonders gesagt, dass auch Reden auf dieser Welt nur wenig umgewälzt haben.
>
> p. 116. ... *For I have to tell all of today's literary knights and dandies: the greatest revolutions in this world were never led by a goose feather.*
>
> H. probably uses a fountain pen. I have to tell him particularly that speeches, too, have not overturned much in this world.

A comment such as this, together with another about Hitler becoming Reich Chancellor out of defiance, strongly suggests that this typescript dates from early 1933. If so, one can understand why it might be broken off as the regime quickly translated words into deeds and stylistic criticism became increasingly irrelevant. The anger and frustration resurfaced in 1942 in the unrelenting assault on the un-named "Wirrkopf".

The Inventorists

Eugen Seidel and Ingeborg Seidel-Slotty

Relatively little is known about the authors of *Sprachwandel im Dritten Reich*. The linguistic scientists Eugen Seidel (1906–1981) and Ingeborg Seidel-Slotty (1910–1973) left the Reich for political reasons in 1933

(Maas 2015), finding temporary refuge from Nazi authorities, first in Prague, where Seidel-Slotty's father Friedrich Slotty, also a vocal anti-Nazi, was a professor of comparative linguistics at the German University; and then in Romania from 1938 or 1939, escaping the German occupation of Prague but evidently retaining access to German newspapers, books, and media, from which they collected and collated thousands of examples of language in use between 1933 and 1943. They returned to Germany (to the GDR) in 1955. The study was published in the GDR in 1961.

The sheer mass of detail contained in *Sprachwandel* can barely be sampled in a review such as this. Its material is organized under four main headings: style, grammar, lexis, and expansion ('Ausbreitung') of the politicolect into general usage. It appears to be based on an index-card system, and the scale of the enterprise can be gauged from the study's 274 paragraphs of data and analysis, supported by commentary essays, and the index of some 1900 words and expressions identified as belonging to Nazi discourse, from ABART (deviant variety, sub-species) to ZWISCHENSCHALTUNG (third-party intervention), including one hundred and seventy five lexical derivations beginning VOLK- or VOLK- (e.g. VOLKSGANZE (entirety of the ethnic nation), VOLKSEINEND (unifying the 'Volk')). The section on style notes six features, some of which overlap: (1) repetitive and tautological expressions ("etwas Einziges und Einmaliges", "something singular and unique"), (2) metaphors, especially those drawn from the military domain ("ein ganzes Regiment kämpft gegen Hunger und Kälte", "an entire regiment is fighting against hunger and cold"), and as an extension of this (3) false pathos, invoking "a tone of passion and overheated tension", a "mood of struggle", (4) affected, bombastic language, trying to sound ever more profound (e.g. the use of "etwas WAGEN" (venture/dare to do something) instead of 'etwas tun' (do something)), (5) clipped expression, adding punchy counterpoint to repetitive style ("wird erbarmungslos ausgemerzt", "is mercilessly purged"), also including the preference for nominal style ("Neuwerdung des Lehrstandes", "regeneration of the teaching profession"), and in contrast to this (6) vagueness of expression, in which apparent explanations turn out to be circular assertions ("Recht ist, was dem deutschen Volke nützt", "What is lawful is what serves the German 'Volk'"). These features are also exemplified in the sections on syntax and word formation. Logical connectors like UND SO (and thus) and DAMIT (in order that) tautologically intensify, rather than logically extend a point ("... zielen auf die Bildung des Bewußtseins und damit auf die des Charakters", "... are aimed at the development of consciousness and consequently of character"). On this last example the authors comment that the connection appears to be neither consecutive nor causal: "The concepts of consciousness and character are brought into some kind of connection, but in a way that assumes it is obvious how they relate to one another" (p. 19). The ideological lexicon gives birth to a potentially infinite number of neologisms with which to populate the new discourse, as keywords generate hundreds of new derivations, such as the collective nouns VOLKHEIT (patterned on 'Menschheit', humanity/human race) and WEHRHEIT (anomalously derived from an abstract noun and apparently equivalent to the semantically concrete WEHRMACHT, armed forces, p. 27). Compound nouns, notoriously non-transparent in their logical structure, change their use: VOLKSSEELE (folk soul) no longer exclusively designates the concept from anthropological psychology ("Völkerpsychologie"), but also the evaluative VÖLKISCHE SEELE (cf. p. 36), which passes judgment on ideological correctness of attitude. New forms proliferate, for example conjoined with GROSS- to conjure a sense of monumental achievement and ambition (often with unintended comic effect[6]): alongside the geo-political GROSSRÜMANIEN the authors note GROSSFILM and GROSSGASTHOF (large restaurant). The section on lexis groups ideological keywords by the grand metaphors to which they contribute, principally: militarization of the discourse (KOMMANDOSTELLEN DER WIRTSCHAFT, command posts of the economy); terms connoting dynamism (the NSDAP styles itself a movement (BEWEGUNG) rather than a 'Partei'); BLUT UND BODEN (Blood and Soil: "der Sieg des Blutes gegen volksfremde Willkür und Verführung", "the victory of the blood over [un-German] alien whim and seduction"); and unity of the 'Volk' (DAS VOLKSGANZE).

As Utz Maas (2015) observes, one of the recurring insights in *Sprachwandel* is the power of ritualized repetition to undermine rational discourse, drain words of their traditional semantic values, and thus communicate an impression of security and power by favouring the dimension of expression over that of content ("Dominanz der 'Ausdrucksbewegung' gegenüber 'rationalen Konturen'"). The unintellectual, indeed anti-intellectual tenor of this kind of discourse often resists analysis in logical categories—for example it exhibits both "Fremdwort mania" and nationalistic-xenophobic language purism without having to account for the contradiction in doing so (cf. Seidel and Seidel-Slotty 1961, pp. 16ff, 123ff). Once we move away from keywords and their ideological content (and in some cases even before we do so), the new discourse is essentially about tone, mood, and impact. The authors find a proliferation of terms which connote "mindestens einen Gefühlswert der Gewaltsamkeit", i.e. at least a feeling of positively connoted violence (p. 60). *Sprachwandel* may be organised around categories of linguistic structure, but its main thrust is firstly as a critique of style, and secondly as a study in how meaning is generated through social praxis, and how Nazi discourse degrades the potential of language as a tool of rational discussion. The section devoted to "expansion" particularly marks *Sprachwandel* out as a work of 'inner exiles':

> Die "Sprache des Ns". ist natürlich nicht von diesem geschaffen. Nur an Breite und Stärke hat unter seiner Herrschaft ins Immense gewonnen, was früher unbeachtet blieb, weil es nur den Stil von einigen "Außenseitern" bestimmte. (Seidel and Seidel-Slotty 1961, p. 144)
>
> The "language of National Socialism" was of course not created by National Socialism. What had previously barely been remarked upon because it shaped the style of only a few "outsiders", gained immensely in breadth and strength under its rule.

An analysis of publications by the same author before and after 1933 evaluates the extent to which their language use changed to incorporate new ideologemes and the new 'tone'.[7] Of particular interest here is their detailed comparison (pp. 139–143) of Leo Weisgerber's *Muttersprache und Geistesbildung* (1929, Mother Tongue and the Formation of Spirit) and *Die volkhaften Kräfte der Muttersprache* (1938/1943, The 'volkhaft' Forces of the Mother Tongue), which reveals Weisgerber's widespread adoption of the term VOLKHAFT after 1933 in arguing his "inhaltbezogen" (semantic-anthropological) approach to language as the expression of the worldview of a speech community. Weisgerber, one of the most sophisticated language theorists writing in German in the twentieth century, was at that time at the beginning of a brilliant academic career. Seidel and Seidel-Slotty, along with other linguistic scientists,[8] were eminently well placed to observe the development of his use of language under the impact of the new discourse norms. The evidence assembled in these pages of *Sprachwandel* illustrates how readily a (Wilhelm von) Humboldtian discourse on language could be aligned with a nationalist discourse on race and culture. By 1961, Weisgerber was arguably the most eminent linguistic scientist in the Federal Republic, its "linguistics pope", creator and head of the Institute of Celtic Studies at the University of Bonn (and in 1964, co-founder of the renowned Institute for German Language in Mannheim). Although there is no reference to it, Seidel and Seidel-Slotty would presumably have been aware of the vitriolic exchanges in the Federal Republic, beginning in 1955, between Weisgerber and his accuser on precisely this issue, Walter Boehlich (Boehlich 1955, p. 892f., 1964; Weisgerber 1956).

This inevitably raises the question: To what extent is *Sprachwandel* a contemporaneous study of the Nazi period, to what extent a work from 1961? The question is difficult to resolve when so little is known about its provenance. At the time of writing there is no trace of a manuscript, or of the data set on which it was based, and thus no substantive information about the genesis of the book which could shed light on how the authors' notes were fashioned into the published work.[9] On closer inspection, the apparently clear statement by the authors in the Introduction (p. vi) that the study "was written during the Nazi dictatorship, and so presents to a greater or lesser extent phenomena as contemporary which today belong to the past", actually highlights the problem of provenance. Subtitled "A critical study of fascist influences", *Sprachwandel* was published in the German Democratic Republic at a particularly strained moment in the Cold War, and contains occasional footnotes relating to contemporary (i.e. 1961) language usage, as when the fascist use of AUSRADIEREN (rub out, eliminate) is found echoed in contemporary West German government circles (p. 44), and the Nazi usage of VOLKSEIGEN (characteristic of a biological race) is disambiguated from the GDR usage in 'volkseigener Betrieb' (enterprise in public ownership, p. 97). From these examples it is apparent that the contemporaneous work has been overlaid with material from the period to 1961. To some extent, then, it is also a document in the competing claims of the two post-war German states to represent the 'better' Germany.[10] Some awareness of this circumstance may be warranted with regard to the sections of commentary, whilst the implication that all the data were recorded in the Nazi period may well be justified. However, in the absence of any archival evidence there is no way of testing either of these assumptions.[11]

The Diarists

The most widespread mode of 'private' oppositional writing, however, was certainly the diary. Alongside the voices of Victor Klemperer, Theodor Haecker, and Erich Kästner, three women diarists, Anna Haag, Ursula von Kardorff, and Thea Sternheim, provide a measure of "counterpoint" (Timms 2015, p. 26) to the generally male-dominated public discourse both of National Socialism, and of opposition to it. These diarists have been selected for what they exhibit about the oppositional, disenfranchised voice of a certain class of 'inner exile' German. It would be extravagant to claim a wider representative significance for them, if indeed one can imagine a truly representative sample of the German population, an ambitious claim even for Walter Kempowski's grand project to map the hidden depths of this private space in *Das Echolot* (The Echo Sounder).[12] Whilst the diaries reviewed below contain politically explicit statements, especially on language use, they are not (with the possible exception of Haecker) conspiratorial political diaries in Heidrun Kämper's sense. Whilst they sometimes exhibit the "economy of concealment" which Kämper (2011) finds in Willi Graf's journal, they just as often exhibit the "generosity of explanation" which she finds in Ulrich von Hassel's (from which the Gestapo was able to extensively reconstruct the membership and aims of the failed *coup d'état* of 20 July 1944 (Operation Walkyre)). The diaries reviewed below typically record random minutiae of private and professional life, daily experience, the communicative acts of friends, colleagues and strangers, and the diarist's own political statements, constituting clandestine contributions to an alternative, albeit fragmented, discourse of dissent. A recurring feature of these diaries is the anecdote or joke which captures words and deeds of opposition to the regime amongst peers or the population at large. Some of these anecdotes, in particular, offer a window onto this world of barely concealed hatred of the regime and its representatives, detailing small acts of courage at some personal risk. Others are more ambiguous, often suggesting a deep-seated sense of political powerlessness and disengagement beneath the surface show of 'Resistenz'. Jokes, and particularly *ad hominem* jokes about the foibles of individual Nazi leaders, often fall into this category. A sub-set of the latter, sexual jokes, arguably occupies a particular low point in this discourse of powerlessness, where the sexual is a displacement of, and subaltern substitute for, the political.

Victor Klemperer

Klemperer (1881–1960) was removed from his post as Professor of Romance Philology at Dresden Technical University in 1935 (2.5.1935)[13] after a process of exclusion from the Faculty beginning already in 1933 (cf. 15.5.1933). Having converted to Protestantism on marrying his wife Eva (for practical rather than religious reasons), his sense of identity, like many other Jewish Germans, was as a German and not, as he was forced to become, a Jew. The metaphor of a man walking a tightrope without a safety net is the one Klemperer chose in 1947 to characterize the importance of his diary as a place of refuge, of self-preservation ("Selbstbewahrung", 29.10.1933), where sanity, clarity, and integrity could be sought in the face of despair at the "Schand- und Wahnsinnstaten" ("outrages and insane acts") of the Nazis, as Klemperer notes in May 1933, giving a telling summary of the *mood* of the time ("*Stimmung* dieser Zeit"): "das Warten, das Sichbesuchen, das Tagezählen, die Gehemmtheit in Telefonieren und Korrespondieren, das zwischen den Zeilen der unterdrückten Zeitungen Lesen" ("the waiting, the visiting each other, the counting the days, the inhibition on the telephone and in correspondence, the reading between the lines of the suppressed newspapers", 15.5.1933). Klemperer's diaries, first published in the 1990s, have been translated into many languages, inspired television films (e.g. Kasten and Kohlhaase 1998, 1999) and YouTube videos.[14] Their loose-leaf pages were smuggled out of the "Judenhaus" in which they were quartered (usually by Eva), to be buried in the garden of a friend's house in the suburbs of Dresden. Had it been discovered, this diary was a death sentence in waiting for all concerned, despite Klemperer's attempts to disguise their names (26.12.1942). That it and they survived was due to extreme caution and immense good fortune, as the Gestapo turned over the flat but failed to find its latest instalments concealed in a Greek dictionary (27.5.1942).

Anecdotes recorded here demonstrate their role in the communicative ecology of fascist society, especially when the victims in these anecdotes were perceived to belong to groups other than one's own—a particular feature, perhaps, of the early years of Nazi rule. In May 1933, a friend (her political sympathies nationalist, not Nazi) relates the story of a communist whose garden is dug up in the search for a machine gun. He denies it, and they find nothing. In order to extract a confession, they beat him to death. The body is brought to the hospital with boot marks in the stomach and fist-size holes in his back, stuffed with wadding. "Offizieller Sektionsbefund: Todesursache Ruhr, was vorzeitige 'Leichenflecke' häufig zur Folge habe". ("Official post-mortem finding: dysentery, which apparently can lead to early 'markings on the corpse'" (15.5.1933)). This anecdote could quite easily be from Kraus's *Walpurgisnacht*.

Increasingly, the diary became a place of angry, determined documentation—much as Bloch had recommended: "Ich will Zeugnis ablegen, und exaktes Zeugnis" ("I shall bear witness, and exact witness", 27.5.1942)—this after surviving the latest house search.[15] Gradually, Klemperer realised that his philological life's calling was not his work on French Enlightenment literature (a haven in which he also sought refuge), but his own journal as a document and exploration of the language circulating around him. Under the rubric "Sprache des 3. Reichs" (1.1.1935) and finally L[ingua] T[ertii] I[mperii] (cf. 1.7.1941) he noted lexical and rhetorical changes in the language used not only by Nazis but also by non-Nazis and even by the victims of Nazism. The entry of 1.1.1935 notes the non-pejorative use, in an announcement by the SA, of their FANATISCHER WILLE (fanatical will), FANATISCHE(R) EINSATZ(BEREITSCHAFT) (fanatical (readiness for) action), and their professed GLÄUBIGKEIT, OHNE ZU VER-

STEHEN (faith without needing to understand, i.e. blind faith). The lexicon of Klemperer's "LTI" includes many familiar lexemes: AUSRICHTUNG, AUSROTTEN, BLUT, BRUTAL, CHARAKTERLICH, the generic DER JUDE, EHRE (honour), EINMALIG (unique), ERBGESUNDHEIT (hereditary [racial] health), FANATISCH, GEMEINSCHAFT, LIQUIDIEREN, LUFTTERROR (referring to Allied bombing), RASSE, SCHÄDLING (parasite), TOTAL, UNERWÜNSCHT, VORSEHUNG (providence), and WEHRKRAFTZERSETZUNG. Fixed phrases include GROSS AUFGEZOGEN (on a gigantic scale), BLONDES BLUT, DAS EWIGE DEUTSCHLAND (the eternal Germany), ENTSCHEIDENDE ERFOLGE (decisive successes), and VERSCHWORENE GEMEINSCHAFT (community united by oath). The metaphors, tropes, and effects attributed to LTI include the language of sport (including "Boxersprache"), threefold repetition ("Dreiklang"), and the predilection for impressively large numbers ("Riesenzahl") and superlatives. The language of the victims also forms part of LTI, as Klemperer notes with frustration their unreflecting adoption of it (a Jewish friend refers to 1933 as the UMBRUCH, 2.2.1944)—but also elements of a resistant counter-discourse, as when Jewish friends talk about their murdered comrades having "been died" (GESTORBEN WIRD, 23.10.1942). Klemperer himself creates the non-grammatical phrase ABGEWANDERT WORDEN in a lucid comment on a returned postcard:

> … und heute kam diese Karte zurück. Blaustempel darauf "zurück", Bleistiftnotiz "Abgewandert". Beachte zu *LTI*: "Abgewandert" für abgewandert *worden*. Harmloses Wort für "vergewaltigen", "vertreiben", "in den Tod schicken". (27.2.1943)

> … and today this postcard was returned. Blue official stamp on it "Return to Sender", in pencil "moved away". NB for *LTI*: "moved away" for *has been* moved away. Harmless word for "violate", "expel", "send to their death".[16]

Small but significant acts of linguistic defiance amongst the 'German' population are also noted in the changing language of the obituary ('Todesanzeige'), as the families of fallen soldiers withhold the expected tribute, for example in the statement that a son has fallen "for the Fatherland" (26.7.1941), instead of "for Führer and Fatherland".

The diary records the systematic ghettoisation of the Jews, as they are banned from using parks, trams, German newspapers, selling furniture, and owning property, including radios and cats (e.g. 15.5.1942).[17] They also record a functioning communication network: In the "Judenhaus" to which the Klemperers are consigned in 1940 there are reports of the apparently systematic extermination of Jews in Warsaw (1.6.1943), of "transports" to Theresienstadt (6.8.1942), and of death announcements from a place called Auschwitz, "das ein schnell arbeitendes Schlachthaus zu sein scheint" ("which seems to be a fast-working slaughter house", 14.10.1942)—evidence that, at least amongst the persecuted Jewish population in Dresden, a communication network existed which carried knowledge of the genocide. The deaths reported from Auschwitz are of two Dresden women ("up till now it was only men who died in a concentration camp") whose "offences" are also recorded: one had had forbidden fish in the fridge, the other had used the tram, which she only should have used to go to her place of work, to go to the doctor.

Heidrun Kämper (2011, p. 235) has called these diaries "a testimony not only to contemporary history but to language and everyday communication under totalitarianism",[18] as a result of which Klemperer has bequeathed us an "archive" (Kämper 2000, p. 26), a record of everyday communication in the 'Third Reich' which goes beyond the registration of lexical items to document actual linguistic events in their contexts of use. Of particular value are the records of oral communication, amongst Klemperer's friends and acquaintances, but also in the *vox populi*, which are typically not captured in audio recordings from the time. Kämper (2000, pp. 27–31) lists some of the salient features of this discourse environment: the devastating impact of the (threat of) postal censorship, the disorienting atmosphere of rumour, the fear of being reported by a 'Spitzel' or tricked into a careless word by an *agent provocateur* working for the Gestapo (e.g. 19.8.1933, 16.2.1934, 11.12.1943). For a STERNJUDE (star-carrying Jew) like Klemperer, there was also the abuse hurled at him on the street by Gestapo and professedly 'Aryan' citizens, but also occasional small acts of "gefährliche Höflichkeit" ("dangerous politeness", 24.9.1942, cf. 16.4.1943) when strangers speak to him humanely, express their sympathy, even solidarity, share their contempt for the regime, albeit in a whisper. Throughout, Klemperer is a witness with fine-tuned powers of observation, for example when he notes the subtle gradations in the raising of the arm and the stiffness of the open hand for the DEUTSCHER GRUSS 'Heil Hitler!', especially amongst strangers (13.6.1934, 2.9.1941).

Theodor Haecker

The Catholic theologian and cultural critic Theodor Haecker (1879–1945), like Karl Kraus a polemical publicist, was a thorn in the flesh of the Nazis long before their accession to power, and a marked man afterwards. In his essay on Vergil (Haecker 1932), published in Innsbruck in the journal *Der Brenner*, he had denounced Nazism as the work of the anti-Christ and the swastika as "the sign of the beast, the caricature of the cross", a symbol of deceit, trickery, perversion ("ein Symbol des Dreh"). As Helena Tomko (2017, p. 55f.) explains, Haecker traces the origins of the symbol to "the spinning motion of a four-legged beast", and turns 'Drehen' (motion) into 'Dreh' ('deceit'), and 'spinning' into 'swindle' ('Schwindel') by "a malevolent sleight of hand". Copies of this issue of *Der Brenner* were delivered to Germany just as the Nazis took power, causing Haecker anguish as he tried desperately to have the issue recalled or to have pages blacked out. He was arrested and briefly detained in May 1933, when a Gestapo house search failed to find copies of the offending *Brenner*. Living in Munich, in close contact with other Catholic opponents of the regime, many of them associated with the journal *Hochland*, Haecker also read extracts from his works to small circles of trusted friends, including members of the White Rose group Willi Graf and Sophie Scholl. Hans Scholl also knew Haecker's writings, and probably Haecker personally, through Carl Muth, the editor of *Hochland*.[19] In February 1943 Haecker had a lucky escape when the Gestapo searched the house following the arrest of the White Rose group, and his daughter Irene left the house with the folder containing his notes, saying she had a piano lesson (Siefken 1989, p. 15). A charge of preparing high treason ('Vorbereitung zum Hochverrat') was subsequently dropped for lack of evidence. In these years Haecker entrusted his invective to a diary spanning the years 1939 to 1945—published posthumously in 1947 as the

Tag- und Nachtbücher (Day and Night Books). He continued to publish occasional essays in *Hochland* into the 1940s, mainly on theological issues, including a short selection of extracts from this diary in 1940. The published extracts stand in stark contrast to the raw diary manuscript.[20] Whilst they contain a general, philosophical and theological rebuttal of the National Socialist worldview, they carry no trace of the savage and personalized polemic conducted in the diary, the topical and *ad hominem* references which would certainly have cost Haecker his life.

Hinrich Siefken (1989, p. 7) describes the *Tag- und Nachtbücher* as a mixture of "aphoristic criticism of the times, philosophical and religious reflection, polemical note, spiritual stock-taking and self definition in lonely conversation with himself, dialogue, diatribe, and prayer". Haecker's viewpoint is one of a combative, even militant Catholic convert, and this also gives him purchase on the language of the time, the willingly worn "straitjacket" of everyday discourse:

> Die Normalsprache, die flüssige Sprache ist eine nivellierende Uniform, ja eine Zwangsjacke, die unter Umständen die stärksten Kräfte bricht; sie wird von manchen freiwillig angelegt. (Haecker 1989, p. 110 (8.9.1940))

> Everyday language, flowing language is a levelling uniform, even a straitjacket, which in certain conditions can break the strongest forces, and is put on voluntarily by many people.

It is the unholy connection between Pflicht (duty) and the Phrase (glib phrase)—a Prussian-German characteristic—that Haecker sees as truly dehumanizing (1989, p. 74). A radical Catholic, he hears the usurpation of religious discourse by Nazi orators, especially Hitler, whom he regarded as the Anti-Christ. Hitler's cultivation of the myth that he was protected by the providence (Vorsehung) of a divine authority (Herrgott) was for Haecker an act of unsurpassed sacrilege. Haecker repeatedly picks out these keywords for scathing commentary (e.g. pp. 38f., 72, 81, 109, 154, 196), as in the following example from September 1940:

> Es gibt einen Gott. Sein Name ist: der Herrgott oder der deutsche Herrgott oder der Allmächtige oder die Vorsehung. Darum gibt es auch eine Religion, eben die deutsche Herrgottreligion. Sie ist ohne Dogma. Also denken kann

> dabei jeder, was er mag. Nur tun nicht. Die Theologie ist einfach. Gott hat als der deutsche Herrgott den Willlen, dass es den Deutschen gut gehe, dass sie über alle herrschen. Kein Wunder! Deutsche Mystiker sind dahintergekommen, dass Gott nicht wäre ohne sie. Da sie nun aber ihrerseits Produkte des deutschen Volkes sind, so gehört nicht viel Logik dazu, einzusehen, dass dann auch Gott selber ein Produkt dieses deutschen Volkes ist. Gott strafe mich, wenn das ein Pamphlet ist. (1989, p. 109f.)

> There is a God. His name is the LordGod or the German LordGod or the Almighty or Providence. Hence there is a religion, this same German LordGod religion. It is without dogma. So anyone can think what he likes, he just can't do it. The theology is simple. It is God's will as the German LordGod that the Germans should do well, that they should rule over everyone. No wonder! German mystics discovered that God would not exist without them. But because they are themselves products of the German 'Volk' it does not take much logic to see that God is also a product of this German 'Volk'. May God punish me if this is a pamphlet.

This is worse than apostasy in Haecker's view: apostates misuse culture, but not the words of Christ. (The insidious power of this para-religious discourse can be seen in the reaction of one Else K. of Wesermünde, recorded later by Walter Kempowski, writing to her husband after Hitler survived the bomb blast of 20 July 1944: "Ein Wunder hat ihn uns gelassen, Liebster. Deutlicher wird der Himmel nie zu uns sprechen können" ("A miracle has preserved him for us, my Dearest. Heaven will never be able to speak to us more clearly")).[21] Haecker names those he finds responsible for preparing the Germans for such godless philosophy: Nietzsche, Wagner, and Houston Stewart Chamberlain (p. 28). It is a particular feature of the Germans that they have elevated such figures to intellectual and spiritual grandees. But Haecker's unremitting attack on the profanity of the HERRGOTT trope is directed specifically at Hitler's repeated self-stylization as the leader sent by Providence, with divine protection, as in his speech on New Year's Eve 1939:

> Im vergangenen Jahr hat unser deutsches Volksreich dank der Gnade der Vorsehung geschichtlich Wunderbares und Einzigartiges geleistet! Wir können am Beginn des Jahres 1940 den **Herrgott** nur bitten, daß er uns

weiterhin segnen möge im Kampf um die Freiheit, die Unabhängigkeit und damit um das Leben und die Zukunft unseres Volkes! In Demut danken wir dem **Herrgott** für seinen Segen.

Thanks to the grace of Providence, our Reich of the German 'Volk' has made historically miraculous and unprecedented achievements in the past year. At the beginning of 1940 we can only ask the **LordGod** to continue to bless us in the struggle for freedom, independence, and so for the life and the future of our 'Volk'. In humility we thank the **LordGod** for his blessing.

The human voice is for Haecker a manifestation of spirituality, effectively a sacrament, or rather, in its public manifestation in the 'Third Reich', a pathological symptom. Several entries are responses to what Haecker hears in the ubiquitous strident voice of the radio presenters, as in the following comment in November 1939:

Ich erschrecke in diesen Tagen über die Fähigkeit der menschlichen Stimme, abgesehen von dem, was sie sagt, allein durch sich selbst, nicht bloß individuell, sondern typisch, repräsentativ, die geistige Ausgestorbenheit eines ganzen Volkes zu verraten, zu ver*lautb*aren,[22] zu proklamieren. (1989, p. 21)

I recoil in these days at the ability of the human voice, regardless of what it says, simply by itself, not just individually, but typically, representatively, to betray the spiritual extinction of a whole people, to announce it, to proclaim it.

The numinous quality of this voice, the "cussing quagmire of a political robot, composed of baritone and lie" ("Schimpfsumpf eines politischen Roboters aus Bariton und Lüge," p. 26), is at the root of Haecker's Cassandra experience which, in April 1944, he feels he cannot communicate even to some trusted friends "who cannot see or hear" when he tries to share his "desperately lucid insight" and "point out the simply unmissable and unmistakeable tone, the tone which is identical with the sense of what is said" (p. 232f.). "What am I to do?", he confides to his diary, "Say nothing at all? Be silent? Or speak up too late?". What Haecker hears in the tone of the time is the incurable and 'unholy' condition of the 'Volk''s soul, *which takes pleasure in this voice* and wilfully draws down the wrath of God on itself. In September 1941, he quotes from a speech by Hans Fritzsche comparing the bombing of London with the destruction of Sodom and Gomorrah and notes: "I already know many reasons why Germany will not win the war. This Fritzsche speech is another one" (p. 198). Haecker hears the undertone of defeat in the announcers' proclamation of victories on the eastern front (p. 240), and the symbolic *faux pas* in the announcement on 31 December 1944 that Hitler's address to the nation has been put back to five minutes *after* midnight. The media managers, he writes, are unwittingly fulfilling a prophecy: the man will not stop until nothing remains (p. 237).

More than any other commentator reviewed in this book, Haecker exemplifies the strength of Christian resilience in the face of fascism, the voice of combative and even militant Christianity in a new crusade against the anti-Christ. The esoteric nature of his position may render him less accessible to today's more secular readers, but he occupies an important place in the spectrum of intellectual opposition to Nazism.

Erich Kästner

Kästner (1899–1974) is a typically ambiguous figure of inner exile in the Nazi era. Carl Zuckmayer's secret report (2002, p. 15f.), compiled for the CIA in the 1940s, classified him as "positive (untouched by Nazi influence, recalcitrant, reliable)", having first grouped him (with Ernst and F.G. Jünger and Hans Fallada) as a "special case, part positive, part negative, not easily classified". Kästner watched his books being burned by the Nazi students on the Opernplatz in Berlin in May 1933. His diary of the war years, begun in January 1941, records his professional life as a writer in the anomalous position of being employed at the personal behest of Goebbels to write film scripts (including the 1943 fantasy comedy *Münchhausen*) whilst being officially banned from publishing and making public appearances. Kästner had friends and acquaintances not only in the film studios but also in the Propaganda Ministry. His diary and outline plans for two novels drawing on the diary material coexist in a symbiotic relationship in a single blue notebook, published in 2006. It is especially interesting for its recording of anecdotes and jokes circulating in Berlin as the city was reduced to ruins, giving an insight into the everyday world of a recalcitrant population suspicious of and hostile to the regime—a world of rumour and bitter humour far removed from the sanitized propaganda image of a unified 'Volksgemeinschaft'. Kästner himself makes jokes at Hitler's expense:

> Heute früh wurden die Luftschutzsirenen ausprobiert. Kurz, Hitler hatte Recht, als er in seiner Rede ausrief: "Es wird wieder Frühling!" (Kästner 2006, p. 30, 26.2.1941)
>
> Early today the air raid sirens were tried out. In short, Hitler was right when he called out in his speech: "It will soon be spring again!"

At the end of October 1941 he notes how the introduction of the yellow star for Jews is met by Berliners with the phrase *Pour le Sémite* (p. 56, a variation on the military honour *Pour le Mérite*). The joke, itself morally indeterminate without a specific context of use, is clearly recounted sympathetically: Kästner writes of a Jew being humiliated in Berlin, and of the deportation of Berlin Jews to the Warthegau which has been underway for five days.

Rumours circulate of bombings and discontent across Germany: from Münster, Essen, Dresden (where Kästner's parents were living), and Hamburg in August 1943, where a 'Flakhelfer' from Munich has been sentenced to six years hard labour for saying there would be a mutiny in Munich if it had been flattened like this (p. 74). There are anecdotal reports of desertions and executions at the front, of mass murders of Jews in Poland, of conditions in the Warsaw Ghetto, and of distrust of the regime, and especially of Goebbels, the city's Gauleiter. There are suspicions that his order to evacuate the city in 1943 is a scheme to seize their property, and resentment of the ban on removing furniture from the city, introduced only after senior members of the military have packed off their own trophies from the French campaign. Kästner caustically notes the vitriol directed at these "Bonzen" (bosses, p. 71) by VOLKSGENOSSEN who were passing by. The BONZEN look after their own: the wife of an SS man is evacuated from the city even though they have no children, and the firm is ordered to continue paying her salary (p. 74, 10.8.1943). Kästner is critical of the lacklustre ("leichtfertig angeordnet") evacuation arrangements, and of Goebbels's assurance, astonishing from the city's chief of defence, that as a father of four he will not leave the city, a statement greeted sarcastically by Kästner as touching ("rührend") and uplifting ("erhebend") (p. 69). The performances of "Pfarrer" ("Vicar") Fritzsche (p. 66), the voice of the Propaganda Ministry known to millions of Germans, are treated with disdain as he 'chats' away ("plaudert") in an attempt to raise morale. The regime is accused of 'sucking up' to the workers ("Anbiederung", p. 64), and of cynical disregard for the civilian population, like a callous second in a duel (p. 70) (or—echoing one of Goebbels's favourite tropes—a boxing match, p. 99) who is prepared to risk all and see his charge killed in the process.

Kästner records jokes which reveal how this resentment is vented by a powerless population: Goebbels will bring out a book in six years' time entitled *Six Years of Blitzkrieg* (p. 5, 16.1.1941). Ley and Goebbels arrive in Heaven, where Ley is given a large schnaps jug, Goebbels a beautiful girl. An old socialist passes by and complains to St. Peter, who consoles him: "Don't get so upset! Ley's jug has got a hole in it, and Goebbels's girl ..." (p. 23, 9.2.1941). The tellers of these two jokes are indiscreetly named. Other jokes are recorded, with obvious pleasure, without naming a source:

> Der Krieg wird wegen seines großen Erfolges verlängert. (p. 16, 26.1.1941)
>
> In view of its great success, the war is being prolonged.
>
> Ein Lehrer gibt das Thema zum Klassenaufsatz: "Hätte sich Werther auch im Dritten Reich erschossen?" Der kleine Fritz gibt schon nach fünf Minuten das Heft ab. Was hat er geschrieben? "Nein, aber Goethe!" (p. 36, 19.3.1941)
>
> A teacher gives the class an essay title: Would Werther have committed suicide in the Third Reich? After five minutes little Fritz hands in his notebook. What has he written? "No, but Goethe would have."

> Eine Synagoge brennt. Ein Brandstifter sagt zu einem alten Juden, der dabei steht: "Na, da sind Sie wohl nicht schlecht verzweifelt?" Der Jude verneint. "Denn", sagt er, "entweder gibt es einen Gott, dann gibt's auch eine Gerechtigkeit; oder es gibt keinen Gott,—wozu brauchen wir dann noch eine Synagoge?" (p. 36, 19.3.1941)
>
> A synagogue is burning. One of the arsonists says to an old Jew standing nearby, "I suppose you are pretty despondent?" The Jew says No. "Either there is a God, in which case there will be justice, or there isn't, in which case why do we need a synagogue?"
>
> Roosevelt and Hitler hätten ein neues Luftabkommen miteinander getroffen: Amerika stellte die Bomber zur Verfügung und Deutschland den Luftraum! (p. 101, 5.3.1945)
>
> Roosevelt and Hitler are rumoured to have signed a new agreement on the use of airspace. America supplies the bombers, Germany the airspace.

There are also indiscreet stories from the front of soldiers parodying Goebbels, of executions for desertion (p. 28, 21.1.1941), and an acquaintance from the Propaganda Ministry tells of a mischievous advert in the Berlin edition of the *Völkischer Beobachter*:

> Zu tauschen gesucht ein fünfzig Zentimeter hoher Sockel mit Hoheitsabzeichen gegen Mehrladepistole. (p. 64, 1.3.1943)
>
> Exchange sought: a fifty-centimetre high pedestal with national insignia [i.e. swastika] for a magazine pistol.

A belated attempt to find the culprit leads nowhere: he paid cash. In August 1943 Kästner notes a new greeting, BLEIBEN SIE ÜBRIG!, a variation on the official slogan BLEIBEN SIE RUHIG!, turning "Stay calm!" into "Stay alive!". A similar inventiveness turned KOHLENKLAU (a propaganda figure weakening the war effort by stealing coal) into HELDENKLAU (the stealer of heroes), a reference to General von Unruh, the regime's recruitment sergeant always on the look-out for new sources of recruits to the armed forces. Following the defeats on the eastern front and the regime's campaign of fear at the prospect of a Russian invasion, the formula KdF

(Kraft durch Freude, Strength through Joy) is reinvented as Kraft durch Furcht (Strength through Fear). In February 1945, Kästner labels as Gräuelpropaganda—a term officially discouraged even for foreign propaganda—the regime's campaign of fear of the Russians, intended to strengthen the 'Endkampfstimmung' (last stand mentality) of the population, and records a Berlin woman's response: "Lieber 'nen Russen aufm Bauch als 'n kaputtes Haus aufm Kopp!" (p. 93, 12.2.1945, "Sooner a Russian on my belly than a ruined house on my head").

One anecdote tells how Reich Youth Leader Baldur von Schirach visits a factory and is given an apparently enthusiastic reception by the workforce, who sing Party songs and chant "Sieg heil!" for two hours without interruption, so that he leaves without uttering a word (p. 14, 23.1.1941). On the same day, Kästner notes with derision an inadvertently comic radio announcement that miners working underground are to receive lemon hard boiled sweets ("Zitronenbonbons") as an extra allowance. He also notes the shift in official pronouncements as German cities suffer under the bombing campaign: Munich, formerly Stadt der Bewegung (City of the Movement), is now Stadt der Kunst (City of Art), and Nuremberg, the Stadt der Reichsparteitage (City of Party Rallies), has become the Stadt Dürers (City of Dürer (p. 65, 13.3.1943)). Kästner clearly sees through these attempts to shift the public mood from triumphalism to pathos, and to disassociate the Party from these now ruined cities. One entry from 1941 rejects the narrative of the Dolchstoss (stab in the back) of 1918 as a right-wing myth, a Dolchstosslegende:

> Die Dolchstoßlegende ist vom Heer, von den Gegnern der Sozialisten, bis zu den Nationalsozialisten, derartig verbreitet worden, dass die Tatsachen, die doch das Gegenteil beweisen, daneben und dahinter völlig verblasst sind. (p. 31, 1.3.1941)
>
> The legend of the stab in the back has been spread so extensively, by the army, by the enemies of the Socialists, all the way to the National Socialists, that the facts demonstrating the contrary have lost all colour in its shadow.

The opportunist behaviour of the Reich's new Russian allies, he notes in 1941, puts the alleged British Charakterlosigkeit (unprincipled 'lack of character', p. 45, 16.4.1941) in the shade. In March 1943 he records how children in their first year of schooling are now being called LERNANFÄNGER (beginning learners) instead of ABC-SCHÜTZEN (alphabet marksmen), presumably because schoolchildren now really are being drafted into national defence as 'Flakhelfer'. As is the case with other commentators, Nazi discourse is also critiqued implicitly, using ironic 'Imitat', as a careful consideration of context usually makes clear. For example, Kästner notes (presumably benefitting from his contacts in the Propaganda Ministry) that the reporting of three VOLKSGENOSSEN being executed for looting has been suppressed, despite the deterrent value of the story, because: "Volksgenossen just don't loot" (p. 58f., 18.2.1943). This anecdote captures not only Kästner's debunking of one of the key ideologemes of the regime, but also his insight into the cynicism of the Propaganda Ministry's news management.

Ursula von Kardorff

Perhaps the most well-known diary by a woman from these years is von Kardorff's *Berliner Aufzeichnungen*, written in 1947, but first published in 1962 (*Diary of a Nightmare*, 1965), with a revised edition and expanded Foreword in 1992. Kardorff accidentally found herself on the fringe of the 20 July plot, and this of course lends her reminiscences a special historical importance, as leading figures in the conspiracy are encountered (Ludwig Beck was being painted by her father in December 1942). We also learn about her situation as a journalist in the 'Third Reich' (although we might learn more from Margret Boveri's account (Boveri 1965) of the *Berliner Tageblatt*, significantly titled "Wir lügen alle" ("we all lie")). As one would expect of a journalist subject to the secret 'Sprachregelungen' of the Propaganda Ministry, she is a language critic, albeit an occasional one. On 20 March 1944, for example, she notes two such instructions affecting religious terminology: "Statt 'Gott' muss es jetzt in der Presse 'VORSEHUNG' heißen, und aus 'Christi Geburt' ist die 'ZEITWENDE' geworden" ("Instead of 'God' the press has to write 'Providence', and 'A.D.' has become the 'Common Age'"). However, at least one sceptical commentator, Volker Ullrich (1992), has dismissed the book as a rewriting of history, and Timms too (2015, p. 149) is inclined to question whether a journalist in Berlin could remain ignorant of Jews' fates (e.g. in the entry for 28.12.1942).[23] There is a case for considering the published text on a par with Klemperer's *LTI* and (to some extent) with Seidel and Seidel-Slotty's study, as part of the post-war discourse on Nazism.

Peter Hartl (1991, pp. 9–21) describes a politically naive young girl from a well-connected Berlin family of artists, whose youth was shaped by the Bohemian ethos of the Weimar Republic in the 1920s (cf. Frei and Schmitz 1989, pp. 150–154). Her father was a successful painter and a professor of art until removed from his post in 1934, her uncle had been Vice President of the Reichstag in the 1920s, German-Jewish family acquaintances included Alfred Kerr and Max Liebermann, who resigned as President of the Prussian Academy of Arts in 1933. Like her pro-Hitler mother, she voted Yes in the plebiscite of August 19, 1934 to confirm Hitler's absolute hold on power, and only gradually acquired a political sense, even after joining the editorial team of the Feuilleton of the national-conservative *Deutsche Allgemeine Zeitung* (DAZ) in 1939. The death of her brother Jürgen on the eastern front in February 1943 was a bitter blow. Acquainted with several of the figures of the Kreisau Circle and the failed coup attempt of 20 July 1944, she was questioned by the Gestapo in September 1944. Preparing the text for the extended and revised edition, Hartl (1991, p. 24f.) describes how Kardorff drew on three sources (preserved in the Institute for Contemporary History in Munich): (1) her diary, begun on 2 January 1943 and interrupted only twice: in February and March 1943, after the death of Jürgen, and between July and November 1944, in the wake of the failed putsch; (2) almost daily notes in small pocket diaries, preserved except for the one which she destroyed in 1944; (3) correspondence with friends. Whilst Hartl generally absolves Kardorff of the charge of falsifying history, finding an "honest reconstruction" of her personal experiences in a "reliable and authentic" testimony (p. 28f.), his editorial overview (pp. 24–30) also describes omissions, additions and elaborations, and alterations to the source material. Much of this is explicable as a process of decoding what was cryptically contained in the original, as when Sergeant S and his sister, referred to as "wunderbare Menschen" on 6 May 1943, are revealed in the book to be Hans and Sophie Scholl. The original entry for 25 January 1943, recording Goebbels's "total war" speech, is followed in the print edition by the interpolated comment: "Das wird die Stalingrader Strategie auch nicht wieder gutmachen. Es ist grotesk" ("That will not compensate for the Stalingrad strategy. It is grotesque"). Such elaborations, we deduce, reflect her words at the time which she could not commit to paper.

More controversially, Nazi terms used uncritically were dropped: FÜHRER was replaced by "Hitler", SCHWEISSTRIEFENDE PLUTOKRATEN (sweat-dripping plutocrats[24]) by "verängstigte Reiche" (alarmed kingdoms), RUSSENWEIBER (Russian women[25]) by "Ostarbeiterinnen" (women workers from the east). Some lexical items were deleted without substitution: SYSTEMZEITHAFT, ("typical of the SYSTEMZEIT"—a derogatory term for the Weimar Republic and its liberal democratic values) and TERRORANGRIFFE (terror attacks, i.e. Allied bombing), as well as some expressions of nationalistic pride. These changes naturally raise questions about the integrity of the published *Notes* proclaimed in Kardorff's first Introduction: "Allzu Persönliches wurde fortgelassen, nichts Neues, später Erfahrenes hinzugefügt" (Kardorff 1965, p. 5; "All too personal details were left out, nothing new, nothing that was learned later, has been added").

However, it would be unfair to Kardorff not to point out that her write-up of her personal history often reveals her own failures and weaknesses in the face of fascism. For example, when she persuaded the general editor of the DAZ, Otmar Best, to exempt her (having already lost a brother) from an instruction by the Propaganda Ministry that every member of the DAZ editorial team must publish an anti-Jewish article, she confessed: "Frage mich mit Schrecken, wieweit ich standhaft geblieben wäre; wenn man mir mit sofortiger Entlassung gedroht hätte: Ich hätte ganz bestimmt nachgegeben" (27.5.1943, "I ask myself, horrified, how far I would have stood my ground if I had been threatened with immediate dismissal. Quite certainly I would have given way"). The honesty of this statement is a relative rarity in post-1945 autobiographical writing in German.

To have retained her original words in 1947 would have required a degree of courage that Kardorff clearly could not find, and she was probably correct in fearing extensive condemnation had she done so. Today, we might be more prepared to recognize in these authorial decisions a profound shame surrounding the 'Sprachlosigkeit' to which she had succumbed, including signs of linguistic conformity in a conscious or unconscious defence mechanism when writing the contemporaneous notes in case they were discovered. Remarking that her treatment of politically sensitive topics is much more reserved and coded ("zurückhaltender und verschlüsselter") in the original notes, Hartl (1991, p. 27) rightly points to cases of executions for 'defaitistisch' comments in private diaries and letters. Kardorff's original notes were evidently characterized by a hybridity born of fear, to which her published text added yet another layer. It is this layered hybridity that makes Kardorff a potentially fascinating study in the discourse history of National Socialism, and for that reason a comprehensive examination of the print editions and their source texts, begun by Hartl, would appear to be an important research desideratum.

Anna Haag

The war diary of Anna Haag (1888–1982), presented for the first time in Edward Timms's recent study, is a valuable addition to this corpus.[26] Begun on 5 May 1940, her diary is, Timms notes, a reaffirmation of family and humane principles: "entries conceived as a means of bonding with the family evolved into a trenchant critique of the regime. The early entries show that keeping a diary was also a form of resistance against the pressures of propaganda" (p. 84). She herself explains her motive in writing it in terms of her determination not to be "found wanting" ("zu leicht befunden") before God (p. 18). In 1940, Anna and her husband Albert belonged to the now marginalized and fragmented intelligentsia in Stuttgart. Anna's values, Timms notes, were "rooted in the turn-of-the-century German liberalism and the pacifist movement of the inter-war period" (p. 7). They admired Friedrich Naumann and Theodor Heuss (pp. 28, 66). Albert's career as a school director had received a set-back when he had been transferred and demoted ("strafversetzt") to teaching girls after delivering a pacifist school assembly in November 1933 (p. 76).

At times her voice is surprisingly reminiscent of Theodor Haecker (of whom she appears to have been unaware). Like Haecker, she continues to refer to "das deutsche Volk" in a non-Nazi sense (but alters 'Volk' to 'Menschen' when railing at the "stupid Germans" who let their thinking be taken over by the relentless propaganda of hate, warfare, and racial difference). Like Haecker, she observes the presentation of Hitler as a mystical Führer figure, asks how much longer God will allow this Sodom and Gomorrah to continue, records her relief at the "deliverance" of the British Expeditionary Force from Dunkirk (cf. Haecker 1989, p. 71f., 1–2.6.1940), and searches for evidence of divine intervention in the setbacks on the eastern front. On learning of the existence of the Verein Lebensborn, she condemns it in terms similar to Haecker, as a stud farm for "SS-Zuchthengste" (SS stallions, p. 167). Nazi rhetoric is turned back on itself as she labels Hitler the ÜBERVERBRECHER (Supercriminal), describes the Nazi state as a KULTURSCHANDE (affront to civilization, p. 147), and comments, as the battle for Stalingrad goes badly, that Germans will come to experience the UNERBITTLICHE HÄRTE (merciless hardness) which they have thus far embraced as a virtue. Although not a religious person, Haag's ethical discourse has remarkable similarities at times with Haecker's. On 6 January 1940, for example, she confides to her diary:

> Die moralische Abwärtsentwicklung des deutschen Volkes in seiner Gesamtheit, das fast dürstige Aufsaugen der falschen Ideale (RASSE, HERRENMENSCHENTUM, WELTMISSION usf.)[27] mit all ihren scheußlichen Folgen beweisen, *wie* hörig ein Volk werden kann, dessen Gliedern jede Möglichkeit genommen wird, selbst zu denken. *Ein* Mensch, *ein* Parteiapparat denkt für alle. Alle Gedanken werden filtriert und in die Gehirne der Masse hineingegossen. Und da es gleichzeitig so eingerichtet ist, dass derjenige, der sich diesem "Gedankengut" widersetzt, verhungern oder im KZ oder Zuchthaus krepieren muss, so legen die allermeisten den eigenen Denkapparat gehorsam still, denn man will ja leben und lieben und essen und trinken. (p. 107f.)

> The collective moral deterioration of the German people, their thirst for gulping down false ideals (race, master race, world mission etc.) with all their appalling consequences, prove just *how* submissive a nation can become whose members have been deprived of all scope for thinking for themselves. A *single* individual, a *single* party apparatus thinks for everyone. All ideas are filtered and poured into the brains of the masses. And since at

> the same time arrangements have been made for everyone who repudiates this "wealth of ideas" to starve or die a miserable death in a concentration camp or prison, the result is that the overwhelming majority obediently shut down their own thinking apparatus, for after all everyone wants to live and love and eat and drink.

Her diary is a valuable testimony, at once documenting and resisting, as Timms notes, "the discourse of invincibility through multiple variations, from the speeches of Hitler, Goebbels and Scholtz-Klink through editorials in the press to gossip overheard on the tram. Extended quotations endow Anna's critique with a documentary authority" (p. 109). Her testimony is especially valuable when she names, for example, the Stuttgart judge Max Hegele, a near neighbour, who sentenced Jan Michalski, a Polish forced labourer, to death in 1942 for sleeping with a German woman. Anna also records a conversation with Frau Hegele, who refers to men like Michalski as GANGSTER and terrible UNTERMENSCHEN who were fortunate to be sentenced ("abgeurteilt") by a respectable German judge rather than being shot on the spot (p. 126). Conversely, Haag withholds the identities of like-minded friends and neighbours, including the "Tankgäste" who joined the Haags to 'tank up' on the truth by listening to the BBC (p. 102f., cf. p. 145). Such gatherings of RUNDFUNKVERBRECHER (radio criminals) were considered an act of WEHRKRAFTZERSETZUNG (undermining of the war effort) and were liable to the death penalty, as a leaflet pasted into her diary makes clear. She listened incredulously, for example, to Thomas Mann's broadcast of January 1942 announcing the gassing of eight hundred Dutch prisoners, and in December 1942 she heard a report of Richard Crossman's joint declaration in the House of Commons on the mass extermination of Jews (pp. 142, 145f.). She appears to have missed Mann's revelation of the mass gassings, broadcast on Christmas Eve 1942, and to have remained ignorant of the extermination camps of the 'Final Solution'. Timms observes: "Sympathy for deported Jews, revulsion at the reports of the mass shootings, and speculations about gas warfare run continuously through her diary—without quite converging" (p. 150). Haag's is yet another diary to reveal how widespread was an awareness of the atrocities being carried out in eastern Europe, as soldiers returning on leave unburdened themselves. She records the tales of mass shootings brought back by soldiers and SS men, as well as the pretence by many of her neighbours not to have heard these accounts (pp. 148–150). She also records the general outrage at the euthanasia policy embarked on in 1936, which in Stuttgart was focused on the nearby sanatorium at Grafeneck, in 1940 and 1941 the site of gassings under the 'T4' Programme,[28] a precursor of the mass gassing techniques employed as part of the 'Final Solution'. From the diary, we know that copies of Cardinal von Galen's sermon denouncing this practice—the only public denunciation—were circulating in Swabia.

Haag is an occasional but astute critic of the "language treasures circulating in the land" at the instigation of the "Maulheld" (loudmouth, p. 185) Goebbels ("im Lande kursierende Goebbels'sche Sprachschatz", p. 113f.). She too notes with horror the expansion of Nazi discourse amongst the gullible and the ambitious. She explicitly marks terms such as ABTRANSPORTIERT (transported away), AUSROTTUNG (extermination), BESTIEN (beasts), (SERBISCHE) GESINDEL ((Serbian) rabble), GROSSTATEN (great deeds), HELDENTUM (heroism), ORDNUNG (order), (GÖTTLICHE) SENDUNG ((divine) mission), and UNTERMENSCHEN (sub-humans) as citation forms in her text, distancing herself from their implicit norms and moral implications (p. 109). These are not just words used by the regime, she notes: ordinary Germans, "even the greatest idiot", are talking like members of the master race.

Amongst the jokes and anecdotes recorded here is the apparently widespread reference to Hermann Goering as Herr Maier, after he proclaimed that if a single bomb fell on Germany, people could "call me Maier"; the ironic apostrophization of Hitler in 1943 as the "GRÖFAZ" (GRÖSSTER FELDHERR ALLER ZEITEN, Greatest Military Strategist of All Time, p. 178), using the truncated style so beloved of the regime and so detested by Karl Kraus; and a graffito in 1944, "Alles tot, Heil Hitler" ("Everyone's dead, Heil Hitler!", p. 189).

Thea Sternheim

Born Thea Bauer, Thea Sternheim (1883–1971) retained her married name after her separation in 1927 from her second husband, the Jewish author Carl Sternheim. Her published diaries, spanning the years 1903 to 1971, run to five volumes.[29] An heiress to her industrialist father's fortune, she could have afforded to stay in Germany in economic hard times, but left in disgust at the political developments, via Brussels, Switzerland and France, finally settling in Paris in 1932. Perhaps because of this early decision to leave, and her financial independence, hers is a constant and steadfast voice in its denunciation of Nazism. Nor was it confined to the diary: before the accession to power, guests with Nazi views were shown the door in her Berlin apartment: "derartige imperialistische Tendenzen sind jedenfalls nicht in meinen 4 Wänden zu dulden" ("those kinds of imperialist views will not be tolerated within my four walls, at any rate", 9.11.1931). Her diaries record stormy arguments with Nazi sympathizers and officials before and after her move to Paris, her connections and friendships with leading figures in the cultural life of Europe (André Gide, Max Ernst, Marc Chagall, Pablo Picasso, Julien Green, Gottfried Benn, Klaus Mann), and her forthright comments on many of the political events of the day. Her friendship with Benn lasted until his death in 1956, despite her bitter disappointment at his "Anpassungsfähigkeit" (conformism) in 1933, when she read, "in the new government paper that calls itself the *Berliner Tageblatt*", Benn's statement on becoming head of the poetry section of the Prussian Academy in Berlin, an act which she describes as a "Beweihräucherung der Fehmemordzentrale" (literally: scattering holy incense on the headquarters of Feme murder—a reference to Benn's Catholicism, 2.5.1933). Her diatribe against Nazis is informed only weakly by her own Catholicism, which she struggled to retain, and more by a strong sense of class superiority, closer to Karl Kraus[30] than to Theodor Haecker. Physical ugliness, foul smells and pestilence often accompany descriptions of Nazis she encounters—reminiscent of the physical disgust driving Ernst Bloch's broadside in "Der Nazi und das Unsägliche":

> Qualvolle, seit langem nicht mehr erlebte Schlaflosigkeit. Groll, Ekel. Wie weit mein Gott ist meine Hoffnung von der Zuchtlosigkeit dieses Volkes entfernt! (Munich, 11.3.1933)

> Tormented sleeplessness, for the first time in ages, anger, nausea. How far removed my God is my hope from the indiscipline of this 'Volk'!

In the Berlin of the late 1920s and early 1930s, she observed with disbelief and horror the rise of a "national tollwütiges Geschlecht" ("rabidly nationalistic type", 26.11.1931) and the idea of a "drittes Reich", in which she sees "düstere Phantasien einiger Gewaltmenschen" ("dark phantasies of a few violent people", 27.11.1931) whom she variously calls "Rowdies", "Kannibalen", "Rinde" (cattle), a "Pest" (plague). In 1935 she was a grateful reader of the devastating biography of Hitler by Konrad Heiden (1935), also in French exile, hoping that this would be a turning point in the fortunes of the man she refers to as the "Anstreicher" (house painter), a "Bluthund und Kleinbürger" (murderer and petit-bourgeois) and the "Oberverbrecher" (criminal in chief), this last term in response to the trial of Herschel Grynszpan for the murder of Ernst vom Rath, third secretary at the German embassy in Paris. Recounting the tragic story of the Grynszpan family, she asks "So who is the real murderer?" (9.11.1938). She notices that border officials are beginning to wear Hitler moustaches and comments that Europe, and especially Germany, was becoming "eine Gefängniszelle [prison cell] par excellence", (11.12.1931). In March 1933 she is invited to old family friends in Berlin. Karl Christian von Loesch, Professor of anthropology at the Friedrich-Wilhelm-Universität, expert on German ethnic populations, co-founder in 1925 of the Institute for Border and Foreign Studies, former adviser to Schleicher and Stresemann, and contributor to the 'deutschnational' journal *Deutsche Rundschau*, was at this time about to join the NSDAP (on 1 May 1933). She picks an argument with this "patriotically roaring roaring mass of flesh" and Rudolf Pechel's ex-wife:

> Bald steht dem teutonischen Paar der Schweiß auf der Stirn. Dazwischen Telefonaden, die Loesch kurz mit "Einsperren!" … "das Schwein ist auszuschalten! …" beantwortet. Welch ein Einblick in das, was diese Leute selbst gern mit Herrenmoral zu bezeichnen pflegen. Mein schüchterner Einwurf: "Und wie vereinen Sie Ihren heutigen Standpunkt mit Ihrem oft angezogenen Christentum?" Er stutzt einen Augenblick, meint, damit sei es ihm nach wie vor ernst. Aber gleich trommelts neuen Ansatz vom Sofa her. Die blonde Pechel mit ihren blitzenden Augen erinnert mich plötzlich an die Verse, die sich der patriotische Deutsche im Krieg gern aufsagte:

"Auf, deutsches Weib, jetzt lehre du den Mann das Schädelspalten ...". Nicht er, aber sie ist die Triebfeder. Er nutzt die Konjunktur aus. Sie befindet sich in regelrechtem Blutrausch. (Berlin, 16.3.1933)

Soon the teutonic pair have sweat on their foreheads. In between, telephone calls, which Loesch abruptly answers "Lock him up!", "the swine should be eliminated". What an insight into what these people like to call master morality (*Herrenmoral*[31]). My modest intervention: "And how do you reconcile your current standpoint with the Christianity you so often wear?" He is dumbstruck for a moment, says he's serious about it now as always. But then a storm of abuse from the sofa. The blonde Pechel with her burning eyes suddenly reminds me of the lines which the patriotic German man liked to recite in times of war: "Go to, German woman, teach your man how to split a skull". She, not he, is the driver. He is an opportunist. She is in a veritable bloodlust.

A similar evening in Paris is recorded in May 1937 when, with Max Ernst and Marc Chagall, she encounters a "Nazi übelster Sorte" ("Nazi of the worst kind"), a "fleischgewordene[r] Bierrülpser" ("beer burper incarnate", 26.5.1937). In the ensuing argument, she decides to leave, and is pursued by the hostess who wants to persuade her to stay. It transpires that the hostess had not realized that some of her guests were Jewish. In Paris, Sternheim remained well informed about events—the number of Germans sentenced for political offences (1931: 14,000, 1935: 86,000, cf. 30.7.1936), the gassing of Jews in Poland (24.9.1942), and the truth about Guernica: "von deutschen Flugzeugen über 3 Stunden mit Brandbomben gelegt, dem Erdboden gleichgemacht worden. Dreiviertel der Civilbevölkerung hingemordet" (29.4.1937), "incendiary-bombed by German planes for three hours [...] flattened. Three quarters of the civil population slaughtered".

Although there is no evidence that she knew of Haecker's or Kraus's writings, there are parallels with both. A Catholic who was struggling with her faith and the "bankruptcy of Christian sentiment" (4.4.1933), she refers to the "Hakenkreuzbestien" (swastika beasts, 2.5.1933) and likens the swastika at one point to the male phallus (5.2.1936). Newspaper cuttings are pasted into the diary, and in July 1937 she types out a twenty-four page copy of Goebbels's speech from the *Völkischer Beobachter* (sadly not reproduced in the printed diary) on the trials of Catholic priests. As Kraus was beginning his *Dritte Walpurgisnacht*, she makes the following entry in her diary on 31 March 1933:

> Steigende Judenhetze in Deutschland. | Aber zu welch peinlichen ausserpolitischen Resultaten müssen bereits die Auftakte des neuen Systems geführt haben, bedarf es bereits eines so grotesken Abwehrkampfes der Greuelberichte, wie ihn die Kölnische Zeitung durchzuführen für nötig hält. Private und Geschäftsleute jüdischer und arischer Abstammung versichern mit hochtrabenden Worten, dass keinem Juden bisher ein Haar gekrümmt worden wäre. Auch den in Konzentrationslagern zusammengetriebenen freiheitlich Gesinnten ginge es prächtig. Bodenlose Missgunst verquickt sich mit machiavellischer Heuchelei und äussert sich diszipliniert. Diszipliniertes Henkertum—das ist's, wofür die Hakenkreuzfahne zum Symbol geworden ist.
>
> Increasing harassment of Jews in Germany. | But to what embarrassing results in international relations must the beginnings of the new system have led already, when it requires such a grotesque rebuttal of the horror stories such as the Kölnische Zeitung thinks it necessary to carry out. Private citizens and business people of Jewish and Aryan background assure us in high-flying words, that not one hair of a Jew's head has been bent to date. Even those with a disposition to freedom who have been rounded up in concentration camps were doing just fine. Endless malevolence mixes here with Machiavellian hypocrisy and expresses itself in a disciplined way. A bunch of disciplined executioners—that is what the swastika has come to symbolize.

In 1938 Leni Riefenstahl's film of the 1936 Olympics, *The Gods of the Stadium*, is angrily dismissed as a "Mystifizierungs-apparat" (apparatus/camera for mystification) in praise of "Kolossaldynamik" (i.e. colossal (classical) sculpture, 9.11.1938). When Madame Ponçet, the wife of the French ambassador to Berlin, returns to Paris with a present from Hitler wrapped in a swastika-motif ribbon, Sternheim expresses her disgust at the "pestilenzielle Fäulungsgestank der Verräter" ("pestilential rotting stink of traitors", 28.10.1938)—this on the same day the death of Ernst Barlach, sculptor of the Güstrow Angel,[32] is announced: "vom Hitlersystem kaltgestellt und verfehmt" ("neutralized and marginalized by the Hitler system"). After the German occupation she is moved from Paris to the south, where her Jewish surname (*nomen est omen*, cf. Bering 1987) causes her problems in encounters with "Sbirren" (political police, agents). Her 'Aryan' credentials are questioned and only after she protests that she is separated from Sternheim is she allowed back to Paris, where she must produce her "Ariernachweis" (certificate of 'Aryan' purity). Her Jewish name is a source of humiliation and a real existential threat (pp. 209–211, Chalons s. Saone, 19.10.1940).

Sternheim's diary is not an intensely language-critical document in the manner of Klemperer or Haecker. It is of interest rather for her forthright voice and her willingness to call interlocutors to task. But this impressive document of mental resilience does at times contain explicit and sustained language criticism. Newspaper cuttings of speeches and articles are pasted in (but sadly not reproduced in the published diaries) and commented on. Here, for example, is part of her treatment of Hitler's speech of 10 September 1943 following the capitulation of Italy:

> Noch immer ich! ich! ich! Als ob die unglückseligen Deutschen nichts wichtigeres zu bedenken hätten, als was sich in der Seele eines von Gott und allen guten Gewissen verlassenen Untermenschen abspielt!
>
> Aber abgesehen vom Ichwahn welch ein Versagen jeder politischen Sensibilität, ein Passus wie dieser: "Als England und Frankreich im September 1939 an das deutsche Reich den Krieg erklärten, wäre Italien durch die Verträge gezwungen gewesen sich mit Deutschland sofort solidarisch zu erklären. Dabei war diese Solidarität nicht nur begründet in den Abmachungen des Paktes, sondern in dem von den Feinden sowohl Deutschland als auch Italien für die Zukunft zugedachten Schicksal."
>
> Was für ein Deutsch! (p. 331, Paris, 11.9.1943)

> Again and again I! I! I! As if the unfortunate Germans had nothing more important to think about than what is going on in the soul of an Untermensch deserted by God and by all good consciences.
>
> But aside from the egomania, what a failure of all political sensibility, a passage like this: "When England and France in September 1939 declared war on the German Reich, Italy would have been obliged by the treaties to

declare solidarity with Germany immediately. This solidarity was grounded not just in the agreements of the pact but in the future fate intended for both Germany and Italy by the enemies."

What awful German!

In truth, there is little to object to in the grammar of the two sentences quoted, and here Sternheim, like Lichnowsky, seems reduced in exasperation to attacking the man and his politics by dismissing his style. In contrast, she is more sure-footed in homing in (as others did) on Hitler's egomaniacal ICH and its fateful consequences for the world,[33] and in throwing the derogatory keyword UNTERMENSCH back at its owner whilst also (implicitly, at least) removing it from its racial context. As we have seen, even Bloch's attempt at detached diagnosis in "Der Nazi und das Unsägliche" is driven by this kind of visceral response.

Conclusion

The impact these private writings had at the time was restricted to a few trusted friends at the most, Haecker's secret readings having perhaps the greatest reach, to members of the White Rose resistance movement. Rather, these documents are exercises in maintaining one's sanity and integrity. The diaries in particular contain valuable testimonies not only of individual lives but also of social and political realities of everyday existence, in which the inner life seeks a kind of sanctuary alongside and in opposition to the mundane and the public, the interactions with neighbours and colleagues, and events on the national and global political stage. These voices speak for the most part in plain language, but are not entirely free from self-censorship. There must have been moments when these writers contemplated the consequences of their writings being discovered, as well as the distinct possibility that they and their documents would not survive the regime. The diarists record, inter alia, anecdotes of subversive behaviour and some courageous individual acts, name victims, perpetrators and fellow-travellers. These small individual acts of 'Resistenz' exhibit varying degrees of language-critical awareness, competence, and political motivation. Jokes, in particular, and especially lewd jokes, whilst clearly a popular outlet for hostility to the regime, occupy an ambiguous place on the spectrum of linguistic opposition to tyranny, sometimes appearing closer to a subaltern retreat from the political rather than an adequate form of subversion in the suppressed popular discourse of opposition.

This chapter has focused on oppositional voices which were withheld from the public domain, confined to a precarious private space to which few if any readers had access at the time. The next two chapters turn to voices which ventured into the public domain to deliver 'resistent' messages. In terms of what these voices could say and how they could say it, they differ quite markedly from the testimonies reviewed in this chapter. It is to these public voices, in various forms of 'inner exile', that we now turn.

Notes

1. See Dodd 2013, pp. 180–183, 259f. von Polenz (1999, p. 311) calls her a direct descendant of Kraus in the genre of the language gloss.
2. German distinguishes between words as connected discourse ('Worte') and words as individual lexical items ('Wörter').
3. It can be inspected at the Deutsches Literaturarchiv in Marbach am Neckar, under the rubric: A: Lichnowsky/Verschiedenes/81.7629/ Konvolut Anmerkungen zu einem Buch, vermutlich 'Mein Kampf' von Adolf Hitler.
4. In the following review, the relevant passage in Hitler's text is set in italics, followed by Lichnowksy's comment. Her page references can be matched against Hitler 1934.
5. An article by Lichnowsky first published in the *Frankfurter Zeitung* in 1941 was titled "Haben und Besitzen sind nicht synonym". Cf. Dodd 2013, pp. 180–183.
6. This was a common source of ironic comment even in public discourse. Cf. Oskar Jancke's gloss "GROSSUNFUG" (grand nonsense), Jancke 1938, p. 89f.
7. In this respect *Sprachwandel im Dritten Reich* would appear to have some affinity—discounting the limitations of its 'inner exile' position—with Carl Zuckmayer's *Geheimreport* (Zuckmayer 2002), produced in 1944 in the USA for the CIA, in which leading figures of German cultural life are evaluated in terms of their entanglement with the regime.

8. See Storz's article on VOLKHAFT and VÖLKISCH, reviewed in Chap. 7, and Dornseiff's review of Weisgerber 1934 (Dornseiff 1934).
9. Correspondence with Akademie der Künste, Berlin (on archival documents relating to Seidel) and conversation with Professor Hartmut Schmidt (Berlin).
10. Cf. Townson 1992, pp. 176–192; Clyne 1993; Stevenson 2002; von Polenz 1999, pp. 424–435, 562–571.
11. On a separate issue, it is difficult to believe that in 1961 the authors were unacquainted with the post-war debates on 'Nazi language', framed largely by Klemperer's *LTI* (1947) and the *Wörterbuch des Unmenschen*, the first book edition of which had appeared in 1957. The possible influence of these works, discussed in Chap. 8, cannot be dismissed.
12. See Kempowski 1993, 1999, 2002, 2005 (English translation 2015).
13. In light of the different editions of the diaries, references are to the date of the entry (or the nearest preceding date). The complete text is available on CD-Rom (Klemperer 2007). Of the print editions, Klemperer 1998a is the most complete version of the text.
14. Cf. https://youtu.be/jeS5ZGJnUco?list=PL1hOdNwUSZZItlLLu9FLXZOimHdrKbcTu (3.12.2016).
15. In the same entry Klemperer gleefully celebrates his victory over the Gestapo as "KdF"—KUNST DER FINGERFERTIGKEIT (the art of prestidigitation), yet another ironic variation on KRAFT DURCH FREUDE.
16. In the sense of 'removal' from one place of residence to another, the misdirection of the official use of ABGEWANDERT lies partly in the suggestion that the person has emigrated. A creative English rendition of the ironic variation might be that these people have "been gone away with".
17. See also 3.12.1938, 8.7.1942, 21.8.1942, 30.1.1943, 24.6.1944, 4.1.1945. For a fuller account, cf. Klemperer 2007; Anhang, p. 11258ff.
18. Whilst this kind of characterization tends to foreground its 'referential' quality, as a factual description of a reality existing independently of the chronicler, Klemperer's account is, like those of all the commentators reviewed in this book, also 'relational' in its subjectivity. On this distinction, applied to Klemperer, see Woods 2014. Kämper does not employ this terminology, but does address the "Bedingtheit" of Klemperer's commentary, its embeddedness in specific cultural-historical contexts.
19. Siefken (1994, p. 20) points to the clear influence of Haecker and Muth's Christian theology on the White Rose's fourth pamphlet in the summer of 1942.

20. Haecker, "Tagebuchblätter", *Hochland* 37 (1939/1940), Heft 12 (September 1940), 470–475.
21. Cf. Damiano 2005, p. 8f.
22. By setting *laut* in italics, Haecker is emphasizing the loud declamatory tone of such language.
23. Cf. Kardorff 1997, p. 33: "doch das ganze Ausmaß des Grauens ahnten wir nicht" ("but we had no idea of the full extent of the horror").
24. PLUTOKRATEN was a common term in Nazi discourse for the governing elites in the UK and USA, implying an international Jewish financial lobby.
25. Unlike 'Frau', 'Weib' often has a derogatory connotation, as it does here.
26. See also Haag's later autobiographical work (Haag 1968).
27. The keywords, whilst not explicitly marked in Haag's text, are clearly identified as such.
28. 'Aktion T4' was the name given after 1945 to the involuntary euthanasia programme, after the address of the relevant department of the Reich Chancellery in Berlin, Tiergarten 4.
29. Sternheim 2002. Quotations, by date, are from volumes 2 (1925–1936) and 3 (1936–1951).
30. Kraus left the Jewish faith and adopted Catholicism in 1911, but left the Catholic church in 1923.
31. The term originates with Nietzsche, its opposite is 'Sklavenmoral' (slave morality).
32. On the history of Barlach's famous "Schwebender Engel" in Güstrow, see MacGregor 2014, pp. 528–542.
33. Cf. my reading (in Chap. 7) of Kircher's "Sprache und Stil" and Sternberger's "Blick der Liebenden"; and Tucholsky 1975, Bd. 9, p. 182 (referenced in Chap. 2).

Bibliography

Bering, Dietz. 1987. *Der Name als Stigma. Antisemistismus im deutschen Alltag 1812–1933*. Stuttgart: Klett-Cotta.

Boehlich, Walter. 1955. Über die Sprache. *Merkur* 9: 889–894.

———. 1964. Irrte hier Walter Boehlich? *Frankfurter Hefte* 19: 731–734.

Boveri, Margret. 1965. *Wir lügen alle. Eine Hauptstadtzeitung unter Hitler*. Olten: Freiburg i.B.

Clyne, Michael. 1993. Who Owns the German Language? In *Das unsichtbare Band der Sprache*, ed. John Flood et al., 357–369. Stuttgart: Hans-Dieter Heinz Akademischer Verlag.

Damiano, Carla A. 2005. *Walter Kempowski's "Das Echolot": Sifting and Exposing the Evidence via Montage*. Heidelberg: Universitätsverlag Winter.

Dodd, William J., ed. 2013. *"Der Mensch hat das Wort". Der Sprachdiskurs in der Frankfurter Zeitung 1933–1943*. Berlin, Boston: de Gruyter.

Dornseiff, Franz. 1934. Sprache und Gesamtkultur. *Geistige Arbeit*, Vol. 1, No. 12, p. 8f. June 20.

Emonts, Anne Martina. 2012. Unmasking Violence and Domination. Mechtilde Lichnowsky and the 20th Century (Word) Wars. In *Plots of War: Modern Narratives of Conflict*, ed. Isabel Capeloa Gil and Adriana Martins, 87–97. Berlin, Boston: de Gruyter.

Haag, Anna. 1968. *Das Glück zu leben. Erinnerungen an bewegte Jahre*. Stuttgart: Adolf Bonz.

Haecker, Theodor. 1932. Betrachtungen über Vergil, Vater des Abendlandes. *Der Brenner* 13: 3–31.

———. 1989. *Tag- und Nachtbücher 1939–1945. Erste vollständige und kommentierte Ausgabe*. Herausgegeben von Hinrich Siefken, Brenner-Studien, Bd. 9. Innsbruck: Haymon Verlag.

Hartl, Peter. 1991. *Einführung zur Neuauflage*. Kardorff 1997, pp. 7–31.

Heiden, Konrad. 1935. *Hitler. Das Zeitalter der Verantwortungslosigkeit*. Band I. Zürich: Europa Verlag.

Hitler, Adolf. 1934. *Mein Kampf. Zwei Bände in einem Band*. Ungekürzte Ausgabe. 97–101. Auflage. München: Franz Eher Nachfolger.

Jancke, Oskar. 1938. *Restlos erledigt? Neue Glossen zur deutschen Sprache*. München: Knorr & Hirth.

Kämper, Heidrun. 2000. Sprachgeschichte – Zeitgeschichte. Die Tagebücher Victor Klemperers. *Deutsche Sprache* 28 (1): 25–41.

———. 2011. Telling the Truth: Counter-Discourses in Diaries under Totalitarian Regimes (Nazi Germany and Early GDR). In *Political Languages in the Age of Extremes*, ed. Willibald Steinmetz, 215–241. Oxford: Oxford University Press.

von Kardorff, Ursula. 1965. *Diary of a Nightmare: Berlin, 1942–1945*. Translated from the German by Ewan Butler. London: R. Hart-Davis.

———. 1997. *Berliner Aufzeichnungen 1942 bis 1945*. Unter Verwendung der Original-Tagebücher neu herausgegeben und kommentiert von Peter Hartl. Ungekürzte Ausgabe, 2. Auflage. München: Deutscher Taschenbuch Verlag.

Kasten, U., and W. Kohlhaase. 1998. *'Mein Leben ist so sündhaft lang': Victor Klemperer—ein Chronist des Jahrhunderts*. Ostdeutscher Rundfunk.

———. 1999. Victor Klemperer—ein Leben in Deutschland. *ARD*.

Kästner, Erich. 2006. *Das blaue Buch. Kriegstagebuch und Roman-Notizen*. Herausgegeben von Ulrich von Bülow und Silke Becker. Aus der Gabelsberger'schen Kurzschrift übertragen von Herbert Tauber (Marbacher Magazin 111/112). Marbach am Neckar: Deutsche Schillergesellschaft.

Kempowski, Walter. 1993. *Das Echolot. Ein kollektives Tagebuch. Januar und Februar 1943*. 4 Bände. München: Knaus.

———. 1999. *Das Echolot. Fuga furiosa. Ein kollektives Tagebuch. Winter 1945*. 4 Bände. München: Knaus.

———. 2002. *Das Echolot. Barbarossa '41. Ein kollektives Tagebuch*. München: Knaus.

———. 2005. *Das Echolot. Abgesang 45. Ein kollektives Tagebuch*. München: Knaus.

———. 2015. *Swansong 1945: A Collective Diary of the Last Days of the Third Reich*. Translated by Shaun Whiteside. New York: W.W. Norton.

Klemperer, Victor. 1978. *LTI. Notizbuch eines Philologen*. Berlin: Aufbau.

———. 2000. *The Language of the Third Reich. LTI: Lingua Tertii Imperii*. Translated by Martin Brady. London: Athlone Press.

———. 2007. *Die Tagebücher (1933–1945). Kommentierte Gesamtausgabe*. Herausgegeben von Walter Nowojski unter Mitarbeit von Christian Löser. Direktmedia (Digitale Bibliothek, CD-Rom Edition).

Lichnowsky, Mechtilde. 1946. Worte über Wörter. *Die Wandlung* 1: 521–526.

———. 1948. Werdegang eines Wirrkopfs. *Die Wandlung* 3: 606–615.

———. 1949. *Worte über Wörter*. Wien: Bergland.

Maas, Utz. 2015. *Ingeborg Seidel-Slotty*. Updated March 5. Universitätsbibliothek Osnabrück. https://esf.uni-osnabrueck.de/index.php/katalog-m-z/s/427-seidel-slotty-ingeborg. Accessed 30 November 2016.

MacGregor, Neil. 2014. *Germany. Memories of a Nation*. London: Penguin (British Museum, BBC, Allen Lane).

Pfäfflin, Friedrich, and Eva Dambacher. 2001. *"Verehrte Fürstin". Karl Kraus und Mechtilde Lichnowsky. Briefe und Dokumente 1916–1958*. Göttingen: Wallstein.

von Polenz, Peter. 1999. *Deutsche Sprachgeschichte vom Spätmittelalter bis zur Gegenwart*. Bd 3: *19. und 20. Jahrhundert*. Berlin, New York: de Gruyter.

Seidel, Eugen, and Ingeborg Seidel-Slotty. 1961. *Sprachwandel im Dritten Reich*. Halle: VEB Verlag Sprache und Literatur.

Siefken, Hinrich. 1989. Einleitung. In *Tag- und Nachtbücher 1939–1945*, Hg. Theodor Haecker, 7–17. Innsbruck: Haymon.

———., ed. 1994. *Die "Weiße Rose" und ihre Flugblätter*. Manchester: Manchester University Press.

Sternheim, Thea. 2002. *Tagebücher 1903–1971*. Herausgegeben und ausgewählt von Thomas Ehrsam und Regula Wyss im Auftrag der Heinrich Enrique Beck-Stiftung. 5 Bde. Göttingen: Wallstein.

Stevenson, Patrick. 2002. *Language and German Disunity: A Sociolinguistic History of East and West Germany, 1945–2000*. Oxford: Oxford University Press.

Timms, Edward. 2015. *Anna Haag and Her Secret Diary of the Second World War. A Democratic German Feminist's Response to the Catastrophe of National Socialism*. Oxford, Berne, Berlin: Peter Lang.

Tomko, Helena M. 2017. The Reluctant Satirist: Theodor Haecker and the Dizzying Swindle of Nazism. *Oxford German Studies* 46 (1): 42–57.

Townson, Michael. 1992. *Mother-Tongue and Fatherland: Language and Politics in German*. Manchester: Manchester University Press.

Tucholsky, Kurt. 1975. *Gesammelte Werke*. Herausgegeben von Mary Gerold-Tucholsky, Fritz J. Raddatz. Reinbek: Rowohlt.

Ullrich, Volker. 1992. Geschönt und darum kaum mehr authentisch. Eine rekonstruierte Neuausgabe der 'Berliner Aufzeichnungen' von Ursula von Kardorff. *Die Zeit*, July 3. http://pdf.zeit.de/1992/28/geschoent-und-darum-kaum-mehr-authentisch. Accessed 20 August 2016.

Weisgerber, Leo. 1929. *Muttersprache und Geistesbildung*. Göttingen: Vanderhoeck & Ruprecht.

———. 1956. Von den Grenzen des Irrtums und der Verantwortung einer Schriftleitung. *Wirkendes Wort* 6: 158–160.

Woods, Roger. 2014. The Referential and the Relational: Victor Klemperer's Diaries in the Nazi Years. *Journal of War & Culture Studies* 7 (4): 336–349.

Zuckmayer, Carl. 2002. *Geheimreport*. Göttingen: Herausgegeben von Gunther Nickel und Johanna Schrön. Wallstein.

6

Voices at Home (II): From Resistance to 'Resistenz' in the Printed Word

Resistance: The Language of Insurrection

The following words could conceivably be from one of Thomas Mann's addresses to the German people from his Californian exile:

> Nichts ist eines Kulturvolkes unwürdiger, als sich ohne Widerstand von einer verantwortungslosen und dunklen Trieben ergebenen Herrscherclique "regieren" zu lassen. Ist es nicht so, dass sich jeder ehrliche Deutsche heute seiner Regierung schämt, und wer von uns ahnt das Ausmass der Schmach, die über uns und unsere Kinder kommen wird, wenn einst der Schleier von unseren Augen gefallen ist und die grauenvollsten und jedes Mass unendlich überschreitenden Verbrechen ans Tagelicht treten? (Siefken 1994, p. 22)

> Nothing is more unworthy of a cultured nation than to allow itself, without resistance, to be "governed" by an irresponsible ruling clique given over to dark instincts. Is it not the case that every honest German today is ashamed of his government, and which of us can imagine the scale of the disgrace that will befall us and our children once the veil has fallen from our eyes and the most gruesome crimes, infinitely transgressing all measure, have come to light?

W J Dodd, *National Socialism and German Discourse*,
https://doi.org/10.1007/978-3-319-74660-9_6

They were, in fact, written by Alexander Schmorell and Hans Scholl, and are the opening lines of the first typewritten, cyclostyled pamphlet distributed by the 'White Rose' group in Munich in June 1942 (Siefken 1994, pp. 19–21). This first pamphlet quotes from Goethe and from Schiller's political writings from 1790 on the tyrannical state (a dimension of Schiller's work conveniently overlooked by Chamberlain and Engel in 1914, and in Nazi cultural historiography), including the sentence: "Alles darf dem Besten des Staats zum Opfer gebracht werden, nur dasjenige nicht, dem der Staat selbst nur als ein Mittel dient" ("Everything may be sacrificed for the good of the state, except for those things for which the state itself serves only as a means").[1] Between June 1942 and February 1943 the White Rose were responsible for political graffiti in Munich and six distributed pamphlets (some co-authored by Sophie Scholl and Professor Kurt Huber). A draft for a seventh pamphlet, by Christoph Probst, was discovered in Hans Scholl's possession following the arrest of Hans and Sophie in the main lecture building of Munich University on 18 February 1943. The group's words (including revelations of the atrocities on the Eastern Front and calls to sabotage) were accompanied by political actions, not just in distributing and couriering leaflets across Germany but in seeking to build networks in other cities and universities and in the Wehrmacht. Links with other conspiratorial networks (the Kreisau Circle, and—through Falk Harnack, who escaped execution—the Red Orchestra) were pursued. An impressive unity of word and action characterizes their behaviour under interrogation and before Roland Freisler's 'People's Court' ('Volksgerichtshof'). Sophie, offered a possible defence by her interrogator that she was led astray by the older males, steadfastly insisted on her authorship. A series of trials led to multiple prison sentences and seven death sentences. Christoph Probst and Hans and Sophie Scholl and were guillotined in Munich on the day of their summary trial, 22 February 1943. Willi Graf, Kurt Huber, and Alexander Schmorell were executed in the following weeks and months, Hans Konrad Leipelt in January 1945. Freisler's show trials and death sentences were designed to intimidate oppositionally minded Germans, and no doubt succeeded in cowing many people into silence and outward conformity. It is a fitting tribute to the White Rose that it should be their words which enjoyed the widest dissemination in

Germany, when the RAF dropped millions of copies of the sixth pamphlet on German towns and cities in 1943.

The voice of Sophie Scholl seems to stand out as a rare example of a woman's oppositional voice in the public sphere, and it is indeed the case that the literature on publicly voiced dissent has focused almost exclusively on men. This gendering of the discourse clearly has something to do with the gender roles of the time, especially under National Socialism. Women were by and large not prominent in the churches, in journalism,[2] and generally in public and underground organizations, so that their discourse is less likely to have been preserved in documents.[3] By some estimates, women accounted for about one in five resisters, often performing tasks as enablers such as typing, translating, duplicating, but also distributing leaflets. One possible reason advanced for the apparent lower participation of women is that they were more susceptible to the threat of SIPPENHAFT (kin liability[4]), which allowed the authorities to arrest, interrogate, incarcerate and torture members of the wider family, including children, for the 'crimes' of an individual. Women targeted by the regime were usually affiliated to known opposition groups such as Communists, Social Democrats, Jehovah's Witnesses, or married to known male opponents. Many in the public eye emigrated (Erika Mann, Lida Gustava Heymann, Helene Weigel, Anna Seghers). Hundreds were brutally killed. Minna Cammens, Social Democrat Member of the Reichstag, was arrested for distributing leaflets in March 1933. Her husband received her ashes a few days later. Similarly, the actress Hanne Mertens disappeared after mocking Goebbels. The Gestapo file reveals "NN" against her name, marking her out for NACHT UND NEBEL (night and fog) summary arrest and disposal. She was murdered in Neuengamme concentration camp on April 21 1945. The first woman to be officially executed for treason was Liselotte Hermann, arrested for revealing details of aircraft production in 1935, and guillotined on 23 June 1938. Margarete Schaeffer was denounced and executed (on 20 July 1944) for calling Hitler "the greatest criminal of all time"—substituting VERBRECHER for FELDHERR (general), as did many Germans, in the much-satirized phrase GRÖSSTER FELDHERR ALLER ZEITEN (GRÖFAZ/GRÖVAZ). Libertas Schulze-Boysen and Mildred Harnack, arrested in 1942 with their husbands as part of the Red Orchestra resistance group in Berlin, received prison sentences but were executed on the personal order of Hitler.

Some women prominent in German cultural life signalled their distance from the regime whilst suffering relatively minor personal consequences. Ricarda Huch wrote her now famous open letter to Max von Schillings, resigning from the Prussian Academy of Arts, on 9 April 1933, stating "What the present government prescribes as national sentiments is not my [idea of] Germanness" ("Was die jetzige Regierung als nationale Gesinnung vorschreibt, ist nicht mein Deutschtum", cf. Bendt and Schmidgall 1994, pp. 325–327). She was insulted by Goebbels in return, but not arrested. Käthe Kollwitz was partially but not completely barred from exhibiting her drawings and sculptures despite signing an appeal (with Heinrich Mann and others) to the SPD and KPD to form a united front against the NSDAP (Schymura 2014, pp. 255–307). Gertrud von le Fort's career as a published author continued to surprisingly little criticism (cf. Klapper 2015, pp. 211–241). The regime's gender stereotype of women as unpolitical beings (only one of the ninety concentration camps set up in 1933—Moringen—was a women's camp) actually gave women opportunities not available to men, such as carrying two shopping bags so as not to give the 'German greeting' (DEUTSCHER GRUSS), transporting leaflets in prams and under maternity dresses, and helping Jewish women and children to escape Germany by giving them ('Aryan') motherhood medals. It seems likely that women also played an important role in the day-to-day maintenance of oppositional groups as 'Quartiermütter', and by gathering local intelligence in exchanges with neighbours and passing it on whilst appearing to conform to the stereotype by 'gossiping' over coffee and cake. The majority of carers for disabled people, however, were women (including nuns), an exposed occupation once the authorities began demanding lists of names for enforced sterilization or unspecified treatment (murder) under the poorly concealed LEBENSUNWERT programme. Many certainly took risks by falsifying official returns in order to subvert these demands, and it has been estimated that some 1500 lives were saved in this way (Oldfield 1986, p. 96). Only rarely, one suspects, has evidence of these courageous acts survived. One of the most defiant of the 'unquiet voices' was that of Countess Erika von Brockdorff, convicted of having radio contact with the Soviet Union, who, taunted by the judge that the smile would soon disappear from her face, replied "Not while I can still see you" (Oldfield 1986, p. 97). Some three hundred women's names have been found in Gestapo execution records. Two hundred and seventy are known to have been executed in Berlin's Plötzensee prison, the majority of them single women (Oldfield 1986, p. 94).

The salience of men in the literature on resistance to Nazism may also reflect a gendered conception of resistance which privileges typically male forms of action. The examples given above should provide an important corrective here. Yet if the forms of opposition engaged in by most women fall more readily into our category of 'Resistenz', it must be said that this is also true of men. Nor is it just women whose achievements may be undervalued by such gendered thinking: lesser forms of opposition offered by men may be judged insufficiently masculine when measured against the actions of those, mainly in the Wehrmacht after 1939, who attempted to assassinate Hitler. Certainly, the oppositional messages in books and periodicals reviewed in the remainder of this chapter fall short of political activism, and here the distinction between resistance ("Widerstand", in the first line of the first White Rose pamphlet) and 'Resistenz' is at its clearest. The authors reviewed in the remainder of this chapter were circumspect in their articulation of distance from and criticism of the regime. Theirs are voices which typically sought to preserve civilized discourse and to articulate their dissent in coded language, insinuating an intellectual and ethical rejection of Nazism, aware that in committing to the printed word they were also potentially providing evidence for their own hearings with the Gestapo. They did so with varying degrees of adroitness and civil courage. The boldest examples challenged the limits of the safely sayable, but even these are still regarded today by some German commentators as a failure to engage politically and, even worse, as acts of obeisance and opportunism. In the shadow of the White Rose, this scepticism is understandable and reflects the robustness with which many Germans confront the Nazi past.

'Resistenz': The Coded Discourse of Inner Exile

The Nazification of German society by concentration camp and guillotine had the understandable effect of silencing expressions of opposition, or in forcing them underground, into the problematic 'private' space, or, in the public arena, into the coded language of 'Resistenz'—the logical correlate of and response to the enforced 'Sprachlosigkeit'. Plain speaking was an act either of great courage or great foolishness, and as Klemperer testifies, Germans were executed "wejen Ausdrücken"—for what they said (Klemperer 1978, p. 299; cf. Militz 1998). Spoken discourse was characterized by extreme caution over who you were talking to, and in public by subtleties of word choice, intonation, tone of voice, and paralinguistic features like eye contact and body language which are impossible to reconstruct today (although the infinite gradations of the DEUTSCHER GRUSS ('Heil Hitler!') are a recurring point of reference in written testimonies, cf. Sternberger 1988, p. 134f.; Kempowski 2002, p. 188 (Ernst Jünger)). In written discourse, where these paralinguistic features are not available, writers and their readers quickly became skilled at using the resources of text and genre as platforms for their dissenting voices, in a set of increasingly recondite discourse practices. This chapter and the next will review the main facets of these coded contributions to the public discourse. The present chapter presents a brief overview of literary responses in books and cultural-philosophical periodicals, before turning to a more narrow consideration of the careers of three language commentators who were to play an influential role in Western Germany in the immediate post-war period: Dolf Sternberger, Gerhard Storz, and Wilhelm E. Süskind. The next chapter will provide a more detailed case study of the *Frankfurter Zeitung*'s attempt to maintain a discourse of 'Resistenz' once Goebbels had decided it suited his purpose not to close it down.

Two seminal contributions to the linguistics of coded communication are available in English translation: Erwin Rotermund's (2011) essay "Concealed Writing ('Verdeckte Schreibweise') in the 'Third Reich'", and Reinhold Grimm's study "In the Thicket of Inner Emigration" (2003). Briefly, Rotermund applies the categories of Quintilian rhetoric to explain the relationship between ostensible and deep meaning in coded texts, and the signals through which the existence of an esoteric meaning can be conveyed. Rotermund argues that in creating such a text, a delicate balance needs to be struck between concealment ("Tarnung") and revelation of the esoteric message, and between the salience of the esoteric message and compensatory measures ("Absicherung") to protect the author in the event of inquisition. The result is a hybrid text whose surface appears to conform to ruling discourse norms, whilst breaches in one or more of Grice's four conversational maxims serve as "stumbling blocks" (Strauss 1952, p. 36) disrupting the communicative flow and inviting the alert reader to look for a deeper frame of reference in the text as a whole. These maxims are that the discourse partner is being as informative as necessary (category of quantity), as relevant as necessary (relation), as clear as possible (manner), and truthful (quality) (cf. Rotermund 2011, p. 84). A "stumbling block" can be created, for example, when a text appears to be dwelling disproportionately long on an apparently trivial piece of information.

Grimm addresses the problem of conceptualizing this kind of discourse as a form of resistance. He argues that the oppositionality of texts produced in 'inner emigration' needs to be assessed in light of a full consideration of the context of their production and use. Silence, for example, could be construed as an act of compliance or of resistance, depending on the expectations placed on the (non-)speaker by the discourse context. The variety of possible performances should be viewed, Grimm continues, as a spectrum, at one end of which there is a discernible "anti-Nazi" discourse, whilst at the other end the discourse is merely "not Nazi". In order for the term to have some coherence, Grimm suggests that the term 'inner emigration' should be reserved for behaviour at the "anti-Nazi" end of the spectrum where the hegemonic discourse norms are actively subverted.

Problems in conceptualizing this field are evident from the various terms which have been used to characterize it, although the everyday metaphor 'between the lines' works equally well in German: 'zwischen den Zeilen'. The oldest and best-established term is Aesopian (or Aesopic) discourse, after the narrative strategies adopted in speaking truth unto power in the slave Aesop's fables. In German, Sternberger's phrase 'verdeckte Schreibweise' (coined in 1950, literally: concealed mode of writing) has been widely used. The ability of oppositional Germans to tune in to these nuances, their 'Hellhörigkeit' (hyper-sensibility), is another key concept which tends to be positively connoted. (Bergengruen (1947, p. 8) likened the instinctive sixth sense developed in inner exile when encountering strangers to the way dogs sniff each other out.) Bergengruen's confident claim of a perfectly elaborated code, whilst almost certainly overstated, reflects the pride of many of these practitioners in their skill:

> So konnten alle Dinge beim Namen genannt werden, scheinbar bei einem uneigentlichen und nicht demjenigen, unter dem sie im Kataster der Wörterbücher eingetragen waren, aber bei dem Namen, der ihr Wesen anrief und in die Deutlichkeit stellte. (Bergengruen 1947, p. 10)
>
> Thus all things could be named, unobtrusively and with a non-literal name, not the one that was entered in the ledgers of the dictionaries, but with the name that summoned forth the essence of the thing and showed it clearly.

Against this, a negative inflection of these phenomena is found in the terms 'Sklavensprache' (slave language), and 'subaltern discourse', which emphasize the fundamental unfreedom of the speaker. Finally, an assessment of the relationship between 'Sprachlosigkeit' (as described in Bauer 1988) and 'Resistenz' (as defined by Broszat (1986, p. 295)) is crucial in coming to an understanding of this field. Following Broszat's lead, I take the view that these are not contradictory, but entirely compatible and complementary concepts: the greater the degree of Nazification, the greater the 'Sprachlosigkeit'; the greater the degree of 'Sprachlosigkeit', the greater the degree of 'Resistenz'.

In talking about the here-and-now of their situation, writers often resorted to a technique of geographical and/or temporal displacement. Historical fiction flourished. In Reck-Malleczewen's *Bockelson* (1937), the Anabaptist terror in sixteenth-century Münster serves as a template. Before the non-aggression pact of 1939, the Soviet Union could be used in the same way. Pechel's "Siberia" (discussed below) adopts this technique, as does Ernst Jünger's (1939) novel *Auf den Marmorklippen* (*On the Marble Cliffs*, 1947), in which the murderous leader-figure of the Forester might be loosely based on Stalin, or Hitler, or Goering, and the central chapter depicting the murderous camp at Köppels-Bleek might be an imaginative response to the Gulag, or to the concentration camps (and an uncannily prescient imagining of future extermination camps). Stefan Andres's 1936 novella *El Greco malt den Großinquisitor* (El Greco Paints the Grand Inquisitor), set in the Spanish Inquisition, could be construed as an attack on the Catholic Church, as could his *Wir sind Utopia* (1943, We are Utopia), set in the Spanish Civil War, although uncertainty seems to attach to which side is which. These examples could be added to at length.

We have now travelled the long and convoluted path from the political pamphlet and the plain discourse of the White Rose to the indirect discourse of inner exiles using the printed word. The print media genres of poetry, imaginative fiction, and the essay became platforms for a wide array of Aesopic voices drawn from diverse social, political, and confessional backgrounds, from the national conservative Ernst Jünger to the liberal Republican Dolf Sternberger, whose improbable friendship in these years was founded on mutual respect and shared anti-Nazi convictions (Schöttker and Hübner 2011). An important feature in this landscape was the resilience of those with a strong Christian faith. Conspicuously absent from the spectrum were, of course, Jewish authors like Klemperer, and the political left, especially Social Democrats and Marxists who, in so far as they were not in territorial exile (like Brecht and Bloch), were probably in a concentration camp, like Carl von Ossietzky. In some cases, bans on publication and public appearances appear to have been local and temporary, or restricted to particular works, and in some cases the precise details of the ban remain unclear.

Literary Responses

The system of post-censorship operating in the field of book publication imposed a culture of self-censorship on authors and publishing houses, leaving it to them to judge where the limits of the safely sayable lay in the new discourse market. It was also inefficient and rather shambolic, being left to a number of organizations such as Alfred Rosenberg's high-faluting but ultimately ineffectual Supervisory Reich Surveillance Office[5] and the SS periodical *Das schwarze Korps*, neither of which had the power to force withdrawal from publication, but only to censure. Even so, the encoding of the oppositional voice became more and more convoluted, in order to escape future retribution, which of course ran the risk that the oppositional import was rendered too abstruse for all but the most determined and cultured readers to find. These readers constituted a small and geographically as well as ideologically disparate minority of Germans, arguably not a community in any material sense, and hardly a potent political grouping. Indeed, the regime seems to have calculated that some kind of safety valve for the venting of frustrations was useful, within limits. Today, readers who thankfully have no experience of living in such a punitive discourse environment may find it difficult to put themselves in the situation of readers who actively seek oppositional content in apparently conformist utterances, performances, and texts. But this was the reality of many Germans in the Reich, just as it was in Soviet Russia and is today under repressive regimes around the world.

This complex and important strand of German discourse history is the subject of myriad studies, and can only be indicated in the briefest of outlines here. Readers wishing to explore it further are recommended to consult the volume of essays titled *Flight of Fantasy: New Perspectives on Inner Emigration in German Literature* (Donahue and Kirchner 2003), and John Klapper's study *Nonconformist Writing in Nazi Germany: The Literature of Inner Emigration* (Klapper 2015).[6] Klapper's study contains an excellent introduction to the situation of oppositional writers and the theoretical and practical problems involved in framing, identifying and evaluating the oppositional voice in works of fiction. Eight chapters are devoted to a detailed consideration of an individual author: Werner Bergengruen, Stefan Andres, Friedrich Reck-Malleczewen, Gertrud von le Fort, Reinhold Schneider, Ernst Jünger, Ernst Wiechert, and Erika Mitterer. The list of authors who have been considered to belong to this diverse category is long and contentious. Ehrke-Rotermund and Rotermund's groundbreaking critical anthology (1999, in German), for example, adds further names to this list: Rudolf Pechel, Herbert Küsel, Albrecht Haushofer, Wolfgang Drews, Ernst Penzoldt, Dolf Sternberger, Hans Carossa, Karl Barth, Hermann Kasack, Carl Linfert, Joachim Günther, Hans Gerth, Adam Kuckhoff, Friedrich Georg Jünger, Werner Finck, Gerhard Nebel, Gottfried Benn, Werner Krauss.

Literary genres are, potentially at least, platforms for the most radical, sustained, and inventive critique of language in use, as the example of Keun's *Nach Mitternacht* demonstrates. Taking a wider view of book production in these years allows us to include books devoted explicitly to language in our field of inquiry: exemplary collections of 'fine writing' (such as *Deutscher Geist* (1936), edited by Oskar Loerke, and *Die deutsche Sprache* (1935), edited by Clemens ten Holder), lay guides to style and 'correct usage' (such as those by Storz and Süskind, discussed below), and monographs on (the state of) 'the German language' (such as Reifferscheidt's *Über die Sprache* (1939)). Special mention needs to be made here of the remarkable Adolf Storfer (1888–1944), whose two copiously researched volumes on the cultural and lexical history of German dialects—*Wörter und ihre Schicksale* (Words and their Fates, 1935), *Im Dickicht der Sprache* (In the Thicket of Language, 1937)—were, amazingly, co-published in Berlin and were clearly received with relish by opponents of the regime. Storfer is in every sense an exceptional figure in this list. A Jew and former member of Freud's circle, he was forced to flee Austria in 1938 on a path of exile which led, via Shanghai, to his untimely death in Melbourne in 1944 (Henneberg 2003, p. 62). The subversive potential of Storfer's books lay not in their explicit political orientation but precisely in their scientific assiduousness which furnished myriad examples of how migration, cultural exchange, and social stratification had widened and deepened the lexical and phraseological resources of the German language. Conversely, Storfer's archaeological excavations revealed a largely forgotten socio-political and socio-pragmatic history of the German speaking peoples in which 'völkisch' ideology had no part to play.

Literary-Philosophical Periodicals

Unlike book publications, periodicals were subject to pre-publication censorship. In line with Goebbels's policy of retaining an outward appearance of tolerance, and also, presumably, because they were adjudged to pose little threat to the regime, a number of 'highbrow' journals, niche publications with relatively small circulations, were allowed to continue. The focus here is on two of the more outstanding examples: *Deutsche Rundschau* and *Hochland*. Other periodicals which occupied an ambiguous "free space" (Klapper 2015, p. 30f.) in the media landscape included *Das Innere Reich*, *Die Literatur* (edited by Wilhelm Emanuel Süskind), *Die Neue Rundschau*, *Die Weißen Blätter*, *Eckhart*, *Europäische Revue*, and *Stimmen der Zeit*. Political considerations may have played a part in allowing these journals to continue. Closing down *Hochland*, a long-established title in Catholic intellectual circles, would run the risk of a clash with the Catholic Church, and to move against the conservative-national *Deutsche Rundschau* might alienate a constituency forming part of the 'Conservative Revolution'.

Rudolf Pechel (1862–1961) belonged to the Young Conservative wing of German politics which opposed parliamentary democracy and Weimar liberalism, and advocated an authoritarian nation state. Under his editorship, *Deutsche Rundschau* was initially sparing in its criticism of the regime in 1933, but this quickly changed (Ehrke-Rotermund and Rotermund 1999, p. 26). Like many National Conservatives, Pechel was repelled by the street violence and strident anti-Jewish rhetoric of the NSDAP. In August 1932 he had called on the Nazi leadership to distance itself from recent outrages against Jews:

> Wir können und wollen nicht dulden, dass der deutsche Name durch rohe Gewalttaten entehrt werde, und dass womöglich das menschenunwürdige Agitationsgeschrei, das die nationalsozialistische Führung immer noch nicht in ihrer Gefolgschaft unterdrückt hat: "Juda verrecke!", zu blutigen Ausschreitungen führt. (Pechel 1947, p. 25 ("Auch die Judenfrage"))
>
> We cannot and will not tolerate the German name being dishonoured by acts of raw violence, and the inhuman language of agitation which the National Socialist leadership has still not suppressed in its ranks: "Juda perish!", leading to bloody excesses.

Edgar Jung, author of von Papen's Marburg speech of 17 June 1934, a member of Pechel's circle and a collaborator on *Deutsche Rundschau*, was the first to be murdered in the 'Night of the Long Knives' of 30 June 1934, and from this point, if not before, Pechel was on a collision course with the regime, penning some of the most daring and disparaging articles to appear in print. The essay "Lob des Scharlatans" (Praise of the Charlatan, February 1938), analyzed in Ehrke-Rotermund 2012, discusses the historical figure of the leader as charlatan, his route to power and means of holding on to it, brow-beating the population into silence: "die Freiheit, zu diskutieren und zu urteilen, wird durch stundenlange Reden gelähmt" ("the freedom to discuss and to judge is hobbled by speeches lasting for hours on end"). Perhaps the most audacious of Pechel's pieces is "Sibirien" (Siberia, Pechel 1947, pp. 94–100) from September 1937, purportedly a review of a Soviet exile's book denouncing Stalin's terror and gulag system, in which Pechel obscures the boundaries between quotation, paraphrase, and commentary, and systematically translates Russian terms into their German equivalents—for example rendering 'comrade' ('tovarisch' in the original) as "Parteigenosse" (party member, the normal German term for a member of the NSDAP),—insidiously describing contemporary reality in Nazi Germany. (A detailed analysis of this article is found in Rotermund and Ehrke-Rotermund 1999, pp. 25–39). Literary history was searched for items with present relevance. In May 1940 *Deutsche Rundschau* printed a review-cum-summary of Victor Hugo's 1852 attack on Napoleon III, "Der kleine Napoleon" (Napoleon the Small, Pechel 1947, pp. 171–181), an exiled writer's rant against a petty dictator. The collection of Pechel's *Deutsche Rundschau* articles between 1932 and 1942 published in 1947 as *Zwischen den Zeilen* (Between the Lines, with a Foreword by Werner Bergengruen) contains almost forty such pieces.

Pechel's right-wing credentials may have provided a measure of protection for a while, but Bergengruen's belief (1947, p. 8) that Nazis were excluded from Pechel's esoteric discourse is contradicted by the evidence, as officials in the Reich Chancellery understood perfectly the true meaning of "Siberien" (Ehrke-Rotermund and Rotermund 1999, p. 38f.). Pechel survived an interview in the Propaganda Ministry but was a marked man and was eventually arrested, and the journal closed down, in 1942, ostensibly because of "Nachrichten-Politik" (News policy, Pechel 1947, pp. 338–341), a thinly concealed attack on Goebbels which was unhelpfully (for Pechel) read out on the BBC. Pechel's strategy here simply quoted a recent Goebbels speech on news management and juxtaposed it with a speech by Siegfried von Kardorff from 1918, attacking German news management in the First World War for withholding the true state of affairs from the German public. Pechel spent the next three years in concentration camps before being released in April 1945. The following month he co-founded the Christian Democratic Union (CDU) in Berlin. In 1952 he was made honorary president of the newly-founded Deutsche Akademie für Sprache und Dichtung.

Hochland, edited by Carl Muth from its inception in 1903 until its enforced closure in April 1941, enjoyed an increase in circulation after 1933, rising from some 5000 in 1934 to 12,000 in 1939/1940 (Schaezler

1965, pp. 225–228). Censorship was initially lax, but increased as better educated censors, including lapsed clerics, were employed. On at least three occasions, the authorities took action: in August 1934 because of Daniel Feuling's "Um ein viel gelesenes Buch", (*Hochland* 31/2 (1933/1934), 457–463), which rejected Rosenberg's *Myth of the Twentieth Century*; in December 1939 on account of Joseph Bernhart's article "Hodie" (On this Day, printed for the first time in *Hochland* 43 (1950), 105–114); and in April 1941 when a review of Nietzsche (correctly) quoted his maxim that God is dead. On the first two occasions, amendments were demanded before the journal was allowed to print; on the third, the issue did not appear. Bernhart's article defied a directive of the Propaganda Ministry, following Hitler's survival of Georg Elser's assassination attempt in Munich on 8 November 1939, that ecclesiastical publications must henceforth emphasize "the rule of providence" ("das Walten der Vorsehung") in protecting the Führer (cf. Kardorff 1997, p. 49 (26.12.1942)). In defiance of this instruction (and in terms strikingly similar to Haecker's diary diatribes against Nazi appropriations of VORSEHUNG and HERRGOTT), Bernhart's end-of-year message warned against "hasty talk of God's will and finger". The implicit rejoinder to the Propaganda Ministry's sacrilegious instruction was a theological-historical meditation on the Christmas message: "Hodie Christus natus est" ("Today Christ is born").

Haecker's response to the accession to power, in the April 1933 issue, was the essay "Das Chaos der Zeit" (The Chaos of the Time, *Hochland* 30/2 (1932/1933), pp. 1–23), which began with the observation that language, especially in Germany, was on the point of expressing nothing more than the "blood lust and brutality" of a chaotic modernity which was no longer centred, religiously, on logos, but on the Faustian deed and hubris of the new 'Übermensch'. Soon, he wrote, "no one will be able to agree with the other about the meaning of a word", since agreement as to the import of language will exist only "in its tone, its sound, in the *flatus vocis*, the breath of the voice, and [...] no longer exists, or is only seldom achieved through heroic efforts, by chance, by consent ("Fügung"), by providence, by grace, through supernatural love, in the imperishable spiritual element of a word—in its meaning". The rise of "incantatory sound" signalled "the dying of language itself", "the demise of thinking solely for the sake of truth". The published extracts from his diary, however, appearing in October 1939, take the form of philosophical musings, betraying nothing of the vitriol and political animus found in the secret diary ("Tagebuchblätter", *Hochland* 37/2 (1939/1940), pp. 470–475).

Hochland used the domains of theology, history, culture, and language as battlegrounds in a broad-front campaign against Nazism's threat to "spiritual freedom in the Christian West" (Schaezler 1965, p. 221; cf. Ackermann 1965). Alongside notable contributors like Haecker, Bergengruen, and Muth himself, contributors choosing language as a battleground included lesser-known figures such as F.M. Reifferscheidt, Karl Schaezler, and Ernst Alker, who in 1935 wrote ironically about the harvest which would come from BLUT UND BODEN, using the popular derogatory term BLUBO to characterize the avalanche of clichéd 'Heimat' literature already being hammered out by thousands of typewriters ("Ernte vom Blut und Boden", *Hochland* 32/4 (1934/1935), pp. 289–302 (289)). Language criticism in *Hochland* was particularly targeted at the Nazis' attempts to appropriate religious discourse, as in the use of vocabulary such as WEIHE (consecration), (DRITTES) REICH, and HEILIG (holy). As early as March 1933, in one of six articles that year devoted to the concept (DRITTES) REICH, Muth suggested that it was the product of resurgent Romantic sentiment, backward-looking political prophecy, mysticism, and an attitude of *ressentiment* ("Das Reich als Idee und Wirklichkeit—einst und jetzt", *Hochland* 30/1 (1932/1933), pp. 481–492). Christendom as an aspiration for all Christians has historical political formations, Muth continues, but these did not and do not correspond with nation states and national agendas. Like Haecker, Muth locates a key moment in this process in "the collapse of the unity of faith" ("Zerfall der Glaubenseinheit") initiated by Luther. Muth goes on to cite Haecker as the only critic to challenge the legitimacy of Bismarck's Reich as the continuation of the idea of a Holy German Reich, thus undermining the 'Second' Reich in the sequence. Astonishingly, Muth quotes at length from Haecker's "powerful and magnificent diatribe" in the 1932 *Brenner*, including the reference to the swastika as "das Zeichen des Tieres, die Karikatur des Kreuzes" ("the sign of the beast, the caricature of the Cross"), and Haecker's view that it would have been better had Luther been burned at the stake, to spare him his shameful legacy:

Prussia, Bismarck, and National Socialism, which is essentially a Protestant movement ("wesentlich eine protestantische Bewegung") leading to the destruction of true religion and to cultural barbarism ("die Zerstörung wahrer Religion und die kulturelle Barbarei"). A close reading of these articles from 1933, including, as Helena Tomko points out, "Das Chaos der Zeit", reveals the not-so-hidden persistence of the "steady analysis of […] linguistic hallmarks of systematic dehumanization" (2017, p. 52) and of the illicit secularization of religious terms which Haecker had articulated in his 1932 essay.

Schaezler took aim at the "misuse" ("Missbrauch") of the terms HEILIG and WEIHE in Wagner and in media reports of initiation ceremonies in the Hitler Youth and BDM (*Hochland* 34/1 (1936), pp. 90–93; the latter was also targeted by Sternberger in the *Frankfurter Zeitung*).[7] In 1938, in a review of two books tracing the secularization of religious terms (*Hochland* 35/2 (1938), 161–164; Papmehl-Rüttenauer 1937; Stange 1937), Schaezler found an opportunity to detail the history of HEILIG, opening with the pointed observation that SEELE (soul) was now used in military terminology to designate the inside of a canon barrel. The historical process of detaching HEILIG from ecclesiastical usage is traced from its beginnings in Luther, to moves towards a personal, subjective use in a religion of feeling, as in Herder, before "degenerating" further in the language of the Romantics. An anonymous letter to Novalis is quoted approvingly: "You retain the words of the Christian religious system and impart other meanings to them". The remainder of the nineteenth century ("that unholiest of all centuries") then led, Schaezler observes, to strange couplings ("absonderliche Verbindungen") between Romanticism and the new materialist philosophies, at which point Schaezler commends Sternberger's *Panorama* (1938) as kindred study. The blame for these developments, Schaezler suggests, lies with the Church itself, for allowing many of its key terms to be "emptied" of meaning (the example given is HIMMELREICH (Kingdom of Heaven)) by surrendering them to positivist rationality ("positivistische Vernünftelei", p. 164). The choice of example, as so often, is suggestive, leaving the reader to complete the connection between the secularized HIMMELREICH and the pseudo-religious DRITTES REICH.

The July 1934 issue reprinted a speech by Ulrich von Wilamowitz-Möllendorf from 1898 ("Nationale Kultur", *Hochland* 32/2 (1934/1935), pp. 383–384), whose lectures on Classical culture and history Haecker attended in Berlin in 1901/1902, in which he insists that the modern nation state should not imagine it has dominion over culture:

> denn er hat sie nicht gemacht, so wenig wie die Religion, die er auch nicht beherrschen kann. Staat, Volk, Religionsgemeinschaft sind Kreise, die sich vielfach schneiden müssen, zum Heile der Menschheit und ihrer Kultur, die rettungslos zersplittern würde, wenn jene Kreise je zusammenfielen. (p. 383f.)

> for it did not create culture, just as it did not create religion, of which it also cannot be master. State, 'Volk', religious community are circles which must overlap extensively, for the good of mankind and its culture, which would fragment disastrously if ever these circles coincided.

In quoting Wilamowitz's assault on 'völkisch' notions of cultural and political autarky in the German political discourse of the 'Second' Reich, the resort to history endorses an earlier voice in the current struggle. In a stark rebuttal of racial doctrine, Wilamowitz continues: "Wer diese Kultur bewußt oder unbewußt als ein Lebenselement in seiner Seele trägt, der ist ein Deutscher; Rasse, Sprache, Staatsangehörigkeit sind alle nicht entscheidend" (p. 384, "Whoever takes this culture into their soul as an element of life, whether consciously or unconsciously, is a German. Race, language, nationality are all not decisive.")

The book review was a favoured genre for recommending authors with a potential for 'Resistenz'. Indeed, it is possible to see a small network of mutual appreciation at work here: Schaezler recommends books by Sternberger and Storz, Oskar Loerke's edited volume *Deutscher Geist* (*Hochland* 38/5 (1940/1941), pp. 220–223), and Oskar Jancke's *Sprachdummheiten* (1936) (*Hochland* 34/1 (1937), p. 379). Storz reviews Reifferscheidt's *Satire und Polemik* (*Hochland* 38/9 (1940/1941), 364–366). Jewish authors are also commended. Remarkably, Karl Kraus is celebrated in an essay by Ludwig Hänsel (*Hochland* 32/3 (1934/1935), 237–250), and accorded a respectful obituary (*Hochland*

33/2 (1935/1936), 477), and Adolf Storfer's *Im Dickicht der Sprache* (1937) is reviewed by Schaezler, who makes no mention of Storfer's Jewishness or his close connection to Sigmund Freud (*Hochland* 35/1 (1937/1938), 155–158. The article also contains a positive review of Storz 1937.) Armed with examples from Storfer, Schaezler commends the study of language to counter the simple beliefs of the ignorant (p. 155), revealing, inter alia, that JUBEL (cheering) is Hebrew in origin, HOCK an English shortened form of 'Hochheimer' wine, that iron technology, in which Germans consider themselves the world leaders, was invented by the Celts, and that in the aftermath of Metternich's notorious secret police, colloquial Viennese idiom has twenty one expressions for SPITZEL (informant). The very mention of this word here is an indication of Storfer's subversive potential. The danger of "Sprachmengerei", Schaezler comments disingenuously, may be less acute in an age of autarky, but newly created words show that language mixing still occurs in German, for example NORDISIEREN ('nordify', its suffix a standard device for Germanizing Romance borrowings) and KNOCKOUT. These neologisms are clearly identifiable items in Nazi discourse, the first belonging to the Nordic myth of 'Aryan' racial superiority, the second belonging to Goebbels's favourite sporting metaphor of life as a boxing match.

Two years earlier, Reifferscheidt had published a detailed rebuttal of the concept of autarky in language, evidently aimed at the Deutscher Sprachverein ("Autarkie der Sprache?", *Hochland* 32/9 (1935), 246–256). "Unsere Muttersprache" (the first two words of the article) is, he explains, "unser Haus trotz den Anleihen bei fremden Völkern" ("our house despite all the borrowings from other peoples"), and the urge which some people have to remove entire 'foreign' blocks from this house is a childish demand ("das kindische Verlangen"). Whole domains of German life still carry the linguistic markers of German indebtedness to foreign inventions and interventions: to the Romans, for example, in wine growing and agriculture, an indebtedness even found in the German suffix '–er', with which a 'good German word' like 'Luftschiff' (airship) can be turned into LUFTSCHIFFER (airship aviator). Those who demand a "KAMPF" against the 'Fremdwort' do not realize that KAMPF is derived from the Latin *campus (martius)* (field of battle).

The picture presented here of a united front against the regime is, however, at best incomplete, and at worst idealized, as becomes evident in the spat—reviewed in the following chapter—between Sternberger and Reifferscheidt in the pages of the *Frankfurter Zeitung* over the latter's book *Über die Sprache* (1939).[8] Whilst one may plausibly detect an oppositional community of purpose in Sternberger, Schaezler, and Storz (and in the last two's admiration for Storfer), Reifferscheidt is a complex figure in this landscape, a recalcitrant spirit who, despite appearances to the contrary in 1935, articulates an understanding of language and nation which, in 1939 at least, shares authoritarian and mystical traits with the 'völkisch' inflection of the MUTTERSPRACHE concept around which Eduard Engel and Houston Stewart-Chamberlain could unite in August 1914.

Three Language Commentators

The focus in this final section narrows to consider the work of three language critics in these years who would play a significant role in the post-war discourse on language and Nazism in Western Germany: Dolf Sternberger (1907–1989), Gerhard Storz (1898–1983), and Wilhelm Emanuel Süskind (1900–1970). All might be seen as examples of the popular genre of journalistic, conservative language criticism. A lament of declining standards, however, was certainly not the sole preserve of oppositional intellectuals (hence its value as camouflage); indeed 'völkisch' variants were also prominent in the Reich, and sometimes co-existed with oppositional discourses, as the cases of Baberadt and Reifferscheidt (reviewed in the following chapter) reveal.

Dolf Sternberger

Sternberger's seminal role in the *Frankfurter Zeitung*'s discourse on language will be reviewed in the following chapter, which also makes clear the formative influence this habitus had on the conception of the "Lexicon of the 'Unmensch'" in autumn 1945. Sternberger published two books in the Reich. *Der verstandene Tod* (Death Understood), a critique of Heidegger's treatment of death in *Sein und Zeit* (*Being and Time*, 1927), was Sternberger's doctoral thesis, completed in 1932 under the sometime supervision of Karl Jaspers and Paul Tillich, and the unofficial supervision of Theodor Adorno. An attack on the perceived meaninglessness and inhumaneness of Heidegger's philosophical language, this study appeared in 1934, when Heidegger was the notoriously pro-Nazi Rector of Freiburg University. For Sternberger, as indeed for many oppositional Germans, Heidegger would remain an apologist for Nazism.

Panorama oder Ansichten vom 19. Jahrhundert (1938, *Panorama or Views of the Nineteenth Century*, 1977), is a coded cultural history of the late nineteenth century and its relationship to 1930s modernity which, on an oppositional reading, contains a critique of the attitudes aiding the popular acceptance of fascist norms by the supposedly Christian and enlightened middle classes. The attack on Darwin, for example, in the central chapter, readily furnishes a host of contemporary analogies between Natural Selection and National Socialism (Dodd 2017). In this respect, *Panorama* is a family relative of exile works on this theme by Benjamin, Bloch, and others (Dodd 2013b). Sternberger's real achievements in the field of language criticism, however, were as an essayist, particularly in the Feuilleton of the *Frankfurter Zeitung*. It was there, on Christmas Day 1941, that "Figuren der Fabel" (Figures of the Fable) appeared. An Aesopian commentary on textual variants of Aesop's fables and their critical reception through the ages, the portion of this essay dealing with the fable of the Wolf and the Lamb was immediately recognized in the Propaganda Ministry as a commentary on the treatment of the Jews. Of particular interest here is Sternberger's insistence on the wolf's need of language (by extension, in the construction of racist laws) to justify his devouring of the lamb: raw power, even in a dictatorship of terror, needs to construct self-justifications using language:

> Die Gewalt tritt ja gerade nicht in ihrer zwar schauderhaften, aber immerhin offenkundigen Nacktheit hervor, sondern—sie ist ja gekleidet in den Mantel des Rechts, sie erhebt ja gerade den Anspruch, nicht die Gewalt, sondern das Recht zu sein. Als ob sie wüßte, daß sie allein und ohne solchen Schein nicht bestehen könnte. (Sternberger 1988, p. 17)

The point is that violence does not show itself in its admittedly terrible but nevertheless blatant nakedness, but instead clothes itself in the mantle of law, it even claims to be not violence, but the law. As if it knew that it could not survive on its own and without such a pretence.

Gerhard Storz

The 'resistent' qualities of Storz's *Laienbrevier über den Umgang mit der Sprache* (1937, Layperson's Guide to Using Language), may not be immediately apparent to today's readers, but like his study of Schiller,[9] it is a book which quietly but firmly rejects National Socialist norms. Extensively pre-published in the *Frankfurter Zeitung*, it was (as the next chapter explains in more detail) fiercely rejected by the purist lobby, who rightly perceived its withholding of the expected patriotic mantras. This hostility becomes understandable from the following passage, in which Storz paints a vivid picture of the nature of language:

> Alles in allem: die Sprache ist nicht etwas Starres; nichts, was auf unser Planen und Wollen geduldig wartete; sie fließt und lebt in einem nicht aufzuhaltenden Strom, in uns, aus uns, in uns hinein, um uns her. Und wie in einem Fluß mehrere Bewegungen zugleich mit der einen, in der Talrichtung ziehenden gehen, so auch in der Sprache: Die Wasser oben fließen anders als die in der Tiefe, Quellen strömen vom Bett her unvermerkt ins obere Wasser ein, saugende Trichter und Strudel bilden sich, Bäche bringen anderes, fremdes Gewässer hinzu, das sich mischt oder sich nicht gesellen will. Wohl kann, wer nur Ohren und Aufmerksamkeit hat, im eigenen Umkreis Richtung und Zug der Sprache von heute erkennen, aber das Vielerlei, die Kreuz und Quer von Ursache, die zur Wirkung, von Wirkung, die zur Ursache wird, mit fremden Wirkungen sich verflechtend—welcher Zeitgenosse könnte diese "Kette der tiefsten Wirkungen ringsumher" mit seinen eigenen Augen übersehen! Wie dem Leben des Flusses nicht zu wehren ist—auch gewaltsame Beschränkungen und Verlagerungen hemmen nicht das eigengesetzliche Spiel seiner Wellen und des Wallens in ihm—so vermögen wir Lebenden nicht, diesen gewaltigen Strom der Sprache, zumal wenn er Muttersprache heißt, nach unserem Wähnen und Gutdünken zu lenken, wir, deren Lebenszeit, gemessen an dem Weg jenes Stromes, nur einen kurzen Wellenschlag bedeutet. (Storz 1937, p. 11f.)

> All in all, language is not inert, not something that would wait patiently on our plans and wishes, it flows and lives in an unstoppable great river, inside us, out of us, into us, around us. And just as in a river many different currents move with the one current, towards the valley, so it is with language. The waters at the surface flow differently from those in the depths, springs flow unnoticed from the river bed up into the surface currents, eddies and vortexes form, streams bring different waters from far afield which mingle or keep themselves apart. Anyone with ears who pays attention can certainly recognize the direction and drift of language today in his own circle, but the diversity, the to and fro of cause leading to effect leading to cause, mingling with foreign influences—who today could not see with his own eyes this "chain of most profound effects around us". Just as there is no gainsaying the life of the river—even massive obstacles and diversions cannot stem the natural laws of its waves and swells—so we human beings are incapable of directing the powerful flow of the language, even when it is called mother tongue, according to our will and thinking; we, whose life span, measured by that of the river, is but a momentary ripple.

This image of language as a river flowing through history contests and counters discursive constructions of fascism as a force of nature. Strikingly reminiscent of Storfer's copious etymologies,[10] it is saturated with 'Resistenz': to a monolithically imposed discourse, and to a racially 'purified' language—and with that to every facet of 'völkisch' ideology rooted in the myth of Teutonic separateness and autarky. It is an eloquent rebuttal of the ideology of 'Sprachmengerei' (linguistic bastardization). Many currents mingle in the great river of (the German) language, including alien ("fremd") waters which may or may not still carry traces of their provenance. Storz asserts and celebrates the intermingling of cultures in contact as an unstoppable historical fact, despite the ultimately futile violent ("gewaltsam") attempts of National Socialism to change the course of history. The unattributed reference in the embedded quotation to the Prologue of Goethe's *Faust* keys in to a discourse on the metaphysics of evil. German readers could easily look up the expanded quotation to find these words are spoken by the Archangel Michael in Heaven before Mephistopheles makes his wager with God about the soul of Faust:

Und Stürme brausen um die Wette,	And storms rage in competition
Vom Meer aufs Land, vom Land aufs Meer,	From sea to land, from land to sea,
Und bilden wütend eine Kette	And raging form a chain
Der tiefsten Wirkung rings umher.	Of the profoundest effects all around.
Da flammt ein blitzendes Verheeren	A lightning flash of destruction
Dem Pfade vor des Donnerschlags;	Flares before the path of the thunder;
Doch deine Boten, Herr, verehren	But Thy messengers, Lord, revere
Das sanfte Wandeln deines Tags.	The gentle movement of Your day.

The passage carries a message, quite typical of inner exile texts, of consolation in adversity, hope, and solidarity[11]: the dominion of evil is temporary, the storm will exhaust itself, and God's gentle ("sanft") law will one day reassert itself. Storz's discourse is one of many reviewed in the present study whose resilience is informed by a strong Christian (Catholic) faith. Mephistopheles' triumph will be short-lived.

Wilhelm E. Süskind

Like Storz's *Laienbrevier*, Süskind's primer on good style, *Vom ABC zum Sprachkunstwerk. Eine Sprachlehre für Erwachsene* (1940, From Alphabet to the Linguistic Work of Art. A Language Guide for Adults), was extensively pre-published in the FZ. One of the most popular books of its kind, over thirty thousand copies were sold before the end of the war. Jürgen Schiewe (2015, p. 91) finds "traces of a concealed mode of writing [verdeckte Schreibweise]" in Süskind's presentation of the hierarchical structures of language, for example in comparing the "Hauptwort" (noun) to a "großer Herr" who, on closer examination, may turn out to be "der schäbigste Hohlkopf und Windbeutel" ("the most despicable hollow head and windbag", p. 23). Süskind's metaphor is ostensibly directed at deverbal nouns such as INANGRIFFNAHME (from the verbal construction 'etwas in Angriff nehmen', to tacke/start on a task) as a feature of

'Verlautbarungssprache' (declamatory language of authority) but the metaphor of the powerful windbag, as Schiewe points out, has obvious real-world correlates. Schiewe plausibly shows how Süskind harnesses metaphors latent in the metadiscourse on grammar to a discourse of implied political dissent which also covers the (breakable) rules of punctuation, and the over-used superlative as a symptom of a "Bedürfnis nach Beschwörung und Vergötterung" (p. 71f., "desire for conspiracy and deification"). Schiewe concludes that Süskind consistently urges his readers to be autonomous users of the language, detaching themselves, for example, from automatically reproducing the language of the (regulated) press ("Zeitungssprache", p. 200)—this a widespread concern of language critics in inner exile.

Schiewe's illuminating reading might be extended to the chapter on the language of advertising ("Die Sprache der Reklame"), pre-published in the journal *Europäische Revue* (16 October 1940, pp. 610–616). This chapter, focused, like the chapter on "Zeitungssprache", on a text-type rather than grammar, and on the reception rather than the production of language, is clearly an invitation to read critically. In focusing (ostensibly) on the advertising industry in America, Süskind appears to conform to cultural expectations that the United States will be criticized. Attentive readers, however, may suspect a sub-text nearer to home, at the latest in the paragraph found towards the end of the chapter, in which the language of advertising is characterized as follows:

> Sie bleibt zum Beispiel immer verständlich erfassbar und geht nie ins Metaphysische. Sie setzt grundsätzlich ein günstiges Ende voraus und behandelt auch die Übelstände, die sie schildert, als leicht abstellbar. Niemand soll abgeschreckt und in moralische Verzweiflung gestürzt werden. Zwar wählt die Reklame kostbare und tiefsinnig klingende Ausdrücke, aber keine tief schürfenden; denn der kaufende Mensch will zwar wichtig genommen und seriös angesprochen, aber nicht angestrengt und erschreckt werden. Die Sprache der Reklame ist grundsätzlich die Sprache der Erleichterung. Sie umgeht, was schwierig ist; sie vermeidet Fragen, indem sie Problemchen aufwirft, und an die Stelle des Änderns

> und Besserns setzt sie die Hygiene und den Komfort. Sie tarnt selbst den Tod. (Süskind 1940, p. 206)

> For example, it always remains easily accessible and never ventures into the metaphysical. It fundamentally assumes there is a positive outcome and treats even the grievances which it depicts as capable of being easily removed. No one is to be frightened off and plunged into moral despair. The advertisement chooses precious and profound sounding phrases, but nothing too deep. After all, the consumer wants to be made to feel important and to be spoken to seriously, but doesn't want to be made to feel uncomfortable and frightened. The language of adverts is fundamentally the language of putting you at ease. It skirts around anything difficult, it avoids questions by throwing up tiny little problems, and instead of change and making things better it offers hygiene and comfort. It even camouflages death.

Even today, readers may "stumble" over the last sentence, five monosyllabic words intruding like hammer blows. Death has not been mentioned thus far, and it will not be mentioned again. This is a classic example of the contrived "stumbling block" alerting attentive readers to the presence of a coded meaning—if we assume that Süskind is communicating competently and the text is both cohesive and coherent. The oppositional subtext can be constructed by a double displacement: for America, read Germany; for REKLAME, read PROPAGANDA. This was not a difficult substitution for Germans to make. As noted in Chap. 3, a 1937 'Sprachregelung' (directive) from the Propaganda Ministry had declared that the use of the word WERBUNG (advert, advertising) should be restricted to the register of business and commerce ("Handelssprache"), while PROPAGANDA was made a legally protected term and the property of the NSDAP:

> Es wird gebeten, das Wort 'Propaganda' nicht mißbräuchlich zu verwenden. Propaganda ist im Sinne des neuen Staates gewissermaßen ein gesetzlich geschützter Begriff geworden und soll nicht für abfällige Dinge Verwendung finden... (Glunk 1970 (26), p. 100; Lämmert et al. 1967, p. 119)

> It is requested that the word 'Propaganda' should not be used wrongly. Propaganda in the meaning of the new state has become in a manner of speaking a legally protected term and should not be used for trivial things.

This directive, a serious miscalculation by the regime (Glunk 1970 (26), pp. 100–116), sought to impose the semantics of internal party usage on the population as a whole. PROPAGANDA was to be positively connoted when referring to the regime's own information management by the PROPAGANDA Ministry, and elevated above its mundane cousins selling the products of industry and commerce. A further instruction was issued via the 'Werberat der deutschen Wirtschaft' (Chamber of Commerce), also in 1937, proscribing the use of PROPAGANDA in commercial contexts in words such as PROPAGANDA-KAFFEE (best quality coffee brand):

> Der Politiker, der Ideen durchsetzen will oder Maßnahmen vorbereiten oder begründen will, treibt Propaganda, der Kaufmann, der Waren (oder Leistungen) absetzen will, treibt Werbung.
>
> Über dieses Verbot, das Wort 'Propaganda' zum Bestandteil einer Warenbezeichnung zu machen, hinaus muß es als grundsätzlich unerwünscht angesehen werden, daß das Wort 'Propaganda' zu Zwecken der Wirtschaftswerbung Verwendung findet. Der Ersatz dieses Wortes durch Werbung wird in fast allen Fällen ohne Schwierigkeiten möglich sein. (Glunk 1970, p. 101)

> The politician who seeks to turn ideas into action or to prepare or justify political measures, engages in propaganda; the salesman who seeks to sell goods (or services), engages in advertising.
>
> Over and above this proscription on using the word 'propaganda' as part of a product name, the use of the word 'propaganda' for the purpose of commercial advertising must be regarded as fundamentally undesirable. Replacing this word with 'advertising' will be possible without any difficulty in almost all cases.

Although not mentioned in these directives, REKLAME is easily recognizable as a synonym for WERBUNG in the sense 'advertisement'. Indeed, as pointed out in Chap. 2, Hitler's own usage in *Mein Kampf* varied between

PROPAGANDA and POLITISCHE REKLAME (e.g. Hitler 1934, p. 200). This raises the possibility that Süskind's paragraph, in addition to being a coded commentary on Goebbels's propaganda practices, is a carefully crafted pastiche of the passage in *Mein Kampf*. The tightly controlled media had no doubt generally observed the instruction to distinguish between the terms since 1937, but it is doubtful that popular usage followed suit, so that REKLAME, WERBUNG, and PROPAGANDA still belonged to a single semantic field in most Germans' mental lexicons and Süskind's readers who were primed to make the leap from America to Germany could re-read the chapter, and perhaps the book, from a new vantage point. To take just one example, Süskind's mention of "hygiene" in the last line of the paragraph quoted seems like a natural fit (like "comfort") in the schema of advertising, but in the substituted schema of propaganda it acquires quite a different meaning, invoking 'racial hygiene' and its consequences for 'non-Aryans' and, in so-called euthanasia programmes, for 'Aryans' too. Readers who followed this hermeneutic trail were led to a stark warning: Take a close look at what the Propaganda Ministry is really selling. Pechel was arrested in 1942 for a very similar message.

Conclusion

The enforced shift from a discourse of open resistance to one of coded 'Resistenz' was the inevitable result of the extreme Nazification of Germany society and the creation of a repressive, potentially murderous discourse environment. The public articulation of dissent, particularly in print media, became increasingly nuanced as writers and their readers resorted to the knowing use of significant topoi (such as history or the contemporary Soviet Union) and tropes (such as analogy, displacement and metaphor) signalled by rhetorical means using the lexical and phraseological resources of text and genre. The cultural field, including literature, theology, history, and language itself, was a favoured site of publicly articulated 'Resistenz'. This chapter has shown how a discourse on language could be and was harnessed to this coded public articulation of dissent. Nowhere was this discourse on language more programmatically embraced than in the *Frankfurter Zeitung*, to which we now turn. The first public debates on language and Nazism in Western Germany would be shaped by this strand of language criticism, with its roots in the sensibilities of inner exile—regrettably so in von Polenz's view (1999, p. 319)—and represented by Sternberger, Storz and Süskind, rather than the more explicitly socio-pragmatic critiques of Kraus and the exiled Brecht or the 'private' observations of actual contemporary usage by Klemperer and Haecker in their diaries.

Notes

1. "Die Gesetzgebung des Lykurgus und Solon" (The Legislation of Lycurgus and Solon). Friedrich Schiller, *Sämtliche Werke in zwölf Bänden*, Stuttgart o.J. Bd. 10, p. 297.
2. Women journalists on national newspapers (such as Margret Boveri on the *Berliner Tageblatt*, Ursula von Kardorff on the *Deutsche Allgemeine Zeitung*, and Luise Kaschnitz on the *Frankfurter Zeitung*) were largely confined to writing for the feuilleton or the women's section, although Heddy Neumeister (*Frankfurter Zeitung*, cf. Dodd 2013a, p. 276) wrote on social issues which were inherently political.
3. The following account is indebted to Koonz 1987 (especially pp. 309–344), Oldfield 1986, and Stephenson 2001, pp. 109–112. Cumulatively, these sources name some thirty women who were executed or murdered.
4. The meaning of this term also extends to include 'guilt by association' and 'collective punishment'.
5. The full title was 'Amt des Beauftragten des Führers für die Überwachung der gesamten geistigen und weltanschaulichen Erziehung der NSDAP' (Office of the Führer's commissioner for the oversight of the whole of the intellectual and political education of the NSDAP).
6. Cf. also (in German) Gołaszweski et al. 2016.
7. Sternberger, "Am Altar", FZ, 7.6.1936. Cf. Gillessen 1986, p. 242.
8. See Dodd 2007, pp. 196–206, Dodd 2013a, pp. 44–46. There is a similar exchange between Reifferscheidt and Franz Wolfgang in *Hochland* in 1940 (36/2, p. 316; 37/2, pp. 358–369).

9. Storz 1938. Storz's quotation from Goethe also belongs to a campaign to resist the regime's attempts to enlist the great authors of Weimar Classicism to a National Socialist literary pantheon.
10. On the links between Storz and Storfer, see Henneberg 2003, p. 62; Dodd 2013a, p. 1f., Dodd 2013c.
11. This self-understanding of many inner exile writers is captured in Torberg 1964, an imaginary retrospective dialogue between an inner exile and a territorial exile.

Bibliography

Ackermann, Konrad. 1965. *Der Widerstand der Monatsschrift 'Hochland' gegen den Nationalsozialismus*. München: Kösel.

Bauer, Gerhard. 1988. *Sprache und Sprachlosigkeit im "Dritten Reich"*. Köln: Bund-Verlag.

Bendt, Jutta, and Karin Schmidgall. 1994. *Ricarda Huch 1864–1947. Eine Ausstellung des Deutschen Literaturarchivs im Schiller-Nationalmuseum Marbach am Neckar 7. Mai–31. Oktober 1994. Ausstellung und Katalog.* Marbacher Kataloge 47. Herausgegeben von Ulrich Ott und Friedrich Pfäfflin. Marbach am Neckar: Deutsche Schillergesellschaft.

Bergengruen, Werner. 1947. *Zum Geleit*. Pechel 1947, pp. 5–22.

Broszat, Martin. 1986. Zur Sozialgeschichte des deutschen Widerstands. *Vierteljahrshefte für Zeitgeschichte* 34 (3): 293–309.

Dodd, William J. 2007. *Jedes Wort wandelt die Welt. Dolf Sternbergers politische Sprachkritik*. Göttingen: Wallstein.

———., ed. 2013a. *"Der Mensch hat das Wort". Der Sprachdiskurs in der Frankfurter Zeitung 1933–1943*. Berlin, Boston: de Gruyter.

———. 2013b. Dolf Sternberger's *Panorama:* Approaches to a Work of (Inner) Exile in the National Socialist Period. *Modern Language Review* 108 (1): 180–201.

———. 2013c. Gegen 'volkhafte' Sprachauffassungen resistent: Der Sprachkritiker Gerhard Storz. In *Mimesis, Mimikry, Simulatio. Tarnung und Aufdeckung in den Künsten vom 16. bis zum 21. Jahrhundert. Festschrift für Erwin Rotermund zum 80.* Geburtstag, Hg. Hanns-Werner Heister and Bernhard Spies, 47–59. Berlin: Weidler Buchverlag.

———. 2017. Darwin's Imperialist Canvas: Dolf Sternberger's *Panorama oder Ansichten vom 19. Jahrhundert* (1938) as Cultural History in the Shadow of National Socialism. In *Biological Discourses. The Language of Science and*

Literature Around 1900, Cultural History and Literary Imagination, ed. Robert Craig and Ina Linge, vol. 26, 135–158. Oxford, Bern, Berlin: Peter Lang.

Donahue, Neil H., and Doris Kirchner, eds. 2003. *Flight of Fantasy: New Perspectives on Inner Emigration in German Literature, 1933–1945*. New York: Berghahn.

Ehrke-Rotermund, Heidrun. 2012. Hitler – ein Massenbetrüger. Bilder als Medium der 'Verdeckten Schreibweise' in Rudolf Pechels Buchbesprechung 'Lob des Scharlatans' (1938). *Jahrbuch der Deutschen Schillergesellschaft* 56: 227–258.

Ehrke-Rotermund, Heidrun, and Erwin Rotermund, Hg. 1999. *Zwischenreiche und Gegenwelten. Texte und Vorstudien zur "verdeckten Schreibweise" im "Dritten Reich"*. München: Wilhelm Fink.

Gillessen, Günther. 1986. *Auf verlorenem Posten. Die Frankfurter Zeitung im 'Dritten Reich'*. München: Siedler.

Glunk, Rolf. 1966–1971. Erfolg und Misserfolg der nationalsozialistischen Sprachlenkung. *Zeitschrift für deutsche Sprache* 22–27.

Gołaszweski, Marcin, Magdalena Kardach, and Leonore Krenzlin, Hgg. 2016. *Zwischen Innerer Emigration und Exil. Deutschsprachige Schriftsteller 1933–1945*. Berlin, Boston: de Gruyter.

Grimm, Reinhold. 2003. In the Thicket of Inner Emigration. In *Flight of Fantasy: New Perspectives on Inner Emigration in German Literature, 1933–1945*, ed. Neil H. Donahue and Doris Kirchner, 27–45. New York: Berghahn.

Henneberg, Nicole. 2003. 'Bohemien, Räuberhauptmann und Sprachforscher'. Der vergessene Wiener Etymologe Adolf Josef Storfer. *Die Horen* 48/4 (212): 61–74.

Hitler, Adolf. 1934. *Mein Kampf. Zwei Bände in einem Band*. Ungekürzte Ausgabe. 97–101. Auflage. München: Franz Eher Nachfolger.

Jünger, Ernst. 1939. *Auf den Marmorklippen*. Hamburg: Hanseatische Verlagsanstalt.

von Kardorff, Ursula. 1997. *Berliner Aufzeichnungen 1942 bis 1945*. Unter Verwendung der Original-Tagebücher neu herausgegeben und kommentiert von Peter Hartl. Ungekürzte Ausgabe, 2. Auflage. München: Deutscher Taschenbuch Verlag.

Kempowski, Walter. 2002. *Das Echolot. Barbarossa '41. Ein kollektives Tagebuch*. München: Knaus.

Klapper, John. 2015. *Nonconformist Writing in Nazi Germany: The Literature of Inner Emigration*. Rochester, New York: Camden House.

Klemperer, Victor. 1978. *LTI. Notizbuch eines Philologen*. Berlin: Aufbau.

Koonz, Claudia. 1987. *Mothers in the Fatherland. Women, the Family and Nazi Politics*. New York: St. Martin's Press.

Lämmert, Eberhard, Walter Killy, Karl Otto Conrady, and Peter von Polenz. 1967. *Germanistik—eine deutsche Wissenschaft*. Frankfurt/Main: Suhrkamp.

Militz, Hans-Manfred. 1998. 'Wejen Ausdrücken': Redewendungen im LTI von Victor Klemperer. *Proverbium* 15: 201–219.

Oldfield, Sybil. 1986. German Women in the Resistance to Hitler. In *Women, State and Revolution*, ed. Sian Reynolds. Wheatsheaf: Brighton.

Papmehl-Rüttenauer, Isabella. 1937. *Das Wort 'heilig' in der deutschen Dichtersprache von Pyra bis zum jungen Herder*. Weimar: Verlag Hermann Böhlaus Nachf.

Pechel, Rudolf. 1947. *Zwischen den Zeilen: Der Kampf einer Zeitschrift für Freiheit und Recht 1932–1942*. Wiesentheid: Droemersche Verlagsanstalt.

von Polenz, Peter. 1999. *Deutsche Sprachgeschichte vom Spätmittelalter bis zur Gegenwart*. Bd 3: *19. und 20. Jahrhundert*. Berlin, New York: de Gruyter.

Reifferscheidt, Friedrich M. 1939. *Über die Sprache*. Leipzig: Hegner.

Rotermund, Erwin. 2011. 'Concealed Writing' (*Verdeckte Schreibweise*) in the 'Third Reich': Forms and Problems of Reception. In *Aesopic Voices. Re-framing Truth Through Concealed Ways of Presentation in the 20th and 21st Centuries*, ed. Gert Reifarth and Philip Morrissey. Newcastle upon Tyne: Cambridge Scholars Publishing.

Schaezler, Karl. 1965. Das *Hochland* und der Nationalsozialismus. *Hochland* 75: 221–231.

Schiewe, Jürgen. 2015. Wilhelm Emanuel Süskinds Stillehre *Vom ABC zum Sprachkunstwerk*. Ein Text (auch) mit verdeckter Schreibweise? *Aptum. Zeitschrift für Sprachkritik und Sprachkultur* 01 (11): 86–96.

Schöttker, Detlev, and Anja Hübner. 2011. Ernst Jünger, Dolf Sternberger. Briefwechsel 1941–42 und 1973–80. *Sinn und Form* 36 (4): 448–473.

Schymura, Yvonne. 2014. *Käthe Kollwitz 1867–2000. Biographie und Rezeptionsgeschichte einer deutschen Künstlerin*. Essen: Klartext.

Siefken, Hinrich., ed. 1994. *Die "Weiße Rose" und ihre Flugblätter*. Manchester: Manchester University Press.

Stange, Erich. 1937. Das Wort und die Wörter. Das Sprachgut der Christenheit in seiner Bedrohung durch die Sprache der Welt. *Pastoralblätter* 78: 1.

Stephenson, Jill. 2001. *Women in Nazi Germany*. Harlow: Longman.

Sternberger, Dolf. 1938. *Panorama oder Ansichten vom 19. Jahrhundert*. Hamburg: Henry Goverts. Also in: Schriften, V. (1981). Frankfurt/Main: Insel.

———. 1988. *Gut und Böse. Moralische Essais aus drei Zeiten.* (*Schriften* IX). Frankfurt/Main: Insel.

Storfer, Adolf Josef. 1935. *Wörter und ihre Schicksale*. Zürich: Atlantis Verlag. Reprinted: Verlag Vorwerk 8, Berlin (2005).

Storfer, Adolf. 1937. *Im Dickicht der Sprache*. Wien: Verlag Dr. Rolf Passer. Reprinted: Verlag Vorwerk 8, Berlin (2005).

Storz, Gerhard. 1937. *Laienbrevier über den Umgang mit der Sprache*. Frankfurt/Main: Societäts-Verlag.

———. 1938. *Das Drama Friedrich Schillers*. Frankfurt/Main: Societäts-Verlag.

Strauss, Leo. 1952. Persecution and the Art of Writing. In *Persecution and the Art of Writing*, ed. L. Strauss, 22–37. Chicago: Chicago University Press.

Süskind, Wilhelm E. 1940. *Vom ABC zum Sprachkunstwerk. Eine Sprachlehre für Erwachsene*. Stuttgart: Deutsche Verlags-Anstalt.

Tomko, Helena M. 2017. The Reluctant Satirist: Theodor Haecker and the Dizzying Swindle of Nazism. *Oxford German Studies* 46 (1): 42–57.

Torberg, Friedrich. 1964. Innere und äußere Emigration: Ein imaginärer Dialog. In *PPP: Pamphlete – Parodien – Post Scripta*, Hg. Friedrich Torberg, 53–69. München, Wien: Albert Langen, Georg Müller.

7

Voices at Home (III): The Case of the *Frankfurter Zeitung*

There was a relationship of mutual hostility between the NSDAP and liberal 'bourgeois' newspapers in the Weimar Republic, and one title in particular, the *Frankfurter Zeitung* (FZ) was reviled by Hitler in *Mein Kampf*, not least because of its Jewish ownership. For Hitler the FZ was

> der Inbegriff aller Anständigkeit. Verwendet sie doch niemals rohe Ausdrücke, lehnt jede körperliche Brutalität ab und appelliert immer an den Kampf mit den "geistigen" Waffen, der eigentümlicherweise gerade den geistlosesten Menschen am meisten am Herzen liegt. (Hitler 1934, p. 267 (Book 1, Chapter 10))
>
> the embodiment of all respectability. It never uses coarse expressions, rejects all physical brutality and always appeals to the struggle with "intellectual" weapons which, remarkably, endears itself to the most insipid people.

Yet the FZ, together with other liberal titles such as the *Berliner Tageblatt,* was not closed down in 1933. The *Tageblatt* was eventually closed down in 1939, the FZ in August 1943. After a brief initial period in which its editors believed the paper could mount a direct political challenge to the

W J Dodd, *National Socialism and German Discourse*,
https://doi.org/10.1007/978-3-319-74660-9_7

regime, they were forced to fall back on an *ad hoc* strategy of "pinpricks" ("Politik der Nadelstiche", Gillessen 1986, p. 221), using a series of secondary discourses as proxies, mainly in the domain of culture.[1] Within this, a discourse on language emerged, certainly by 1936, as a favoured site of coded dissent, its most prolific practitioner being Dolf Sternberger. Choosing language as a site on which to oppose the now well-entrenched regime was certainly a tacit admission of defeat in the political sphere, an attempt to counter the 'Sprachlosigkeit' in which they and their readers found themselves. The rationale of this emerging language-critical programme had a simple but compelling logic. As a topos, language lends itself to this purpose more than culture in general, of which it is an integral part, because language is in the truest sense of the word everyone's business. Speakers possess the competences not only to form grammatical and appropriate utterances, to encode and decode communication, but also to reflect on these utterances and form judgments about them. These competences exist, however, as potential which needs to be activated and developed. This is particularly true of the reflective, critical competence, and in reality this is (also) distributed unevenly in the language community. Thus, a tension arises between, on the one hand, the ideal of language as the property of all, and, on the other, the very different levels of access to and impact on public discourse by individuals in a given society.

Invoking and insisting on the inherently democratic nature of language in this case offered a stratagem of resistance to the regulated discourse market which allowed the paper to champion literacy, or rather the need to promote people's competence to reflect on both their language production and especially their consumption of others' utterances and texts. This discourse was profoundly shaped by the limits of the sayable in the new print media landscape, and the most noticeable consequence of this was that, with some (by definition, remarkable) exceptions, the FZ's oppositional language critique was deflected away from the kind of *ad hominem* targeting of named speakers and their utterances exemplified by Kraus, Brecht, and indeed Sternberger's own counterfactual lexicon of 1932 (see Chap. 2), towards a generalized critique of 'the (state of the) language' impelled by anxieties about the spread of Nazi norms in the general population. Irony, in coded and referred meanings, is the basic tool of these commentaries, which combined ostensible conformity with subterfuge. This was an increasingly elite discourse, characterized by a literary and philosophical intensity which only educated and determinedly 'resistent' readers might be expected to access. There is no way of knowing how many readers were reached in this way, but their number must be put at a few thousand at most, dispersed throughout the Reich and therefore unlikely to constitute an organized community of opposition. Because of the complexity of many of these texts, a selection of those reviewed in this chapter is reproduced, with English translation, in the Appendix.[2]

The years of inner exile produced a habitus not only in the way these critics talked about language, but also in the way they thought about language. Deeply shaped by the 'Sprachlosigkeit' of their situation and the fear that the everyday speech and thought of Germans was being contaminated by witting or unwitting adoption of fascist usage, this habitus would inform one of the first and most influential attempts in 1945 to come to terms with the role of language in the Nazi period, the "Lexicon of the 'Unmensch'", orchestrated by Sternberger and written in collaboration with two fellow-contributors to the FZ, Gerhard Storz and Wilhelm Emanuel Süskind. Before turning in more detail to the use of language and the oppositional discourse on language in the FZ, however, a brief account of its situation in the media landscape of the Reich, and of its self-understanding in this situation, is necessary.

Situation

The position of the FZ has been described as an "Aushängeschild" for the regime (cf. Hagemann 1970, pp. 298–305 (p. 304)), a shop sign or showpiece. Its editors also referred to it, ironically, as a "Naturschutzgebiet", a nature reserve (Sternberger, "Kinder und Narren sagen die Wahrheit", FZ, 3.5.1936; a similar statement by Theodor Heuss is recorded in Sänger 1977, p. 279). That it was allowed to continue after 1933 is due to the fact that Goebbels wanted a press landscape which would be "monoform in will, but pluriform in the articulation of that will" (*Deutsche Presse* 23 (1933), p. 278, 4.10.1933). The FZ and other 'bürgerlich' titles such as the *Kölnische Volkszeitung* and the *Berliner Tageblatt* were to be showpieces in this landscape, to counter the negative image of the Reich in the liberal democracies, and to reach Germans who would never read a Nazi publication. In January 1933 the editorial conference of the FZ, under its Jewish owner Heinrich Simon, decided not to move the paper to Switzerland, fearing that in exile it would lose touch with the events it reported, and resolving instead "to stay in the country and to dare to try to carry on in the same spirit, as long as this was possible" (Sänger 1975, p. 12). The measures regulating the press, described in Chap. 3, meant that the opportunities for free expression and dissemination of information were quickly reduced, but Goebbels's game also meant that the editors sensed opportunities for pushing the boundaries of the sayable in ways that might not be tolerated in other titles. A game of poker began between the paper and the Propaganda Ministry, a battle of wits to exploit the paper's cultural capital as a voice of 'bürgerlich' opinion, which would run, though they could not know it in 1933, for ten years. The paper was subject to control through the various measures for regulation at the institutional, economic, and content levels outlined in Chap. 3. Editors were liable for their copy under the 'Schrifleitergesetz', so self-censorship was the principal mode of control, and in particular a system of in-house second readers ('Gegenleser') who cleared colleagues' copy before sending it to the type-setters. Heinrich Simon emigrated, and eventually the regime secured financial control of the paper. Since the 'crisis year' of 1929, the paper had been owned by the Imprimatur GmbH, in which IG Farben had an as yet not fully explained financial interest. It was evidently a benign owner, after all the FZ had always been close to business interests, having begun as a 'Handelsblatt' (trade paper). But in 1939, the FZ succumbed, like so many newspapers and publishing houses, to being bought up by the NSDAP's Franz-Eher-Verlag. This does not seem to have materially altered the way the paper operated. Throughout its ten years of existence after 1933, the paper never had a National Socialist manager or chief editor imposed on it.

The special status of the FZ can be seen in the fact that in 1934, by personal permission of Goebbels, an editor (Sternberger) with a Jewish wife was accredited, and three editors with Jewish wives (Sternberger, Wilhelm Hausenstein, Otto Suhr) were employed until May 1943, despite ordinance 5.3 of the 'Schriftleitergesetz' stating that accreditation would not be granted to Jews or those married to Jews (JÜDISCH VERSIPPT). There is also some evidence of latitude in the Ministry's treatment of the FZ, an example being the reported tearing up of a file on Sternberger following the publication of "Figuren der Fabel" (Figures of the Fable, cf. Sternberger 1988, pp. 13–26) in the Christmas Day edition in 1941, a beautifully illustrated full-page article and a thinly veiled commentary on the treatment of the Jews. Sternberger had delivered the text at the last minute, and it had been set without being seen by the 'Gegenleser'. Goebbels darkly intimated to Fritz Sänger, the FZ representative at the Berlin 'Pressekonferenz', that he had not been fooled, and soon afterwards the head of the FZ office in Berlin, Heinrich Scharp, pleaded for the endangered author with Hans Fritzsche, Head of Press Affairs in the Propaganda Ministry, who agreed not to proceed (Gillessen 1986, p. 353).

In the early years of the Reich, the circulation of the FZ increased, in contrast to most titles. Toepser-Ziegert (2007, p. 79f.) gives a circulation of 102,731 for 1934, settling to around 77,000 in the years before the outbreak of war, and falling to around 30,000 in the year of its closure, 1943.[3] It is difficult to quantify the reach of the paper, but even allowing for second and third readers, it is true to say that the FZ attracted a niche readership: educated, liberal in outlook, cosmopolitan and business-oriented, and typically not members of the Party. Indeed, a subscription to the FZ tended to be viewed with suspicion by the local Gestapo. Even so, in quantitative terms, it is likely that only a small percentage of these readers would be able and willing to 'read between the lines' of an increasingly erudite, coded discourse on language and culture once the paper was forced to abandon its overt political stance—at the latest, with the political murders of 30 June 1934. The withdrawal from overtly political commentary was of course a significant defeat for the FZ. On 31 January 1933, the front page carried an article by the chief political editor Rudolf Kircher, addressed to the Hitler-Papen cabinet and titled "Under what conditions? With what guarantees?". In bold type, a central paragraph declared:

> Es wird nötig sein, die Rechte des werktätigen Volkes, die Grundelemente der Demokratie, den Sinn für Geistesfreiheit und Gerechtigkeit, die wirtschaftliche und soziale Vernunft und manches andere mit allen erdenklichen Mitteln gegen diese Regierung zu verteidigen und zur Geltung zu bringen. (FZ, 31.1.1933)

> It will be necessary to defend with all imaginable means at our disposal the rights of working people, the basic foundations of our democracy, the sense of intellectual freedom and justice, economic and social reason, and much besides, and to insist on them.

But with the ruthless consolidation of power, this programme of democratically holding a government to account proved to be an illusion. A discourse of dissent in the political sphere gave way to discourses in secondary domains, mainly in art and culture, amongst which the discourse on language would emerge, from 1936, as one of the most important. In the primary political sphere, the oversight of the Ministry was intense, with the result that the freedom of the editorial team was increasingly constrained by the 'Sprachregelungen' and 'Tagesparolen' handed down in Berlin. The language of the regime occupied the most prominent sections of the paper, and the efforts of the editorial team went into an attempt to differentiate their language from that of the regime, so that readers could recognize the provenance of texts. Frequently, decrees and speeches were given verbatim, often in quotation marks. There is little known about the reactions of the readers, or indeed who they were, as the Nazis burned the archives of the paper in March 1945 in an act of sabotage to prevent them passing into posterity. Thus, the regime determined the continuation of the FZ in 1933, its incorporation into the Franz-Eher-Verlag in 1939, its closure in 1943, and its destruction as a source of historical information in 1945. These facts demonstrate where the real power lay in this relationship, and give some indication of the extent and depth of 'Sprachlosigkeit'.

Self-understanding

The view from the paper's offices in the Eschenheimer Gasse in Frankfurt was clear from the start. The decision not to move the paper abroad was motivated by a sense of patriotism as much as a fear of exile. The FZ would set its entire cultural capital against the regime. In the words of Fritz Sänger, the regime "encountered a tradition in this newspaper which had its origins in the social and political realities and socio-political movements of the nineteenth century. This tradition had its fertile soil in the south German, western European orientation of liberal thought and was supported by the cosmopolitan openness of the then Free City of Frankfurt" (Sänger 1977, p. 275). The editors believed they could cultivate a house style which would set the voice of the FZ apart from that of the regime and the 'co-ordinated' public discourse. A 'humane' language would stand in contrast to the dictated language. An in-house list of proscribed words and expressions was drawn up which were seen as belonging to the sullied language of the times, and sections of the paper, notably the third page and the Feuilleton, were reserved as 'oases' in the desert of National Socialist verbiage. It was a strategy to retain "integrity" (Reifenberg 1964, p. 14), based on a belief that there could be a "clean" and "upright" house style which produced "distance" from the discourse of the regime by means of "style, syntax, word choice, language ethos" (Brück 1956a, p. 28). Through this linguistic ethos, the paper would stand aside from the "jargon of the time" (Wilhelm Hausenstein, quoted in Gillessen 1986, p. 364). This house style had some idiosyncratic features, for example the preference for ph over f in the spelling of a word like "Telegraph", and the avoidance of words and expressions whose Nazi connotations are not at all obvious to most German speakers today, such as "the lax WISSEN UM" (to know of) and "fixed mode words like EINMALIG (unparalleled), UNERHÖRT (unprecedented), ERLESEN (chosen), which had become insufferable" (Gillessen 1986, p. 364). Some of these expressions became the target of a hostile gloss, as in Sternberger's "Die Darumwisser" (The Know-it-alls, FZ, 5.7.1942). The shrillness of the public discourse was also a target of commentary, as in Ernst Benkard's "Das Ausrufzeichen" (The Exclamation Mark, FZ, 31.8.1940), in which the bullying exclamation mark intimidates the other punctuation signs, or the anonymous "Ablativus absolutus" (FZ, 31.12.1936), a metaphor of the language of diktat.

Today, many of the moves in this discursive struggle against Nazism seem obscure, *ad hoc*, and rather tame. The 'Sprachlosigkeit' of this position meant that a direct attack on Nazi keywords such as FÜHRER, (NICHT-)ARIER, RASSENSCHANDE (miscegenation) and DRITTES REICH (such as we find in Haecker, Kraus, and Klemperer, for example) was beyond the limits of what was sayable in print. The challenge, then, was to attack them in coded language. Alongside this negative campaign was a positive one, the central keyword of which, ideally suited to opposing racism, was MENSCH, and its derivations MENSCHLICH (human/humane), MENSCHHEIT (humanity) and MENSCHLICHKEIT (humaneness). A full-page spread on 16 May 1937, titled "Der Mensch hat das Wort" (a typically many-layered slogan[4]) programmatically endorsed this message by reproducing passages from writers and philosophers on language—Hamann, Vico, Herder, Wilhelm von Humboldt, Kierkegaard, Novalis, Schopenhauer, and Ernst Jünger. The subversive use of MENSCH and other keywords such as TREUE (fidelity, in implicit opposition to its use in Nazi discourse) did not go unnoticed in the Ministry. But academics and local Gestapo officials who tried to object to what the paper was up to were given short shrift by the Ministry and warned to keep quiet. Heinrichsdorff 1937 is one such case (cf. Hagemann 1970, p. 313).

Coverage of daily domestic and international politics in words other than those dictated by the regime became increasingly difficult, and virtually impossible once war began, and there was at least one attempt by the Propaganda Ministry, in May 1942, to use the FZ for misinformation regarding Germany's military intentions on the eastern front (Sösemann 2007, p. 27; Goebbels 1995, vol. 4, pp. 291, 319). But on occasions, editorial cunning did find a way round the strictures of the Ministry, as in the case of the announcement of the Nuremberg Race Laws in 1935.

Reporting the Race Laws

At first sight, the reporting of the Nuremberg Laws on 17 September 1935, under the simple heading "Der Wortlaut" (The Text), might appear a prime example of the paper's tactic of separating out government pronouncements from the editors' own language. But this is not the case, as a study of the accompanying 'Sprachregelungen' makes clear.[5] Any ambiguity in the directive of 16 September, which stated that an interpretation of the new laws was of course not possible at the moment, was quickly clarified in a supplementary note which stated "daß die Presse sie nicht auslegen koenne, d.h. duerfe" ("that the press cannot, that is, may not, interpret them [the new laws]", Bohrmann/Toepser-Ziegert Bd. 3/2,

p. 586). Thus, additional commentary and interpretation was expressly forbidden. But when one follows the text of the new laws onto the inside front page and looks across to page three, one finds Sternberger's article *"Ein merkwürdiges Jubiläum" (A Noteworthy Anniversary), an essay on the extraordinary coincidence that on this day one hundred years ago Charles Darwin stepped onto the Galapagos Islands, to change human history, and not for the better. A careful reading of this essay reveals the full force of this thinly coded commentary on the Race Laws.

The Language Discourse of the *Frankfurter Zeitung*: An Overview

A critique of language use has three main variants. It can focus on: (1) named speakers and their utterances on given occasions; (2) the language of identifiable groups within society (such as young people, members of occupations and professions, or people of a certain political persuasion); (3) general trends in usage in society as a whole. It is an inevitable paradox of the FZ's attempt to overcome 'Sprachlosigkeit' that most of its commentaries on language belong to the second and particularly the third of these variants. Whilst the first focuses on named individuals, the second and third tend to be aimed at unnamed or unknown persons, producing a shift in focus to the language as an apparently independent phenomenon. A clear view of language as discourse operating in a socio-pragmatic field gives way, on the surface at least, to an implied view of language as a rule-governed system of which (unidentified) users are adjuncts, if they are visible at all. That named speakers tend not to be found in these commentaries is the clearest manifestation of the critics' 'Sprachlosigkeit'. In the third variant there was, in the case of the FZ, a very noticeable shift of focus onto the feared and observed expansion of the hegemonic discourse into everyday usage, either through unreflected use by non-Nazis, or because speakers were consciously adjusting their usage in search of prestige ('little Hitlers') or indeed in an effort not to stand out from the crowd. Schopenhauer's dictum: "Fremden Stil nachahmen heißt eine Maske tragen" ("to imitate someone else's style is to wear a mask"), quoted in "Der Mensch hat das Wort" (FZ, 16.5.1937), is an ever-present, if implicit, leitmotif of this commentary on style which often takes on the character of moral philosophy, in the form of a practical manual on character and virtue—but again without naming and shaming individual speakers. In the FZ, all three variants targeted a restricted range of words and expressions. With a few remarkable exceptions, prominent ideological and administrative keywords of the regime are avoided.

The main characteristics of this discourse on language were: (1) an opportunist, *ad hoc* critique, a correlative of the "policy of pinpricks"; (2) a discourse lamenting the decline of values, centred on the 'state of the language'; (3) complaints about general language use, rarely criticizing a named speaker/writer; (4) a belief in the power of language to unmask the speaker; (5) metaphorical extensions of the concept of language as a paradigm for freedom and democracy; (6) metonymic extensions of language to its designata (which I will call the 'hinge function').

Language as a metaphor for democracy underpins many of these glosses: the bullying exclamation mark, the ablative absolute as the language of decree, the alphabet as a closed sequence to be recited or as a resource for infinite, and free, expression. The metonymic hinge function derives from the connectedness of language and the world it designates. Like the two flanges of a hinge, word and world are inextricably bound together. To speak of the use of a word typically entails speaking about objects and practices designated by that word, and the FZ authors sought to exploit the opportunity this offers to manoeuvre these objects and practices into public view. This tactic, especially in the critiquing of individual words and their use, was the precise counter-initiative, in the public arena, to the regime's attempts to dictate the meanings and therefore the uses of words. As Walter Dirks remarked, "Whoever knows how to regulate language regulates a great deal more, the ideologies, and in the extreme case the life of feelings and one's picture of the world. We wanted to resist that" (Südwestfunk 20.7.1980, quoted in Gillessen 1986, p. 367). Sternberger's "Brot kosten Geld" (Bread cost Money, FZ, 1.12.1942), for example, in reporting on a programme to teach forced labourers a rudimentary functional command of German, reveals a great deal about their conditions and the attitudes of their German masters. In many of these articles one senses a surreptitious reporting of events against the wishes of the Ministry, so that proscribed issues become tractable and are placed on public view. The covert purpose of the critique of a word was to reveal the socio-political context of its use. Today it is difficult to re-create the sensibility of the 'resistent' FZ reader, but almost certainly, many readers would be quick to pick up the slightest tangential reference to contemporary persons and events. Especially in the critiques of single words, the hinge function is subtly present. As Sternberger wrote in *"Menschen als Material" (FZ, 21.4.1940, discussed below): "A word is never just a word, it is always the precise name of a reality".

The Great Orator Hitler

Three articles engage in an explicit discussion of Hitler's use of language. The earliest of these, "Sprache und Stil" (Language and Style, FZ, 23.9.1934), by the political editor Rudolf Kircher, lays an important foundation for the subsequent language discourse which would gain serious momentum in 1936, and in particular for two later articles by Sternberger on Hitler. It is not without significance that this groundbreaking essay should be written by the paper's foremost political correspondent, author of those words of warning in January 1933, and in regular contact with leading figures of the regime. Legend has it that Kircher feared for his life during and in the aftermath of the 'Night of the Long Knives' on 30 June 1934, and left Berlin for several weeks. His article, it would appear, marks a turning point in the way the FZ would seek to engage with the regime.

Kircher focuses his concern (ostensibly, at least) not on Hitler's language, but on his unworthy imitators. This is clearly tactical, but not without risk, and probably reflects a genuine anxiety about seepage into general usage. This new way of talking, Kircher notes, is characterized by "die ganze Skala der Schwülstigkeit, des Wortpomps und der Superlative" ("the full gamut of bombast, pomp and superlatives") "gerade im Kreise der Gebildeten (und noch mehr der Gebildet-sein-wollenden)" ("in educated circles, and even more amongst those who would like to be seen as educated"). But there is also criticism of Hitler, if one reads closely. After the obligatory compliments and praise, we read: "Was er meint, wird, selbst wenn das Thema schwierig und Diktion nicht leicht ist, all denen klar, die den gleichen Ausgangspunkt zu nehmen vermögen" ("What he means, even when the topic is difficult and the diction not easy, is clear to all those who are able to share the same point of departure"). But to the uninitiated, Kircher observes, this is a struggle. In other words, Hitler's words are anything but clear. And clarity, to pick up an observation elsewhere in the text, is "unerreichbar ohne Gleichgewicht der Seele und ohne die Beherrschung ihrer Regungen durch die Kühle des Verstandes" ("not achievable without equilibrium of the soul and without mastery of its movements through the coolness of reason"). The reader who could connect these two passages understood that Kircher was warning that Hitler lacked these essential qualities. The article, closely read, is an example of Kircher's legendary "cold sarcasm" (Frei and Schmitz 1989, p. 154).

Kircher's coded critique also paints a picture of a German discourse community divided not just by ideology, but by intimidation. A comparison with the "Konfliktstimmung" (atmosphere of conflict) in the Wilhelmine era serves *ex negativo* to point up the enforced suppression of political discourse in the Nazi state, resulting in "Schweigen" (silence/falling silent). In one of the earliest and boldest proclamations of the new 'Sprachlosigkeit', Kircher declares that whilst tens of thousands are speaking the new language of Nazism (although many, it is implied, may not understand it), there are "Unzählige, die hinausschreien möchten, was sie empfinden, Menschen, die echte Nationalsozialisten sind und solche, die es nicht sind" ("countless numbers who would like to cry out what they are feeling, people who are genuine National Socialists and those who are not"). The inclusion of "genuine National Socialists" here, presumably a reference to the victims of June 30, some of them close confidants of Kircher's, may have been prompted by a belief that the author still had the right to speak to the Party in these terms. If so, it was a mistaken and dangerous ploy. Hitler, Kircher observes, is determined to communicate his message "nach der Idee der deutschen Volksgemeinschaft" ("according to the idea of the National Socialist 'Volk' community"), but the picture painted by Kircher is one of a discourse community wilfully cleft asunder by the Nazis, in contrast to that of the Kaiserzeit, which was "nicht dazu bestimmt […] große Volksteile von vornherein abzustoßen" ("not designed […] to jettison whole sections of the 'Volk' from the outset").

The main features of Kircher's strategy—a tightly constructed web of ostensible conformity and camouflaged irony, relying on the reader's ability to re-assemble disparate parts of the text carrying the oppositional commentary—are also found in two pieces by Sternberger in 1937. "Tempel der Kunst" (Temple of Art, FZ, 19.7.1937) and "Ein guter Ausdruck" (A Good Expression, FZ, 22.8.1937). In the first of these, Sternberger, deputed to report on the opening of the Haus deutscher Kunst (House of German Art) in Munich on 17 July 1937, fell into a hapless attempt at an ironic paraphrase of Hitler's opening speech, despite beginning promisingly with the observation that it was "obwohl verzweigt, deutlich und entschieden genug" ("although *verzweigt*, clear and decisive enough"). It is difficult to find a polite equivalent in English for "verzweigt" (branching, multi-faceted?), but the immediate colloquial word that springs to mind is "rambling" (and the echoes of Kircher are unmistakeable here.) But as the article progresses, the strategy of ironic 'Imitat' loses its edge, leaving, to the untrained ear, a mere paraphrase of the speech, including the section headed "Deutsch sein heißt klar sein" ("To be German means to be clear")—a saying much loved by Hitler. It is no coincidence that Walter Benjamin, in exile in Paris, and a hostile reader of the FZ, underlined this passage in Sternberger's piece as evidence of his perfidy (Dodd 2007, pp. 101–106, 191–196; Dodd 2008). The problem of the ironic 'Imitat' as a device, especially in such a prominent place, is well illustrated by this case. As Rudolf Stöber (2010, p. 291) observes, this technique was successful only "wenn der Leser den NS-Stil erkannte, den FZ-Artikel als Imitat der offiziellen Sprache identifizierte, als Kontrast zur ansonsten in der FZ gepflegten Diktion interpretierte und die Diskrepanz als bewusste Distanzierung wahrnahm" ("if the reader recognized the Nazi style and identified the FZ article as an 'Imitat' of the official language, as a contrast to the diction cultivated elsewhere in the FZ, and registered the discrepancy as an act of deliberate distancing").

Sternberger's subsequent article, "Ein guter Ausdruck", looks like a second attempt on the target, from a greater spatial and temporal distance, an act of some daring, indeed, but also, perhaps, motivated by shame and anger over the compromised first attempt. This piece, which, unusually, occupied the title page and provided the front page headline, contains a remarkable example of an *ad hominem* attack on Hitler. Closely read, its message is as forthright as that of Kraus writing in Vienna, or Haecker in his secret Munich diary. The concluding paragraph, found on page three, ostensibly reproduces the standard tribute to the Führer's vision and oratory:

> Die von Adolf Hitler gebrauchte Definition "Deutsch sein heißt klar sein" verpflichtet auch im Bereich der Sprache und gerade dort. Denn ein guter, das ist ein genauer, bewegter, tüchtiger, bildlich treffender und also wahrhaft "gebildeter" Ausdruck ist so viel wert als ein guter Gedanke. Indem man sprechen lernt, lernt man sogleich auch denken. Und was wäre nützlicher, was auch angenehmer als dies?
>
> The definition given by Adolf Hitler, "To be German is to be clear", also lays obligations on us in the sphere of language, and especially there. For a good, that is to say a precise, emotionally felt, honest, visually striking and therefore truly "well formed" expression is worth as much as a good thought. As we learn to speak, we learn at the same time to think. And what could be more useful, more enjoyable than this?

A 'resistent' reading of the article as a whole, however, reveals the daring irony of this 'Imitat' of a tribute which notably withholds the title of FÜHRER from the man whose sentence, measured by the standards set out in the article, is a platitudinous self-contradiction, one of those modes of speaking which, to quote from an earlier passage in the article, "sich freilich mit einem gewissen Brustton füllen lassen und dem Sprecher Bedeutung zu verleihen scheinen" ("are filled with a certain sonorous tone and appear to endow the speaker with importance"). The style is the man, we infer, and Hitler's sentence is indeed a "good expression" because it lays bare the man's dangerous vagueness. To be German is to be clear—about what, exactly?

Other articles may well have contained coded references to specific individuals, as in two of Sternberger's glosses on proverbs, for example, discussed below. In "Zwischen A und B" (Between A and B, FZ, 28.4.1936), the warning against "Verführer" (seducers) could allude to

Goebbels or indeed the Führer himself. As in "Ein guter Ausdruck", the implied question here is: What exactly are Germans being asked to sign up to? In the final section of *"Blick der Liebenden" (The Lovers' Gaze, FZ, 5.4.1936), 'resistent' readers may well have detected a word picture of the Führer as a petulant and dangerous spoilt child.

Critiquing the Language of Groups

A critique of language belonging to a recognizable group, but without named speakers, forms an intermediate stage in the movement away from *ad hominem* critiques. This variant, too, is relatively uncommon in the FZ. The campaign against the word DURCHFÜHREN (to implement, carry out, push through), for example in "Kuriose Heilswege" (Curious Cures, FZ, 19.7.1936) is an example of a thinly concealed critique of fascist governmental language (and policies). The metonymic hinge function of the key lexical field HEIL/HEILEN, already alluded to in the title, extends the commentary to the policy of racial 'hygiene' which was being "durchgeführt" (rolled out) by decree over the hapless Germans in 1936. Posing as a philosophical reflection on illusory universal remedies (using the metaphor of perpetual motion machines) in a world full of problems, the essay ends with a warning about the current pedlars and their "curious cures":

> Zumal, wenn man sich dem in jüngster Zeit üblich gewordenen Wunsche anschließt, die nationalsozialistische Staatsführung möchte im Verordnungswege das jeweilige Heilsprogramm oder Erneuerungssystem kurzerhand "durchführen". Nicht so hoffnungsvoll und sehr bedenklich gegenüber allen deutenden Reden von "dem Geist der Zeit" stimmt hingegen der Blick in das Labyrinth des *wirklichen* Geisteslebens, zu welchem alle diese kuriosen Wege und krummen Gänge (indem sie doch auf lichte Höhen zu führen meinen) sich zusammensetzen. Das Dunkel, das darin herrscht, ist so eigenwillig, daß das Licht der Vernunft es nur selten zu durchdringen vermag.

> Especially if one signs up to the recently widespread wish that the National Socialist government should simply roll out [durchführen] the latest programme of cures or system of renewal by decree. But a glance into the

> labyrinth of *real* life on which all these curious cures and crooked paths converge (although they say they will lead to the sunlit heights) does not inspire one with hope, it is worrying. The darkness reigning there is so wilful that the light of reason is able to penetrate it only rarely.

Somewhat more obliquely, an elite discourse is targeted in a lead article, "Deutsch reden" (Speaking German, FZ, 19.6.1941), which takes exception to the notion of "soldiers of the language" propagated by the Deutsche Akademie under the directorship of August Miller (a rare example of an institution and a person being mentioned by name), with which—in a reprise of Engel and Chamberlain's linguistic imperialism of 1914 (see Chap. 2)—the war is greeted as an opportunity to impose German on conquered territories.

A rather different but equally subversive example of this kind of commentary is Erik von Wickenburg's "Soldatenausdrücke" (Soldiers' Expressions, FZ, 2.6.1942), reporting on overheard conversations between recruits in the junior ranks. Wickenburg speculates on the psychology of this class of recruit to the "Verein für deutliche Aussprache" (Association for Plain Speaking), as the soldiers refer to themselves, before giving examples of current slang expressions used by the lower ranks for debunking the braided uniforms of their decorated superiors, including RAUPENSCHLEPPER (caterpillar track) and ALLERHEILIGENSTRIETZEL (All Saints braid—a pastry design). Although presented as a light entertainment, Wickenburg's article reveals the fault lines in the myth of the unified VOLKSGEMEINSCHAFT, and could conceivably have incurred the charge of WEHRKRAFTZERSETZUNG (undermining morale).

Critiquing Unknown and Unnamed Speakers

The greater part of the language criticism in the FZ, however, belongs to the third variant, the commentary on general trends in society as a whole, and here especially the lack of a clearly identified target is noticeable. In consequence, this commentary on language runs the risk of appearing to hypostasize language as a force in its own right, making of it an independent, autonomous entity free from human agency. There is a certain irony in the fact that the campaign whose rallying keyword was Mensch and whose rallying call was "Der Mensch hat das Wort" was fought out mainly in this third variant, impelled by the fear of the creeping influence of Nazi discourse and values on everyday language and thought. The general avoidance of naming individual speakers is paralleled by a similar avoidance of prominent National Socialist keywords—the critique of durchführen perhaps coming closest to that position. Nevertheless, this third variant did have some notable successes in commentaries on proverbs and individual words.

On the Use of Proverbs

Between March and June 1936 (perhaps significantly, just before the Berlin Olympics when the regime was intent on projecting a positive image abroad), the FZ published a series of nine glosses by Sternberger, a "Vademecum zum Gebrauch von Sprichwörtern" (Guide to the Use of Proverbs). By this time all hopes that the regime would collapse had vanished, indeed it was enjoying considerable acceptance among Germans in light of the forthcoming Olympiad. Sternberger's stated aim, in an Introduction to the first gloss, was to expose the illusion of consolation ("Trost") such proverbs provided for those suffering life's setbacks. In thinly coded commentaries, these glosses were calls to resist both the coercion to conform and the illusory solace which confers a kind of spiritual nobility and moral superiority on the powerless victims and opponents of the regime as they shrug their shoulders in acquiescence. As Sternberger observed, the meaning of proverbs lies quintessentially in their use by particular individuals in particular discursive situations. The Vademecum betrays the author's anxiety that these encapsulations of folk wisdom were now increasingly serving to endorse the National Socialist worldview and reconcile non-Nazis with their gestures of resignation.

The proverbs chosen for this analysis were: (1) Es wird nichts so heiss gegessen, wie es gekocht ist (No meal is served as hot as it is cooked in the kitchen) ("Das heiße Essen", FZ, 15.3.1936); (2) Eine Krähe hackt der anderen kein Auge aus (One crow does not hack out the eye of another) ("Krähen untereinander", FZ, 22.3.1936);

(3) Liebe macht blind (Love is blind) ("Blick der Liebenden", FZ, 5.4.1936); (4) Wer a sagt, muss auch b sagen (If you say A you have to say B) ("Zwischen A und B", FZ, 28.4.1936); (5) Kinder und Narren sagen die Wahrheit (Children and fools speak the truth) ("Das Asyl der Wahrheit", FZ, 3.5.1936); (6) Ende gut, alles gut (All's well that ends well) ("Ende gut, alles gut", FZ, 10.5.1936); (7) Dummheit und Stolz wachsen auf einem Holz (Stupidity and pride grow on the same branch) ("Der stolze Dumme und der dumme Stolze") (FZ, 26.5.1936); (8) Es ist noch nicht aller Tage Abend (We're not at the Last Judgment just yet) ("Aller Tage Abend", FZ, 7.6.1936); (9) Es sind die schlechtesten Früchte nicht, woran die Wespen nagen (The wasps never go for the worst fruit) ("Frucht und Wespe", FZ, 30.6.1936).

To greatly simplify Sternberger's commentaries, their gist is as follows: (1) If you keep believing this, you will end up getting burned; (2) On the contrary, one crow will attack another, to save itself; (3) Love makes us see, custom makes us blind; (4) Did you really say A? The coercive alphabet of Satan has no A, it begins with B, and who knows what you will be saying when you get to Z?; (5) This is true, and a sad reflection on the rest of us; (6) In other words: the end justifies the means?; (7) This is true, although there are many combinations. We see vanity making people stupid, and stupidity making people vain; (8) Saying this simply postpones the Day of Judgment forever. It will come, and you will have to account for your actions. Every day is a day of judgment; (9) Why blame wasps for doing what wasps do? And how comforting to ennoble their victims and to identify with them after the event. A fuller discussion of these glosses, and their intricate allusions and insinuations, is given in Dodd 2007 (pp. 177–191).

The outline given in the preceding paragraph may give some idea of the discourse environment being targeted in the Vademecum: coercion to fall in line, to share complicity; resignation in the face of insuperable power; excuses to remain passive, whilst retaining a sense of integrity; the Nazis as a force of nature (crows, wasps); fond hopes that their words won't be translated into deeds; their appeal to the vain and stupid; warnings to be careful what you say (the truth is dangerous); acceptance of the new norms and abdication of all personal responsibility.

In order to give a deeper insight into the critiques contained in these glosses, it may be helpful to review one in more detail. The third gloss, *"Blick der Liebenden", is reproduced in the Appendix, with an English translation. In reading it, we need to try to put ourselves in the position of the 'resistent' German reader in 1936. This means seeing what is not there on the surface of the text because 'Sprachlosigkeit' forbade it. But conversely, the particular conditions of this 'Sprachlosigkeit' meant that it did not need to be on the surface of the public text. Today the piece may seem innocuous and over-written, but in spring 1936, just six months after the Nuremberg Race Laws, the pragmatic force of LOVE IS BLIND in many German conversations was perfectly clear: its use was racialized. Although the words JUDE, MISCHEHE (mixed marriage) and RASSENSCHANDE (miscegenation) are not found in this text, they were accessible in the sub-text. Readers who, like Sternberger, had a Jewish spouse, would certainly see that their own situation was being addressed in this gloss. Love affairs between a Jew and an 'Aryan' had become an existential threat to both. The pressure, particularly on the 'Aryan' to separate from the Jewish partner, was immense. Some Jewish partners agreed to separation out of love for their spouse and children, whilst others were effectively abandoned by their 'Aryan' partner in an act of political accommodation. It is against these betrayers of love, one senses, that Sternberger's invective is directed. To the keywords which are found only in the sub-text, one could add a positive one: TREUE—faithfulness in the face of custom ("Gewohnheit") which saps love and makes the husband abandon his wife so he can return to the company of friends in the pub and the café. But then the commentary abruptly alters tack. The last six sentences assert that there is one case in which the proverb is justified. These sentences have a quite different target—Adolf Hitler. He is the man who is falsely declaiming his love, parading his labours and sacrifices, demanding to be loved, out of complacency or insecurity. In this case, it is for the German people to stand up and denounce *his* blindness. But, the final sentence asks, at what cost? (A literal translation of this sentence is: "The cataract in this blind man's eye can be lanced only at the cost of great pain".) If this reading of "Blick der Liebenden" accurately captures its historical 'Resistenz', it demonstrates a curious paradox in the discourse community of the 'Third Reich': the very ubiquity of 'Sprachlosigkeit' massively expanded the competence of writers and readers to talk about their circumstances without referring to them literally. Compare especially the absence of the word 'Spitzel' (informer) from Storz's *"Der 'Angeber'" ("The Blagger/Informant", FZ, 23.3.1941), discussed in the next section.

The Word as a Window on Worldview

Commentary on the use and meaning of a single word ('Einzelwortkritik') is the stock-in trade of popular journalistic language criticism. This tradition is also closely associated with value conservatism: changing use is generally construed as wrong use, and as evidence of declining standards. 'Modish' innovations are frowned upon. It is not surprising, then, that 'Einzelwortkritik' was the favoured mode of language criticism in the FZ. Even today, the best of these glosses open a window on the social and political contexts of use: in addition to DURCHFÜHREN, the list includes ANGEBER (bragger/informer, FZ 23.3.1941), RAUM (room, space, FZ, 9.4.1940, 5.5.1940), KRANKENMATERIAL (human pathology) and MENSCHENMATERIAL (human material, FZ, 21.4.1940), VÖLKISCH, VOLKHAFT (FZ, 7.8.1942), FRONTABSCHNITT WISSENSCHAFT (science as front line, FZ, 8.5.1937), ZUGRIFF (grip, FZ, 10.12.1942), LEISTUNG (achievement, work, FZ, 20.10.1942) and UMBETREUUNG (redesignating industries as part of the war economy, FZ, 26.9.1942). In the case of RAUM, two articles engage on an apparently light-hearted discussion on the increasing geopolitical use of this word. Erik Graf Wickenburg's "Räume" (FZ, 9.4.1940), bemoaning the grandiose use of the humble RAUM, prompted a response, allegedly from an (unidentified) reader, which reignited the debate in "Für und gegen den 'Raum'" (For and against 'Raum', FZ, 5.5.1940). A staged debate ensued as to whether the word, more diffuse in its semantics than other geographical terms such as 'country' or 'region', can be said to be "innocent" but misused by "gossips, inflated egos, and the self-important". But amidst the banter there is also serious political comment: in its new, geopolitical use, RAUM is found to have a touch of the (pseudo-)scientific, designating an undefined area of territory and not only the land, but, more importantly, the space above (Luft-Raum, airspace) and below the ground, where valuable natural resources are to be found. Without mentioning the most obvious member of the word family, Lebensraum, a discourse of territorial expansionism and its material motivations is called into view.

After Sternberger, Gerhard Storz (later to become Minister of Culture in Baden-Württemberg) was the most prolific contributor to the language discourse in the FZ. Two of his glosses deserve special mention here. A brilliant philologist and literary critic, his erudite pieces, one suspects, were too densely argued for the average censor. The persistent reader, however, was rewarded. *"Der 'Angeber'" (FZ, 23.3.1941) is a schoolmasterly discussion of the changing use of the word. For Storz's pupil (he was at the time a schoolteacher in Schwäbisch Hall) the word denotes a show-off, whilst for Storz's generation the word's primary meaning has always been 'informer'. In a *tour de force* of learned misdirection, and with breathtaking irony, Storz deliberates on the reasons why the old meaning is falling out of use. Of course, there is no need for it, he muses, as there are no informers in Germany. The reader who tuned in to the (outrageous) irony of this piece would readily have identified the everyday word all Germans knew but which could not be mentioned here: Spitzel (informer, 'grass'). This gloss is a classic example of the uses of the hinge function and the defiance of 'Sprachlosigkeit' in breaking through the limits of the sayable. On a 'resistent' reading, the hermeneutic circle is closed, reader and author united in subversive insight: "We are surrounded by informers but cannot say it". Equally impressive is Storz's learned philological disputation on lexical suffixes in the word family 'volkhaft'/'volklich'/'völkisch' (FZ, 7.8.1942), in a dense but humorously revealing study of their different ideological, semantic, and by implication, pragmatic positions. Storz demonstrates the clear distinction between the purely descriptive volkhaft (typical of or pertaining to a people) and the appellative and evaluative völkisch, establishes that this semantic demarcation is being lost in contemporary usage, and condemns this woolly ("schwammig") usage as unfounded. Presented with philological meticulousness as a "chapter on suffixes", it is designed to defeat even the most conscientious censor, who would surely have given up before the examples are listed. Only the most dedicated reader will persevere and notice that Storz's examples seem to suggest that the relationship of VOLKLICH (pertaining to a people) to VÖLKISCH is likened to that between 'kindlich' (childlike) and 'kindisch' (childish). The more recent derivation pattern in '–isch' is said to belong to "the exemplary present". One target of this commentary appears to be speakers who began to use VOLKHAFT to create an ingratiating but ambiguous kind of 'mood music' suggesting a general conformity with the ideological and political implications of the aggressively racist VÖLKISCH, without actually using that word. This opportunistic use of VOLKHAFT was also noticed, as we saw in Chap. 4, by Seidel and Seidel-Slotty (1961, pp. 139–142) in the writings of Leo Weisgerber. Storz's piece, in conformity with the FZ practice, mentions no names.

"A word is never just a word, it is the precise name of a reality." This sentence is found in Sternberger's *"Menschen als Material" (Human Beings as Material, 21.4.1940), arguably the most daring example of a word gloss in the whole of the FZ's campaign (cf. Dodd 2007, pp. 207–210). Ostensibly a commentary on the scruples some doctors were displaying about using the term KRANKENMATERIAL (pathology) to refer to their patients,[6] the real force of this gloss results from the hinge function of the half dozen words it thematizes in a *tour de force* of misdirection, not least in the excursus into the role of the 'Fremdwort' 'Krankengut'. The oblique invocation of (long-since emasculated) lexical purism in this article is a diversionary tactic helping to disguise the structural ploy which allows Sternberger to forge a link between the initial medical discourse on human beings as exemplars of pathology (KRANKENMATERIAL) and the discourse—invoked, but not specified, at the end of the article—of the völkisch ideology of superior Germanic stock ((ERSTKLASSIGES) MENSCHENMATERIAL). Without the feint towards the 'Fremdwort' question, the references to "Güterzüge" and "Güterbahnhöfe" (words with immediate and specific associations for many readers in 1940) in this tightly-constructed revelatory piece would not be possible. The 'Fremdwort' detour provides a crucial link in the lexical chain which runs through the article: MENSCH—MATERIAL—GUT ('Güter'—'Güterzüge'—'Güterbahnhöfe')—TRANSPORTIEREN: (human being—material ['Fremdwort']—material [German word] (goods—goods trains—goods stations)—to transport), a sequence which darkly alludes to what members of the 'master race', the (ERSTKLASSIGES) MENSCHENMATERIAL (first class human material), mentioned at the close of the article (and a key term in nationalist biological discourses since the nineteenth century, cf. Mehring 1960, p. 142; Schmitz-Berning 2000, pp. 399–403) are doing to the KRANKENMATERIAL mentioned at the beginning. The dramatic 'resistent' reading contained in this article can be constructed by placing the keywords, in order of occurrence, in a simple passive sentence: KRANKENMATERIAL is regarded as a GUT, as MATERIAL and such MATERIAL can be/is being TRANSPORTIERT using GÜTERZÜGE and GÜTERBAHNHÖFE, supervised by those who consider themselves ERSTKLASSIGES MATERIAL. Amongst the real-world events to which the gloss alludes, readers may well have identified the racial 'hygiene' programmes initiated already in 1933, the euthanasia programme since 1939, and more recently the deportations from occupied territories, which had begun to circulate in the German population, as we saw in Chap. 5, through soldiers returning on leave. A strictly confidential 'Pressekonferenz' instruction dated 9.2.1940 about the "Germanisierung" of the Warthegau in western Poland, which Sternberger may well have known about, had concluded "Es gilt dort 350.000 Juden loszuwerden" ("The objective is to get rid of 350,000 Jews there", cf. Gillessen 1986, p. 449f.). In the year 2000, MENSCHENMATERIAL was chosen as the 'Unwort' (abominable word) of the Twentieth Century (see Chap. 9). Sternberger's little-known gloss adds importantly to our understanding of the reasons underpinning this choice.

Critiquing Style: Syntax Meets Politics

Whilst the critiques of single words contain some of the boldest and most brilliant exposés of the regime, the critique of what the editors saw as a fascist style must be counted less satisfactory, at least from today's vantage point. This not to say, however, that it did not resonate with readers at the time. Stylistics is here understood as the study of stretches of discourse larger than the word, and crucially of features which display speakers' linguistic choices when not subject to the constraints of grammar. This takes us into an analysis of running text and syntactic phenomena such as clause structure and (in written text) sequences of sentences; into questions of choice regarding the ordering of elements in a sequence; and, in spoken language, into questions of tone, intonation, and loudness. It also entails analysing the choice between available grammatical options, most obviously in the choice between active and passive constructions, or between verb-centred and noun-centred constructions.

There are points of convergence and agreement here with the analysis of Seidel/Seidel-Slotty (see Chap. 5), the two main ones being the shrillness of tone in the public sphere, and the increased use of nominal style in written and spoken texts, in which the verb is relegated from prominence, often being reduced to a semantically empty place holder in an utterance or sentence dominated by (de-verbal) nouns. As Kraus's lampoon in *Dritte Walpurgisnacht* (see Chap. 4) shows, opponents of Nazism frequently identified an excess of nominalized style as one of its distinctive linguistic markers.

The shrillness of tone in the public space was the butt of lightly ironic commentaries. Theodor Heuss wrote of the "loudspeaker" which language had become (FZ, 9.5.1937). Ernst Benkard's article "Das Ausrufzeichen" humorously presented the exclamation mark as the new boss of all the punctuation marks, which cowered before it (FZ, 31.8.1940). An article on the "Trumped Superlative" (FZ, 1.8.1936, possibly by Hans Kallmann) gently lampooned the inflated use of hyperbole. Fritz Kraus called for a return to a trim or trimmed use of language (FZ, 28.1.1938). Even a gloss on the use of the ablaut (FZ, 10.9.1936) belongs in this category. Superficially, what was at issue here was the correct grammatical form of the imperative (also found in Kraus' *Dritte Walpurgisnacht*, see Chap. 4). But in the FZ article, the real issue is the false tone in the example given: "TRETE/TRITT EIN IN DIE NSV!" ("Join the NSV!" ['Nationalsozialistische Volkswohlfahrt', the National Socialist People's Welfare organisation]). Here, the grammatical uncertainty regarding the second person singular form of the verb, it is implied, unwittingly reveals a clumsy attempt to disguise a command (in reality, joining the NSV was often not a voluntary act) as a friendly commendation. This example illustrates an underlying tenet of the FZ campaign on language, that (to put it in Schopenhauer's words, quoted in "Der Mensch hat das Wort") "Der Stil ist die Physiognomie des Geistes. Sie ist untrüglicher als die des Leibes" ("Style is the physiognomy of the spirit. It is less capable of deception than that of the body").

The spread of nominalized style was viewed with suspicion in glosses such as "Verschriebene Schreiber" (Sternberger, FZ, 6.6.1937), "Das Universalverbum" (FZ, 28.1.1940), "Unbegrenzte Fähigkeiten?" (Storz, FZ, 14.2.1943), and "Unter Beweis stellen" (FZ, 9.5.1942). This last example serves to illustrate the point: instead of using the verb 'beweisen' (to prove), a de-verbal noun is created, accompanied by a semantically empty verb (STELLEN, to place). Other verbs identified for their role in abetting this "Substantivitis" included ERFOLGEN, STATTFINDEN, GESTALTEN, and, most prominently, DURCHFÜHREN.[7] The FZ authors, and Storz in particular, saw these constructions as a device to undermine the semantic transparency of plain language (subject—verb—object: instigator of the action—action—recipient of the action) in order to present a static inventorized view of the world as *fait accompli* through thinking in nouns ("das substantivische Denken", Storz, FZ, 14.2.1943). Grammatical structures thus created "Gedankenbahnen in der Sprache" (Thought Paths in the Language, Storz, FZ, 18.4.1942) with potentially ominous consequences for freedom of thought. Sternberger lampooned this trend in "Verschriebene Schreiber" (Writers who have lost the plot, FZ, 6.6.1937): "Und der Gipfel der Wonne wird erreicht, wenn man es fertigbringt, die Gestaltung etwa eines Feierabends durchzuführen" ("And the summit of joy seems to be attained when one manages to DURCHFÜHREN [implement] the GESTALTUNG [formation] of, let's say, a night out"). The example is manufactured (also a feature of this language discourse) for sarcastic effect, but seems to reflect a real trend in language use which was noted, for example, by Seidel/Seidel-Slotty. In "Das Universalverbum" Sternberger gave a more sober critique of the "Übermacht der Dingwörter" ("excessive power of thing-words"):

> Alle Handlung [...] schrumpft und verhärtet sich zum Ding, und solches Ding kann dann nur noch durchgeführt werden. Wo der Vorgang, das Geschehen, der Prozeß, die Geschichte anfangen sollte—da ist nun nichts mehr übrig, da ist es leer, und in diese Leere hinein wird nun durchgeführt. Das Durchführen (und das Erfolgen) will das bewußte Handeln und das vielfältige Geschehen selber verdrängen. So wissen wir wenigstens, wessen wir uns schuldig machen, indem wir das Universalverbum gebrauchen.

> All action […] shrinks and hardens into a thing, and this thing can then only be implemented [durchgeführt]. Where the course of action, the event, the process, the story ought to begin, there is nothing left, an empty space, and everything gets durchgeführt into this empty space. All this durchführ-ing (and erfolg-ing) is intended to banish conscious doing and the many different ways in which things happen. So we know, at least, what we make ourselves guilty of when we use the Universal Verb.

It is worth dwelling on the last sentence of this passage, which speaks of the guilt "we" incur in adopting this way of speaking. Here the sensitized outsider trapped in inner exile includes himself and his readers in the potential ranks of the linguistically culpable. This is quite different from Kraus critiquing the nominal style of Nazi pronouncements. Kraus's was a view from the outside: "This is how *they* talk".

The limits of this approach to fascist language also need to be noted, however; for example when we find the very same objection to "universal verb" constructions within the fascist discourse. A notable example is found in 1941 in the pages of *Deutsche Presse*, the journal of the embedded Propaganda Companies who reported from the front on military actions. There we find exactly the same objections raised in a gloss by Karl Friedrich Baberadt, sometime correspondent of the FZ:

> Da ist zuerst das fürchterliche und, ach so bequeme *durchführen*! Ist es wirklich notwendig, zu sagen: "… ihre Ausmerzung durchzuführen" oder klingt es nicht besser, zu sagen: "… sie ausmerzen"? (Baberadt 1941)[8]

> Then there is the terrible and oh so convenient *durchführen*! Is it really necessary to say "… carry out their extermination" or is it not better to say "… exterminate them"?

This counter-example is a sobering reminder of the limitations of the FZ campaign in so far as here we apparently have a representative of a movement for 'plain speaking' who objects on aesthetic but also on ethical grounds to dressing up actions of warfare in stylized nominalized language.

A related concern in the FZ was the use of syntactic constructions to deprive free human subjects of their autonomy. Here, grammar and moral philosophy blend in the use of the concepts 'subject', 'object', 'active' and 'passive', and syntactic choices are revealed to be motivated by intentions that are fundamentally "unmenschlich". The fear was that citizens were being converted, and not just in the discourse, from free subjects into manipulable objects. Storz wrote on the dangers of this discursively created passive human subject, for example in "Unbegrenzte Fähigkeiten?" (Unlimited Capabilities?, FZ, 14.2.1943), hinting that the logical end-point of this trend was cannibalism. An important complement was the campaign against a perceived increase in the use of transitive verbs beginning with the prefix 'be-', in preference to alternative constructions. In German, verbs with this prefix take a direct object in the accusative case. Shortly before the enforced closure of the FZ, Walter Dirks delivered an impassioned broadside ("Bekochen und beschirmen", FZ, 25.8.1943), listing scores of such verbs and insinuating their antidemocratic credentials. The argument, to take Dirks's example, was that it was a humane thing to cook a meal for someone ('für jemanden/jemandem etwas kochen'), but a usurpation of their autonomy to 'becook' them (JEMANDEN BEKOCHEN). The anger and frustration directed at a sub-set of the lexical and syntactic system of the German language may seem fanciful today, but the underlying thesis (presented with rather more sophistication than in Sternberger's reprise of it in the "Lexicon of the 'Unmensch'") has a substantive point: the language of care ('taking care of' others) can readily be recruited to a dehumanizing discourse of patronage and control.

The Demise of the 'Fremdwort' Issue and 'German Script'

There are responses in the FZ to the double *coup de grâce* delivered belatedly by the regime to two aspiring nostrums of linguistic fascism: lexical purism and the so-called DEUTSCHE SCHRIFT, 'Fraktur'. As noted in Chap. 3, Hitler's decree of 19 November 1940 finally (after Goebbels's orchestrated attack on Eduard Engel's Jewishness in 1937) killed off the 'Fremdwort' question as a political issue and ended any political aspirations of 'völkisch' language enthusiasts to claim BLUT UND BODEN status for the 'Muttersprache'. It is interesting that even after the fall of Engel, an opportunistic, and gleeful mocking of the "Fremdwort hunters" continues,[9] for example in Theodor Heuss's article on 'völkisch' purists (13.6.1937) and Storz's reviews of Storfer 1937 (19.9.1937) and Jancke 1938 (13.3.1938, in which Storz also commends Jancke's gloss "GROSSUNFUG" (monumental nonsense, Jahnke 1938, p. 89f., cf. Dodd 2013, p. 120), a lampoon on the spread of compounds beginning 'Groß-'). Two articles deserve special mention here. Storz's "Der Eifer für die Sprache" (Zeal for the Language, FZ, 13.6.1937) is a carefully crafted rejection of Ewald Geißler's advocacy, at the 1937 Conference of the Language Association, of "artbegründete Sprachzucht" ("racially grounded cultivation of the language") and his demand, in *Sprache als Rassenpflicht* (Language as Racial Duty) for a consistent "WORTAUFARTUNG" ("racial alignment of the lexis").[10] Although Geißler and the Language Association are not mentioned in Storz's reply, the targets of his piece would be clear to many readers, most clearly in Storz's rejection of the concept of WORTAUFARTUNG. His response to this racialized approach to language is clear: love for one's own language, yes, but not through hatred of the foreign.

As was also noted in Chap. 3, the decree in January 1941 announcing that 'Fraktur' was to be abandoned in favour of 'Antiqua' (now to be called DEUTSCHE NORMALSCHRIFT) demolished long-held assumptions, on the political left as well as the right, about the print iconography of Germannness. Whereas party publications tended to report this decision as a matter of fact, the "seismographic shock" (Rück 1993, p. 231) caused by this announcement was reflected in the FZ, which sought to spice factual reporting with a hint of critical comment in the unsigned articles "Die neue 'deutsche Normalschrift'" (FZ, 13.9.1941) and "Hand-Schrift" (FZ, 14.9.1941). The first of these, with the raised-eyebrow quotation marks in the title, contains a detailed description of the new orthography, including graphic illustrations, not dissimilar to those in a primary school textbook, of how the letters of the alphabet are now to be written. It concludes with the observation: "Die Veränderung, die der Erlaß einleitet, hat also keine geringe Bedeutung für den ganzen Habitus des Schreibenden" ("The change which the decree introduces has, therefore, no little significance for the entire habitus of the writer"). The change-over to 'Antiqua' in the FZ is formally and factually announced on 5 April 1942. In the 1942 Christmas Day edition—a favoured time for pieces in the Feuilleton reflecting on major ethical challenges of the day—Sternberger published an essay "Über die Nachahmung" (On Imitation), in which he reflected on his own unsettled sense of identity in relation to his handwriting, and his sense of shame when he finds himself writing a 'sharp s' (*ſ*) instead of an ordinary s in copying out a seventeenth-century manuscript. This leads to an intense philosophical reflection, with reference to Immanuel Kant, on character and the aesthetic and moral implications of our individual style, which begins of necessity in imitation before developing, if it does develop, into self-fashioned freedom. The letters, or "characters", of the alphabet are the main actors in this drama, in which language as a metaphor for freedom and allusions to the present day are not far beneath the surface. The theme of inauthentic and often unconscious imitation, a recurrent concern of the FZ's language discourse, is particularly intense in this essay, in which Sternberger's professed pangs of conscience seem ludicrously overstated if one is talking just about the shape of a letter:

> Was für eine Unselbständigkeit! Dieses kleine gedrungene, manchmal etwas knorpelige runde "s" war doch einmal das meinige. Mußte ich ihm nicht die Treue wahren? Ihm?—nein: mir selbst hätte ich sie wahren müssen (denn nun war es ja schon geschehen, der Verrat begangen und perfekt).

> What an act of dependency! This small, compressed, sometimes rather ungainly "s" was, after all, once my own. Did I not have to be loyal to him? No, it was to myself I should have been loyal (for now it was too late, the betrayal was done and complete).

Is it far-fetched to imagine that a 'resistent' reading invoked the aesthetic seductions of Nazism, particularly in the use of "German script"? A close contemporary analogue to deserting the plain and honest s for the flamboyant *ſ*, in that case, might be found in the then ubiquitous cultic Siegrune ϟ. The 1942 analogues, once located, render the urgency of Sternberger's soul-searching understandable, together with the Kantian warning of the dangers of slavish imitation with which he concludes: "Nachahmung ist menschlich, nur Nachäffung ist äffisch" (Literally: "Imitation is human, only aping is ape-like").

The Unspeakable Objection to Reifferscheidt (1939/1940)

As was the case in *Hochland*, books on language with 'resistent' potential were favourably reviewed in the FZ, indeed the book review was a favoured genre in this discourse. When faced with books which endorsed 'völkisch' positions, however, the review often resorted to proxy arguments. A case in point is the publication of F. M. Reifferscheidt's *Über die Sprache*, which led to an intense exchange[11] between Reifferscheidt and Sternberger in the FZ.[12] Reading these exchanges today, one has the impression of a philosophical difference being aired in public: Reifferscheidt is presented as a proponent of an elite view of language as a shrine, to which speakers must pledge allegiance (Speakers must serve their language), whereas Sternberger insists that language is the property of individual human beings, whose 'lowly' use of it is also worthy of respect (Language must serve its speakers). Only when we turn to Reifferscheidt's book does a deeper reason for this public argument become apparent. As Clemens Knobloch (2005, p. 84f.) observes, *Über die Sprache* stands in a tradition which "despite occasional brickbats aimed at the National Socialists, in many respects pays obeisance to a substrate of NS ideology", containing "a potpourri of strategies typical amongst the 'educated' which can be mobilised in the form of language for including and excluding" whole groups of speakers, in effect mirroring the binary friend/foe discourse of the regime. Knobloch's analysis is helpful in revealing just how closely some strands of conservative language criticism could run alongside the fascist discourse, even whilst taking aim (as Reifferscheidt had done in the pages of *Hochland*) at some of its manifestations. For example, Reifferscheidt's comments on the current state of American English ("ein immer dürftiger werdendes Natur-Volapük, das sich am Ende nur noch für die Verkaufswerbung eignet":

"an increasingly deficient natural volapuk which at the end of the day is only good for advertising", Reifferscheidt 1939, p. 75) and on the Jews' relation to language ("das Volk ohne Sprache"), the people who have given up and lost their language "um der Gewalt über anderen willen": for the sake of gaining power over others, and who therefore bear the sign of their demise on their brows ("das Zeichen des Untergangs auf der Stirn", p. 96) reveal proto-fascist and racist attitudes which were, presumably, the real bone of contention for Sternberger—although, of course, he could not say this in the pages of the FZ. The negatively connoted "volapuk", for example (according to the OED "an artificial language, invented by the German priest Johann M. Schleyer as a means of international communication") echoes 'völkisch' scorn for the artificial language Esperanto. Reifferscheidt's book, in Knobloch's words, reproduces "the widespread 'anthropological' ("völkerpsychologisch") prejudices about language, on the basis of which an essentialist view of culture (including language) could find public and political purchase".

The "Law of Silence" (1940)

A leader in September 1940 titled "Das Gesetz des Schweigens" (The Law of Silence, FZ, 24.9.1940.) addressed the situation of the populations of Alsace and Lorraine. After the capitulation of France in 1940, arguably the high-point of the regime's popularity, the FZ commissioned essays on French history from Franz Schnabel, a distinguished historian close to the Catholic Zentrum Party, who had been deprived of his academic chair in 1936.[13] Schnabel's piece on the linguistic and political history of Alsace and Lorraine, which appeared on 1 September, is a classic example of non-Nazi writing. He presents a factual account of the historical development of French national identity since the French Revolution from which evaluative nationalist rhetoric is noticeably missing and, in particular, contemporary German claims to 'rightful' ownership are nowhere endorsed. Instead, the populations of Alsace and Lorraine are presented as victims of the recurring territorial claims of two nationalisms. At times it seems, indeed, that the French approach to nationhood is being sympathetically contrasted with the German, as when Schnabel cites Ernest

Renan's voluntarist theory of the nation state and observes that the French "have not made belonging to the nation dependent on genealogy […] but have located it in the will of the individual, the will to belong" ("die Zugehörigkeit zur Nation nicht von der Abstammung abhängig gemacht […], sondern in den Willen des einzelnen, in den Willen zur Zusammengehörigkeit verlegt"). Here, the 'resistent' reader could find an unfavourable comparison of the two national revolutions, of 1789 and 1933, and a rejection of coercive 'völkisch' politics.

The very title "Das Gesetz des Schweigens" sensationally breached the Propaganda Ministry's gagging orders on the paper by thematizing censorship. The first impression, that it is the enforced silence of the FZ which is under discussion, is dispelled on a literal reading, but confirmed on a deeper, 'resistent' reading. This editorial was not signed; in conformity with the genre convention it presented the collective voice of the paper taking a position on a matter of high political importance, the occupation of much of France and the incorporation of these French *départements* into the German state as a vital war and foreign policy aim. This position was articulated with understandable care and caution, and it is unsurprising that the text is characterized by a high degree of hybridity, by aporias, paradoxes, and apparent concessions to the regime. On the one hand there is acknowledgment of the *de facto* "new European order" (neue Ordnung Europas, a recognizable Nazi ideologeme) and the "secular defeat of France". But on the other, there was no endorsement of the historical German claims. Instead, a French newspaper, *Le Jour*, is quoted, without revealing that this was a publication in the *zone libre* and in no way supportive of the Vichy regime. In quoting from *Le Jour*, the plaintiff voice of its editor Fernand Laurent, in his address to the people of Alsace and Lorraine, not only gains direct access to a German readership but, uncannily, merges momentarily with that of the FZ, so that a coded message to its own readers, suffering in occupied Germany, is produced through a simple technique of substitution: for France, read Germany, for *Le Jours*, read FZ—ignoring the disingenuous parenthesis when the editorial quotes Laurent saying "daß wenigstens in dieser Zeitung (im "Jour") wir euch gehört und verstanden haben. Ich möchte, daß ihr eurerseits euch anstrengt, unsere Situation zu verstehen, daß in eurem eigenen Interesse die schmerzlichen Probleme, die ihr hervorruft, nicht öffentlich diskutiert werden können und dürfen" ("that at least in this newspaper (in *Le Jour*) we have heard and understood you. I would like you to try to understand our situation, that in your own interests the painful problems which you call us to address cannot and may not be discussed"). The explosive implications of this passage, culminating in the quoted words of Laurent: "Wir erleiden wie ihr das harte Gesetz des Schweigens" ("We are suffering like you under the harsh Law of Silence") are buried in a complex and multi-layered text and compensated for by apparently conformist statements, for example in mentioning Germany's "festen und klaren Führungsanspruch" ("firm and clear claim to leadership") in the "new European order", in which the suffering of the people of Alsace and Lorraine is to be extinguished ("ausgelöscht"). A careful reading of this editorial shows that whilst German supremacy is presented as a fact, it is not presented as a desirable fact. Indeed, the concluding section appears to warn the victorious Germans that their military successes bring an enormous responsibility for the future of Europe.

Conclusion: The Habitus of Inner Exile and the Origins of the "Lexicon of the 'Unmensch'" (1945ff.)

The discussion in this chapter has, perhaps inevitably, promoted a largely positive view of the achievements of the FZ authors in finding ways of gainsaying the regime and saying the unsayable. But it must be noted that these achievements, such as they were, were not a daily phenomenon. Half of the glosses reviewed in this chapter appeared on a Sunday (a day for adults to take their children to see the animals kept on display in the nature reservation ("Naturschutzgebiet"), according to Sternberger in "Asyl der Wahrheit" on 3 May 1936—a Sunday), and nearly all were placed in the Feuilleton or on the third page, whilst the main sections of the paper were increasingly dominated by the voice of the regime. It would be remiss to conclude this chapter without pointing to critics who believe the price paid for these achievements was too high. In their view, the editors were mistaken, and irresponsible, in taking on and persisting with this devil's bargain, in not seeing that the continuation of this famous title enhanced the standing of the regime in Germany and abroad, and in not closing the paper once it effectively became a mouthpiece of the regime. Were its journalists freedom fighters of the word, or "servants of the state" (Sösemann 2007; Frei and Schmitz 1989, p. 131)? The question still divides critical opinion.

The discourse on language developed in the FZ as a strategy of voicing a dissenting alternative to government proclamations and also, increasingly, to general usage, bears the hallmarks of the conditions of 'Sprachlosigkeit' under which its journalists worked. From the beginning, the paper found it difficult to mount explicit attacks on named speakers and prominent ideologemes. As a result, its critical discourse on language was deflected towards coded, and therefore potentially obscure assaults on these targets, and, more commonly, towards a focus—ostensibly at least—on THE LANGUAGE in general, driven by anxiety over the spread of Nazi norms into general usage. Much of the time, the implied targets of this critique were 'little Nazis' giving themselves airs, non-Nazis trying not to draw attention to themselves, and indeed anti-Nazis searching their own use of language. It was for the most part an *ad hoc* enterprise, seizing opportunities where they presented themselves, and dependent on the ingenuity of the commentators. The situation represented by the FZ certainly deserves our attention as an example of the intellectual and ethical challenges facing public expressions of dissent under Nazism. I would suggest that its best achievements, most of them focused on the critique of single expressions, but also including coded references to Hitler himself, deserve an honourable place in the discourse history of German anti-fascism in the twentieth century. The critique of style, however, and the focus on THE LANGUAGE, apparently unpopulated by individual speakers answerable for their words, must be counted less successful from today's perspective. Against this, we need to remember how far removed we are today from the situation of the readers at the time, who looked to the FZ for a mood music of 'Resistenz'.

Some of the features of this linguistic habitus would be carried over into the "Lexicon of the 'Unmensch'" in 1945, most importantly in the predominance of the third variant of language criticism, focused on THE LANGUAGE in general, which is held to exercise power over the unwary speaker. Other features also carry over: a focus on individual words, a discourse of linguistic and moral decline, a belief in the power of language to unmask its user, the thesis of the inhumane 'accusativization' of the human subject. Amongst the expressions targeted in the "Lexicon" between 1945 and 1948, several (BETREUUNG, CHARAKTERLICH, DURCHFÜHREN, GESTALTUNG, RAUM, WISSEN UM) immediately betray their origins in the FZ discourse. Even the origins of the 1945 Foreword (discussed in the next chapter) can be traced back to the public exchange with Reifferscheidt. In "Wer spricht?" (FZ, 5.1.1940) Sternberger had written:

> ... wir sind, indem wir reden, stets auch gefangen in diesem Mittel, dessen wir uns bedienen. Jedes Wort legt uns fest, jedes Wort, das wir selber sagen, ist zugleich ein kleines Element unseres Schicksals. Und bisweilen scheint eines hinter uns aufzustehen wie ein Kobold und bedeutet auf einmal etwas ganz anderes, als wir "meinten", indem wir's aussprachen. [...] der Gefangenschaft in der Sprache entrinnen wir einzig durch die Freiheit der Sprache. Denn redend sind wir zugleich immer daran, uns zu befreien, ja wir sprechen nur, um uns zu befreien, und die Sprache ist das Signum dieser unsrer Freiheit. Wir haben sie nicht, aber wir müssen—dürfen—können—wollen—sollen—nein, wir werden sie gewinnen. Indem wir begehren, verstanden zu werden. Nichts weiter.
>
> ... we are, when we speak, always caught in this medium [language] which we are making use of. Every word pins us down, every word that we say ourselves, is at the same time a small element of our fate. And from time to time one seems to stand up behind us like a cobold and suddenly means something completely different to what we "meant" when we spoke it. [...] we escape imprisonment in language solely through the freedom of language. For in speaking we are always freeing ourselves, indeed we speak only to free ourselves, and language is the sign of this, our freedom. We do not have this freedom, but we must—may—can—desire to—should—no, we shall gain it. In striving to be understood. Nothing more.

The controversy which engulfed the "Lexicon" in the 1960s and 1970s would have a significant impact on the course taken by political 'Sprachkritik' in (Western) Germany, an impact whose positive consequences inform much of the academic, if not (yet) the lay discourse on language and society in Germany today. In the "Lexicon", Sternberger, Storz and Süskind picked up where they had left off in their contributions to the FZ, in some cases even polishing off old glosses. The climate in 1945 was conducive: the Allies and Germans alike saw the need for a 'denazification of the language'—everyone's language. As the first and second, expanded and partially rewritten book editions appeared, however, in 1957 and 1967, a new generation of readers would begin to question the principles and efficacy of this discourse on language as a critique of Nazism. The history of the reception of the "Lexicon" in its various incarnations is therefore a central theme in the next two chapters.

Notes

1. I am indebted to Professor Günther Gillessen for permission to consult the notes and documentation for his study on the FZ between 1933 and 1943, *Auf verlorenem Posten* (Gillessen 1986), and for discussion and correspondence on this topic.
2. This chapter is a revised English version of Dodd 2013, pp. 1–55. That volume contains an annotated selection of eighty texts from the FZ, not all of which can be mentioned here.
3. Higher figures are given by Gillessen (1986, p. 353f.).
4. Apart from the special connotations of Mensch, the words "hat das Wort" mean "has the word", i.e. has language, but also "is invited to speak". The formula is used when introducing a public speaker.
5. This is a correction of my earlier reading (Dodd 2007, p. 106).
6. Sternberger was a protégé and admirer of Viktor von Weizsäcker (1886–1957), an advocate of a medicine "nicht der fachlichen Absonderung, sondern der Zusammenarbeit" ("not based on specialist isolation, but on cooperation") with the patient (Sternberger 1987, p. 172). Sternberger's review of Weizsäcker's book *Der Gestaltkreis*, part of this 'humane' discourse, is titled "Der Mensch ist kein Ding" (The human being is not a thing, FZ, 7.5.1940). See also Dodd 2007, p. 110f.
7. In German linguistic science, this structure is known as a 'Funktionsverbgefüge'. English grammars of German also refer to 'light verb' structures containing delexicalized verbs.
8. The possibility that Baberadt is being ironic here cannot be completely dismissed, but appears improbable in this particular publication.

9. Most examples of attacks on the lexical purists post-date the 1937 humiliation of the Language Association. Exceptions include Sternberger's "Das arme C" (Poor C, 9.1.1936), a commentary on purists' demands to replace C with K in German place names, and "Man nehme" (Let's take..., 11.12.1936), a scathing rejection of Alexander Matschoß's article, in *Muttersprache*, demanding Germanized terms for 'Natur', 'Kristall', and 'Elektrizität'.
10. Geißler's comments had just been published in *Muttersprache* (52 (1937), Heft 6, col. 252, 258). This issue also contained (251f.) a hostile review of Storz's *Laienbrevier* (1937) by Hans Sacher ("I reject this book, it does not speak to the lay person, does not tell him what he would like to and ought to know, and does not say it in a way he would like to hear it"). Sacher also notes that Storz does not mention the Language Association anywhere in the book, and suspects that he "wishes it harm".
11. A similar exchange is found in *Hochland*, with Franz Wolfgang. See Chap. 6.
12. Sternberger, "Weiter nichts? Über die Verständgung in der Sprache" (FZ, 26.11.1939); Reifferscheidt, "Verständigung und Ausdruck" (FZ, 5.1.1940); Sternberger, "Wer spricht?" (FZ, 5.1.1940). The texts are reproduced in Dodd 2007, pp. 319–327. See also Dodd 2007, pp. 196–206, and 2013, pp. 44–46, 142–154.
13. Schnabel was the author of *Deutsche Geschichte im neunzehnten Jahrhundert*, of which only four volumes (1929–1937) appeared. Publication of subsequent volumes was effectively suppressed. Financial support for his Chair of History at the Technical University Karlsruhe was "reallocated" in 1936.

Bibliography

Baberadt, Karl Friedrich. 1941. Das unvermeidbare Schmarotzerwort. *Deutsche Presse* 31, Nr. 1 (4. January 1941), p. 16.

Dodd, William J. 2007. *Jedes Wort wandelt die Welt. Dolf Sternbergers politische Sprachkritik*. Göttingen: Wallstein.

———. 2008. '... dem Kaiser gegeben was des Kaisers ist': Walter Benjamin's Reading of Dolf Sternberger's 'Tempel der Kunst' (1937). In *The Text and Its Context. Studies in Modern German Literature and Society Presented to Ronald Speirs on the Occasion of His 65th Birthday*, ed. Nigel Harris and Joanne Sayner, 63–77. Oxford: Peter Lang.

———., ed. 2013. *"Der Mensch hat das Wort". Der Sprachdiskurs in der Frankfurter Zeitung 1933–1943*. Berlin, Boston: de Gruyter.

Frei, Norbert, and Johannes Schmitz. 1989. *Journalismus im Dritten Reich*. München: Beck.

Gillessen, Günther. 1986. *Auf verlorenem Posten. Die Frankfurter Zeitung im 'Dritten Reich'*. München: Siedler.

Goebbels, Joseph. 1995. Die Tagebücher von Joseph Goebbels. Teil 2. Diktate 1941–1945. Hg. von Elke Fröhlich. München: K. G. Sauer.

Hagemann, Jürgen. 1970. *Die Presselenkung im Dritten Reich*. Bonn: Bouvier.

Heinrichsdorff, Wolf. 1937. *Die liberale Opposition in Deutschland seit dem 30. Januar 1933 (dargestellt an der Entwicklung der "Frankfurter Zeitung". Versuch einer Systematik der politischen Kritik*. Dissertation zur Erlangung der Doktorwürde der Philosophischen Fakultät der Hansischen Universität zu Hamburg.

Hitler, Adolf. 1934. *Mein Kampf. Zwei Bände in einem Band*. Ungekürzte Ausgabe. 97–101. Auflage. München: Franz Eher Nachfolger.

Jancke, Oskar. 1938. *Restlos erledigt? Neue Glossen zur deutschen Sprache*. München: Knorr & Hirth.

Knobloch, Clemens. 2005. *Volkhafte Sprachforschung. Studien zum Umbau der Sprachwissenschaft in Deutschland zwischen 1918 und 1945*. Tübingen: Niemeyer.

Mehring, Marga. 1960. Menschenmaterial. *Zeitschrift für deutsche Wortforschung* 16: 129–143.

Reifenberg, Benno. 1964. Einleitung. In *Facsimile Querschnitt durch die Frankfurter Zeitung*, Hg. Ingrid Gräfin Lynar, 6–14. Bern: Scherz Verlag.

Reifferscheidt, Friedrich M. 1939. *Über die Sprache*. Leipzig: Hegner.

Rück, Peter. 1993. Die Sprache der Schrift. Zur Geschichte des Frakturverbots von 1941. In *Homo scribens. Perspektiven der Schriftlichkeitsforschung*, Hg. Jürgen Baurmann et al., 231–272. Tübingen: Niemeyer.

Sänger, Fritz. 1975. *Politik der Täuschungen. Missbrauch der Presse im Dritten Reich. Weisungen, Informationen, Notizen 1933–1939*. Wien: Europaverlag.

———. 1977. Zur Geschichte der 'Frankfurter Zeitung'. *Publizistik. Zeitschrift für die Wissenschaft von Presse, Rundfunk, Film, Rhetorik, Öffentlichkeitsarbeit, Werbung und Meinungsbildung* 22: 275–294.

Schmitz-Berning, Cornelia. 2000. *Vokabular des Nationalsozialismus*. Berlin, New York: de Gruyter.

Seidel, Eugen, and Ingeborg Seidel-Slotty. 1961. *Sprachwandel im Dritten Reich*. Halle: VEB Verlag Sprache und Literatur.

Sösemann, Bernd. 2007. Journalismus im Griff der Diktatur. Die Frankfurter Zeitung in der nationalsozialistischen Pressepolitik. In *"Diener des Staates" oder "Widerstand zwischen den Zeilen"?*, Hg. Christoph Studt, 11–38. LIT: Berlin.

Sternberger, Dolf. 1987. *Gang zwischen Meistern.* (*Schriften* VIII). Frankfurt/Main: Insel.

———. 1988. *Gut und Böse. Moralische Essais aus drei Zeiten.* (*Schriften* IX). Frankfurt/Main: Insel.

Stöber, Rudolf. 2010. Presse im Nationalsozialismus. In *Medien im Nationalsozialismus,* Hg. Bernd Heidenreich and Sönke Neitzel, 275–294. Paderborn: Wilhelm Fink/Ferdinand Schöningh.

Storfer, Adolf. 1937. *Im Dickicht der Sprache.* Wien: Verlag Dr. Rolf Passer. Reprinted: Verlag Vorwerk 8, Berlin (2005).

Storz, Gerhard. 1937. *Laienbrevier über den Umgang mit der Sprache.* Frankfurt/Main: Societäts-Verlag.

Toepser-Ziegert, Gabriele. 2007. Die Existenz der Journalisten unter den Bedingungen der Diktatur. In *"Diener des Staates" oder "Widerstand zwischen den Zeilen"?: die Rolle der Presse im "Dritten Reich": (XVIII. Königswinterer Tagung Februar 2005),* Hg. Christoph Studt, 75–88. Münster: LIT Verlag Münster.

8

Aftermath: ENTNAZIFIZIERUNG

This chapter reviews key developments in the German public discourse in the period from the defeat of the regime in May 1945 to the founding of the Federal Republic and the German Democratic Republic in the summer and autumn of 1949. Its focus is the discourse on German guilt and the concept of denazification: ENTNAZIFIZIERUNG. In particular, this chapter reviews the first attempts at a linguistic denazification, typically conceptualized as a "denazification of the language" (ENTNAZIFIZIERUNG DER SPRACHE), and provides a detailed review of the two most significant and enduring works of language criticism in this period, *L(ingua) T(ertii) I(mperii)* by Victor Klemperer, and the "Lexicon of the 'Unmensch'" by Dolf Sternberger, Wilhelm Emanuel Süskind and Gerhard Storz.

Key events in this period include the Potsdam Conference of the Allies from 17 July to 2 August 1945, which agreed in general terms a programme of "denazification" and "re-education", established four zones of occupation (French, British, American, Soviet) under an Allied Control Council, and divided Berlin into four sectors each under the control of one of the Allied powers; a mass migration of people throughout this period into the western part of Germany (estimated at fourteen

W J Dodd, *National Socialism and German Discourse*,
https://doi.org/10.1007/978-3-319-74660-9_8

million people); the 'Stuttgart Declaration of Guilt' by the Evangelical Church (EKD) in October 1945 confessing to inadequacies in opposing Nazism; the fusion of the American and British zones into an economic 'Bizone' in January 1947; the inclusion of the French zone to form a 'Trizone' in March 1948; the introduction of the Deutschmark in the Trizone in June 1948; the founding of the Federal Republic of Germany on the territory of the Trizone in May 1949; and the founding of the German Democratic Republic in the Soviet zone in October 1949. The exact point at which the 'Cold War' between the Soviet Union and the western Allies began is a moot point. The dropping of the atomic bomb by the United States on Hiroshima on 6 August 1945, shortly after the Potsdam Conference, may mark the point at which the course of a 'cold war' was sealed.

Denazification as a Discourse Event

The term ENTNAZIFIZIERUNG (also initially DENAZIFIZIERUNG), a loan translation of a concept originating in the Pentagon, denoted the legal and administrative process imposed on millions of Germans by the Allies for the removal of Nazis and Nazi institutions as part of the democratic REEDUCATION of Germany. Initially supported by a majority of the population, the concept fell into disrepute with Allies and Germans alike because of its failure to bring middle-ranking and many senior Nazis to account.[1] The Allies handed over the process in 1948 to German-chaired SPRUCHKAMMERN (tribunals) as their attention began to focus more on the Cold War. As Heidrun Kämper (1998) points out, denazification is an important chapter in German discourse history, a "linguistic manifestation of an ethical concept" with its own discourse conventions based on the speech acts: accusation, defence, justification. The reluctance of victims to give evidence, and the willingness of friends and neighbours to write supporting statements, resulted in the process being widely perceived already in 1945 as a 'whitewash' issuing PERSILSCHEINE (Persil certificates) instead of fines, confiscations, and prison sentences. Another disparaging term for the process was MITLÄUFERFABRIK (factory turning out Category IV certificates, the weakest grade of culpability in the five categories pronounced by the tribunals).[2] Kämper notes the exculpation strategies used by known Nazis: the impossibility of physical resistance; confessions of political misjudgment (misguided idealism), naivety, and guilt by inaction (PASSIVE MITSCHULD); fictions about struggles with one's conscience whilst in office and claims to have harboured an "inner resistance" without the slightest empirical evidence—which no doubt brought the concept of INNERER WIDERSTAND and the 'good German' into lasting disrepute.[3] Kämper (1998, p. 320) cites a case in which a notorious 'Ortsleiter' (local Party boss) simply lifted the wording of his statement from the helpfully framed Law—a cynical 'cut and paste' exercise. Exasperation amongst Germans even led to the coining of the ironic RENAZIFIZIERUNG, attested in 1946 (Eitz and Stötzel 2007, p. 202).

The most ubiquitous word in German life at this time, however, was SCHULD (guilt), the commonest variant of which was KOLLEKTIVSCHULD (collective guilt). At times the Allies, with the possible exception of the Russians, seemed to endorse the implication that all Germans were 'guilty' of unleashing war and genocide, a thesis which was vigorously contested by many Germans. One can perhaps understand why: 'German collective guilt' bears a certain resemblance to the generic attributions characteristic of the deposed ideology (THE Jew, THE Slav…). Now accusations were being levelled at THE GERMANS rather than individual Germans. An important intervention on the complex notion of guilt was Karl Jaspers' treatise DIE SCHULDFRAGE (Jaspers 1946), in which he distinguished four concurrent (not hierarchical) categories of guilt: criminal, political, moral, and metaphysical. Criminal guilt was now the jurisdiction of criminal courts such as the Nuremberg tribunals, which Jaspers supported. Political guilt for supporting the regime was now a matter for the Allies to pronounce on, since Germans had forfeited the right to determine the civil and material conditions of their country by voting for the NSDAP. For moral guilt attaching to actions short of criminal which had helped to maintain the regime, each German must answer to his or her conscience. And for metaphysical guilt attaching to the decision to stay alive whilst others died for their beliefs, they would have to answer to God.

Denazification "of the Language"

As Deissler (2004) demonstrates, the Allies' plans for the "re-education" of a defeated Germany generally agreed that a denazification of THE (GERMAN) LANGUAGE (ENTNAZIFIZIERUNG DER SPRACHE) was essential. In the American programme—evidently the most extensive and sophisticated of the four occupying powers'—this project was implemented by a cadre of cultural officers (some of them Germans returning from territorial exile in Allied uniform) working with trusted Germans who had demonstrated 'Resistenz' to the 'language *of* National Socialism' and, perhaps more importantly, to the nuances of 'language *in* National Socialism'. Deissler remarks (2004, p. 249) that the programme of reform implemented in 1945 was essentially a constructive version of a negative critique developed in the propaganda war with Nazism, and here one can see how it was possible for such a programme to incorporate the 'unquiet voices' of German criticism. In the immediate post-war period, some of them would play an influential role in shaping the ethos of denazification and the debate on 'Nazi language'.

The most immediate effects of linguistic denazification were seen in the denazified 'Straßenbild' (appearance of the streets) through the removal of the regime's propaganda paraphernalia (insignia, statues, pictures), the re-naming of streets and squares, and the dropping of propagandistic descriptors such as STADT DER BEWEGUNG (City of the Movement, i.e. Munich) from public signs and franking on postage. A lot of the vocabulary of the kind contained, for example, in Paechter's study, designating now defunct institutions, offices, and ranks of party, military, and state structures (GESTAPO, TOTENKOPFVERBAND, PROPAGANDAMINISTERIUM) quickly became historic. In these domains, linguistic denazification was a relatively straightforward affair. The deeper problems lay with lexical and phraseological items typically designating non-concreta and/or having strong connotational value, with matters of tone and 'Sprachduktus' (style), with metaphors, and with the perceived continuation of a Nazi value system in various contexts of use.

Directives issued to print and broadcast media targeted three main areas: typeface, text type, and lexicon. 'Fraktur' (and runes) needed to be replaced by Roman typefaces. Text types, especially in journalism, needed to distinguish rigorously between fact and opinion. The German vocabulary needed to be "purged" (Deissler 2004, p. 247) of items carrying Nazi ideology. The reasons for relegating 'Fraktur' (thus continuing the Nazi policy since 1941) presumably rested on the twin concerns of readability and political semiotics discussed in Chap. 3. American officers, notably Eugene Jolas, Walter Brockmann, Alfred Jacobson and Shepard Stone, played an important role in implementing linguistic denazification in their occupation zone (Deissler 2004, p. 254). Jolas, arguably the most influential of the American press officers,[4] and head of DANA (Deutsche Allgemeine Nachrichten-Agentur), the newly-established news agency in the American zone, issued guidelines for "the American style of newswriting", including: "Essential facts should be given in the lead, that is, in the introductory paragraph, to be followed by paragraphs dealing accumulatively with the chronological enumeration of details". A separate point in the same memo states: "Elimination of all nazi terms must be steadily kept in mind and denazification of the vocabulary should be one of the prime tasks of every news-writer" (Deissler 2004, p. 220). The beginnings of a warm collegial friendship between Jolas and Dolf Sternberger can be traced to the autumn of 1945, when they discussed ideas for a new political, literary and philosophical journal (Deissler 2004, p. 220). Jolas was instrumental in the issuing of the first licence for such a publication in October 1945, to Sternberger and a team of distinguished co-editors, Karl Jaspers, Werner Krauss, and Alfred Weber. The first issue of *Die Wandlung* (The Turn[5]), dated 30 November 1945, contained the first language-critical gloss under the rubric (reviewed below) "From the Lexicon of the 'Unmensch'". Werner Krauss's language-critical essay (Krauss 1946) on the "power and impotence of dictionaries" also deserves mention here. As part of its re-education agenda, *Die Wandlung* contained an array of essays on social questions, literary pieces by suppressed German-language authors (such as Kafka), translations of foreign authors (such as T.S. Eliot), but also contributions about Nazi atrocities such as Sternberger's commentary on (the language of) an SS report documenting the "extermination" (VERNICHTUNG) of the Warsaw Ghetto (Sternberger 1947) and Hannah Arendt's essays "Die organisierte Schuld" ("Organized Guilt", Arendt 1946) and "Konzentrationsläger" (Arendt 1948).[6] In the Foreword to the first issue, in November 1945, Jaspers had stated:

> Was und wie wir erinnern, und was wir darin als Anspruch gelten lassen, das wird mit entscheiden über das, was aus uns wird. ("Geleitwort", *Die Wandlung* 1/1)

> What and how we remember, and what we allow as a valid claim on us, will help to decide what will become of us.

With a print-run of twenty thousand copies, *Die Wandlung* was distributed throughout the American zone and in Berlin, and was the first of a number of impressive such journals which found eager readerships in the period to 1949, when currency reform made many of them economically unviable.[7] The first newspaper to appear under Allied control, already in January 1945, was the *Aachener Zeitung*. The Americans in particular were steadfastly against the resuscitation of old titles from the Nazi era, resisting for example attempts to revive the *Frankfurter Zeitung*. The launch of the *Frankfurter Allgemeine Zeitung* in 1949 followed protracted negotiations on this issue.

Language-critical essays were also broadcast on the newly licensed radio stations, reaching a much wider audience than the print media (Deissler 2004, pp. 210–216). In the American zone, Radio Munich broadcast a three-piece item on "Nazi-Deutsch" in 1946 by Oskar Jancke. The list of lexemes critiqued in Jancke's article suggests, as Deissler implies, a more grounded and immediate connection with National Socialist ideology and crimes than is found in Sternberger's Lexicon. Jancke cites from Hitler's speeches to critique the use of intensifying adjectives, nominal style, "pseudo-scientific" 'Fremdwörter', and an array of political keywords: GNADENTOD (mercy death), ENDLÖSUNG, ENDSIEG, VOLKSGEMEINSCHAFT, WELTANSCHAUUNG, SOZIALISMUS, DEMOKRATIE. A minor figure in the coded inner exile discourse on language in the 1930s, Jancke became one of the most influential language critics of the post-war years, arguing for a new academy of language which would counter the linguistic remnants of Nazism. (Jancke went on to co-found the Deutsche Akademie für Sprache und Dichtung in Darmstadt in 1948). Deissler plausibly suggests that Jancke was familiar in 1946 with Heinz Paechter's 1944 study, to which he was presumably introduced by an American control officer. Radio Stuttgart and Radio Frankfurt also broadcast language-critical items, the latter including pieces by Sternberger. In the British zone, Axel Eggebrecht's four-part study of "Braundeutsch" was broadcast by NWDR in 1946–1947. In the Soviet zone, Theodor Mühlen's series "1000 Worte Deutsch" was broadcast from September 1945 to June 1946 (Mühlen reportedly called on listeners to paint over anti-Jewish signs), and was followed in 1947 by Horst Lommer's "Sprachglossen", which were also broadcast in the American zone by Radio Munich. (Mühlen also broadcast in the western zones, on SWR and NWDR). This suggests a wide-ranging if unconcerted campaign with ambitions to reach the German population as a whole in a media landscape in a state of flux. Despite being conceptually and methodologically disparate (Deissler 2004, p. 148) it is clear that this language criticism was valued by the occupying powers as integral to the denazification programme. It also seems that, like most of the language criticism in the print media, they were focused on the lexicon. (Deissler provides an index of some two hundred "lexemes, phrasemes and names" targeted in these various campaigns.) In at least one case (Eggebrecht), the critique of concepts extended to ENTNAZIFIZIERUNG itself, on account of its vagueness. This suggests that not all language criticism was necessarily in line with the Allies' aims and objectives. Some, for example, still took a purist view of the 'Fremdwort'.

Despite the existence of various news agencies in the French zone, relatively little is known about French policy and personnel. It seems probable that cultural officers came from the bilingual Alsace and Lorraine regions. Deissler (2004, pp. 250–254) reports that the French, keen to prevent the rebuilding of a strong centralized Germany, were sensitive to any mention of a German REICH, and that French control of radio continued after the founding of the Federal Republic in May 1949 (cf. Stötzel 1989, p. 40f.).

Today, many of these language-critical glosses, especially those broadcast on radio, must be presumed lost, and most of those in the print media are accessible only in research libraries. A definitive list of German authors participating in the wider programme of linguistic denazification does not exist, but includes figures as diverse as Hans Habe, Stefan Heym, Rudolf Pechel, Werner Krauss, Mechtilde Lichnowsky, Wilhelm Süskind and Victor Klemperer, who is known to have given a talk on language in

Nazism in Berlin in 1946 to the 'Kulturbund zur demokratischen Erneuerung Deutschlands' (Cultural Federation for the Democratic Renewal of Germany) and also published in its journal *Aufbau*. Krauss and Lichnowsky also contributed language-critical pieces to *Die Wandlung* outside the 'Unmensch' rubric. Hans Habe was editor-in-chief of the *Neue Zeitung* in Munich, the newspaper of the American military government, which regularly published language-critical pieces, including those by Habe himself before he parted from the paper for reasons which remain unclear but apparently had to do with personal and professional disagreements with DANA (dismissed by Habe as a "Narrenschiff" (ship of fools)) and specifically with Eugene Jolas. On a benevolent reading, Habe's metier was language criticism, while Jolas was interested in language regulation. This internecine dispute seems to have generated one of the earliest examples of the "Nazi-Complex" (discussed in the following chapter) in Habe's likening of Jolas to Goebbels (Deissler 2004, p. 229). Süskind also published at least three articles on language in 1945 and 1946 in the *Neue Zeitung*, when he was also reporting on the Nuremberg Trials for the *Süddeutsche Zeitung* and contributing to the *Wandlung* series on the 'Unmensch'—suggesting that his German colleagues and American masters understood his anti-Nazi stance in inner exile better than many later commentators, including Deissler.[8] Finally, it is worth noting Rudolf Pechel's contributions in *Aufbau* and *Die Auslese*, journals published in the Soviet zone after he had co-founded the CDU in Berlin in June 1945 as part of the Soviet initiative to license political parties. In a piece in *Die Auslese*, Pechel praised the "Lexicon of the 'Unmensch'", lamented the Nazis' defiling ("Schändung") of the German language and called on Germans to eradicate ("ausmerzen") all traces. In September be became (briefly) the editor of a CDU newspaper *Neue Zeit*, and in April 1946, also in Berlin, relaunched the *Deutsche Rundschau*, licensed by the British. These few examples may serve to counter any assumptions we may have today that the politics of linguistic denazification in these years, even amongst anti-fascists, were straightforward and predictable.

Anti-fascist language criticism and regulation was at its most intense in the years 1945–1947, perhaps because the educational and administrative objectives had been substantially achieved by 1947, although a more plausible explanation is the American "transformation of focus" (Koszyk, quoted in Deissler 2004, p. 252) from Nazism to Soviet Communism as the chief propaganda target. Beginning with preparations for the merging of the British and American zones into a single Bizone on 1 January 1947, some evidence can be adduced for this thesis. The journal *Der Monat*, for example, launched in 1948, is known to have been secretly funded by the CIA (as indeed was George Orwell's *1984*, a novel from 1948, cf. Saunders 1999). This might also explain the rise of the term TOTALITARIAN in political and popular discourse in this period, also in Germany (TOTALITÄR, TOTALITARISMUS) as an umbrella term equating or conflating National Socialism and Soviet Communism.[9]

The denazification discourse often continued the tradition, found in both fascist and anti-fascist discourses, of using biological metaphors in talking about 'cures' for a 'sick' language, with an implicit focus on THE LANGUAGE as opposed to patterns of usage by individuals and groups. It is instructive to note that Eugene Jolas, writing in 1998, stated that his achievement had been to rid the (German) language of his childhood of the "militaristic and autocratic bacteria that Nazi ideology had poured into its veins" (Jolas 1998, p. 270, quoted in Deissler 2004, p. 258). In the context of 1945, facing the full extent of the devastation precipitated by Nazism, there was little time for reflecting on the implications of one's own metaphorical language, especially when it offered a way of making sense of a chaotic world. To continue the metaphor, the regulation of language ('Sprachregelung') rests of necessity on a critique of language ('Sprachkritik') in much the same way as curing an ailment proceeds from a diagnosis, which in turn rests on identifying and accurately describing the symptoms. In the immediate post-war years, scores of German critics provided the detailed language critiques underpinning the larger task of reform and regulation of attitudes and the public discourse. In retrospect, the significance of many of these German critiques of 'Nazi language' may lie not so much in their accuracy or methodological rigour as in their contribution to increasing the level of sensitivity to language in the general population. It is time now to turn to the two most influential of these early critiques—by Klemperer and Sternberger/Storz/Süskind—and to consider more closely their contributions to linguistic denazification.

Lingua Tertii Imperii (1947)

Victor Klemperer's *LTI: Notizbuch eines Philologen* (LTI: Notebook of a Philologist[10]), published by Aufbau Verlag in Berlin in 1947, is a series of narrative sketches using material excerpted from the diaries. This section will review the genesis of the book, its value as an early contribution to denazification, and the changing perceptions of it, particularly following the publication of the diaries in the mid-1990s. Klemperer's significance in the post-1945 period can scarcely be overstated. His writings constitute the single most enduringly influential body of work, documenting and commenting on the L(ingua) T(ertii) I(mperii), a term which is still widely used to refer to the whole problematic complex of 'Nazi language'. More than 400,000 copies have been printed, mainly in the GDR but also, from 1966 until 1989, in western Germany. After unification in 1990 a massive print run of 50,000 copies was published by Reclam in Leipzig. It has been translated into several languages, including Dutch, French, Italian, Polish, Hungarian, and Russian (Fischer-Hupe 2001, pp. 454–461).

Klemperer began work on *LTI* in July 1945, and by December 1946 (when "Heroismus" was written as the book's Foreword) he had produced thirty six "chapters", most of them in intense, short bursts. Kristine Fischer-Hupe's detailed study reveals a process of "commentating compilation" (2001, p. 53) as Klemperer trawled his diaries for material, from which he constructed not a lexicon (he never made a list of the lexical items attributed to *LTI*, omitting at least 170 items mentioned in the diary (2001, p. 36)), but a sixty-four page typescript the organizing principle of which was categorial, allocating diary references, recorded events, reminiscences and additional commentaries to categories such as technical language, military language, affective language, Jewish-related language, and "Prinzipielles", a category for overarching commentary and theorizing. The book is a "kaleidoscope" in terms of genre (2001, p. 235), not diary, not historiography, but a narrative in conversational style and, significantly, from the retrospective viewpoint of the survivor determined to "bear witness" by addressing his compatriots directly, in a series of standalone but interconnecting narratives in which the linguistic and non-linguistic material is embedded in a specific attested social context of use. Comparing the excerpted diary passages with the resulting passages in *LTI* reveals an amalgam of direct quotations and paraphrases from the diary, interpolations, and narrative bridges. Separate passages from the diary are sometimes fused in the resulting *LTI* passage, whilst the historical chronology is generally observed when different diary passages are invoked. Documentation and commentary are not always clearly distinguishable. What was only implicit in the diary (either because of self-censorship or because the author was 'talking to himself') is elaborated and made explicit in *LTI*. Whilst many persons are still not fully identified, Klemperer's tormentors are named. Some linguistic material is included (for example the term REICHSKRISTALLNACHT for the pogrom of 9 November 1938) which Klemperer became aware of only after the fall of the regime.

A question arising from this process of creative excerpting is whether *LTI* gives a representative impression of the diary, and in particular whether anything significant was omitted. One such omission, noted by Klemperer, is an account of Ina Seidel's and other German writers' "slide into betrayal" ("In-den-Verrat-Gleiten") by accommodating their themes and language to Nazi norms. For this, Klemperer ran out of space and time. Other authorial decisions suggest Klemperer's reluctance to criticize the Soviets and indeed a desire to emphasize a narrative of shared antifascist values. A comparison of Italian and "Bolshevik" propaganda (29.10.1932) is conspicuously omitted in *LTI*, and Klemperer himself notes a decision not to include a passage in which he had agreed with a Goebbels remark on "Russian imperialism" (a passage also missing from the diary editions, cf. Fischer-Hupe 2001, p. 34f.).

The Foreword to the book, "On heroism", written in late 1946, dethrones the militarized HERO discourse in favour of the heroism of ordinary people like Klemperer's 'Aryan' wife Eva, who never abandoned him and effectively saved his life. As it is not possible to cover all thirty six sections of the book here, I will focus on the first chapter, "LTI", completed in the autumn of 1945. It is a contemporary and in many ways a parallel text to Sternberger's Introduction to his "Lexicon" (discussed below), notable for its programmatic statements, metaphorical language, and concerns about a perceived continuation of Nazi discourse practices even in the language of anti-fascists. The corrupting power of the endless repetition of fascist language is described through biological metaphor: LTI impregnates words, phrases and sentences with its poison ('Gift'), permeating the "flesh and blood of the people" (2000, p. 15)

("Fleisch und Blut der Menge", 1978, p. 21) and being absorbed unconsciously until it takes control of people's thoughts and, more importantly, their emotions:

> Sprache dichtet und denkt nicht nur für mich, sie lenkt auch mein Gefühl, sie steuert mein ganzes seelisches Wesen, je selbstverständlicher, je unbewusster ich mich ihr überlasse. (1978, p. 21)
>
> But language does not simply write and think for me, it also increasingly dictates my feelings and governs my entire spiritual being the more unquestioningly and unconsciously I abandon myself to it. (2000, p. 15)

Klemperer notes that the regime did not invent the words FANATISCH und FANATISMUS, but "changed their value and used them more in one day than other epochs used them in years..." (2000, p. 16, "in ihrem Wert verändert und [...] sie an einem Tage häufiger gebraucht als andere Zeiten in Jahren" (1978, p. 21)). The LTI had turned language into political power's "most powerful, most public and most surreptitious means of advertising" (2000, p. 16) ("stärkstes, ihr öffentlichstes und geheimstes Werbemittel", 1978, p. 22). Klemperer concludes this essay with a remarkable comparison:

> Wenn den rechtgläubigen Juden ein Essgerät kultisch unrein geworden ist, dann reinigen sie es, indem sie es in der Erde vergraben. Man sollte viele Worte des nazistischen Sprachgebrauchs für lange Zeit, und einige für immer, ins Massengrab legen. (1978, p. 22)
>
> If a piece of cutlery belonging to orthodox Jews has become ritually unclean they purify it by burying it in the earth. Many words in common usage during the Nazi period should be committed to a mass grave for a very long time, some for ever. (2000, p. 16)

The image of the mass grave is symptomatic of the brutalized public consciousness in 1945, and was certainly intended to shock, conjuring up an image of the millions who had perished under German fascism (although it should be noted that Klemperer envisages only a temporary 'burial' for some of these expressions). The book is explicitly linked to the denazification project, and Klemperer is typical of many language critics at this time in his perception that the LTI has not disappeared with the regime. Indeed, he even calls this continuing, often involuntary mouthing of fascist discourse the Language of the Fourth Reich (a term first encountered in the final pages of the sixty-four page typescript: "LQI. Beobachtet seit Juni 1945" ("LQI. Observed since June 1945", cf. Fischer-Hupe 2001, p. 46)). The issue is also broached in the "LTI" chapter[11]:

> Es wird jetzt soviel davon geredet, die Gesinnung des Faschismus auszurotten, es wird auch soviel dafür getan. Kriegsverbrecher werden gerichtet, "kleine Pgs"[12] (Sprache des Vierten Reichs!) aus ihren Ämtern entfernt, nationalistische Bücher aus dem Verkehr gezogen, Hitlerplätze und Göringstraßen umbenannt, Hitler-Eichen gefällt. Aber die Sprache des Dritten Reiches scheint in manchen charakteristischen Ausdrücken überleben zu sollen; sie haben sich so tief eingefressen, dass sie ein dauernder Besitz der deutschen Sprache zu werden scheinen. Wie viele Male zum Exempel habe ich seit dem Mai 1945 in Funkreden, in leidenschaftlich antifaschistischen Kundgebungen etwa von "charakterlichen" Eigenschaften oder vom "kämpferischen" Wesen der Demokratie sprechen hören! Das sind Ausdrücke aus dem Zentrum—das Dritte Reich würde sagen, aus der Wesensmitte—der LTI. (1978, p. 20)

> So much is being said at the moment about eradicating the fascist mentality and so much is being done to that end. War criminals are being executed, "little Pgs" (the language of the Fourth Reich!) are being removed from office, nationalist books are being withdrawn from circulation, Hitler Squares and Goering Streets are being renamed, Hitler oaks are being felled. But it appears that the language of the Third Reich is to survive in the form of certain characteristic expressions; they have lodged themselves so deep below the surface that they appear to be becoming a permanent feature of the German language. For example, since 1945 I have on countless occasions, in speeches broadcast on the wireless and passionately anti-fascist demonstrations, heard reference to such things as innate qualities "of character" and the "aggressive" nature of democracy. These are expressions from the heart—the Third Reich would say "from the very lifeblood"—of the LTI. (2000, p. 14)

The critical reception of *LTI* has been generally favourable, although its early reception by the professional linguistics establishment was coloured by prejudices about language criticism lying outside of the scientific ('wissenschaftlich') study of language. (This issue will be elaborated in the following chapter in connection with the reception of the "Lexicon of the 'Unmensch'"). Once this prejudice subsided, *LTI* was praised for its empirical documentation of real scenarios and instinctive focus on language as *parole*. Klemperer has been seen as a modern discourse analyst *avant la lettre*, and has been compared to Foucault in his insistence on the power of discourse and his broad understanding of language as part of the larger discursive environment, along with paralinguistic and non-linguistic "dispositives" (sites, manifestations) of cultural norms (Fischer-Hupe 2001, pp. 231–233). In (para-)linguistic terms, Klemperer's modernity is seen in his understanding of the importance of text types, metaphors, style, euphemisms, and argumentation structures in the deployment of language.

The appearance of the diaries in the mid-1990s was a publishing sensation (English translations are available, cf. Klemperer 1998, 1999), rekindling international interest in the book but also prompting questions about the relationship between diary and book. Heidrun Kämper (2000, p. 40) draws a distinction between the diary as an "archive" resource, and the book as an example of "the language-critical engagement with National Socialism refracted through the mirror of communist interpretive models" ("die sprachkritische Aufarbeitung des Nationalsozialismus gebrochen vom Spiegel kommunistischer Deutungsmuster") in which the sufferings of Jews are under-represented. Kämper had earlier suggested (1996, p. 338) that Klemperer is a case study for a chapter of German discourse history which asks whether and how a critique of language written under dictatorship differs from a critique of dictatorial language written after its collapse—a question which applies equally to Sternberger/Storz/Süskind, as we shall see.

"The Lexicon of the 'Unmensch'" (1945–1948)

The most important thing to know about the "Lexicon of the 'Unmensch'" is that it exists in three distinct versions: the series of glosses published between 1945 and 1948, and the two book editions of 1957 and 1967, in which new glosses were added, others omitted, and several texts, including the Introduction, amended or substantially rewritten. (A tabular overview of these three iterations is provided in the Appendix.) The implications of these acts of continuous rewriting ('Fortschreibung') were considerable, and will be discussed at length in the following chapter. The focus here is on the first phase of the "Lexicon".

Sternberger was given the first licence in the American zone of occupation, to edit and publish a monthly cultural and political journal, *Die Wandlung* (with Karl Jaspers, Werner Krauss and Alfred Weber). His early sketches for this journal make the connection with the re-education agenda of the Allies clear:

> Es geht darum, ebenso sorgfältig wie entschieden den Anfang damit zu machen, daß die Deutschen gewissenhaft und selbständig denkende, ihres Rechts und ihrer Pflicht bewußte Personen werden, die nicht bloß Befehlen gehorchen, sondern das Wahre selbst einsehen, die nicht Schlagworte nachplappern, sondern eine eigne Sprache reden. (Cf. Waldmüller 1988, p. 14)
>
> The purpose is to make a start, carefully but decisively, on the Germans becoming conscientious and independent thinkers conscious of their rights and of their duties, who do not just follow commands but see the truth for themselves, who do not just parrot slogans but speak their own language.

From its inception, Sternberger planned a regular series of glosses under the rubric "Aus dem Wörterbuch des Unmenschen" ("From the Lexicon of the 'Unmensch'"), for which he subsequently recruited Storz and Süskind, trusted colleagues who had also published in the *Frankfurter Zeitung* in the 'Third Reich'. (He also tried unsuccessfully to recruit Franz Dornseiff, cf. Dodd 2007, pp. 252–254). Writing to Storz in October 1945, Sternberger characterized the new discourse environment thus: "Es wimmelt von 'Betreuung', und kein Mensch merkt, was er da tut. Es ist kaum zu ertragen. Wir müssen die Kraus'sche 'Fackel' von neuem anzünden […]" ("It's crawling with 'Betreuung' and no one notices what they're doing when they say it. It is almost unbearable. We must light Kraus's 'Torch' again […]", cf. Dodd 2007, p. 243). The resulting series of glosses reveals a habitus, formed in inner exile, in the way of thinking and talking about language which is harder to understand today than, for example,

Klemperer's work. Twenty three glosses were published, in alphabetical order but with egregious omissions, between November 1945 and April 1948. The terms attributed to the UNMENSCH were: AUSRICHTUNG (way of thinking), BETREUUNG (care), CHARAKTERLICH (character-wise), DURCHFÜHREN (carry out, implement), EINSATZ (effort, contribution, operation), FANATISCH (fanatical), GESTALTUNG (shaping), HÄRTE (hardness), INTELLEKTUELL (intellectual), KULTURSCHAFFENDE (those who create culture), LAGER (camp), MÄDEL (girl), ORGANISIEREN (organize), PROPAGANDA, QUERSCHIESSEN (to carp), RAUM, SCHULUNG (training), SEKTOR, TRAGBAR/UNTRAGBAR (person (un)suitable for political support), VERTRETER (representative), ZEITGESCHEHEN (current events). Perhaps the most striking thing about this list is the absence, with one or two possible exceptions, of what might be considered high-profile keywords of Nazi ideology, terms like ENDLÖSUNG (final solution), JUDENFRAGE (Jewish question), ARISCH, or SCHICKSALSGEMEINSCHAFT (community of fate). The calculation behind this decision appears to be the observation that most such words were now marked in the public awareness as tainted. Instead, the Lexicon targets a sub-stratum of words still in unmarked everyday usage. Most of them are still in everyday use today and carry no sinister overtones for the vast majority of German speakers. In 1945, however, I think we must accept the evidence that it was precisely in this sub-stratum (in terms of political discourse) of the vocabulary that sensitized Germans perceived fascist norms persisting in patterns of everyday speech—an LQI, to adopt Klemperer's term.

The correspondence between the three authors reveals the journalistic frenzy in which they worked (Sternberger in Heidelberg, Storz in Schwäbisch Hall, Süskind on the Starnberger See south of Munich), which also explains the missing glosses for the letters J und N (for which JUDE and NORDISCH were briefly considered) and W (for which WELTANSCHAUUNG was dismissed, cf. Dodd 2003, 2007, pp. 241–254). All three signed their contributions with the same abbreviated signatures used in the *Frankfurter Zeitung*, and fell back on material they had developed (and published) in the Reich. Perhaps the most striking example of this is Sternberger's Foreword in November 1945, many of whose formulations (as noted in the previous chapter) reiterate those found in his criticism of Reifferscheidt in 1940. Intriguingly, Sternberger began with a tribute to the recently deceased Haecker:

"Sie sind die tiefsten Sprachverständigen, weil sie Sachverständige sind, und werden tiefere Sachverständige, weil sie Sprachverständige sind"—sagt Theodor Haecker (dessen Hingang wir vor wenigen Monaten erfahren und beklagen mussten, und dessen Wort als das eines christlichen Abendländers wir nun sehr entbehren) von gewissen metaphysischen Schriftstellern. Sprache ist die Gabe des Menschen, das verwirrende und befreiende, verräterische und erhellende, ausgreifende und fesselnde, lösende und bindende, selige und gefährliche Medium und Siegel seines Wesens. Soviel und welche Sprache einer spricht, soviel und solche Sache, Welt oder Natur ist ihm erschlossen. Und jedes Wort, das er redet, wandelt die Welt, worin er sich bewegt, wandelt ihn selbst und seinen Ort in dieser Welt. Darum ist nichts gleichgültig an der Sprache, und nichts so wesentlich wie die façon de parler. Der Verderb der Sprache ist der Verderb des Menschen. Seien wir auf der Hut! Worte und Sätze können ebensowohl Gärten wie Kerker sein, in die wir, redend, uns selbst einsperren, und die Bestimmung, Sprache sei allein die Gabe des Menschen oder eine menschliche Gabe, bietet keine Sicherheit. Denn der Begriff des Menschen schließt die Möglichkeit (und Wirklichkeit) des Unmenschen in sich; im anderen Falle ist er ein unzulänglicher Begriff, und eben daran können und müssen wir ihn prüfen, da wir das Unmenschliche kennen. So hat der Mensch auch als Unmensch seinen Wortschatz, seine eigentümliche Grammatik und seinen eigentümlichen Satzbau. Wir wollen hier seinem Wortschatz nachspüren und in der Sprache jeweils der Sache auf die Sprünge kommen, die sie bedeutet. Sie ist—leider—keine fremde Sprache, aber dieses Wörterbuch hat eine Aufgabe, die derjenigen der übrigen und gewöhnlichen Wörterbücher genau entgegengesetzt ist: es soll uns diese Sprache fremd machen. (*Die Wandlung* 1/1, p. 75. Cf. Hay et al. 1995, p. 69.)

"They have the most profound understanding of language because they understand the world, and gain a more profound understanding of the world because they understand language"—says Theodor Haecker (whose death we had to lament some months ago, and whose word as that of the Christian West we sorely miss at this moment) about certain metaphysical writers. Language is the gift of humankind, the confusing and liberating, treacherous and illuminating, extending and enslaving, blessed and dangerous medium and seal of our being. How much and which language we speak determines how much and which world or nature is available to us. And every word that we speak changes the world in which we move,

> changes us and our place in this world. That is why there is nothing indifferent about language, and nothing so essential as the *façon de parler*. The ruin of language is the ruin of mankind. Let us be on our guard! Words and sentences can be gardens or just as easily prisons in which, as we speak, we incarcerate ourselves, and the definition that language is the gift of humankind alone or a human gift, offers us no security. For the concept of the human being includes within it the possibility (and reality) of the inhuman being. Otherwise it is an inadequate concept, and it is precisely on this point that we can and must examine language, since we have come to know the inhuman. Thus the human being as inhuman being [Unmensch] also has his vocabulary, his characteristic grammar and his own syntax. We set out here to examine his vocabulary and uncover in his language the hidden meanings. This language is, sadly, not a foreign language, but the purpose of this lexicon runs directly counter to other, conventional dictionaries: to estrange us from this language.

It is worth quoting this programmatic statement in full as a reflection on the searing experience of alienation from one's own language, and the overwhelming sense of the dangerous power of language to 'imprison' us, a form of the manipulation thesis of language. In this respect, the parallels with Klemperer are unmistakeable. Unlike Klemperer, however, Sternberger's approach was lexical, in the form of an illustrative counter-dictionary of morally tainted expressions for sensitized readers to supplement from their own experience. The trope of the UNMENSCH marks a move into mythical thinking that is quite unlike Klemperer's worldly approach, although in the immediate context of denazification there could be little doubt that the UNMENSCH was not so much a mythical figure as a generic concept: THE NAZI.

All the glosses were to have a two-part structure (though this was not always adhered to). In Part A, the use and meaning of the word before the advent of the 'Unmensch' was described; in Part B, its perversion in the usage of the 'Unmensch'. Explicitly, a model of meaning was invoked in which the 'true' (and humane) meaning was recovered through its etymology. A recurring theme in these glosses is that the perverted use by the 'Unmensch' is a strategy to subjugate people, turning them into objects of his dealings, passive recipients of power. Although not expressly stated, the impression given, especially if we equate UNMENSCH and NAZI, is that the process of perversion started with the rise of Nazism, perhaps even in 1933. But this is one of the questions about the Lexicon to which there is no clear answer. There is space here to look in detail at only one of the glosses, "Betreuung" (24.1.1946)—and this gloss, in its 1957 incarnation, will also be at the centre of the critical discussion in the next chapter. It is perhaps the most controversial of all the glosses, with the most complex argumentation. The following is a summary:

From the adjective 'treu', a verb is derived using the prefix 'be-' ('betreuen': to care for, supervise, look after), from which the abstract noun is then derived. The prefix 'be-' produces a transitive verb with an accusative grammatical object ('jemanden betreuen') in place of the construction in which the person to whom the action is directed appears in the dative case ('jemandem treu sein'). The accusativizing prefix 'be-' is associated with an "inhumane urge to action" ("unmenschlichen Tätigkeitsdrang"), replacing a relationship of equality between two people with one in which one person dominates the other. Part B of this gloss is reproduced here in full:

> Die Hortnerin oder besser: der Kindergarten betreut die Kinder. Der Lehrer oder besser: die Schule betreut die Schüler—ihre Aufgabe ist die "schulische Betreuung". Der Arzt betreut die Kranken oder besser: das Krankenmaterial (auf deutsch und etwas einschmeichelnder: das Krankengut). Insbesondere betreut die Landesirrenanstalt die Geisteskranken. Die NSV betreute Mutter und Kind, der Reichsnährstand die Bauern, die DAF die Arbeiter: die Wirtschaftsgruppen, Wirtschaftsämter, Rüstungsinspektionen und andere Behörden, alle zusammengefaßt im ausdrücklich so genannten "Betreuungsausschuß", betreuten die industriellen Betriebe. Die Geheime Staatspolizei betreute die Juden, der Verteiler betreute die Käufer und der Führer Adolf Hitler betreute das ganze deutsche Volk. Niemand darf unbetreut bleiben, und zu keiner Zeit seines kurzen Lebens soll der Mensch unbetreut bleiben, denn niemand soll zu irgendeiner Zeit Rechte geltend machen und Ansprüche erheben, niemand zu irgendeiner Zeit auch Liebe, Hilfe und Treue erhoffen können. Er wird ja betreut und damit basta. Die Betreuung wuchs und dehnte sich im gleichen Maße aus, in dem die Werke der christlichen Barmherzigkeit abnahmen oder gewaltsam verdrängt wurden. Wenn erst eines Tages der Gatte die Gattin oder die Gattin den Gatten betreut, dann wird endlich auch die Ehe begraben sein. Am Ende löscht die

Betreuung den Jemand als Jemand, als eigenes Wesen, aus, dem sie gilt oder zu gelten scheint. Hat man je schon gehört, daß jemand von sich selbst sagte: "ich werde von der und der Organisation, von der Schule oder von der Polizei usw. betreut"?—Nein, das hat man noch nicht gehört, denn diese beiden Dinge vertragen sich nicht miteinander, das "ich" und das "betreut werden". Das ist eben ein wahres Tätigkeitswort, strotzend von Aktivität. Im Passiv läßt sich das Verbum nicht in allen Personen durchkonjugieren, jedenfalls nicht in der ersten (ich), kaum in der zweiten (du), aber ohne weiteres in der dritten (er, sie, es), die einen nichts angeht; im Plural geht es überhaupt ganz gut, da ist man ja auch zu mehreren. Und auf den einzelnen, der da (passiv) leidet, kommt es im Plural nicht so genau an. Daß es in der ersten Person des Singulars nicht geht, das ist gut so. Denn der Unmensch mag es nicht, wenn andere Leute "ich" sagen. (*Die Wandlung*, 1/2, p. 67f.)

The kindergarten teacher, or rather: the kindergarten looks after the children. The teacher, or rather: the school looks after the pupils—its job is "schooling supervision". The doctor looks after the ill, or rather: the pathological material (in German and rather more accommodatingly, pathological stuff). Specifically, the regional mental asylum looks after the mentally ill. The NSV looked after mother and child, the Reichsnährstand the farmers, the DAF the workers, the business divisions, economic offices, weapons inspections and other authorities, all gathered together in the precisely so called "Supervisory Committee", looked after the industrial enterprises. The Gestapo looked after the Jews, the [black market] supplier looked after the customers and the Führer Adolf Hitler looked after the whole of the German people. No one is allowed to remain un-looked after, for no one is supposed to claim their rights at any time or make claims, no one to ever hope to find love, help, and personal commitment. He gets looked after and that's the end of it. Supervision grew and expanded in proportion as the institutions of Christian charity shrank or were forcibly suppressed. If one day the husband looks after the wife or vice versa, then marriage will be buried once and for all. In the end, supervision effaces the person as a person, as the independent being they once counted, or appeared to count as. Has anyone ever heard of someone saying of themselves "I am being looked after by this and that organization, by the school or the police etc"? No, you never hear that, because these two things are incompatible, the 'I' and the 'am being

> looked after'. It is a real action word, bristling with activity. In the passive the verb does not conjugate in all persons, at least not in the first (I), hardly in the second (you), but without a problem in the third (he, she, it), which is no one's concern. It goes very well in the plural, for there you are one of many. And the individual who is suffering there (passively) is not really the issue in the plural use. And it is good that it does not work so well in the first person singular. Because the 'Unmensch' does not like it when other people say "I".

Another striking difference to Klemperer becomes apparent here: the example sentences are unattested, without names, places, settings. They are vouched for by Sternberger's own experience rather than by documented record. Institutions rather than individuals are the grammatical subject of these examples, some of which, it is worth noting, have the verb in the past tense, clearly referring to the 'Third Reich',[13] whilst others use the present tense. In at least two of these cases, however, there are allusions to the Nazi period. The reference to the "schulische Betreuung" of the school is resonant of SCHULUNG (included later in the Lexicon), which carried implications of ideological 'training'. And in the doctor's BETREUUNG of KRANKENMATERIAL or the 'all-German' synonym KRANKENGUT (pathological case material), we can detect the clear echo of Sternberger's magisterial essay in the *Frankfurter Zeitung* in April 1941 (reviewed in Chap. 7), *"Menschen als Material".

To conclude: the task of a social and political denazification, supported by the Allies and many Germans, lost momentum long before the founding of the two German states. The Allies' notion of a denazification "of the language" was also enthusiastically taken up by many Germans, but with little co-ordination and no agreed methodology. A comparison of Klemperer and Sternberger/Storz/Süskind reveals much common ground in their urgency of purpose and perception of an 'LQI'. It also reveals profound differences in their understanding of what language is, how it works, and how to describe it. The authors of the "Lexicon", in particular, would face many difficult questions in the Federal Republic in the 1960s and 1970s.

Notes

1. Eitz and Stötzel 2007, p. 197, class ENTNAZIFIZERUNG as a "Stigmavokabel" of the time. On the use of PERSILSCHEIN in 1945, cf. p. 200. On the problematic concept of the 'good German', cf. O Dochartaigh and Schönfeld (eds.) 2013.
2. The categories were: I: HAUPTSCHULDIGE (major offenders), II: SCHULDIGE (offenders), III: MINDERBELASTETE (lesser offenders), IV: MITLÄUFER (followers), V: UNBELASTETE (exonerated). Cf. Eitz and Stötzel 2007, p. 201.
3. Related concepts were already being used in this period to characterize the 'Resistenz' of 'inner emigrant' discourses, for example in the FZ. Cf. Hepp 1949. For an example of the enduring nature of this scepticism in the case of Pechel, see Ehrke-Rotermund 2014.
4. Jolas grew up in bilingual (French/German) Lorraine before emigrating to the USA. In the 1920s he had been prominent in the modernist literary scene in Paris, editing the journal *Transition*.
5. 'Wandlung' can also designate an inner, spiritual change.
6. Waldmüller 1988 contains a catalogue of all contributions to *Die Wandlung*.
7. On journals in this period, cf. Hay and Rambaldo et al. 1995, Flanagan 2000. Journal titles include *Aufbau*, *Frankfurter Hefte*, *Die Gegenwart*, *Der Monat*, *Neue Auslese*, *Ost und West*, and *Der Ruf*.
8. Deissler (2004, p. 241f.), following Köpf 1995, p. 92, finds it "astonishing" that the "Goebbels propagandist" Süskind was "allowed" to pursue these activities in light of his publications during the Reich. This does Süskind the double disservice of failing to engage with his writings, reviewed in Chap. 6 of the present study, whilst letting other authors pass either with a much more carefully formulated note (as with Jancke, cf. p. 213), or without comment of any kind (as in the dubious case of Reifferscheidt, cf. p. 243).
9. TOTALITÄR occurs for the first time in the Kerncorpus 20 in 1934 in the writings of Kurt Tucholsky. Occurrences before 1939 reflect the anticipation of war between 'liberal' and 'totalitarian' societies, whereby from most contexts it is clear that fascist regimes are being referred to. An example from Poland in 1938, however, talks of the need to resist "totalitäre Bestrebungen von links und rechts" ("totalitarian designs from left and right"). dwds.de, Search term 'totalitär', Kerncorpus twentieth century [18.8.2017].

10. English quotations in this section, with page numbers, are from Martin Brady's translation (Klemperer 2000). German quotations are from Klemperer 1978.
11. The LQI trope would later be cited by conservative commentators drawing an equivalence between Nazism and Soviet Communism as 'totalitarian' social systems (cf. Fischer-Hupe 2001, p. 233f.). Klemperer was indeed dismayed by the similarities with the language of the Soviet authorities (cf. Watt 1998). This first occurrence, however, suggests a broader critique of the general population.
12. Pg is a short form of PARTEIGENOSSE (party comrade), which is also the German equivalent of Russian TOVARISCH (comrade). Klemperer may be alluding to this parallel here but it seems more likely that he is objecting to the qualifying adjective and the relativizing concept of 'little' Nazis.
13. Other institutions mentioned in this gloss are the NSV, Reichsnährstand, Deutsche Arbeitsfront, and the economic organizations in the 'Betreuungsausschuss' allocating resources to the war economy.

Bibliography

Arendt, Hannah. 1946. Die organisierte Schuld. *Die Wandlung* 1 (3): 333–344.

———. 1948. Konzentrationsläger. *Die Wandlung* 3 (4): 309–329.

Deissler, Dirk. 2004. *Die entnazifizierte Sprache*. Frankfurt/Main: Peter Lang.

Dodd, William J. 2003. 'Wir müssen die Kraus'sche 'Fackel' von neuem anzünden'. Zur Entstehung der Rubrik 'Aus dem Wörterbuch des Unmenschen' in der Zeitschrift 'Die Wandlung'. *Jahrbuch der Deutschen Schillergesellschaft* 47: 342–375.

———. 2007. *Jedes Wort wandelt die Welt. Dolf Sternbergers politische Sprachkritik*. Göttingen: Wallstein.

Ehrke-Rotermund, Heidrun. 2014. Rudolf Pechel und Wilmont Haacke – zwei Intellektuelle im 'Dritten Reich' oder: Vom 'guten Bekannten' zur Unperson. *Euphorion. Zeitschrift für Literaturgeschichte* 108 (4): 417–448.

Eitz, Thorsten, and Georg Stötzel. 2007. *Wörterbuch der 'Vergangenheitsbewältigung'. Die NS-Vergangenheit im öffentlichen Sprachgebrauch*. Hildesheim, Zürich, New York: Olms.

Fischer-Hupe, Kristine. 2001. *Victor Klemperers "LTI. Notizbuch eines Philologen". Ein Kommentar*. Hildesheim: Olms.

Flanagan, Clare. 2000. *A Study of German Political-Cultural Periodicals from the Years of Allied Occupation, 1945–1949*. Lewiston, NY: E. Mellen Press.

Hay, Gerhard, Hartmut Rambaldo, et al., eds. 1995. *Als der Krieg zu Ende war. Literarisch-politische Publizistik 1945–1950. Eine Ausstellung des Deutschen Literaturarchivs im Schiller-Nationalmuseum Marbach a.N.* Marbach am Neckar: Deutsche Schillergesellschaft.

Hepp, Fred. 1949. *Der geistige Widerstand im Kulturteil der 'Frankfurter Zeitung' gegen die Diktatur des totalen Staates 1933–1943.* Dissertation, Ludwig-Maximilians-Universität München.

Jaspers, Karl. 1946. *Die Schuldfrage.* Heidelberg: Lambert Schneider.

Jolas, Eugen. 1998. *Man from Babel.* Edited, Annotated and Introduced by Andreas Kramer and Rainer Rumold. New Haven, CT: Yale University Press.

Kämper, Heidrun. 1996. Zeitgeschichte – Sprachgeschichte. Gedanken bei der Lektüre des Tagebuchs eines Philologen. *Zeitschrift für Germanistische Linguistik* 24: 328–341.

———. 1998. Entnazifizierung—Sprachliche Existenzformen eines ethischen Konzepts. In *Das 20. Jahrhundert. Sprachgeschichte—Zeitgeschichte,* Hg. Heidrun Kämper and Hartmut Schmidt, 304–329. Berlin, New York: de Gruyter.

———. 2000. Sprachgeschichte – Zeitgeschichte. Die Tagebücher Victor Klemperers. *Deutsche Sprache* 28 (1): 25–41.

Klemperer, Victor. 1978. *LTI. Notizbuch eines Philologen.* Berlin: Aufbau.

———. 1998. *Tagebücher 1933–1945.* Herausgegeben von Walter Nowojski unter Mitarbeit von Hedwig Klemperer. Berlin: Aufbau Taschenbuch Verlag.

———. 1999. *To the Bitter End: The Diaries of Victor Klemperer, 1942–1945.* Translated by Martin Chalmers. London: Weidenfeld & Nicolson.

———. 2000. *The Language of the Third Reich. LTI: Lingua Tertii Imperii.* Translated by Martin Brady. London: Athlone Press.

Köpf, Peter. 1995. *Schreiben nach jeder Richtung. Goebbels-Propagandisten in der westdeutschen Nachkriegspresse.* Berlin: Links.

Krauss, Werner. 1946. Macht und Ohnmacht der Wörterbücher. *Die Wandlung* 1 (9): 772–786.

O Dochartaigh, Pól, and Christiane Schönfeld, eds. 2013. *Representing the 'Good German' in Literature and Culture after 1945. Altruism and Moral Ambiguity.* Rochester, NY: Camden House.

Paechter, Heinz. 1944. *Nazi-Deutsch. A Glossary of Contemporary German Usage.* New York: Frederick Ungar.

Saunders, Frances Stonor. 1999. *Who Paid the Piper? The CIA and the Cultural Cold War.* London: Granta.

Sternberger, Dolf. 1947. Die Vernichtung des Warschauer Ghettos im April und Mai 1943. Auszug aus dem Bericht des verantwortlichen SS- und Polizeiführers Stroop. Mit einer Vorbemerkung von Dolf Sternberger. *Die Wandlung* 2 (6): 524–553.

Stötzel, Georg. 1989. Nazi-Verbrechen und öffentliche Sprachsensibilität. *Sprache und Literatur* 20: 32–52.

Waldmüller, Monika. 1988. *Die Wandlung. Eine Monatsschrift.* Marbach am Neckar: Deutsche Schillergesellschaft.

Watt, Roderick. 1998. Victor Klemperer's 'Sprache des Vierten Reiches': LTI = LQI? *German Life and Letters* 51 (3): 360–371.

9

Legacy: Vergangenheitsbewältigung

It is not much of an exaggeration to say that almost every contribution to German cultural and intellectual life since 1945 has in some way had to address the Nazi past. Today, the German achievement in doing so does indeed appear extraordinary and may well be unique in the history of nations, as Micha Brumlik maintains:

> Gemessen an anderen Staaten, in denen Massenverbrechen, Genozide und Politozide begangen wurden, hat die Bundesrepublik Deutschland, ein vernünftiger Zweifel ist nicht möglich, Außerordentliches vollbracht. (Brumlik, "Vorwort", Fischer and Lorenz (eds.) 2015, p. 12)
>
> Compared to other states in which there have been mass crimes, genocides and political murders, the achievement of the Federal Republic, there can be no reasonable doubt, has been extraordinary.

This chapter has two sections, focusing on the period from 1949 to 1989, and on the post-unification period from 1990 to the present. Instrumentalizations of the Nazi past play a role in the discourse history of these periods, alongside contestations of concepts encapsulated in

W J Dodd, *National Socialism and German Discourse*,
https://doi.org/10.1007/978-3-319-74660-9_9

keyword expressions. The chapter begins with the belated process of VERGANGENHEITSBEWÄLTIGUNG (coming to terms with the past) in the late 1950s, mainly in the Federal Republic, but including a review of the role of Nazi tropes in the Cold War division of Germany to 1989. A significant moment in the development of the discourse on language in this period was the reception of Sternberger/Storz/Süskind in the so-called 'Streit um die Sprachkritik' (argument about language criticism) in the 1960s and 1970s. The section on the period from 1990 to the present reviews the impact of unification on the discourse on Nazism in Germany and abroad, particularly in Britain. This is followed by a brief review of taboo expressions in contemporary German discourse, resurgent nationalist discourses in post-unification Germany, and the contribution of a modern 'politolinguistics' in describing and contesting these discourses.

VERGANGENHEITSBEWÄLTIGUNG I (1949–1989)

Major events in this period include the economic boom (Wirtschaftswunder) in the Western German state in the 1950s; the Auschwitz trials and other trials of Nazi criminals in the late 1950s and early 1960s; the migration of some three million Germans from the GDR to the Federal Republic before the building of the Berlin Wall in 1961; the generational conflict of '1968' which challenged the silence of parents and grandparents regarding their actions under National Socialism; Chancellor Willy Brandt's symbolic KNIEFALL (kneeling) at the memorial in the Warsaw Ghetto in 1970; the televising of films about the Nazi era, most notably the American television series *Holocaust* in 1979; Federal President Richard von Weiszäcker's magisterial speech on German responsibility and penance on the fortieth anniversary of the 'liberation' (BEFREIUNG) by the Allies, 8 May 1985; President Reagan and Chancellor Kohl's visit in 1987 to the military cemetery in Bitburg where SS officers are buried; Federal President Philipp Jenninger's disastrous speech on 10 November 1988, the fiftieth anniversary of the Reich pogrom, which gave offence because of the inappropriate prominence of Nazi discourse which Jenninger failed to mark as 'Imitat'.

The generational upheaval which hit the Federal Republic in the 1960s grew out of a discontent with the economic and military policies of the Adenauer government (the Wirtschaftswunder, NATO membership in 1955), and the failure to pursue denazification and the SCHULDFRAGE. As Eitz and Stötzel remark, the Federal Republic in the 1950s was focused less on the crimes of National Socialism, and more on their consequences (which included formal agreement with Israel in 1952 on the payment of reparations (WIEDERGUTMACHUNG)). The denazification process was ended formally in 1954 in the Federal Republic. Chancellor Adenauer had already announced in October 1949 that it was better for the past to be left as the past ("Vergangenes als vergangen sein zu lassen"), and calls for a SCHLUSSSTRICH (line to be drawn under the matter), already heard in 1946, were now more common (Eitz and Stötzel 2007, p. 601f., 2009, pp. 456–482).

Kämper's analysis (2005, 2007) of the SCHULDDISKURS in the period to 1955, tracing the discourse practices of three groups: OPFER, TÄTER, NICHTTÄTER (victims, perpetrators, non-perpetrators) finds evidence of an incomplete reckoning with the past and an extensive SCHULDABWEHR (suppression of guilt). This was indeed the diagnosis of Alexander and Margarete Mitscherlich (1967), whose psychoanalytic study of the nation's "inability to mourn" (UNFÄHIGKEIT ZU TRAUERN) pinpointed a persistent repression of the past in a country where Willy Brandt, a former exile fighting against Nazi Germany, could be traduced as unpatriotic while those who fought for the regime ('for Germany') could still parade their medals. Their prognosis was bleak: "Die Betrachtung unserer stilisierten Vergangenheit wird also nicht zu einer Erschütterung unserer nationalen Identität, die tiefer gehen würde, führen" ("Contemplation of our stylized past will not lead to a shaking up of our national identity which would go deeper", 1967, p. 68). The psychoanalytical analogy was prescient. The "shaking up" duly occurred rather like Freud's "return of the repressed", culminating in the fierce generational conflict apostrophized as the '1968' phenomenon. This conflict had several themes, including protests against American-led foreign policy, the Vietnam war in particular, but also anger at their parents' and grandparents' silence about the Nazi period. The origins of the term VERGANGENHEITSBEWÄLTIGUNG appear to go back to 1955, to a conference of the Evangelische Akadamie in Berlin titled "Hitler oder die unbewältigte Vergangenheit" (Hitler or the un-overcome Past). The collocations of 'Vergangenheit' and 'bewältigen' (a term used in psychotherapy for 'processing', 'overcoming', 'managing', or 'dealing with' problems) eventually settled in the compound abstract noun at some point around 1960. Theodor Adorno's 1959 essay "Was bedeutet: Aufarbeitung der Vergangenheit" (What does 'Working through the Past' Mean?) was also an influential contribution to this debate in intellectual circles, in which AUFARBEITUNG was (and is) preferred to BEWÄLTIGUNG because it implies a form of remembering rather than forgetting. A significant moment in the discourse on language was the 1966 conference of Germanists in Munich, at which academic 'young Turks' began the process of critically reviewing the role of their academic discipline in the Nazi state. Peter von Polenz delivered a paper on the connection between linguistic purism and Nazism (Lämmert et al. 1967, pp. 111–160). At this time, also, von Polenz was one of several young linguistic scientists who were unhappy with Sternberger/Storz/Süskind's analysis of 'tainted' words as a coming-to-terms with the role of language in fascism. This dispute, reviewed below, would play an important role in the reorientation of the academic study of language-as-discourse in Germany.

The Instrumentalized Past: The "Nazi Complex"

Georg Stötzel has traced arguably the most disturbing feature of German political discourse after 1945 in respect of National Socialism, namely the instrumentalizing use of opportunistic Nazi comparisons calculated to traduce a political opponent (Stötzel and Wengeler 1995, pp. 355–382 (also pp. 300–303); Stötzel 1986, 1989). In this tradition of political discourse, Stötzel notes, the temptation of momentary political advantage ("Augenblicksvorteil") overrides respect for history, elevating emotional appeal over intellectual and moral honesty. Far from furthering historical understanding, the "Nazi Complex" breeds and thrives on historical amnesia. In an active democratic culture, we would expect these instrumentalizations to be the subject of critical comment by contemporaries. This is not always the case in the examples collected by Stötzel.

In the wake of the 'Spiegel Affair' in 1962—the first major political crisis of the Adenauer chancellorship, in which police arrested editors of the Hamburg magazine *Der Spiegel* and searched its offices for a month after it had published details of a NATO assessment critical of West Germany's defence capabilities—one liberal newspaper labelled this intervention a NACHT UND NEBEL exercise, invoking the Gestapo's practice of furtive arrests (and disappearances) in the middle of the night. Adenauer objected to the insinuation that GESTAPO-METHODEN were being employed by the government, countering that he had evidence of acts of treason. This 'scandal', widely interpreted as an attempt to intimidate free investigative journalism, illustrates the complex moral issues around this trope, in that Adenauer and his defence minister Franz Josef Strauss appear as the wronged parties, being compared to Nazis, whilst the charge against them was breach of the constitution. This raises the question whether the use of Nazi comparisons can ever be justified in the cause of democratic values—as Stötzel believes is the case here, and in another in which the writer, political activist, and alleged "sympathiser" with the terrorist scene, Heinrich Böll, complained publicly in 1975 about the VOLKSGERICHTSHOF-TON (People's Court tone) in media attacks on him, invoking the invective hurled at defendants by Roland Freisler and other notorious judges before issuing their summary verdict. Franz Josef Strauss was himself at the centre of a controversy in 1983 when he described some modern art as ENTARTETE KUNST (degenerate art, attested in 1955 and as early 1946, cf. Stötzel 1989, p. 41f., 1995, p. 358, 368). The interesting feature of this controversy is the trivialization strategy used by Strauss in rejecting the charge of using 'Nazi language': the Nazis also presumably used toothbrushes, but nobody was seriously suggesting that we all stop using toothbrushes. As Georg Stötzel points out, this argumentation posits a false equivalence between a central ideologeme of Nazism which led to persecutions and murders, and neutral discourse items (toothbrushes) which have no connection with Nazi crimes. This is a bizarre but characteristic illustration of how any word, here the humble ZAHNBÜRSTE, can become relevant to the discourse precisely because of its irrelevance to the discourse.

In the 1980s Heiner Geissler, the CDU's "semantic strategist" in countering the popularity of SPD policies, was the target of Nazi comparisons made by SPD politicians. In 1983, in angry exchanges about the stationing of nuclear-armed rockets in Western Germany, Hermann Heinemann called Geissler a fascist, accusing him of using NAZI-METHODEN, adding: "Wenn heute die Nazis an der Macht wären, wäre er vielleicht bereits Propagandaminister" ("If the Nazis were in power today, he would perhaps already be Propaganda Minister").[1] In 1985 Willy Brandt took up the attack against the background of the fortieth anniversary of the 8 May, regional elections, and President Reagan's state visit (when Reagan declined to meet Brandt). Geissler, according to Brandt, was a demagogue, "seit Goebbels der schlimmste Hetzer in diesem Land" ("since Goebbels the worst persecutor in this country").

The first instrumentalizations of HOLOCAUST appeared shortly after the term established itself in the public consciousness in the late 1970s. Neologisms ending in -CAUST are attested from the early 1980s, when NUKLEARER/ATOMARER HOLOCAUST entered the discourse of campaigners against nuclear energy and particularly nuclear weapons, and not just in Germany. The Federal government were condemned by Alfred Mechtersheimer (Die Grünen) in 1988, in a Bundestag debate on the defence budget, of being potential EICHMÄNNER DES NUKLEAREN HOLOCAUST ("Eichmanns of the nuclear holocaust", cf. Eitz and Stötzel 2007, p. 342f.). The discourse of anti-abortionists also used this defamatory Nazi comparison, attested in 1991 in a statement by Pope John Paul II and in 1988 by the Bishop of Fulda, who spoke of abortion in terms of SELEKTION for a KINDERHOLOCAUST (Eitz and Stötzel 2007, p. 342f.).

The "Nazi Complex" in the Cold War

Stötzel discerns three phases during which the "Nazi Complex" was instrumentalized in the Cold War between East and West: around the founding of the two German states in 1949, the building of the Berlin Wall in 1961, and by the Kohl government in the 1980s. The first instance (and the only one directed at the west by the east in Stötzel's corpus) dates from May 1948, when the law preparing the introduction of the

Deutschmark in the western zones was labelled an ERMÄCHTIGUNGSGESETZ. Other examples from this period label the extension of the SED's powers in the Soviet zone a "MACHTERGREIFUNG" (quotation marks in the original), an SED/KPD spokesman the GOEBBELS of the Soviet zone, and Walter Ulbricht its GESTAPOCHEF. After the building of the Berlin Wall, Adenauer stated that the Soviets had turned their occupation zone (sic!) into a KONZENTRATIONSLAGER and a West German newspaper referred to Walter Ulbricht as the KZ-CHEF (boss) DER ZONE. None of these usages so far was the subject of critical commentary in the West German media, unlike the instances from the 1980s, when Chancellor Helmut Kohl's statement that the GDR had over two thousand political prisoners in jails and concentration camps provoked outrage in the opposition and the liberal press. Stötzel suggests (1995, p. 372) that this shows a change in the political climate in the West German state, a weakening of West Germans' ideological allegiance to the American-led campaign against Communism. The SPD accused Kohl of blackening (ANSCHWÄRZEN) the GDR with a "terrible error" in the use of history, and the GDR writer Wolf Biermann, in exile in the Federal Republic, called it a derision (VERHÖHNUNG) of the millions who died in Nazi camps. Stötzel (1995, p. 378) notes that the most authoritative condemnation came from the Anne Frank Foundation: Kohl's comparison was a trivialization (BAGATELLISIERUNG) of the Nazi crime. It is interesting to note the authority of this voice with a direct association to the historical victims of Nazism, which raises the question of how such authoritative voices will be heard in times even further removed from the real historical events. Even in 1987, Kohl's political allies were not cowed, one commentator responding that the Soviets had taken over the Nazis' network of detention and concentration camps in their 'liberated' zone. A more calculated response came from the CDU in the claim that Willy Brandt as mayor of Berlin in 1961 had also compared the GDR to a concentration camp, saying "Berlin wird die Landsleute in Ulbrichts KZ nicht abschreiben" ("Berlin will not write off our fellow countrymen in Ulbricht's KZ").

That the majority of these Cold War comparisons target the GDR is explained by the fact that Stötzel's is a study of West German discourse history. There can be little doubt that the political leadership of the GDR employed similar tactics in its attempts to demarcate itself morally and linguistically from its western neighbour (Clyne 1993; Stevenson 2002). One has only to recall the official name of the Berlin Wall—the 'antifascist protection barrier' (ANTIFASCHISTISCHER SCHUTZWALL), labelled in the West the SCHANDMAUER (wall of shame)—to appreciate this fact (cf. Stötzel and Wengeler 1995, pp. 300–303). The reference in Seidel/Seidel-Slotty's study (reviewed in Chap. 5) to the use of AUSRADIEREN in West German government discourse and their catalogue of Weisgerber's conformist use of VOLKHAFT in the 'Third Reich' also seem to belong in this context. The discourse on the GDR's own Nazi past could be described as stable, or as sterile. The youth-led questioning of the past by the '1968' generation in the west had no real counterpart in the east. In a tightly controlled public discourse, the GDR defined itself as the anti-fascist state, distancing itself from any historical connection with Nazism (thus absolving itself of the responsibility to make reparations) and claiming the legacy of Soviet Communism as the only force capable of explaining and overcoming fascism. Its denazification, it claimed, had been completed, whilst leading Nazis were still in positions of power in the Federal Republic. This narrative gained credibility as hidden Nazi pasts gradually emerged in the West German media: Kurt-Georg Kiesinger, Federal Chancellor from 1966 to 1969, had been a member of the NSDAP; Hans Filbinger, Minister-President of Baden-Württemberg from 1966 to 1978, who was obliged to resign following revelations by the dramatist Rolf Hochhuth about his role as a military judge in the navy dispensing death sentences; and Heinrich Lübke, Federal President from 1959 to 1969, who had helped to build the V1 and V2 research centre in Peenemünde, to name but three prominent examples.

The Prolongation of the "Lexicon of the 'Unmensch'"

An overview of headwords in the 1945–1948, 1957, and 1967 iterations is given in the Appendix to this study. At the centre of this dispute was the first book edition of the *Wörterbuch des Unmenschen* which, as outlined in the previous chapter, differed in important respects from the original series of glosses published between 1945 and 1948. Sternberger's Foreword in 1957 proclaimed the prolongation of the authors' critique beyond the immediate post-1945 period[2]: "Das Wörterbuch des Unmenschen ist das Wörterbuch der geltenden deutschen Sprache geblieben" ("The "Lexicon of the 'Unmensch'" remains the lexicon of the German language today"). This assertion also marks the moment at which the Lexicon begins to lose its traction as a critique of Nazism. The reception of this book by a new generation of language scholars "hungry", as von Polenz put it, ("Geleitwort", Dodd 2007, p. 9) to understand the role of language in fascism, led to a far-reaching debate on method, the 'Streit um die Sprachkritik'.

The subsequent popular understanding and most of the academic debate about the Lexicon assumed that the 1957 texts were identical with those of 1945–1948. This is not the case. Two glosses (FANATISCH, HÄRTE) were omitted, six new ones (ANLIEGEN, FRAUENARBEIT, HERAUSSTELLEN, LEISTUNGSMÄSSIG, MENSCHENBEHANDLUNG, PROBLEM) were added. Small changes were made in most texts, substantive changes were made to BETREUUNG, CHARAKTERLICH, GESTALTUNG, LAGER und ORGANISIEREN, whilst DURCHFÜHREN and EINSATZ were effectively re-written. Sternberger alludes to changes in his 1957 Foreword, but gives no indication of their extent, especially in relation to the rewritten pieces. He himself contributed to the ahistorical reception of the Lexicon by deleting the first sentence of his 1945 Introduction, with its reference to Theodor Haecker. It was never restored. The most illuminating formulation of the logic behind the continuation of the 'Unmensch' project is found not in the book, but in an exchange of letters between Sternberger and Süskind, who wanted to omit KONZENTRATIONSLAGER from the new version of LAGER on the grounds that it would be inappropriate to speak in the present tense about (concentration) camps in the context of the 'Unmensch' of the 1950s. Sternberger objects:

> Wir haben ja allgemein unsere Beiträge von ehedem nicht so radikal aktualisiert, daß die totalitäre Epoche zugunsten der bundesrepublikanischen verschwunden wäre; vielmehr haben wir nur die Ausschließlichkeit der Konzentration auf den Sprachgebrauch des Dritten Reiches gelockert. (Sternberger to Süskind, 10.4.1957. Cf. Dodd 2007, p. 285)

> But we have not updated our contributions from then [1945–48] so radically that the totalitarian era would disappear to be replaced by the Federal Republic. Rather, we have only relaxed the exclusiveness of our concentration on the use of language in the Third Reich.

Sternberger is effectively trying to strike a balance, to create a dual focus entailing, from his point of view, a looser, less exclusive concentration on the 'Third Reich', and the results of this can be seen in many of the new texts. The changes to BETREUUNG in 1957, for example, were as follows. The first part of the gloss (Part A) remained unchanged, whilst new example sentences with no direct connection to the Nazi period were added to Part B: "Der Geschäftsreisende betreut die Käufer, der Dirigent betreut die Solisten, aber auch die Partitur und das Werk des Komponisten" ("The travelling salesman looks after the customers, the conductor looks after the soloist, but also the score and the work of the composer"). Once again, the choice of tense is significant. Although the example sentence referring in 1945 to the mental institution used the present tense of the verb (which must have shocked readers then), this example is deleted in 1957, as are several explicit references to the Nazi past, notably to Hitler looking after the whole of the German people. In 1945 this example followed directly on that of the black marketeer. In 1957 this example is expanded: "Als es keinen Markt und keinen Handel mehr gab, als die Konsumenten daher machtlos, zu Objekten, geworden waren, 'betreute' der Verteiler die Käufer" ("When there was no market and no trade any more, when consumers were powerless as a result, had become objects, the black marketeer 'looked after' the customers"). In 1945, the past tense strongly suggested this was a picture of the 'Third Reich'; in 1957 this was not so obviously the case. The 1957 text is more explicit about the continuation of 'Betreuung' after 1945: "Aber das ist mit dem Dritten Reich keineswegs untergegangen" ("But this did not disappear at all with the Third Reich"). In post-war Germany it is "Verbände, Wirtschaftsverbände wie Berufsverbände" ("associations, business and professional associations alike") which have adopted this word. Even the modern concept of customer service ('Kundendienst') is chided for its "kundendienstmäßige Betreuung" (customer service care). In accepting this way of speaking, people had "abdicated" their autonomy and helped to consolidate the power of "the regiment of managers and secretaries". 'Betreuung' belongs equally in a dictionary of contemporary organizational jargon, Sternberger continues, and in a dictionary of "Lager- und Terror-Sprache". This assertion is bolstered by a footnote to H.G. Adler's book on Theresienstadt (1955), in which Adler confirms that 'betreuen' was indeed used to denote the guards' relation to the inmates, and Sternberger finds his judgment of 1946 corroborated: "Ja wahrhaftig: Die Geheime Staatspolizei betreute die Juden". Finally, the sentence from the 1945 text asserting that one never hears "ich werde von der und der Organisation [...] betreut" is changed to "Nein, das hat man noch nicht oder nur selten und dann mit Verblüffung und mit Scham sagen hören" ("No, one has not heard that before or only rarely and then heard it said with consternation and shame").

Changes to Süskind's 1946 text Härte (omitted in 1957) are found in the 1967 edition. In 1946 Süskind had written: "Der Unmensch behandelt die Wörter wie die Bodenschätze: er nimmt sie, wo er sie findet, und fabriziert Kriegsmaterial daraus. Was die Anwendbarkeit angeht, hält er es mit Hermann Göring: die Anwendung bestimme ich" ("The 'Unmensch' treats words like natural resources in the earth: he takes them where he finds them and makes weapons of war out of them. As far as their use is concerned, the 'Unmensch' agrees with Hermann Goering: I determine their use"). In the 1967 text, "Kriegsmaterial" is replaced by "Kampfgerät" (weapon) and the reference to Goering is deleted. In place of this, however, the historical perspective is restored when slogans from the Second War are quoted: "Räder müssen rollen für den Sieg" (Wheels must roll for victory).

In 1986, in the Introduction to a reprint of the 1967 edition, Sternberger conceded defeat in his campaign ("Feldzug") against some of these words, notably 'betreuen', which had "spread like an epidemic", and become one of the identifying marks of the era ("eigentliche Kennmarke der Epoche"). The "triumphal march since the beginnings of the dictatorship irrespective of all political and social changes" ("Siegeszug seit den Anfängen der Diktatur über alle politischen und sozialen Veränderungen hinweg") would require a study illuminating all the dark corners "in which has taken root" ("worin sie sich festgenistet hat") and all the other words "which it has overrun, suppressed and squashed" ("die sie überrollt, verdrängt und zerquetscht hat").

The prolongation of the 'Unmensch' critique produced a hybrid, positioned between a critique of fascist language and a critique of the "inhuman" management and administrative practices in the 1950s and 1960s. This problem certainly contributed to the criticisms levelled at the Lexicon in the course of the 'Sprachstreit'. In the Foreword to the second book edition (which again added new glosses), Sternberger sought to deflect these criticisms, describing the idea that the authors' concerns had been limited to the 'Third Reich' as a misunderstanding—a statement which von Polenz (1999, p. 319) called a "denial" ("Leugnung") of the original political intention of the 'Unmensch' as a figure representing Nazi dictatorship. It is time now to turn to the 'Sprachstreit'.

The 'Sprachstreit' and the Socio-pragmatic Turn

The confrontational but collegial exchanges between Sternberger and a number of academic 'Sprachwissenschaftler' can be viewed in three phases: (1) the attack on the Lexicon's methodology and findings, (2) Sternberger's counter-attack, (3) reform of academic linguistics and beginnings of a "professionalized", linguistically-grounded discipline of language criticism.[3]

(1) There is room here only to summarize the main objections raised by Peter von Polenz, Herbert Kolb, Werner Betz and others. It is important to note that this was a clash not just of generations but also of intellectual traditions. Linguistic science ('Sprachwissenschaft') in Germany in the 1960s was dominated by the structuralism of Ferdinand de Saussure and/or the formalism of Noam Chomsky. Von Polenz was a Saussurean structuralist, which meant that he accepted two main tenets: that the scientific study of language should concern itself with *langue*, the language system (as distinct from *parole*), and that it should concern itself primarily with the synchronic (as distinct from the diachronic) axis. Sternberger, like many of his generation, had not come across Saussure's ideas. His understanding of language was a traditional 'altgermanistisch' one going back to Herder and Wilhelm von Humboldt, in which evalu-

ating judgments on language use, in a largely diachronic framework, were acceptable. Like Kraus, he was terminologically imprecise, tending to speak of 'die Sprache' even when he was talking about the use of language. The second important point is that von Polenz and the others knew next to nothing about the biographies of the *Lexicon* authors, and this remained the case during the dispute.

From this basically structuralist standpoint, there was a long litany of criticisms against the *Lexicon* (listed in von Polenz 1999, p. 317f.), including: (a) the selected words were not a homogeneous group, (b) none of them was a prominent NS ideologeme such as ARISCH, ARTEIGEN, BLUTSCHANDE…, (c) metaphor is inimical to scientific discourse, (d) its evaluative vocabulary was binary: good/bad, 'Mensch'/'Unmensch'…, (e) the concept of the 'Unmensch' was mythic, imprecise and undefined, and not confined to a critique of fascism, (f) talk of the state of "THE LANGUAGE today" ("das heutige Deutsch") ignored basic features of a language such as register variation and text types, (g) the *Lexicon* failed to distinguish clearly between *langue* and *parole*, leading to unacceptable critiques of the language system, especially in the so-called "inhuman accusative", (h) quoted examples were not attested authentic examples of use in specified situations, (i) the critical discourse was an outmoded conservative one lamenting the 'decay' and 'decline' of society, belonging to the genres of journalism ('Publizistik') and the feuilleton, (j) the word-centred approach adopted ('Einzelwortkritik') failed to appreciate that meaning does not reside lexico-semantically in single, isolated words but is constituted in (linguistic and social) contexts, (k) meaning is primarily a synchronic construct, the 'true' meaning of a word cannot be established through its etymology, (l) the critiques of language were subjective, based on biographical experiences, and not intersubjectively verifiable (and so not scientific), (m) lexemes, as units of the language system, cannot be labelled good or bad regardless of their present or future contexts of use, (n) the assertion that verbs beginning 'be-' (using a morphological resource of the language system) are the invention of the 'Unmensch' reflected an ignorance of the history of German. In fact, such verbs were much more frequent in the seventeenth century, (o) the critique of the "inhuman accusative" failed to take account of its functional role in the language system.

With regard to this last point, Herbert Kolb (cf. Sternberger et al. 1986, pp. 229–245) explained the systemic benefits of the 'accusativizing' prefix 'be-' in terms of its structural "Bequemlichkeit" (convenience). The existence of a verb like BELIEFERN alongside 'liefern' (to deliver) makes possible a range of structures which increase the semantic and expressive options of speakers. Lexicalization creates concepts for the person receiving the delivery ('der/die Belieferte'), the act of delivering ('die Belieferung') and an adjectival attribute ('der belieferte Kunde', the customer to whom something is delivered). These lexicalizations allow speakers to topicalize (foreground) different aspects of the transaction, giving the sentence a new focus. Kolb's structural explanation was a serious challenge to Sternberger's moral objection, flatly rejected in Kolb's dictum that to BETREUEN someone was as far removed from being inhumane as it was to BEKLEIDEN (clothe) them.

A further objection to the argumentation of the *Lexicon* was that it reified (hypostasized) language as a monolith, overstating the manipulation theory of language and potentially presenting a picture of speakers as helpless victims. Werner Betz (1963) summarized this position ironically: It's not the speaker but the language that lies? ("Nicht der Sprecher, die Sprache lügt?"). This, together with the closeness of the UNMENSCH trope to Nazi discourse (UNTERMENSCH) made the *Lexicon* authors susceptible to the charge of HILFLOSER ANTIFASCHISMUS (helpless anti-fascism, cf. Haug 1967, 1982).

From today's vantage point it is possible to see the problems with Sternberger/Storz/Süskind's discourse on THE GERMAN LANGUAGE as partly conceptual, partly terminological, and quite different in kind to the wholesale "vilification" ("Schmähung", von Polenz 1999, p. 320) of German by literary and cultural critics like George Steiner, whose 1959 essay "The Hollow Miracle" (Steiner 1969, pp. 136–151) went beyond Sternberger's critique to locate "latent hysteria, confusion, and the quality of hypnotic trance" in THE GERMAN LANGUAGE since 1870, exploited by Hitler, and its "death" in the age of the Wirtschaftswunder, lamenting that it was "no longer the language of Goethe" and no longer capable of sustaining great literature.

(2) Sternberger rejected the criticisms and stood his ground defiantly. His belief in the rightness of his critique was unshakeable. Despite the entrenched positions, a very German public debate developed in the

press, on radio, and on television. Sternberger, now an eminent professor of political science at Heidelberg, was also a natural 'Publizist' and a prominent public intellectual. His chief antagonist in these public exchanges was von Polenz, who accepted the challenge to enter the public arena, and a collegial friendship developed between the two. By any objective assessment, Sternberger did not answer most of these charges. Kolb's "Bequemlichkeit" was rhetorically thrown back: convenient for whom?—for those who use language to control others! (Sternberger et al. 1986, p. 316f.). The debate, which lasted roughly the whole of the 1960s, petered out inconclusively. In one respect, however, Sternberger landed a decisive blow. Reading Saussure's *Course on General Linguistics*, which von Polenz had sent him, he objected to Saussure's elevation of a theoretical concept (*langue*) to a position of dominance over the actual spoken word (*parole*). Saussure's vision of language had no place for the speaking individual, it was, in the truest sense of the word, "unmenschlich". Sternberger, a student of Karl Jaspers, also plausibly rejected the notion that his critique of language was not concerned with 'Sprachgebrauch' (*parole*, language use): he did sometimes use the term 'Sprachgebrauch' and, like Jaspers, distinguished between 'Sprache' (language in general) and 'Rede' (language in use). In the Foreword to the 1967 edition, which also carried essays from the 'Sprachstreit', Sternberger insisted: "Wörter sind nicht unschuldig, können es nicht sein, denn die Schuld der Sprecher wächst der Sprache zu" ("Words are not innocent, they cannot be, for the guilt of the speakers grows onto the language"). This counter-attack raised serious issues about the deficiencies of linguistic structuralism, convincing von Polenz and others that their model of language was inadequate for the study of political language.

(3) The 'Sprachstreit' was one of the decisive moments in the history of recent German linguistic thought, part of a paradigm shift which stands at the beginning of a line of research which applies the insights of linguistic science to the study of *parole*, and accepts some degree of diachrony. Without these basic tools, discourse history is unthinkable. In many ways von Polenz is its inspirational figure. Forced to reflect on his own professional practice, he sought to rectify the shortcomings of his approach in search of a linguistic science which could address and analyze language as a social and political phenomenon (Heringer 1982; von Polenz 2005). This had to include a scientifically grounded study of language as *parole*.

The course correction he embarked on led to important studies such as his *Deutsche Satzsemantik. Grundbegriffe des Zwischen-den-Zeilen-Lesens* (1985) and the monumental *Deutsche Sprachgeschichte* (1991–1999), an impressive example of the socio-pragmatic approach to the history of language use and language sensibilities. A new generation of scholars (many of them von Polenz's students) have developed the socio-pragmatic approach in a number of directions. Already in the 1960s Cornelia Berning produced a text-based historical lexicon of National Socialist vocabulary (Berning 1964), since reworked as one of the standard discourse-historical studies of the language of the NSDAP (Schmitz-Berning 2000). Rolf Glunk's large-scale study of the "successes and failures" of the regime's 'Sprachregelungen' (Glunk 1966–1971) also deserves mention here. Other important milestones in this German tradition include Walther Dieckmann's study of political language (Dieckmann 1969), Utz Maas's analyses of rhetorical techniques in Nazi speeches (Maas 1984), Josef Klein's analysis of political "semantic battles" (Klein 1989), studies in "historical semantics", "concept history" ('Begriffsgeschichte') and "the history of attitudes" ('Mentalitätsgschichte') (e.g. Busse et al. 1994), and the "Bozen Manifesto" (Lanthaler et al. 2003) referred to in the Introduction to the present study. This selective list leaves many distinguished scholars unmentioned, including several whose work feeds into the present study. Since the 'Sprachstreit' there has been a gradual reinstatement of the *Lexicon* authors as discourse analysts *avant la lettre*. Their work has been steadily reappraised, for example by Hans Jürgen Heringer, Horst Dieter Schlosser, Georg Stötzel, Rainer Wimmer (Wimmer 1982) and von Polenz himself (Dodd 2007, pp. 55–68; Stötzel 1989, 1995; von Polenz 2005, 2007). An important stage in this process is Konrad Ehlich's essay of 1998, to which we now turn.

Re-reading *LTI* and the *Lexicon of the 'Unmensch'*

Ehlich, editor of an important volume of essays on "language in fascism" (Ehlich 1989), offered a "re-reading" of the *Lexicon* (and *LTI*) in 1998. The criticized words, he affirms, were not central ideologemes of the regime, most of which became 'tainted' with the fall of the regime. For the authors, the continued circulation of these other words meant that there was no catharsis, no STUNDE NULL (zero hour) in 1945. That most of the criticized words are considered normal in today's usage, as they were before the fascist period, is the point we need to reflect on. The irresolvable internal contradictions (aporias) of these early works of language criticism demonstrate the difficulty of identifying the object we want to describe. The attempt of the *Lexicon* authors to inventarize the meaning of words "lexicalistically" was bound to fail because of their traditional linguistic model of language as a combination of lexicon and grammar. Linguistic reality resists description in these terms, leading to "semantic reification" and a hypostatization of the language as an independent entity—a view of language which is close to fascist conceptions and prone to overstate the power of the text producer over that of the text consumer (the 'manipulation theory'). The closeness of this position to narratives of exculpation ascribing all guilt to the FÜHRER or a fascist elite is unfortunate. Ehlich's analysis here tacitly acknowledges criticisms of the inadequacies of the *Lexicon* authors' theory of fascism (e.g. Voigt 1967, 1974).

The high-profile ideological keywords of National Socialism, Ehlich points out, actually formed a very small sub-set of the vocabulary. The contribution of works like the *Lexicon* is to draw attention to a "substratum" of lexical and phraseological items which can combine with ideological vocabulary in a "Mischungsverhältnis". Investigating this 'mix' of linguistic resources is for Ehlich the important research desideratum of the *Lexicon*. For this, the lexical-semantic approach needs to be "pragmatized" and the investigation needs to focus more on describing how an "ideological substrate" is articulated in language, a substrate of habitual, normative styles which also has a discourse history reaching back into the early nineteenth century and beyond. Such an investigation, Ehlich believes, would focus on "discourses of social normalization". The *Lexicon* authors' "ensemble" of Enlightenment and Christian values, the platform for their critiques, fed directly into the discourse on German guilt, Sternberger's dictum on the guilt of THE LANGUAGE being an example of "fleischgewordene Schuld" (guilt incarnate).

Citing Klemperer's concept LTI/LQI in his title, Ehlich invites a reconceptualization of the role of language in fascism, and in present-day discourse. As Heringer had suggested to von Polenz in 1982, the full implications of the *Lexicon* for the Federal Republic had been little understood. The kind of re-reading suggested here would not exclude (as the present study does) the thirteen new headwords added in 1957 and 1967 but make them an integral part of the research project, as Stötzel (1989, p. 38f.) had indeed suggested. Such a study should of course also examine the rewriting of glosses. These "re-readings" of the *Lexicon* might, for example, encourage us to revisit the issue of BETREUUNG and reflect that a discourse of care ('looking after', 'seeing to', 'taking care of') is always available for instrumentalization as a cover for inhumane actions. That these English expressions are classic gangster jargon ("I'm going to take care of you") may give us pause for thought.

'Pragmatized' Dictionaries

The 'pragmatization of semantics' demanded by Ehlich in 1998 had of course already begun. A particularly impressive development since the 1980s has been the genre of the 'pragmatized' discourse-historical lexicon, an early example of which is *Brisante Wörter* (Strauss et al. 1989). This distinctively German genre is epitomized in the work of Georg Stötzel, Martin Wengeler, and the 'Düsseldorf School', in works such as *Kontroverse Begriffe* (1995), *Die Sprache des Migrationsdiskurses* (Jung et al. 1997), the *Zeitgeschichtliches Wörterbuch der deutschen Gegenwartssprache* (Stötzel and Eitz 2003), the two-volume *Wörterbuch der 'Vergangenheitsbewältigung'* (Eitz and Stötzel 2007, 2009), and Kämper's 'Diskurswörterbuch' of the SCHULDDISKURS in the period 1945–1955 (Kämper 2007). These reference works are the product of an empirical search in text corpora for meta-discursive manifestations of a term being contested or "thematized" (commented on in some way). In their study of the VERGANGENHEITSBEWÄLTIGUNG discourse, Eitz/Stötzel identify four meta-discursive categories: (1) speech acts objecting to 'tainted' language ("belastete Vokabeln"), (2) instrumentalizing Nazi comparisons ("Nazi-Vergleiche") to damage opponents, (3) objections to Nazi terms used uncritically in academic literature, (4) use of a meta-vocabulary to describe the argumentation structures of the discourse (e.g. VERGLEICH (comparison), RELATIVIEREN, VERHERRLICHEN (glorify), VERHARMLOSEN (render harmless), bagatellisieren (trivialize), belastet (compromised, 'tainted')). Taking up Cornelia Schmitz-Berning's work on the discourse history of expressions belonging to an identifiable language *of* National Socialism, and the Mitscherlichs' psychoanalytic study of Germans' inability to process the national guilt (Unfähigkeit zu trauern, Mitscherlich and Mitscherlich 1967, p. 67), the authors trace linguistic manifestations of contestation, denial, and suppression in contemporary discourse. They also argue that discourse history conducted in these terms differs from the grand narratives of most historiography, such as the history of ideas, in its "micro-diachronic" focus on relatively small periods of time. The forty headwords in Eitz/Stötzel 2007 are Anschluss, Auschwitz, Auschwitz-Lüge, Auschwitz-Vergleiche, ausmerzen, Befreiung/Niederlage, Drittes Reich, Elite, Endlösung, entartete Kunst, Entnazifizierung, Ermächtigungsgesetz, Euthanasie, Gestapo, Gleichschaltung, grossdeutsch, Hitler-Vergleiche, Holocaust, Holocaust-Vergleiche, Invasion/Landung der Alliierten, Kollektivschuld, Konzentrationslager, lebensunwertes Leben, Machtergreifung, Mischehe, (Ende der) Nachkriegszeit, Nazi-methoden, Nazi-Vergleiche, NSDAP, Reichskristallnacht, SA, Schreibtischmörder, Selektion, SS, Stunde Null, Vergangenheitsbewältigung, Viertes Reich, Wehrmacht, Widerstand, Wiedergutmachung. Researching them generated some five thousand further expressions deemed "discourse-relevant" by the research team, one thousand of which are listed in the index. On a crude average, then, each lexical item is part of a dynamic network of about a hundred further "discourse-relevant" expressions for articulating differing views on the topic. This is more than a family of semantic relations, it is the linguistic manifestation of contested values on the market for ideas and attitudes. At best, traditional dictionaries handle the discourse potential and ideational orientation of such words poorly, if at all. For example, the contested nature of Machtergreifung (seizure of power) as an uncritical adoption of Nazi mythology is evident from its co-occurrence in texts with terms seeking to replace it with a more neutral, factual term: Macht übergeben, Machtübergabe, Machtübertragung (hand over (of) power), and with terms carrying a different evaluative tenor: Machterschleichung (gradual, devious attainment of power, a negatively-inflected term which implies criticism of the Weimar constitution). Instrumentalizing neologisms since

1945 include, as noted above, MACHTERGREIFUNG DER SED (the 'takeover' of the SPD by the KPD in the Soviet zone in 1946 to create the Workers' Unity Party (SED)). A further twenty nine terms are covered in the second volume: ANTISEMITISMUS, BEFEHLSNOTSTAND, DISPLACED PERSONS/FREMDARBEITER, FLÜCHTLINGE/VERTRIEBENE, GASKAMMER/VERGASEN/VERGASUNG, GOEBBELS-VERGLEICHE, JUDE, KRIEGSVERBRECHER, MILITARISMUS, NATIONALISMUS, NAZI/NEONAZI, NESTBESCHMUTZER, OPFER, PATRIOTISMUS, PAZIFISMUS, RASSE/RASSISMUS/HERRENRASSE, REEDUCATION/UMERZIEHUNG, REMILITARISIERUNG, REVANCHISMUS, SCHLUSSSTRICH, STÜRMER-VERGLEICHE, TÄTER, VERSÖHNUNG/AUSSÖHNUNG/NORMALISIERUNG, ZIGEUNER. One has to wonder how extensive and deep these discursive-argumentational-conceptual-lexical networks are. Rather like the roots of a plant, they seem to become ever finer, the further back you chase them. It is probably not possible to be encyclopaedic, and impractical to try, since the 'micro-diachronic' timescales are so short and the discourse is constantly changing.

VERGANGENHEITSBEWÄLTIGUNG II (1990–)

The period begins with the accession of the former GDR to the Federal Republic under article 23 of the Grundgesetz. Significant events in this period include the relocation of the Bundestag from Bonn to Berlin, housed in the former Reichstag building, now refurbished and with the deputies' chamber visible from the walkway inside the glass cupola designed by British architect Norman Foster; Martin Walser's speech in 1998 criticizing the "instrumentalization" (INSTRUMENTALISIERUNG) of the Holocaust abroad; the Wehrmacht exhibition of 1998 documenting the involvement of the army in mass killings in Eastern Europe; Haacke's installation DER BEVÖLKERUNG in the north inner courtyard of the former Reichstag building in the year 2000, and its reception[4]; the introduction of the Euro in 2002; the opening of the HOLOCAUST MAHNMAL (warning-commemoration) to the "murdered Jews of Europe", in the government quarter in Berlin, next to the Bundestag, in 2005; the recent emergence of Hitler as a comic figure, for example in Timur Vermes' novel *Er ist wieder da* (2012, *Look Who's Back*, 2014). The (re-)unification of the two states was accompanied by tax levies in the West and job insecurity in the East. Since the mid-1990s popular movements and political parties espousing nationalist and 'völkisch' positions have made inroads in regional and national elections. The period also sees a growth in academic studies of political and public discourse, and, since 1991, of public and media interest in the Unwort des Jahres (the 'un-word' of the year) selected each year by a jury from suggestions sent in by the public. The 'un-word' is an expression in the public discourse deemed to discriminate, euphemize, or otherwise articulate an inhumane or undemocratic norm. The first 'Unwort', in 1991, was ausländerfrei ([country] free of foreigners), from the right-wing discourse on immigration (an echo of judenfrei in National Socialist discourse). In 2000 the jury selected Menschenmaterial as the 'un-word' of the century.[5] In 2016 controversy surrounded the publication of a historical-critical edition of *Mein Kampf* (Hitler 2016) by the Institut für Zeitgeschichte (Institute for Contemporary History) in Munich.[6]

The Instrumentalized Past: doppelte Vergangenheitsbewältigung?

The unification of the two German states following the Two-plus-Four Treaty of 1990 gave rise to more contestations and instrumentalizations in the public discourse. Some on the political right objected to the term Wiedervereinigung (reunification) on the grounds that Germany (in the borders of 1937) was still not united. The term is still found today, together with the more prosaic Vereinigung (unification), not necessarily with the political nuance in mind. Those on the left who viewed the process as a take-over by the (capitalist) west talked of the Federal Republic "swallowing" the GDR ('schlucken'), and Nazi analogies critical of this process included Anschluss (i.e. of Austria in 1938) and Gleichschaltung (now a ubiquitous term to negatively connote any kind of 'top-down', 'imposed' rearrangement of society or an organization). A less sympathetic view of the GDR was encapsulated in terms invoking National Socialism: DOPPELTE VERGANGENHEITSBEWÄLTIGUNG implied that the GDR needed to go through its own much delayed process of facing the Nazi past whilst simultaneously working through the traumatic legacy of SED-HERRSCHAFT (SED dictatorship) in a process of ENTSTASIFIZIERUNG (destasification).

Instrumentalizations continue to be found in other discourses. The anti-abortion neologisms BABYCAUST and EMBRYOCAUST, originating in the USA, and significantly found today predominantly on the internet, enter German discourse in the early 1990s. The metadiscursive term HOLOCAUST-VERGLEICH (typically used in contexts condemning these usages and lamenting the disrespect they show for the victims of the Nazi genocide) also dates from this period (Eitz and Stötzel 2007, pp. 342–360). An example of an instrumentalization in the discourse on migration, attested in 1998, is "MACHTÜBERNAHME DER TÜRKENKINDER in Deutschland durch kriminelle Türkenkinder" ("seizure of power by Turkish children in Germany through criminal young Turks", Eitz and Stötzel 2007, p. 444f.).

Nazi Comparisons Abroad: The British 'Eurosceptic' Discourse

The term INSTRUMENTALISIERUNG entered the broader German public discourse in the uproar surrounding a high-profile speech in 1998 by Martin Walser, in which he criticized the "instrumentalization of the German past" *abroad* (cf. Eitz and Stötzel 2007, p. 336f.). At this point, at the latest, a history of the discourse on Nazism needs to acknowledge its international dimension (which often feeds back into the German discourse). The British discourse on German unification, for example, was marked in 1990 by a Nazi comparison predicated on European integration being, in the words of Nicholas Ridley, Trade and Industry Secretary in Margaret Thatcher's government, a "German racket to take over the whole of Europe". In an interview with Dominic Lawson for *The Spectator*,

Ridley went on to say that handing over British sovereignty to Europe was like handing it "to Adolf Hitler, quite frankly", and declined to affirm Lawson's suggestion that Chancellor Kohl was surely preferable to Hitler, saying "I'm not sure I wouldn't rather have the [air raid] shelters and the chance to fight back". Ridley's outspoken candour, which led to his dismissal by the Prime Minister, is significant today as an example of the instrumentalization of the German Nazi past in a sustained 'Euro-sceptic' discourse on the right of British politics and in the print news media, which culminated in the 'Brexit' referendum vote of 2016. Two of the many further contributions to this discourse were the Juncker: Junker comparison, and an implicit instrumentalization of new european order (Neuordnung Europas). The first of these was an intervention in the House of Commons in 2014 following Prime Minister Cameron's failure to prevent the confirmation of "the German-backed Luxembourger Jean-Paul Juncker"[7] as President of the European Commission, when Conservative MP Stephen O'Brien "bellowed across the Chamber [...] that the PM should 'take inspiration from the fact that in a previous Battle of Britain we saw off many Junkers before'". The second example centres on senior Conservative politician Boris Johnson's comparison in the *Sunday Telegraph* on 15 May 2016 between the European Community and Napoleon and Hitler's "disastrous" attempts to "unite" Europe. The headline "The EU wants a superstate, just as Hitler did" homed in on the German theme, but the Nazi comparison lurking in Johnson's words was more fully elaborated by UKIP MEP Gerard Batten: "In 1942 when the Germans still thought they were going to win the war they produced a report entitled the Europäische Wirtschafts Gemeinschaft—which translates as the European Economic Community."[8] Johnson's remarks were condemned by some but not all Conservative politicians and by Labour MP Hilary Benn, who called them "deeply offensive", also to the victims of Nazism. Finally, in the *Daily Mail* article by Dominic Lawson in which he recalls his interview with Ridley and refers to the defamatory images of Chancellor Angela Merkel currently in the Greek media with Hitler moustache and swastika armband, a picture of Merkel (not the caricature) is captioned "German Chancellor Angela Merkel declared that her government would have to have 'oversight'—Uberwachung [sic!]—of the over-indulged Greek public sector". The inclusion of the (anglicized)

German word ÜBERWACHUNG here, in a newspaper most of whose readers do not have even a working knowledge of German, can only be appellative, reflecting a calculation of its negative affective function (based presumably on the recognizability of UBER, as in "Deutschland Deutschland UBER alles", still associated in the Anglophone world with German national hubris rather than von Fallersleben's egalitarian ideals). For those who do know German, the 'totalitarian' associations of 'surveillance' are invoked. These examples of instrumentalization by British 'Eurosceptics', especially in the period 2014–2016, could be multiplied many times in a discourse history of the UK and other countries.[9]

Memory Traces and Taboos in Contemporary Usage

Collective memory of Nazism appears still to influence patterns of language use in the German-speaking world today. Perceptions of 'tainted' words and expressions in everyday discourse are relatively rare now, as Fiedler's (2005) corpus study of the words in the *Lexicon of the 'Unmensch'* demonstrates. Rather, there seems to be a settled pattern of taboos. An analysis of discursive taboos has the obvious difficulty that it seeks to identify what is *not* there on the surface of discourse. In some cases, official proscriptions help to identify these gaps, as with certain combinations of letters on vehicle registration plates: AH, KZ, SA, SS are proscribed in all federal states, NS in most (!), and in some states combinations of letters and numbers are not allowed, such as HH 18 and HH 88 (codes for HEIL HITLER! and Hitler's initials). A fairly straightforward lexical example, which can be deduced from a traditional dictionary, is the use of 'Führer' to designate people. (In the sense of guidebook ('Reiseführer') it has never been seen as problematic). Here we find uncontentious terms like 'Lokführer/in' (train driver), 'Führer/in' (tour ('Führung') guide), and 'Führerschein' (driver's licence), although in this latter case we also find 'Fahrerlaubnis', apparently a legacy of the GDR which may reflect a sensitivity to the term 'Führer' (Stötzel 1989, p. 43). The existence of both lexemes seems to be generating a semantic differentiation in contemporary usage, 'Führerschein' designating the document,

'Fahrerlaubnis' the legal right to drive. (In Switzerland, 'Führerausweis' is the norm.). Of course, all of these have the potential for ironic or sarcastic instrumentalization, but to do so would appear to cross the line to taboo, or at least to bad taste. In the domain of politics, however, there is an asymmetry. The leader of the opposition is the 'Oppositionsführer', but the Chancellor and leader of the government is the 'Regierungschef(/in)'. This last example reveals a wave of secondary impact on the German lexicon and in part explains the openness since 1945 to lexical imports, in this case from French ('Chef' is attested already in the Kerncorpus 20 in 1900), which allow speakers to circumvent 'tainted' usage. The foreign word is not the only solution to this problem, however: German 'Leiter/in' (leader) is also widely used to denote people in leading positions in an organization.

As one reviewer (Smith 2008) of Eitz/Stötzel 2007 commented, it is simply essential to know that certain lexical items are still "so tainted by their use by the Nazis that they are now completely taboo": ENDLÖSUNG "will forever be associated with Hitler's genocidal 'Final Solution to the Jewish Question'", and SELEKTION with "the death camp practice of 'selecting' inmates to be executed". To navigate this typically unmarked ideological minefield, one needs to be aware not just of no-go pathways (taboos) but also of alternative pathways (nuance), as memory traces and attitudinal markers attach to lexical expressions.

It is easier to determine whether features once attributed to 'Nazi language' *are* there in today's discourse, and whether they continue to be perceived as 'tainted'. Leaving aside expressions (like ENDLÖSUNG, JUDENFREI, VOLKSBREI) which are prominent in the public memory as carriers of Nazi ideology, and are therefore candidates for Eitz/Stötzel's study when used outside a discourse of historiographical, critical debate on Nazism, Mark Fiedler's (2005) corpus-based study of the expressions targeted in the *Lexicon of the 'Unmensch'* finds that virtually all the words listed there have 'returned' to common use with no overt indications of an awareness of their involvement in Nazi discourse. This finding was in effect already conceded by Sternberger in 1957. For example, DURCHFÜHREN commonly collocates with 'Untersuchung' (investigation) and other terms denoting a complex and painstaking process that must be gone through. The verb has a tendency to connote administrative, repetitive, and sometimes dull work. German friends tell me a lecture that they would describe as being DURCHGEFÜHRT would not be inspiring to listen to. (English speakers would be likely to say that they had to 'sit through' it). Similarly, CHARAKTERLICH appears to have quickly lost its discursive link with WELTANSCHAUUNG despite the latter term's continuing historical association with Nazism. Today it can be used when drawing a distinction between a person's narrow professional skills (with several instances of use by football coaches) and his or her general qualities as a person.

The Discourse of/on Contemporary Nationalist Politics

The period from 1990 is marked by a series of outstanding political discourse studies on the one hand (without which this book could not have been written), and on the other by a re-emergence of nationalist discourses in the unified Germany, including a narrative on THE GERMAN LANGUAGE. The discipline of 'politolinguistics' has never been better equipped to analyze and critique these contemporary developments and their relation to earlier nationalist discourses. This is one of the achievements of which Brumlik (quoted at the beginning of this chapter) is rightly proud, and in the present day it has an important role to play in critiquing the resurgence of nationalist norms in German public and political discourse.

Since the 1990s a nationalist discourse on THE GERMAN LANGUAGE has made inroads in the public consciousness, reviving many of the shibboleths of the Deutscher Sprachverein, with echoes of, for example, Eduard Engel's inventarizing attacks on the 'Fremdwort', notably in the (on-line) 'Anglizismen-Index', also in print form (Junker 2011). Electronic media have enabled the Verein Deutsche Sprache, in particular, to make an impact on the lay discourse on 'the state of the language', lamenting loss of national identity and its 'betrayal' by elites in academia and mainstream politics.[10] Commentators on these developments tend to view them as nationalistic rather than 'völkisch', but as Smith (2008) notes, the new right in Germany today are careful to avoid using the kind of 'tainted' expressions for which other citizens are often taken to task.

In 1999, when the Republikaner and Deutsche Volksunion (DVU) parties were well established, Jäger and Jäger noted a "creeping rightwards development in the 'centre' of German society" ("schleichende Rechtsentwicklung in der 'Mitte' der deutschen Gesellschaft")—'völkisch' and racist notions, they observed, were being encountered more often in the media, in everyday discourse, and even in statements by the traditional political parties (1999, p. 11). Whilst extreme nationalist ideas had never completely disappeared in the Federal Republic and the GDR, their appearance in public pronouncements had been "beyond the limits of the publicly sayable" ("jenseits der Grenze offener Sagbarkeit"). Now, however, mainstream politicians (including Chancellor Gerhard Schröder (SPD)) were making such discourse respectable ("hoffähig") by courting popular opinion. Mainstream political discourse was increasingly tending to 'völkisch' positions in domestic policies and especially on immigration; the multicultural society was being presented as a nightmare ("Schreckgespenst"); Islam had filled the role of a new Feindbild (opposed by the christliches Abendland (Occident)); the discourse on immigration was couched in a new stylized Opfer: Täter perspective in which Deutsche were the victims and Einwanderer the perpetrators, also with regard to the 'social questions' of welfare and employment. The authors also note the extreme right's instrumentalization of the concept of political correctness in a strategy to normalize these views (Jäger and Jäger 1999, pp. 100–104).

This study is part of Victor Klemperer's legacy. The authors were published experts on Klemperer's *LTI*, and the book begins with a section on Klemperer's language commentary as an example of how to do language criticism, and the need for it in the present day, in which Klemperer's foreboding that the "dangerous legacy" of a "new Hitlerism" would return had taken on a new urgency. The authors warn: "Das, was in dieser Gesellschaft an undemokratischen Positionen sagbar ist, wurde in den letzten Jahren erweitert und allmählich akzeptiert" ("The undemocratic positions that can be articulated in this society have been extended and gradually accepted in recent years"). Mainstream politicians in the 1990s were warning of this trend. Ignaz Bubis (FDP, Chairman of the Central Council of Jews) identified extreme ideology in "so-called conservatives". Friedrich Pflüger (CDU) found that "Conservative Revolutionaries" (a clear reference to the 1920s) were becoming fashionable ("salonfähig") because of the trivialization (BAGATELLISIERUNG) of Nazi crimes and the demonization of the political left. Heiner Geissler (CDU) observed a "return to 'kleindeutsch' nation-state thinking" ("Rückkehr zum kleindeutschen nationalstaatlichen Denken") in which the "homogeneous ethnic state" ("der homogene Volksstaat") was once again being "proclaimed as the only natural and legitimate form of political community" ("wird wieder als die einzig natürliche und legitime Form des politischen Gemeinwesens verkündet").

Moving forward to the present (2017), the main mouthpieces of nationalist politics in Germany are Pegida ('Patriotische Europäer gegen die Islamifizierung des Abendlandes', Patriotic Europeans against the Islamification of the West) and the Alternative für Deutschland (AfD). Heidrun Kämper's (2017) analysis of the latter's election manifesto (AfD 2017) will serve here to illustrate the nature of the AfD's discourse and serve as an exemplary case study in the methods of critical 'politolinguistics'. The following is a summary of her analysis.

As a text-type, the manifesto of a political party is a highly deliberated ("reflektiert") document with an appellative and a suasive function. That is to say, it is a calculated statement aimed at strengthening the resolve of members and supporters, and at persuading others to give the party their vote. The main characteristics of this document are (1) a superficial appellative plurality, with generalized formulations of nostrums which resemble formulations found in other parties' manifestos; (2) a much more elaborated narrow appeal to core voters, indicating hard-line attitudes towards migrants; (3) statements creating a misleading impression of the powers provided for in current legislation; (4) statements implying a biologized view of the world ("Weltanschauung") and the nation state; (5) a binary argumentation structure contrasting "das Eigene" (what is ours) with "das Fremde" (what is foreign/alien), creating an in- and an out-group in Germany. This last point becomes clear in the high frequency of DEUTSCH, UNSER (our), and EINHEIMISCH (native German) in this document, and their collocations, in which DEUTSCH designates an intrinsic value ("Wert an sich") rather than a geographical or ethical one (for example, a commitment to the ethical values of the constitution, as proposed in Sternberger's concept, framed in 1979, of constitutional patriotism (Verfassungspatriotismus, cf. Sternberger 1990, pp. 13–16, 17–31)). deutsche Literatur and deutsche Sprache are thus regarded as cultural goods to be cherished, a deutsche Leitkultur (German dominant culture, claiming allegiance to Christianity, the European Enlightenment and Renaissance, and Roman law, to which immigrants must assimilate) is promoted, in which actions will be taken for the Wohl des deutschen Volkes (wellbeing of the German people). The contexts of use of deutsch, unser, and einheimisch reveal an "evaluating, demarcating function" ("wertende, abgrenzende Funktion") articulated in a "classification into 'valuable' and 'not valuable'" ("Klassifizierung in 'wert' und 'unwert'"). A striking example is the declaration of a Willkommenskultur (culture of welcome) encouraging more pregnancies of deutsche Frauen and pledging support for an increase in the 'German' birth rate, which currently lags behind that of Migranten. The logic of this argumentation structure is that the AfD regards children of nichtdeutsche Frauen as a lower category of 'Germans'. This example is striking for its provocative manufacture of an ideological polysemy, taking the positively inflected keyword Willkommenskultur from the Merkel government's discourse on migration and using it in a politically antagonistic sense. In pragmatic terms, this is a combination of 'tearing down' the rallying standard of the opposing army, and 'appropriating' it for one's own call to arms. The discussion here invokes the concept on ideological polysemy (Dieckmann 1969, pp. 70–75; Klein 1989), as indeed had Klemperer's defiant re-definition of Heroismus in *LTI*.

Thus far, my reiteration of Kämper's findings has not included explicit comparisons with National Socialism. Attentive readers will have noticed a number of implicit comparisons, however: the description of the AfD's vision as a Weltanschauung, the analysis of deutsch invoking the designation völkisch, and the binary pair wert/unwert invoking the historical concept lebensunwert. Wohl des deutschen Volkes may invoke gesundes Volksempfinden and other formulations of Nazi ideology. In the contexts from which these have been quoted thus far, Kämper refrains from explicit comparisons, perhaps in order to allow the reader to make these connections. But these associations are then drawn together in an explicit commentary, when the cumulative argument issues into explicit summation: “konfrontativ ausgedrückt: Ausländer sind Feinde…” (“to put it confrontationally, foreigners are enemies…”):

> Hohe deutsche Kultur ist nicht gleichzustellen mit niederer nicht-deutscher Kultur. Was deutlich wird im Zuge der exkludierenden Argumentation der AfD: Das AfD-Programm beruht auf einer biologistischen, kulturalistisch-nationalistischen Weltanschauung mit gegen ‘Nicht-Zugehörige’ gerichteten Ungleichheitsvorstellungen und bedient nationalistische Ressentiments, die historisch aus dem völkisch-nationalistischen Geist des frühen 20. Jahrhunderts ableitbar sind (der wiederum im rassistisch-nationalistischen Denken des späten 19. Jahrhunderts seine Wurzeln hat…).
>
> High German culture cannot be equated with low non-German culture. What becomes clear in the process of the excluding argumentation of the AfD is that the AfD programme rests on a biological, culturally nationalistic view of the world with concepts of inequality directed at ‘those who do not belong’ and which serves nationalist resentments which historically can be seen to derive from the völkisch-nationalistic spirit of the early twentieth century (which in turn has its roots in the racist nationalistic thinking of the late nineteenth century…).

Kämper demonstrates this finding by quoting from the 1920 programmes of the Deutschnationale Volkspartei and the NSDAP (see Chap. 2), and a parallel reading of these texts bears out Kämper’s finding. (One could also find textual parallels in *Mein Kampf*, for example in a sentence such as “[d]ass jede solche Germanisation in Wirklichkeit eine Entgermanisation ist” (1934, p. 428: “that any such Germanisation in reality is a de-Germanisation”. The context here is the language discourse.)) The AfD’s programme is extensively formulated, for example, in a series of demands whose ‘völkisch’ tone is evident:

> Wir fordern, die Einbürgerung Krimineller zuverlässig zu verhindern, den Anspruch auf Einbürgerung abzuschaffen, den früheren Status Quo des Abstammungsprinzips (galt bis 2000) wieder einzuführen.

> We demand that the naturalization of criminals be reliably prevented, that the right to naturalization be abolished, that the previous status quo of the genealogical principle (in force until 2000) be reintroduced.[11]

The articulation of a political programme whose goal is (in Kämper's words) "the closed society of 'ethnic Germans'" ("die geschlossene Gesellschaft der 'Deutschstämmigen'") is an act of "linguistic violence" ("sprachliche Gewalt") against the post-1945 consensus in German politics, articulated in 1949 in the first article of the Grundgesetz: "Die Würde des Menschen ist unantastbar" ("The dignity of the human being is inviolable"). The principle enshrined in that article, Kämper points out, is itself an implicit reference to and rebuttal of the norms of Nazism. The manifesto and public pronouncements of the AfD are carefully calibrated to avoid being banned under the constitution, and this calculation may prove correct, but its pronouncements should not be allowed to pass uncontested ("unwidersprochen akzeptiert"). "Politolinguistics", Kämper argues, has a role to play in preventing the normalisation of this discourse.

The evidence of the discourse analyses presented here suggests a shift in the norms of public and political discourse in the united Germany at some point in the (late?) 1990s. Fritz Hermanns (1995, p. 308), in his survey of the affective value of the word family DEUTSCH/DEUTSCHE(R)/DEUTSCHLAND in a linguistic history of public attitudes ('Mentalitätsgeschichte') since 1990 had reported no significant change in its semantic and deontic value, and in his *Deutsche Sprachgeschichte* von Polenz (1999, p. 287) still felt able to aver that nationalistic linguistic purism had no significant impact in Germany after 1945. Neither of these confident assertions from the 1990s can stand without qualification in Germany today, where historical amnesia or indifference manifested in apparently trivial divergences in the use of language, for example in referring to the Bundestag, now housed in the Reichstag building, as the REICHSTAG (Smith 2008), may have intended or unintended political implications.

In the election of 24 September 2017 the AfD polled 12.6% of the vote, receiving ninety-two of the 707 seats in the Bundestag.

Notes

1. Source for this and the following example is *Der Spiegel,* 20.5.1985. [http://www.spiegel.de/spiegel/print/d-13514192.html] (11.9.207).
2. A detailed account of the book editions and the differences between the three phases of the Lexicon can be found in Dodd 2007, pp. 277–299. It has not been possible to establish how many copies of the books were sold. There were at least three editions in 1957 with Claassen, with licensed paperback editions with dtv in 1957 and 1962. The 1967 edition with Claassen had at least three editions (the third dated 1968) and a licensed paperback edition with dtv in 1972. The third edition of 1968 was the basis for the Ullstein paperback edition of 1986, which went through at least three editions.
3. For a detailed account, see Dodd 2007, pp. 42–62; von Polenz 1999, pp. 314–322. The main critical essays are published in Sternberger/Storz/Süskind 1986, pp. 225–339.
4. On the debate surrounding Haacke's installation, see the summary of the 'Haacke-Diskurs' in Girth 2015, pp. 92–96.
5. This action was founded by Horst-Dieter Schlosser and initially run under the auspices of the Gesellschaft für deutsche Sprache in Wiesbaden, before becoming independent of government funding after a row with the CDU government in 1994. A list of these 'un-words' can be found at: [http://www.unwortdesjahres.net] (18.9.2017).
6. A prominent voice raised in objection was that of Jeremy Adler, son of H.G. Adler (1955). Cf. https://ec.europa.eu/epale/en/blog/hitlers-mein-kampf-edition-public-enlightenment (1.10.2017).
7. This and the following quotation are from Dominic Lawson's article in the *Daily Mail* on 4.7.2014 (Mail Online): [http://www.dailymail.co.uk/news/article-2680183/Is-EU-just-German-racket-Europe-Nearly-25-years-ago-Tory-minister-told-DOMINIC-LAWSON-lost-job-firestorm-followed-right-along.html] [17.9.2017].
8. "Nazis created 'basic plan' for European Union, UKIP MEP Gerard Batten says". The Independent (online edition), 16.5.2016. [http://www.independent.co.uk/news/uk/politics/eu-referendum-nazis-created-basic-plan-for-the-european-union-ukip-mep-gerard-batten-says-a7032221.html] (17.9.2017).
9. In the interests of balance, an example on the British political left should also be noted, for example Labour politician Ken Livingstone's hapless

claims in March and April 2017 of "Nazi-Zionist collaboration" before 1939, and that Hitler was a supporter of Zionism. Widely criticized in the British press, this instrumentalization served an anti-Israel (pro-Palestinian) political discourse. See David Baddiel's rejoinder in *The Guardian* on 6.4.2017: https://www.theguardian.com/commentisfree/2017/apr/06/ken-livingstone-hitler-zionism-jews [17.9.2017].

10. Interested readers may care to check the on-line presence of *Deutsche Sprachwelt* and the Verein Deutsche Sprache. For a more detailed consideration of this topic see especially Pfalzgraf 2006; also Dodd 2015, Schiewe 2010, Jung 1995.
11. The law governing the right to German citizenship was amended in 2000, allowing the (geographical) *ius solis* principle under certain conditions and ending the dominance of the *ius sanguinis* principle of citizenship by descent from German parents. The German term for this latter principle, ABSTAMMUNGSPRINZIP, carried unfortunate echoes of Nazi terminology (ABSTAMMUNGSNACHWEIS: genealogical passport testifying to 'Aryan' descent). Cf. Berning 2000, pp. 4–7.

Bibliography

Adler, H.G. 1955. *Theresienstadt. 1941–1945. Das Antlitz einer Zwangsgemeinschaft. Geschichte Soziologie Psychologie*. Tübingen: Mohr.

Alternative für Deutschland (AfD). 2017. *Grundsatzprogramm*. https://www.alternativefuer.de/wp-content/uploads/sites/111/2016/03/Leitantrag-Grundsatzprogramm-AfD.pdf. Accessed 19 December 2016.

Berning, Claudia. 1964. *Vom 'Abstammungsnachweis' zum 'Zuchtwart'. Vokabular des Nationalsozialismus*. Berlin: de Gruyter.

Betz, Werner. 1963. Nicht der Sprecher, die Sprache lügt? *Sprache im technischen Zeitalter* 6: 461–464.

Busse, Dietrich, Fritz Hermanns, and Wolfgang Teubert, Hgg. 1994. *Begriffsgeschichte und Diskursgeschichte. Methodenfragen und Forschungsergebnisse der historischen Semantik*. Opladen: Westdeutscher Verlag.

Clyne, Michael. 1993. Who Owns the German Language? In *Das unsichtbare Band der Sprache*, ed. John Flood et al., 357–369. Stuttgart: Hans-Dieter Heinz Akademischer Verlag.

Dieckmann, Walther. 1969. *Sprache in der Politik. Einführung in die Pragmatik und Semantik der politischen Sprache*. Heidelberg: Carl Winter.

Dodd, William J. 2007. *Jedes Wort wandelt die Welt. Dolf Sternbergers politische Sprachkritik*. Göttingen: Wallstein.

———. 2015. Under Pressure? The Anglicisms Debate in Contemporary Germany as a Barometer of German National Identity Today. *German Politics and Society* 33 (1&2): 58–68.

Ehlich, Konrad, Hg. 1989. *Sprache im Faschismus*. Frankfurt/Main: Suhrkamp.

Eitz, Thorsten, and Georg Stötzel. 2007. *Wörterbuch der 'Vergangenheitsbewältigung'. Die NS-Vergangenheit im öffentlichen Sprachgebrauch*. Hildesheim, Zürich, New York: Olms.

———. 2009. *Wörterbuch der 'Vergangenheitsbewältigung'. Die NS-Vergangenheit im öffentlichen Sprachgebrauch*. Band 2. Unter Mitarbeit von Katrin Berentzen und Reinhild Frenking. Hildesheim, Zürich, New York: Olms.

Fiedler, Mark. 2005. *Sprachkritik am öffentlichen Sprachgebrauch seit 1945: Gesamtüberblick und korpusunterstützte Analyse zum 'Wörterbuch des Unmenschen'*. Tönning: Der andere Verlag.

Fischer, Torben, and Matthias N. Lorenz, Hg. 2015. *Lexikon der 'Vergangenheitsbewältigung'*. Bielefeld: Transcript.

Girnth, Heiko. 2015. *Sprache und Sprachverwendung in der Politik. Eine Einführung in die linguistische Analyse öffentlich-politischer Kommunikation*. 2., überarbeitete und erweiterte Auflage. Germanistische Arbeitshefte, Band 39. Berlin, Boston: de Gruyter.

Glunk, Rolf. 1966–1971. Erfolg und Misserfolg der nationalsozialistischen Sprachlenkung. *Zeitschrift für deutsche Sprache* 22–27.

Haug, Wolfgang Fritz. 1967. *Der hilflose Antifaschismus*. Frankfurt/Main: Suhrkamp.

———. 1982. Die Sprache des hilflosen Antifaschismus. In *Holzfeuer im hölzernen Ofen. Aufsätze zur politischen Sprachkritik*, Hg. H. J. Heringer, 150–160. Tübingen: Gunter Narr.

Heringer, Hans Jürgen. 1982. Der Streit um die Sprachkritik. Dialog mit Peter von Polenz im Februar 1981. In *Holzfeuer im hölzernen Ofen. Aufsätze zur politischen Sprachkritik*, Hg. H. J. Heringer, 161–175. Tübingen: Gunter Narr.

Hermanns, Fritz. 1995/2012. Deutsch und Deutschland. Zur Semantik deutscher nationaler Selbstbezeichnungswörter heute. In *Fritz Hermanns: Der Sitz der Sprache im Leben. Beiträge zu einer kulturanalytischen Linguistik*, Hg. Heidrun Kämper, Angelika Linke, and Martin Wengeler, 295–310. Berlin, Boston: de Gruyter.

Hitler, Adolf. 2016. *Mein Kampf. Eine kritische Edition*. Herausgegeben von Christian Hartmann, Thomas Vordermayer, Othmar Plöckinger, Roman Töppel. Unter Mitarbeit von Pascal Trees, Angelika Reizle, Martina Seewald-Mooser. München, Berlin: Im Auftrag des Instituts für Zeitgeschichte München.

Jäger, Margret, and Siegfried Jäger. 1999. *Gefährliche Erbschaften. Die schleichende Restauration rechten Denkens*. Berlin: Aufbau Taschenbuch Verlag.

Jung, Matthias. 1995. Amerikanismen, ausländische Wörter, Deutsch in der Welt. Sprachdiskussionen als Bewältigung der Vergangenheit und Gegenwart. In *Kontroverse Begriffe. Geschichte des öffentlichen Sprachgebrauchs in der Bundesrepublik Deutschland*, Hg. Georg Stötzel and Martin Wengeler, 245–283. Berlin, New York: de Gruyter.

Jung, Matthias, Martin Wengeler, and Karin Böke, Hgg. 1997. *Die Sprache des Migrationsdiskurses. Das Reden über "Ausländer" in Medien, Politik und Alltag*. Wiesbaden: Westdeutscher Verlag.

Junker, Gerhard H., Hg. 2011. *Der Anglizismen-Index. Erste Auflage in Verbindiung mit dem INDEX-Arbeitskreis des Vereins Deutsche Sprache und dem Sprachkreis*. Bern, Paderborn: IFB Verlag Deutsche Sprache GmbH.

Kämper, Heidrun. 2005. *Der Schulddiskurs in der frühen Nachkriegszeit. Ein Beitrag zur Geschichte des sprachlichen Umbruchs nach 1945*. Berlin, New York: de Gruyter.

———. 2007. *Opfer – Täter – Nichttäter. Ein Wörterbuch zum Schulddiskurs 1945–1955*. Berlin: de Gruyter.

———. 2017. Das Grundsatzprogramm der AfD und seine historischen Parallelen. Eine Perspektive der Politikolinguistik. *Aptum. Zeitschrift für Sprachkritik und Sprachkultur* 01 (17): 16–41. Also in: *Sprachreport* 33 (2): 1–21. Mannheim: Institut für deutsche Sprache.

Klein, Josef. 1989. Wortschatz, Wortkampf, Wortfelder. In *Politische Semantik. Beiträge zur politischen Sprachverwendung*, Hg. J. Klein, 3–50. Opladen: Westdeutscher Verlag.

Lämmert, Eberhard, Walter Killy, Karl Otto Conrady, and Peter von Polenz. 1967. *Germanistik—eine deutsche Wissenschaft*. Frankfurt/Main: Suhrkamp.

Lanthaler, Franz, Hanspeter Ortner, Jürgen Schiewe, Richard Schrodt, and Horst Sitta. 2003. Was ist der Gegenstand der Sprachbetrachtung?. *Sprachreport* 2/2003, Mannheim: Institut für Deutsche Sprache, 2–5. ("Bozener Manifest").

Maas, Utz. 1984. Als der Geist der Gemeinschaft eine Sprache fand. In *Sprache im Nationalsozialismus*. Opladen: Westdeutscher Verlag.

Mitscherlich, Alexander, and Margarete Mitscherlich. 1967. *Die Unfähigkeit zu trauern. Grundlagen kollektiven Verhaltens*. München: R. Piper.

Pfalzgraf, Falco. 2006. *Neopurismus in Deutschland nach der Wende*. Frankfurt/Main, Berlin, Bern, Bruxelles, New York, Oxford, Wien: Peter Lang.

von Polenz, Peter. 1999. *Deutsche Sprachgeschichte vom Spätmittelalter bis zur Gegenwart*. Bd 3: *19. und 20. Jahrhundert*. Berlin, New York: de Gruyter.

———. 2005. Streit über Sprachkritik in den 1960er Jahren. *Aptum. Zeitschrift für Sprachkritik und Sprachkultur* 02 (05): 97–111.

———. 2007. Geleitwort. *Dodd* 2007: 7–9.

Schiewe, Jürgen. 2010. Sprachreinheit als Kompensation fehlender nationaler Identität. In *Kommunikation für Europa II. Sprache und Identität*, Hg. Schiewe et al., 25–36. Frankfurt/Main: Peter Lang.

Schmitz-Berning, Cornelia. 2000. *Vokabular des Nationalsozialismus*. Berlin, New York: de Gruyter.

Smith, David Gordon. 2008. From 'Anschluss' to 'Zyklon B'. New Dictionary Highlights Words to Avoid. *Der Spiegel Online International*, January 30. http://www.spiegel.de/international/zeitgeist/from-anschluss-to-zyklon-b-new-dictionary-highlights-nazi-words-to-avoid-a-531900.html. Accessed 1 September 2017.

Steiner, George. 1969. *Language and Silence: Essays 1958–1966*. Harmondsworth: Penguin.

Sternberger, Dolf. 1990. *Verfassungspatriotismus*. (*Schriften* X). Frankfurt/Main: Insel.

Sternberger, Dolf, Gerhard Storz, and Wilhelm E. Süskind. 1986. *Aus dem Wörterbuch des Unmenschen. Nach der erweiterten Ausgabe von 1967*. Frankfurt/Main, Berlin: Ullstein.

Stevenson, Patrick. 2002. *Language and German Disunity: A Sociolinguistic History of East and West Germany, 1945–2000*. Oxford: Oxford University Press.

Stötzel, Georg. 1986. Normierungsversuche und Berufungen auf Normen bei öffentlicher Thematisierung von Sprachverhalten. In *Kontroversen, alte und neue. Akten des VII. Internationalen Germanisten-Kongresses Göttingen 1985*, 86–100. Tübingen: Niemeyer.

———. 1989. Nazi-Verbrechen und öffentliche Sprachsensibilität. *Sprache und Literatur* 20: 32–52.

———. 1995. Der Nazi-Komplex. In *Kontroverse Begriffe. Geschichte des öffentlichen Sprachgebrauchs in der Bundesrepublik Deutschland*, Hg. Georg Stötzel and Martin Wengeler, 355–382. Berlin, New York: de Gruyter.

Stötzel, Georg, and Martin Wengeler, Hgg. 1995. *Kontroverse Begriffe. Geschichte des öffentlichen Sprachgebrauchs in der Bundesrepublik Deutschland*. Berlin, New York: de Gruyter.

Stötzel, Georg, and Thorsten Eitz, Hgg. 2003. *Zeitgeschichtliches Wörterbuch der deutschen Gegenwartssprache: Schlüsselwörter und Orientierungsvokabeln*. Hildesheim: Olms.

Strauß, Gerhard, Ulrike Haß, and Gisela Harras. 1989. *Brisante Wörter von Agitation bis Zeitgeist. Ein Lexikon zum öffentlichen Sprachgebrauch (Schriften des Instituts für Deutsche Sprache 2)*. Berlin: de Gruyter.

Voigt, Gerhard. 1967. Zur Sprache des Faschismus. *Das Argument* 9: 154–165.

———. 1974. Bericht vom Ende der 'Sprache des Nationalsozialismus'. *Diskussion Deutsch* 5: 451–456.

Wimmer, Rainer. 1982. Überlegungen zu den Aufgaben und Methoden einer linguistisch begründeten Sprachkritik. In *Holzfeuer im hölzernen Ofen. Aufsätze zur politischen Sprachkritik*, Hg. H. J. Heringer, 290–313. Tübingen: Gunter Narr.

10

Conclusion

This concluding chapter briefly reviews the main findings of the present study and brings them into the present day, reflecting on the legacies of National Socialism for the German discourse community, the state of political discourse analysis in the German-speaking world, and the lessons which might be learned for the future. To the extent that the national disaster of National Socialism has spurred German linguistic science to a *retrospective* understanding of the workings of political discourse, the question arises: what if any lessons can be learned for our understanding of political discourses today and in the future? Is there a body of experience here that might help in the task of 'confronting the present' (GEGENWARTSBEWÄLTIGUNG)?

National Socialist Discourse: Provenance, Reality, Legacy

Discourses have histories, they evolve. The discourse practices *of* National Socialism did not appear out of nowhere in the 1920s, nor did they begin to exercise an influence on German society only on 30 January 1933.

W J Dodd, *National Socialism and German Discourse*,
https://doi.org/10.1007/978-3-319-74660-9_10

Political history and discourse history do not map onto each other here. Narratives on German nationhood and identity which with hindsight appear as 'precursor' discourses *leading to* or *culminating in* National Socialism already dominated much of the public sphere in the latter years of the Weimar Republic, also in the statements of constitutional conservatives like von Papen. These discourses of 'Conservative Revolution' were in turn ensembles of political discourses in the long nineteenth century, dating back at least to the trauma of the Napoleonic occupation. Debates on topics as diverse as language, culture, ethnicity, and Empire served a grand narrative of German essentialism, natural superiority, but also, paradoxically, of envious outrage at the economic and military superiority of Britain and France, in particular. Discursive 'othering' played a vital role in the formation of a rallying narrative of Germanness, identifying "enemies" without and within. As Robertson (1999, p. 184f.) notes, the techniques of 'othering' remained largely constant whilst their targets changed: THE French, THE Jews, THE English, THE Catholics, THE 'liberals'. The moment which propelled these narratives into a potent political force was, notably, another national trauma, the humiliation of 1918.

The power of discourse to create a psychological 'reality' (Schiewe and Wengeler 2005, p. 7) in which logical thinking defers to raw emotions and contradictions disappear in a kind of mass 'cognitive dissonance', is documented repeatedly by the 'unquiet voices' at the centre of this study. The rhetoric of KAMPF—itself a standard trope of political discourse—transferred easily from the mental to the physical realm, as the violence latent in the conventionalized use of language (the 'Phrase') was "revindicated" (Kraus 1989, p. 140) in a binary friend/foe worldview, inciting and justifying acts of physical violence, and intimidating those who were repelled by it. The testimony of the diarists reviewed in Chap. 5, the proliferation and intensity of the hegemonic discourse as documented, for example, by Seidel/Seidel-Slotty, helps us today to imagine how intimidating everyday discourse *in* National Socialism must have been for non-Nazis imprisoned in their own country, where the 'private' space was under threat from informers and *agents provocateurs*, even in the family home (cf. Brecht's *Fear and Misery of the Third Reich*).

Whilst the language of those in territorial exile from the regime continued to be forthright, the problem, identified by Ernst Bloch, of finding the appropriate form and the 'right words' with which to combat National Socialism, perhaps proved insuperable. A discourse of righteous indignation proved inadequate to the task, as Kraus and Bloch realized, as did satire—though this did not prevent such verbal attacks. Once violence was established as the 'language' of power, the language and genres of factual documentation (also in fictionalized form, if based on documented fact) proved perhaps the most powerful tools, but by themselves they could not dislodge the regime without the intervention of (external) physical force. For those in inner exile, forms of mental opposition, of 'Resistenz' articulated in language, were the logical correlative of the almost total Nazification of German society (Broszat 1986), and were defined by the conditions of discursive disempowerment ('Sprachlosigkeit', Bauer 1988) against which they rebelled.

The reality of living in a brutal, near-hegemonic discourse environment is thankfully difficult for most people in democratic societies to appreciate (although those subject to anonymous abuse in electronic social media may disagree). The testimonies of our 'unquiet voices' in forms of inner exile are important here, both those bearing witness in private (such as Klemperer) and those who sought to articulate 'Resistenz' in the print media (such as Sternberger). The circumstances of text production and propagation are certainly pertinent here: the 'private' testimonies are typically more forthright in naming and documenting, and thus more valuable as records than the public voices, which, as Chaps. 6 and 7 demonstrate, were deflected into an increasingly coded and elite discourse on culture as a proxy for political criticism. It is not a straightforward matter, however, to compare the two situations, as they perform different functions. The 'private' notes document reality for a future time which the writer may not see, whilst the published texts are intended for daily consumption in an ongoing battle for and with words and meanings, employing a strategy of "pinpricks" against the overwhelming power of the regime. Both are attempts to assert personal integrity and humane values. In the latter case, there is also an attempt to form a counter-discourse of solidarity. Equally, self-censorship is not entirely absent from the ostensibly 'private' writings, and in this respect they, too, are often documents of 'Sprachlosigkeit'. To this extent, none of the 'unquiet voices' quite escaped the situation of Brecht's Herr Egge, described in the

Introduction to this study, and in Bauer's pointed reference (1988, p. 13) to Erving Goffman's ethnography of speaking.

With the defeat of the regime in 1945, the majority of terms designating institutions of the 'Third Reich' became historical. The Allies' attempt to "denazify the language" was largely unco-ordinated and was ultimately abandoned, its main achievements lying more in raising the level of language awareness in the population at large in the months and years following the liberation. Here, the efforts of the occupying powers towards "re-education" were enthusiastically supported by many of the 'unquiet voices'. As the discourse on Nazism became retrospective, it also acquired a new current relevance. This is evident from the concerns over the continuing use of expressions (e.g. in the "Lexicon of the 'Unmensch'") whose moral taintedness, evident to many in 1945, appears to have dwindled and disappeared quite quickly after 1945, to the dismay of observers like Sternberger for whom words like BETREUEN and DURCHFÜHREN would forever carry the stigma they had acquired in his personal linguistic biography between 1933 and 1945. The rapid re-normalization of these words would appear to suggest that the "Lexicon's" analysis is flawed, and von Polenz (1999, p. 317f.) lists sound arguments in support of this view. Nevertheless, as Ehlich (1989) suggests, it may be that it is precisely these unobtrusive words and expressions, constituting a "substratum" of ideological discourse, which possess a latent potential for activation as a reservoir of resources for popularizing, enforcing, persuading, and coercing speakers into acceptance of norms. As suggested in Chap. 9, for example, the discourse of 'care' is open to such mis-use.

More pressingly, the instrumentalization of Nazi tropes for present political advantage has proved a persistent feature of the retrospective discourse on Nazism, not only in the German-speaking world, but globally. The examples reviewed in Chap. 9 demonstrate the high level of sensitivity in Germany, manifest in the way in which these "Nazi comparisons" (Stötzel 1995) are contested. Contestation is evidence of a continuing historical awareness in German society: it is very difficult for a public speaker to plead ignorance of the Nazi past, or that s/he was guilty only of 'mis-speaking'. The level of expectation is perhaps lower in other countries, where knowledge of German history is not a national imperative. Speaking from ignorance or without due thought (absent-minded 'mis-speaking') may incur less public censure abroad, although we should perhaps not allow such excuses from those in positions of public prominence, and certainly not when there is a demonstrable attempt to knowingly manipulate the Nazi past to bolster nationalist or Germanophobic sentiment. The level of linguistic taboo in contemporary German discourse, reviewed in Chap. 9, is also a testament to the deep social memory entrenched in language use. That it can still be detected seventy years after the fall of the regime is evidence of the longevity of the German national trauma.

In Germany as in perhaps no other society, nationalism is still viewed with great suspicion. German nationalist political discourses are inevitably measured against the historical warning example of National Socialism. It may well be the case that nationalist political discourse in Germany today is hyper-sensitive to the charge of echoing Nazism, and more careful, or strategic, in its use of language. However, as Kämper's analysis of the AfD programme (Kämper 2017) demonstrates, this may be changing, particularly in regard to expressions implying a biological concept of the nation. This is an area in which the 'politolinguistics' championed by Kämper and others can make an important contribution to public understanding in Germany and abroad.

Linguistic Discourse Analysis: A German Model

This brings us to a consideration of the distinctive German achievements in the description and criticism of political discourses, on which the present study has drawn. This achievement has been impelled to a very considerable extent by the need to contribute to the German 'Vergangenheitsbewältigung'. The 'Sprachstreit' in the 1960s marks an important departure in this respect, impelling von Polenz and others to a kind of Damascene conversion at a time when the very notion of a critical linguistics was held to be invalid in the structuralist (Saussurean) and formalist (Chomskyan) models of language which were still the orthodoxy in the universities. Since the 'socio-pragmatic' turn to the study of *parole* of the 1960s, a 'pragmatized semantics' has played an increasingly influential role in the description of discourse practices and indeed the production of 'pragmatized' historical lexical reference works spanning "micro-diachronic" periods (Eitz and Stötzel 2007). The role of individual lexical items in this dynamic field of language-as-discourse is now better understood, particularly in the concept of the 'Schlagwort'—much more ubiquitous than Williams's 'keywords' and not quite captured in the English 'slogan'—and its role in rallying supporters to the banner or stigmatizing the banners of opponents (Dieckmann 1969; Klein 1989). Schmitz-Berning's (2000) study of the discourse histories of key terms in the 'language *of* National Socialism', begun in the 1960s, marks an important early step in this process. The 'pragmatized' studies of contested discourse items produced by the 'Düsseldorf School' (including the works by Stötzel, Jung, Wengeler, Böke, and Eitz) and others cited in the course of this study are examples of a corpus-based empirical method for discovering and describing discourses. A linguistically grounded 'Sprachkritik' in the tradition begun by von Polenz is now established as an academic university discipline and is beginning to be studied in schools (cf. Heringer and Wimmer 2015). There is still much work to do before this professionalized discourse on language can counter the often mistaken lay discourses on language which can still be activated in the population at large, for example by equating THE GERMAN LANGUAGE with the 'German nation', describing both using the metaphor of a living organism under attack from 'foreign bodies'. The characteristics of such discourses are now well understood, as is their role in contributing to a discriminatory discourse on national identity.

Discourse Analysis: A Cassandra Experience?

Nevertheless, lay discourses in the population at large continue to be more powerful than the body of knowledge assembled in the academies. Turning to the present and the future, one has to ask whether the lessons learned from the academic study of the discourse *of*, *in*, *resulting in*, and *reflecting on* National Socialism can be transferred to the understanding and critiquing of present and future political discourses. Some of the experiences of our 'unquiet voices', admittedly operating in a society in which the freedom to articulate dissent had been all but eliminated, are not encouraging here. In a sense, they are rather like crime scene investigators, perhaps helping to identify perpetrators and even motives, but unable to broadcast their findings or to prevent future crimes. The frustrations articulated by many of them frequently lend support to a view of discourse analysis as a Cassandra experience, most notably Theodor Haecker's (1989, p. 232f.) realization in April 1944 that even other opponents of the regime cannot hear what he hears in the discourse, or see where it is leading: "What am I to do? Say nothing at all? Be silent? Or speak up too late?". Kraus's rhetorical question: "Is what they say and what they deny not enough to reveal what they do?" (1989, p. 108) also voices the frustration of one for whom the discourse is transparent, while to others it remains opaque. Kraus's falling silent ("Not one word that hit home") and Bloch's desperate search for an adequate linguistic response to Nazism might also be seen in the same light.

Turning to the present and the future, perhaps the best one can hope for is that the lessons learned from the study of National Socialism and German discourse will serve as a flexible model with which to approach future variations on past themes, and not only in Germany. To do so, they must take the step from academic knowledge to the general knowledge enshrined in public discourse if they are to contribute to the ideal of a "deliberative democracy" (Teubert 2014, p. 104):

> Denn alle Diskursteilnehmer, nicht nur Experten, sind dazu aufgerufen, über das, was moralisch ist, was als Trick zulässig ist und was nicht, zu diskutieren. Was die Sprachwissenschaft beitragen kann, ist eine mehr oder weniger systematische Übersicht aller solcher Tricks als unabdingbarer Lehrinhalt für alle Schulen, in denen künftige Staatsbürger unterrichtet werden. (Teubert 2014, p. 98)
>
> For all participants in the discourse, not just experts, have the task of discussing what is moral, what is admissible as a rhetorical ploy and what is not. What linguistic science can contribute is a more or less systematic overview of such ploys as an essential subject for all schools in which the citizens of the future are taught.

In the case of nationalist discourses, at a time when global migration has provoked unsettled national identities across the world to aggressively reassert themselves, the prospects are arguably better in the German-speaking than in the English-speaking world, precisely because of the enduring retrospective national conversation about National Socialism since 1945, and the legacy of German 'unquiet voices'. There is clearly the danger, for example, that the 'othering' of Jews in 1920s Germany is being reincarnated in the discourse on Muslims in Europe (including the UK) and the USA, and that assertive nationalist discourses will once again rally around the stigmatization of "enemies within" as well as without. CITIZENS OF NOWHERE and ENEMIES OF THE PEOPLE have featured, for example, in recent British public discourse in the aftermath of the EU referendum of June 2016. In both cases, the choice of words was contested, but largely in a partisan way that reinforced the political divide exposed by the vote. It could be argued in their defence that these high-profile contributors to the public discourse (a Prime Minister, headline writers of the popular press) were unaware of the echoes which become apparent when these expressions are cited in the context of the present study. On the other hand, it seems reasonable to expect a higher level of awareness and sensitivity from our politicians and opinion formers, and a willingness to debate and even to modify their use of language in light of an informed public discussion of its implications, in the interests of "deliberative democracy". An extensive culture of democratic 'politolinguistics' would appear to be an urgent requirement as democratic societies face the challenges of the future.

Bibliography

Bauer, Gerhard. 1988. *Sprache und Sprachlosigkeit im "Dritten Reich"*. Köln: Bund-Verlag.

Broszat, Martin. 1986. Zur Sozialgeschichte des deutschen Widerstands. *Vierteljahrshefte für Zeitgeschichte* 34 (3): 293–309.

Dieckmann, Walther. 1969. *Sprache in der Politik. Einführung in die Pragmatik und Semantik der politischen Sprache*. Heidelberg: Carl Winter.

Ehlich, Konrad, Hg. 1989. *Sprache im Faschismus*. Frankfurt/Main: Suhrkamp.

Eitz, Thorsten, and Georg Stötzel. 2007. *Wörterbuch der 'Vergangenheitsbewältigung'. Die NS-Vergangenheit im öffentlichen Sprachgebrauch*. Hildesheim, Zürich, New York: Olms.

Haecker, Theodor. 1989. *Tag- und Nachtbücher 1939–1945. Erste vollständige und kommentierte Ausgabe.* Herausgegeben von Hinrich Siefken, Brenner-Studien, Bd. 9. Innsbruck: Haymon Verlag.

Heringer, Hans Jürgen, and Rainer Wimmer. 2015. *Sprachritik. Eine Einführung.* Stuttgart: UTB.

Kämper, Heidrun. 2017. Das Grundsatzprogramm der AfD und seine historischen Parallelen. Eine Perspektive der Politikolinguistik. *Aptum. Zeitschrift für Sprachkritik und Sprachkultur* 01 (17): 16–41. Also in: *Sprachreport* 33 (2): 1–21. Mannheim: Institut für deutsche Sprache.

Klein, Josef. 1989. Wortschatz, Wortkampf, Wortfelder. In *Politische Semantik. Beiträge zur politischen Sprachverwendung*, Hg. J. Klein, 3–50. Opladen: Westdeutscher Verlag.

Kraus, Karl. 1989. *Dritte Walpurgisnacht.* Herausgegeben von Christian Wagenknecht. Frankfurt/Main: Suhrkamp taschenbuch.

von Polenz, Peter. 1999. *Deutsche Sprachgeschichte vom Spätmittelalter bis zur Gegenwart.* Bd 3: *19. und 20. Jahrhundert*. Berlin, New York: de Gruyter.

Robertson, Ritchie. 1999. *The 'Jewish Question' in German Literature 1749–1939: Emancipation and Its Discontents.* Oxford: Oxford University Press.

Schiewe, Jürgen, and Martin Wengeler. 2005. Einführung der Herausgeber zum ersten Heft. *Aptum. Zeitschrift für Sprachkritik und Sprachkultur* 01 (05): 1–13.

Schmitz-Berning, Cornelia. 2000. *Vokabular des Nationalsozialismus.* Berlin, New York: de Gruyter.

Stötzel, Georg. 1995. Der Nazi-Komplex. In *Kontroverse Begriffe. Geschichte des öffentlichen Sprachgebrauchs in der Bundesrepublik Deutschland*, Hg. Georg Stötzel and Martin Wengeler, 355–382. Berlin, New York: de Gruyter.

Teubert, Wolfgang. 2014. Die Bedeutung von Sprachkritik für die Demokratie. *Aptum. Zeitschrift für Sprachkritik und Sprachkultur* 02 (14): 98–114.

Appendix

Texts

This Appendix contains texts or excerpts of texts marked in this study with an asterisk, with English translations; and a tabular overview of the iterations of the "Lexicon of the 'Unmensch'".

Ein merkwürdiges Jubiläum (extract)
Dolf Sternberger
Frankfurter Zeitung, 17 September 1935, p. 3

Heute, am 17. September, ist genau ein Jahrhundert vergangen seit dem Tage, an dem Charles Darwin, 26jährig, den Strand von Chatham-Island, einer Insel der Galapagosgruppe, betrat. [....] Ja, es handelt sich wirklich nicht bloß um das wissenschaftliche, nicht einmal bloß um das "geistige" Leben im dem eingeschränkteren Sinne eines Schauspiels, welches noch die eigentlichen nationalen und gesellschaftlichen Ordnungen ungeschoren ließe: Darwins Theorie der natürlichen Entwicklung und der genetischen Einheit alles Lebendigen hat diese Grundlagen selber mit in Bewegung gebracht. Ohne Darwin kein Nietzsche, ohne Nietzsche zum Beispiel—wahrscheinlich—kein

W J Dodd, *National Socialism and German Discourse*,
https://doi.org/10.1007/978-3-319-74660-9

Mussolini! Schon sind wir mitten in der Politik des gegenwärtigen Moments, wenn auch gewiß mit einigen Sprüngen, einigen Auslassungen, Abkürzungen und Vereinfachungen, denn es waren ohne Zweifel krümmere Gänge, in denen sich jener Ruck von Galapagos durch die Geschichte des 19. Jahrhunderts bis in unsere eigene fortgepflanzt hat. [...]

[...] Die Aufzeichnungen [...], die [...] Darwin währenddessen nach Europa brachte, bewirkten, nachdem sie zur Theorie sich gruppiert und ausgebildet hatten, daß der christliche Glaube an den Schöpfergott—Fundament dieser selben Zivilisation—ins Wanken geriet, schließlich offen mit dem Ziele seiner völligen Destruktion angegriffen wurde, weiter, daß der Mensch (in Europa) als ein selbstmächtiges Naturwesen erklärt wurde, dem es nur aufgegeben sei, sich vollends zum "prachtvollen Untier" zu entwickeln (Nietzsche).

A Noteworthy Anniversary

Today, the 17 September, it is exactly one hundred years since the day the twenty-six year-old Charles Darwin stepped on to the beach of Chatham Island, an island of the Galapagos group. [...] Indeed, it is really not just a matter of the scientific nor even merely the "spiritual" life in the narrower sense of a spectacle that would leave the real national and social orders untouched: Darwin's theory of natural development and the genetic unity of all living things has itself helped to cause these foundations to move. Without Darwin, no Nietzsche, without Nietzsche, for example—probably—no Mussolini! We are already in the midst of the politics of the present moment, albeit certainly with a few jumps, a few omissions, abbreviations and simplifications, for without doubt there were more crooked paths by way of which the jolt of Galapagos has perpetuated itself through the history of the nineteenth century into our own history. [...]

[...] The notes [...] which Darwin brought back to Europe, after they had formed themselves into a theory, caused the Christian faith in God the creator—foundation of this same civilization—to begin to waver, finally to be attacked with the clear goal of its complete destruction, and further that the human being (in Europe) was declared to be an autonomous being of nature whose only task was to develop into a "magnificent animal" (Nietzsche).

Blick der Liebenden
(Vademecum zum Gebrauch von Sprichwörtern: III).
Dolf Sternberger
Frankfurter Zeitung, 5 April 1936, p. 7 (Feuilleton)

Meist sagt es ein alter Schulkamerad des Mannes, der sich soeben verliebt oder gar verheiratet hat: "Ich weiß nicht, was er an dieser Frau findet, sie ist weder intelligent noch besonders hübsch, und über ihren Charakter wollen wir schon gar nicht reden—man kann's nicht ändern: *Liebe macht blind*."

Und er wendet sich resigniert ab, überzeugt, daß er den Freund so bald nicht wieder allein zu fassen kriegen wird, und gewillt, sich den Einladungen des jungen Paares so oft als möglich durch Ausflüchte zu entziehen, die vielleicht nicht einmal ganz ungern gehört werden. Seine Resignation wird freilich in den seltensten Fällen vollkommen und endgültig sein, denn die geheime Hoffnung, daß auch für ihn wieder bessere Tage kommen werden, hält ihn davon ab, sich grimmiger Menschenverachtung anheimzugeben. Wer gewiß ist, daß Liebe blind mache, hat den mit solcher Blindheit Geschlagenen noch lange nicht aufgegeben. Denn es ist ja *nur* die Liebe, die blind macht—so denkt er im stillen—, und die geht vorüber. Die Gewohnheit aber wird ihn eines Tages schon wieder sehend machen, und ich kann's abwarten.

Oft genug wird einem solchen Kenner der menschlichen Leidenschaften der Freund, der geheiratet hat, nach einigen Monaten schon bei sich selber und nach einigen Jahren auch offen recht geben. Dann nämlich, wenn er wieder anfängt, allein auszugehen und sich im Wirtshaus oder Café mit den alten Schulkameraden zu treffen, gereift an Einsicht und Erfahrung, wie er meint. Dann scheint alles beglichen und die Wahrheit außer Zweifel.

Dieses späte Einverständnis des Ehemannes beweist indessen gar nichts. Schon darum nicht, weil er, den die abgelaufene Zeit so vergeßlich hat werden lassen, am wenigsten befugt ist, über die Liebe etwas auszusagen. Es kann sich ja auch so verhalten, daß er vordem als Liebender sehend gewesen und nun durch Gewohnheit erst blind geworden ist. Daß sein Überdruß nicht in der Erkenntnis, sondern seine—ach wie zweifelhafte—Erkenntnis im Überdruß begründet ist. Überdruß aber ist eine Folge von Faulheit. Ein Liebender, der faul und bequem wird—man erkennt ihn unzweifelhaft an den deklamatorischen Versicherungen, die er über gebrachte Opfer und dergleichen abgibt—, hat es schon satt, selber zu lieben. (Denn die Liebe ist zwar heiter, aber doch kein bloßer Spaß.) Und wenn er es satt hat und wenn er satt ist, dann glaubt er, sehend zu werden—während der Satte sonst zwar nicht gerade blind, aber doch schläfrig zu werden pflegt. Über all das aber, was er vordem mit dem frisch aufgetanen Blick des Liebenden entdeckt und erkannt hatte—all die tausend kleinen Mienen, Gebärden und Regungen nämlich des geliebten Wesens, welche jener Schulkamerad mit seinem Sprichwort im Munde oder vorm Kopf niemals hätte sehen können—, über all das hat sich dann ein anfangs dünner, später immer dichter werdender Schleier gesenkt. Die Liebe machte ihn sehend, seine Faulheit machte ihn blind. Es gibt allerdings einen Fall, in dem das Sprichwort gleichwohl zu Recht gebraucht werden kann: dann nämlich, wenn Liebe und Faulheit zusammenfallen oder die Liebe der Faulheit entstammt. Wer—sei es aus Selbstgefälligkeit, sei es aus Unsicherheit—einzig zu dem Zwecke liebt oder zu lieben vorgibt, um selber mit Liebe bedient und gestärkt zu werden, den freilich macht Liebe blind. Er pflegt sich auf seine Verdienste, seine Arbeiten und vorzüglich seine Leiden zu berufen und fordert Liebe zum Dank dafür. Hier gilt's. Hier ist aber nicht an irgendeinem dritten, sondern an dem derart falsch geliebten Wesen selber, aufzustehen und zu sprechen: *Solche* Liebe macht *dich* blind. Diesem Blinden kann der Star nur unter großen Schmerzen gestochen werden. (Cf. Sternberger 1988, pp. 41–43.)

The Lovers' Gaze.
(Guide to the Use of Sayings: III)

Often an old classmate of the man who has just got engaged or even married will say "I don't know what he sees in this woman, she is neither intelligent nor particularly pretty, and let's not even start on her character—there's nothing to be done: *Love is blind.*"

And he turns away in resignation, convinced that he will not have his friend to himself again for a long time and resolved to evade the young couple's invitations in the meantime through a variety of excuses, which may even not be unwelcome to them. His resignation will admittedly in most cases not be complete and final, for the secret hope that better days will come even for him prevents him from giving himself over to bitter misanthropy. He who is certain that love makes you blind has not by a long chalk given up on the one who has been smitten. For, he thinks to himself, it is after all *only* love that makes you blind—and that passes. Familiarity will one day make him see sense, and I can wait.

Often enough the friend who has married will, after a few months, admit secretly to himself, and after a few years openly to this expert on human passions that he was right—when he starts to go out on his own again and to meet his old school friends in the pub or the café, older in understanding and experience, as he believes. Then everything seems settled and the truth beyond doubt.

But this late concurrence of the husband proves nothing at all. For the simple reason that he whom the passage of time has made so forgetful is the least qualified to say anything about love. It may be that as a lover he could once see and now, through custom, has become blind. That his satedness is not caused by his new way of seeing, but that his—oh so dubious—new way of seeing is caused by satedness. But satedness is a consequence of laziness. A lover who becomes lazy and comfortable—you can recognize him unmistakeably by his declamatory assurances of the sacrifices and the like that he has made—has already stopped loving. (For love is indeed jolly, but no joke.) And when he is fed up and has had enough, then he believes he can see—when in fact he who is fed up, though he doesn't usually go blind, usually becomes drowsy. And a veil, at first just thin but growing ever thicker, has fallen over everything that he had discovered and seen with the newly opened eyes of a lover—all the thousands of little expressions, gestures and movements of his loved one, which his old schoolmate with his proverb could never have seen. Love made him see, his laziness made him blind. But there is one case in which the proverb is justified, namely when love and laziness coincide or love springs from laziness. Whoever—be it out of complacency or out of insecurity—loves or pretends to love solely in order to receive love and be strengthened by it, he is indeed made blind by love. He is accustomed to cite his achievements, his hard work, and above all his suffering, and demands love as thanks for these. In this case the proverb is true. And in this case it is not for a third party, but for the falsely loved one, to stand up and say: *This* kind of love makes *you* blind. This blind man's eyes can be opened only at the cost of enormous pain.

Menschen als Material

Dolf Sternberger

Frankfurter Zeitung, 21 April 1940, p. 3

Manche Kliniker pflegten—und das war lange Zeit selbstverständlich, fiel niemand weiter auf—bei Berichten in der Fachliteratur, wenn sie etwa die Wirkungen eines Heilverfahrens beschrieben und statistisch ordneten, die Menschen, an denen sie es erprobt hatten, als ihr "Krankenmaterial" zu bezeichnen. Man schien, indem man so sprach, in der Klinik wie in einer Fabrik zu hantieren, wo das "Ausgangs-" oder "Rohmaterial" durch gewisse Weisen der Bearbeitung aufbereitet, verändert, geformt oder auch veredelt, im Analogiefalle also behandelt oder auch geheilt wird. Diese Assoziation oder dieses drastische Gleichnis, dem das Wort "Krankenmaterial" mindestens unbewußt seine Entstehung dankt, ist aber in neuester Zeit doch offenbar als peinlich empfunden worden. Jedenfalls suchte man nach einem neuen Wort, das weniger "materialistisch" klänge. Und man fand es auch. Es war obendrein ein deutsches Wort und hörte sich edler an. Es hieß "Krankengut". Man kannte bis dahin zwar Massengüter und Stück- güter, immerhin aber auch das Kulturgut und das Gedankengut, also "immaterielle" Güter, so schien also gegen diese neue Prägung kaum etwas einzuwenden zu sein. In Wahrheit war dies fast nichts anderes als eine Verdeutschung des "Materials", nur daß diesmal an die Stelle der Fabrik das Handelshaus getreten ist. Güter besitzt man—dies gilt zumal vom Landgut oder Rittergut—oder man kauft, verkauft und transportiert sie, wozu unter anderen Mitteln Güterwagen, Güterzüge und Güterbahnhöfe dienlich sind. Güter sind allemal Dinge, und wenn man von "immateriellen" oder auch von "höheren" Gütern spricht, so macht man sie im gleichen Atemzug eben zu Dingen oder man spricht es aus, daß sie zu Dingen geworden sind. Die Verschönerung des Krankenmaterials zum Krankengut enthüllt also, daß man sich nur terminologisch unbehaglich gefühlt hat, daß in der Sache aber alles beim alten geblieben ist. Kürzlich aber ist in der Münchener Medizinischen Wochenschrift ein Kliniker, Professor von Baeyer, aufgetreten, der beide Wendungen, die alte wie die neue, auszuräumen trachtet und am Ende rund und klar empfiehlt: "Man sage einfach: die Kranken". In der Tat, die Kranken sind Wesen und nicht Dinge. Man sage es einfach! Es wird sich zu zeigen haben, ob es so einfach ist, dieses einfache, natürliche, würdige Wort zu gebrauchen. Man muß es auch meinen, denken, fühlen, tun—kurz, die Kranken müssen auch wirklich aufhören Krankengut zu sein, sie müssen wirklich Kranke werden für den Arzt. Denn solch ein Wort ist ja niemals bloß ein Wort und nichts weiter, es ist stets der genaue Name einer Realität. Als "Menschenmaterial", und sei es auch ein "erstklassiges", sind die Menschen wirklich Material, es steckt ein Zustand, ein objektives Verhältnis in dem Wort. Und wenn aus dem Menschenmaterial die Menschen erstehen, wie dort aus dem Krankengut die Kranken; so ist nicht bloß ein Wort verändert, sondern ein Zustand. Man sage es einfach—aber man meine es auch ernstlich! (Cf. Sternberger 1991, p. 316f.; Dodd 2013a, p. 156f.)

Human Beings as Material

In their specialist journals it was customary for many clinicians when they described the effects of a course of treatment and considered them statistically—and this was long considered natural, did not strike anyone as strange—to refer to the persons on whom they had tested it as their "pathological material". Speaking in such terms one seemed to be operating in the clinic as in a factory where the "initial" or "raw material" was prepared, altered, shaped, or even processed by means of certain methods of working on it, by way of analogy, then, was treated or even healed. This association or this drastic metaphor which at least subconsciously gave rise to the word 'Krankenmaterial', has obviously come to be regarded with embarrassment in recent times. At any rate, they looked for a different word that would sound less "materialistic", and they found it. What is more, it was a German word and sounded nobler. It was 'Krankengut'. One was familiar with bulk goods and parcelled goods, but also with cultural and intellectual goods, "immaterial goods", so there seemed little to object to about this new formulation. In fact it was little more than a

Germanizing of the "material", only that this time the firm had replaced the factory. You can possess goods (this also holds for nobles' and country estates) or you can buy, sell, and transport them, for which amongst other things goods wagons, goods trains, and goods stations are useful. Goods are always things, and when one talks about "immaterial" or "higher" goods one turns them in the same breath into things or one states that they have become things. The embellishment of 'Krankenmaterial' to 'Krankengut' thus reveals that they were just uncomfortable about the terminology and that nothing had changed in practice. Recently, however, a clinician, Professor von Bayer, wrote in the Munich Medical Weekly, seeking to do away with both terms, the old and the new, and finally stating quite clearly: "Let us just say 'those who are ill'". Indeed, the ill are beings and not things. Just say it, then! It remains to be seen whether it will be simple to use this simple, natural, noble word. One also has to mean it, think it, feel it, do it—in short, those who are ill really have to stop being pathology, they must really become ill human beings for the doctors. For a word like this is never just a word and nothing more, but always the exact name of a reality. As "Menschenmaterial", even if it is "first class", human beings really are material, there is a condition, an objective relation in the word. And when the human beings arise from the human material, like the ill people from the pathology, then it is not just a word that has changed, but a state of affairs. So let us say it—and really mean it!

Der 'Angeber' (extract)
Gerhard Storz
Frankfurter Zeitung, 25 March 1941, p. 3

[…] Die Aelteren verstehen nicht anders als unsere klassischen Schriftsteller und alle Wörterbücher unter "Angeber" den Denunzianten. Ein Primaner aber übersetzt den lateinischen Passus "*secretarum epistularum delator*" heute folgendermaßen (und glaubt gewiß, seine Sache besonders geschickt gemacht zu haben): "Der Mann, der mit seiner Kenntnis von geheimen Briefen zu prahlen pflegte." Das wahrlich blinde Vertrauen des Schülers zu seinem Vokabelbüchlein, in dem kurz und kahl steht "delator = Angeber", sah sich mit einem roten Strich im

Extemporale-Heft übel belohnt. [...] Der Sprachreiniger aber möchte sich bald dem Uebelstand gegenüber sehen, daß "Denunziant" zu den schwer ersetzbaren Fremdwörtern gehört. Dann wird ihn vielleicht der sprachdeutende Kulturhistoriker mit dem Bemerken trösten, die gemeine Handlungsweise dessen, den die Römer "*delator*" nannten, sei erfreulicherweise so selten geworden, daß sie die Bezeichnung durch ein deutsches Wort gar nicht mehr verdiene. (Cf. Dodd 2007, p. 311f.; 2013a, p. 183f.)

The 'Angeber' (Blagger/Informant)

[...] For the older ones amongst us, the word "Angeber" means, just as it did for our classical writers, an informant. Today however a sixth-former translates the Latin passage "*secretarum epistularum delator*" as "the man who used to boast about his knowledge of secret letters" (and certainly thinks he has done his job well). The student's truly blind trust in his vocabulary notebook, in which he finds, brief and bald: "delator = Angeber", was rewarded with a red line. [...] The language purist, however, may soon find himself confronted with the unwelcome situation that "Denunziant" is one of those 'Fremdwörter' that can't be done without. In which case the philologically informed cultural historian may console him with the observation that the shameful behaviour which the Romans called "*delator*" has thankfully become so rare that it no longer merits being designated by a German word.

Tabular Overview of the Headwords in the Iterations of the "Lexicon of the 'Unmensch'"

Die Wandlung 1945–48	First Book Edition 1957	Second Book Edition 1967/68
	Anliegen (Sternberger)	Anliegen (Sternberger)
		Auftrag (Sternberger)
Ausrichtung (Sternberger)	Ausrichtung (Sternberger)	Ausrichtung (Sternberger)
Betreuung (Sternberger)	Betreuung (Sternberger)	Betreuung (Sternberger)
Charakterlich (Sternberger)	Charakterlich (Sternberger)	Charakterlich (Sternberger)
Durchführen (Storz)	Durchführen (Storz)	Durchführen (Storz)

Die Wandlung 1945–48	First Book Edition 1957	Second Book Edition 1967/68
	Echt, einmalig (Süskind)	Echt, einmalig (Süskind)
Einsatz (Storz)	Einsatz (Storz)	Einsatz (Storz)
		Erarbeiten (Sternberger)
Fanatisch (Storz)		
	Frauenarbeit (Storz)	Frauenarbeit (Storz)
Gestaltung (Storz)	Gestaltung (Storz)	Gestaltung (Storz)
Härte (Süskind)		Härte (Süskind)
	Herausstellen (Süskind)	Herausstellen (Süskind)
Intellektuell (Sternberger)	Intellektuell (Sternberger)	Intellektuell (Sternberger)
		Kontakte (Sternberger)
Kulturschaffende (Süskind)	Kulturschaffende (Süskind)	Kulturschaffende (Süskind)
Lager (Süskind)	Lager (Süskind)	Lager (Süskind)
	Leistungsmäßig (Sternberger)	Leistungsmäßig (Sternberger)
Mädel (Storz)	Mädel (Storz)	
		Menschen (Sternberger)
	Menschenbehandlung (Sternberger)	Menschenbehandlung (Sternberger)
Organisieren (Süskind)	Organisieren (Süskind)	Organisieren (Süskind)
	Problem (Storz)	Problem (Storz)
Propaganda (Süskind)	Propaganda (Süskind)	Propaganda (Süskind)
Querschießen (Süskind)	Querschießen (Süskind)	Querschießen (Süskind)
Raum (Storz)	Raum (Storz)	Raum (Storz)
		Ressentiment (Sternberger)
Schulung (Storz)	Schulung (Storz)	Schulung (Storz)
Sektor (Süskind)	Sektor (Süskind)	Sektor (Süskind)
Tragbar (Storz)	Tragbar (Storz)	Tragbar (Storz)
Untragbar (Storz)	Untragbar (Storz)	Untragbar (Storz)
Vertreter (Sternberger)	Vertreter (Sternberger)	Vertreter (Sternberger)
		Verwendung (Sternberger)
Wissen um ... (Sternberger)	Wissen um ... (Sternberger)	Wissen um ... (Sternberger)
Zeitgeschehen (Storz)	Zeitgeschehen (Storz)	Zeitgeschehen (Storz)

Discourse-Relevant Expressions Identified in the course of this study (page number followed by n indicates endnote)

-berg, -eles, -heim, -itzig, -stein 17 | ABC-Schützen 136 | Abart 118 | abgewandertworden 125 | Abstammungsnachweis 285n11 | Abstammungsprinzip 285n11 | abtransportiert 142 | Adolf-Hitler-Schulen 106 | AH 276 | Ahnenerbe 65 | Allerheiligenstrietzel 202 | Allgemeine SS 105 | Angeber 206 | Ängstliche Gemüter 34 | Anliegen 261 | Anschluss 271, 273 | anschwärzen 259 | Antifaschistischer Schutzwall 260 | antijüdisch 56 | Antisemitismus 272 | Arier 17, 30, 58, 102, 193 | Ärger 34 | Arierparagraph 17 | arisch 242, 265 | Art 50, 51 | arteigen 78, 83, 265 | artfremd 50, 51 | artgegründete Sprachzucht 61 | artvergessen 52 | Asphaltliteratur 98 | atomarer Holocaust 258 | Aufarbeitung 256 | aufarten 57 | Aufbauwille 101 | Auferstehung 15 | aufnorden 57 | aufräumen 91 | Auschwitz 271 | Auschwitz-Lüge 271 | Auschwitz-Vergleiche 271 | ausländerfrei 273 | ausländische Sprachsudelei 24 | ausmerzen 16, 271 | ausradieren 121, 260 | ausrichten 105 | Ausrichtung 105, 125 | ausrotten 16, 125 | Ausrottung 142 | aussaugen 16 | Außenbürtigkeit 108n11 | ausscheiden 16 | Autarkie 172 | autarkisch 78 |

Babycaust 274 | bagatellisieren, Bagatellisierung 259, 271, 280 | Bazillen 16 | Befehlsnotstand 272 | Befreiung/ Niederlage 254, 271 | Begleitbataillon des Führers 105 | Bekennende Kirche 65n1 | bekleiden

W J Dodd, *National Socialism and German Discourse*,
https://doi.org/10.1007/978-3-319-74660-9

266 | bekochen 213 | belastet 271 | beliefern 266 | besitzen 116 | Bestien 142 | betreuen, Betreuung 221, 241, 242, 247, 261-263, 266, 270, 294 | Betrübnis und Beschämung 34 | Bevölkerung vii, 92-94, 272 | Bewältigung 256 | Bewegung 29, 119 | Bezogenheit 106 | Bleiben Sie ruhig!/ Bleiben Sie übrig! 134 | Blockwart 101 | blondes Blut 16, 80, 125 | Blut und Boden/ Blubo 64, 119, 169, 213 | Blutschande 265 | Boden vii, 92 | Bourgeoisie 16 | Bonzen 132 | Brüderlichkeit 15 | brutal 51, 125 | Bücherjude 17 | Bundestag/ Reichstag vii, 283 | bündisch 16 |

Charakter 23, 29, 30, 34 | charakterlich 125, 221, 242, 261, 278 | Charakterlosigkeit 135 | christliches Abendland 279 | Cohn 17 | coventrieren 51 |

damit 119 | das ewige Deutschland 125 | das neue Deutschland 101 | Daseinskampf 20 | dem deutschen Reiche 63 | dem deutschen Volke vii, 63, 93 | Demokratie 232 | Denazifizierung 228 | der Bevölkerung vii, 93, 272 | der Jude 17, 30, 125, 134 | der/ die/ das (generic definite article) 125, 229, 244, 292 | Desinfektion 16 | deutsch 279, 280, 281, 283 | Deutsch sein heißt klar sein 199-201 | Deutsche Christen 46n1 | deutsche Frau/en 101, 281 | deutscher Gruß 127, 158, 160 | deutsche Kultur 16 | deutsche Leitkultur 281 | deutsche Literatur 281 | deutsche Mutter 101 | Deutsche Normalschrift 61, 214 | Deutsche Schrift 61, 63, 213 | deutsche Sprache 22, 59, 82, 165, 278, 281 | deutsches Blut 17, 28 | deutsches Wesen 16, 20 | Deutschheit 15 | Deutschland 283 | Deutschland erwache! 82 | Deutschtum 30 | Die Juden sind unser Unglück 17 | DINATAG 53 | Displaced Persons/ Fremdarbeiter 272 | Disziplin 92 | DNB 54 | Dolchstoß/ Dolchstoßlegende 25, 135 | doppelte Vergangenheitsbewältigung 274 | Doppelverdiener 27 | Drittes Reich 26, 56, 169, 170, 193, 271 | Dummheit und Stolz wachsen auf einem Holz 204 | durchführen 201, 206, 211, 221, 242, 261, 277, 294 |

Echtbürtigkeit 108n11 | Ehre 19, 92, 94, 125 | ehrliches Erstaunen 34 | Eichmänner des nuklearen Holocaust 258 | eine Krähe hackt der anderen kein Auge aus 203 | einheimisch 280, 281 | einmalig 125, 193 | Einsatz 242, 261 | Einwanderer 279 | Elite 271 | Embryocaust 274 | Endausleselager 106 | Ende der Nachkriegszeit 271 | Ende gut, alles gut 204 | endgültig lösen 16 | Endlösung 16, 232, 242, 271, 277 | Endsieg 59, 232 | entartet 16 | entartete Kunst 257, 271 | Entartung 60 | Entjudung 58 | Entnazifizierung 227-247, 248n1, 271 | Entnazifizierung der Sprache 227-247 | entpolonisieren 15 | entscheidende Erfolge 125 | Entstasifizierung 274 | Entwöhnung 24 | erbarmungslos 51 | erbgesund, Erbgesundheit 57, 125 | Erbwert 51 | erfolgen 211 | erlesen 193 | Ermächtigungsgesetz 271 | Erregung des Volksempfindens 102 | Erregung öffentlichen Ärgernisses 102 | erstklassiges Menschenmaterial 208, 209 | Es ist noch nicht aller Tage Abend 204 | es sind die schlechtesten Früchte nicht, woran die Wespen nagen 204 | Es wird nichts so heiß gegessen, wie es gekocht ist 108n8, 203 | Euthanasie 271 | evakuieren 47, 50 | ewiger Jude 17 |

fanatisch/ Fanatismus 125, 238, 242, 261 | fanatische Einsatzbereitschaft 124 | fanatischer Wille 124 | Feindbild 279 | Feminismus 58 | Flüchtlinge/ Vertriebene 272 | Flut 25 | Frauenarbeit 261 | Frauenschaft 57 | Freiheit 15 | fremde Wurzeln 23 | fremdrassig 57 | fremdvölkisch 15, 58 | fressendes Gift 32, 33 | Frontabschnitt Wissenschaft 206 | Führer 16, 56, 193, 269 | Führer und Reichskanzler 56 | Führerautorität 29 | Führerprinzip 46 |

Gangster 141 | ganz 51, 116 | Ganzheit 106 | gänzlich 51, 116 | Gaskammer/ vergasen/ Vergasung 272 | Gau 36n4, 16 | Gefolgschaft 16, 29 | Gefüge 106 || Gehorsam 16, 92 | Geist 16 | Gemeinnutz vor Eigennutz 52 | Gemeinschaft 16, 106, 125 | Gendarm 34 | Genfer Entente 56 | Germanentum 16 | Gesamtheit 106 | Gesamtorganisation der gewerblichen Wirtschaft 106 | Gesellschaft 16 | Gesindel 142 | Gestalt 106 | gestalten 211 | Gestaltung 211, 221, 242, 261 | Gestapo 230, 271 | Gestapo-Methoden 257 | Gestapochef 259 | gestorben wird 125 | gesundes Volksempfinden 102, 281 | Gesundung 91 | getaufter Jude 17 | Gift wie Gift behandeln 16, 39n42 | Gläubigkeit, ohne zu verstehen 124 | gleichgeschaltet, Gleichschaltung 10, 46, 53, 57, 83, 271, 273 | Gnadentod 232 | Goebbels/Gobbeles 36n8, 77 | Goebbels-Vergleiche 234, 259, 272 | Gott, Kaiser, Vaterland 20 | gottgewollt 32 | göttliche Sendung 142 | granites Fundament 117 | Greuelpropaganda 56, 135 | Greuelhetze 56 | Gröfaz (Größter Feldherr aller Zeiten)/ Grövaz (Größter Verbrecher aller Zeiten) 142, 157 | groß aufgezogen 125 | groß- 119, 142 | großdeutsch 56, 271 | Großdeutsches Reich 56 | Großdeutschland 28 | Großfilm 119 | Großgasthof

119 | Großrümanien 119 | Großtaten 142 | Großunfug 149n6, 213 | Gut 208, 209 | Güterbahnhöfe 208, 209 | Güterzüge 208, 209 |

Handelsjude 17 | hart wie Kruppstahl 34 | Härte 242, 261, 263 | Hauptschuldige 248n2 | Heil 201 | Heil Hitler! 276 | heilen 201 | heilig 169, 170 | heilige deutsche Sprache 22 | heilige Landmarken 15 | Heimat 100, 101 | Heimatkräfte 32 | Heimschulen 106 | Heimtückegesetz 48 | Heldentum 142 | herausstellen 261 | Heroismus 237, 281 | Herrenmenschentum 140 | Herrenmoral 151n31 | Herrgott 128, 168 | HH18/HH88 276 | hilfloser Antifaschismus 266 | Himmelreich 170 | Hitler-Vergleiche 271 | HJ 106 | höchste deutsche Heiligkeit 25 | Hock 172 | Hoheitszeichen 102 | Holocaust 258, 271 | Holocaust-Mahnmal 272 | Holocaust-Vergleiche 271, 274 | Horden 16, 20 | Hörgoi 105 | HSSPf 105 | Humanität 15 |

ich 33, 148 | Imitat 10, 78, 79, 85, 91, 101, 136, 199, 200, 254 | Inangriffnahme 177 | innerer Widerstand 229 | Innungsverbände 106 | Instinkt 16 | Instrumentalisierung 272, 274 | intellektuell 242 | Invasion/ Landung der Alliierten 271 | Isidor 38n35 | Itzig 17 |

Jubel 172 | Juda verrecke! 82 | Jude 205, 242, 272 | Judenfrage 36n7, 66, 242 | judenfrei 51, 273, 277 | Judenknecht 102 | Judenzählung 38n29 | jüdisch versippt 191 | jüdischmaterialistischer Geist 28 | Jugendertüchtigung 34 | Juncker: Junker 275 |

Kampf 50, 172 | Kampf gegen die bewusste politische Lüge 28 | Kampf ums Dasein 16, 30 | Kanonenfutter 34 | Kraft durch Freude (KdF)/ Kraft durch Furcht/ Kunst der Fingerferigkeit 150n15, 135 | Kinder und Narren sagen die Wahrheit 204 | Kinder, Küche, Kirche 27, 52 | Kinderholocaust 258 | klassisch 34 | kleindeutsch 56 | Kniefall 254 | Knockout 172 | Kohlenklau/ Heldenklau 134 | Kollektivschuld 229, 271 | Kommandostellen der Wirtschaft 119 | Konzentrationslager 57, 259, 261, 271 | Konzertlager 50 | körperliche Ertüchtigung 28, 29 | Kosmopolitismus 15 | Krankenmaterial 206, 208, 209, 247 | Krebs 16 | Kriegsverbrecher 272 | Kultur 16, 20, 21 | Kulturschaffende 242 | Kulturschande 140 | KZ 47, 259, 276 | KZ-Chef 259 |

Lager 242, 261 | Landbesitz vii, 92 | Landmarken 15 | Lebensraum 83, 207 | lebensunwertes Leben 48, 158, 271, 281 | Lebenswille 32 | Leistung 206 | leistungsmäßig 261 | Lernanfänger 136 | Ley/Levy 77 | Liebe 32 | Liebe macht blind 203 | liquidieren 125 | LQI 239, 269 | LTI 236-240, 269 | Luft-Raum 207 | Luftschiffer 172 | Luftterror 125 |

Macht übergeben, Machtübergabe 271 | Machtergreifung 57, 259, 271 | Machtergreifung der SED 272 | Machterschleichung 271 | Machtübernahme der Türkenkinder 274 | Machtübertragung 271 | Mädel 242 | Mark 36n4, 32 | Material 208 | materialistische Weltordnung 28 | Mauscheldeutsch 64 | Mengselsprache 24 | Mensch 194, 208 | Menschenbehandlung 261 | Menschenmaterial 51, 83, 206, 208, 209, 273 | Menschenwürde 92 | Menschheit 15, 194 | menschlich, Menschlichkeit 194 | Migranten 281 | Militarismus 272 | Mimikry 64 | Minderbelastete 248n2 | Mischehe 51, 56, 205, 271 | Mischling 102 | Missgeburt 30 | Mitläufer 248n2 | Mitläuferfabrik 228 | Moderne 27| Mörder Jesu 17 | Muttersprache 24, 60, 64, 173, 213 |

Nacht und Nebel 157, 257 | Nation 15 | Nationalismus 272 | Nationalpolitische Erziehungsanstalten 106 | Nazi-Complex 256-260 | Nazi-Methoden 258, 271 | Nazi-Vergleiche 271 | Nazi/ Neonazi 272 | Nestbeschmutzer 272 | Neuordnung (Europas) 59, 218, 275 | Nicht-Deutsche 28 | Nicht-Staatsbürger 29 | Nichtarier 30, 48, 102, 193 | nichtdeutsche Frauen 281 | Nichttäter 255 | noch nie da gewesen 85 | Nomade 17 | nordisch 52, 242 | nordisieren 172 | Novemberverbrecher 25 | NS 276 | NSDAP 271 | nuklearer Holocaust 258 |

OGW 106 | Opfer 255, 272, 279 | Opferbereitschaft 29, 34 | Opferwilligkeit 29 | Ordnung 142 | organisch 32 | organisieren 242, 261 |

Parasiten 16 | Parteigenosse/ Pg 167, 249n12 | passive Mitschuld 229 | Patriotismus 272 | Pazifismus 272 | Persilscheine 228 | Pflicht 19, 128 Phrase 128 | Plutokrat 17, 138, 151n24 | Political Correctness 279 | politische Reklame 31, 180 | Polypen 16 | Problem 261 | Propaganda 31, 56, 57, 179-181, 242 | Propagandaministerium 230 |

Querpfeifer 50 | querschießen 242 |

radebrechen 30 | Rasse/ Rassismus/ Herrenrasse 56, 125, 140, 272 | Rassenbrei 30 | Rassenschande 30, 52, 193, 205 | Raum 206, 221, 242 | Raupenschlepper 202 | Reeducation/ Umerziehung 228, 272 | Reformjude 17 | Reich 57, 169, 233 | reichsdeutsch 58 | Reichserbhofgesetz 57 | Reichsfeinde 15 | Reichsfrauenführerin 52 | Reichskristallnacht 237, 271 | Reichstag/ Bundestag vii, 283 | Reklame 31, 179-181 | relativieren 270 | Remilitarisierung 272 | Renazifizierung 229 | resistent, Resistenz 11, 123, 148, 159-182, 187-222 | Revanchismus 272 | rücksichtslos 51 | rücksichtsloser Kampf 29 | Rundfunkverbrecher 141 | Russenweiber 138 | russische Horden 16, 20 |

SA 57, 84, 105, 271, 276 | Sabotage gegen das Winterhilfswerk 101 | säubern, Säuberung 51, 58, 78 | Schacher 17 | Schädling 16, 125 | Schar 16 | Schicksal 32 | Schicksalsgemeinschaft 242 | Schieber 29 | Schimmelpilz 24 | Schlagwort 31 | Schlussstrich 255, 272 | Schmachfrieden 58 | Scholle 101 | Schreibtischmörder 271 | Schuld 229 | Schuldabwehr 255 | Schulddiskurs 255, 270 | Schuldfrage 229, 255 | Schuldige 248n2 | Schulung 242, 247 | Schutzhaft 47, 50, 101 | Schutzstaffel 105 | Schwarze Liste 101 | Schweigen 73, 74, 198, 217-219 | schweißtriefende Plutokraten 138 | SED-Herrschaft 274 | Seele 170 | Sektor 242 | Selbstaufopferung 20 | Selbstmord verübt an 77 | Selbstüberwindung 34 | Selektion 258, 271, 277 | serbische Gesindel 142 | sich am Aufbauwillen des deutschen Volkes vergehen 102 | Sippenhaft 57, 157 | sittliche Grundlagen 32 | Sittlichkeits- und Moralgefühl der germanischen Rasse 28 | slawische Flut 15 | Sohn 32 | Sondergerichte 48 | Sozialismus 232 | Spitzel 89-91, 172, 207 | sprachlos, Sprachlosigkeit 10, | Sprachmengerei 172, 176 | Spruchkammer 228 | SS 57, 65, 84, 105, 106, 271, 276 | SS-Verfügungstruppen 105 | SS-Sicherheitsdienst 105 | SS-Totenkopfverbände 105 | Staatsfeinde 16, 298 | Stadt der Bewegung/ Stadt der Kunst 135, 230 | Stadt der Reichsparteitage/ Stadt Dürers 135 | Stählung 34 | Stände 32 | stattfinden 211 | Stehsärge 109n15 | stellen 211 | Sternjude 126 | Stunde Null 269, 271 | Stürmer-Vergleiche 272 | Systemzeit 138 | systemzeithaft 138 |

T4 142 | Täter 255, 272, 279 | Terrorangriffe 138 | Thing 16 | total 51, 125 | totalitär, Totalitarismus 235 | Totenkopfverband 230 | tragbar 242 | transportieren 47, 208, 209 | Trete/Tritt ein in die NSV! 210 | Treue 19, 194, 205 | Treue und Gehorsam 16, 29 |

uber 276 | Überflutung 25 | Überverbrecher 140 | Überwachung 276 | Umbetreuung 206 | Umbruch 125 | Umsturz 78 | Unbelastete 248n2 | und so 119 | undeutsch 58 | unendlich 116 | unerbittliche Härte 140 | unerhört 193 | unerwünscht 125 | Unfähigkeit zu trauern 255, 271 | Ungeziefer 16 | Unmensch 10, 240-247, 266 | unser 280, 281 | Untermensch 51, 141, 142, 147, 266 | untragbar 242 | unwert 281 | Unwort des Jahres 273 |

Vaterland 19 | vaterlandslos 15, 298 | Verbrechen am Volke 28 | Verfassungspatriotismus 281 | Vergangenheitsbewältigung 253-283, 271, 274 | Vergeltung 51 | Vergleich 270 | verharmlosen 270 | verherrlichen 270 | Verhöhnung 259 | Verkehrsgruppen 106 | vernichten, Vernichtung 16, 231 | Vernunft 15, 16 | Verschwiegenheit 29 | verschworene Gemeinschaft 125 | verschwunden worden 77 | Versöhnung/ Aussöhnung/ Normalisierung 272 | vertilgen 16 | Vertreter 242 | Verwertbarkeit 29, 51 | Viertes Reich 271 | Volk/ Volk(s)-/ volk(s)- vii, 10, 17, 50, 51, 92-94, 106, 118 | volkhaft 10, 120, 206, 207, 260 | Volkheit 119 | völkisch 10, 29, 206, 207, 281 | völkische Seele 119 | volklich 208 | Volksbefragung 102 | Volksbrei 17, 277 | volksdeutsch 56, 58, 65 | Volksdeutsches Reich 56 | volkseigen 121 | volkseinend 118 | Volksempfindung 102 | Volksganze 118, 119 | Volksgeist 15 | Volksgemeinschaft 29, 58, 202, 232 | Volksgenosse 28, 29, 50, 132, 136 | Volksgericht 48, 50 | Volksgerichtshof-Ton 257 | Volksgesundheit 28 | Volkskörper 16 | Volksschädling 57 | Volksseele 119 | Volkstum 15 | Vorsehung 19, 125, 128, 136, 168 |

Wachmannschaften 105 | Waffen-SS 105 | wagen 118 | wegsehen und weghören 81 | Wehrheit 119 | Wehrkraftzersetzung 125, 141, 202 | Wehrmacht 119, 271 | Weihe 169, 170 | weiße Rasse 20 | welsch 58, 63 | Welscher und Fälscher 24 | Welscherei 61 | Weltanschauung 29, 101, 117, 232, 242, 278, 281 | Weltmission 140 | Weltsprache 23 | Wer A sagt, muss auch B sagen 204 | Werbung 181 | wert/ unwert 281 | Wesen 30, 60 | Widerstand 11, 155, 159, 271 | Wiedergeburt 32 | Wiedergutmachung 255, 271 | Wiedervereinigung 273 | Willens- und Entschlusskraft 29 | Willkommenskultur 281 | Wirtschaftsgruppen 106 | wissen um 193, 221 | Wohl des deutschen Volkes 281 | Wortaufartung 61, 213 | Wucherer 17, 29 |

Zahnbürste 257 | Zeitgeschehen 242 | Zeitungsjude 17 | Zeitwende 136 | zersetzend 28, 101 | zersetzender Einfluss 28 | Zigeuner 272 | Zivilisation 16, 21 | Zugriff 206 | zum Schwerte greifen 19 | Zwischenschaltung 118 |

Bibliography

Abraham, Max. 2003. Juda verrecke. Ein Rabbiner im Konzentrations-Lager, mit einem Vorwort von K. L. Reiner. In *Konzentrationslager Oranienburg*, Hg. Irene A. Diekmann and Klaus Wettig, 117–167. Potsdam: Gerhart Seger und Max Abraham.

Ackermann, Konrad. 1965. *Der Widerstand der Monatsschrift 'Hochland' gegen den Nationalsozialismus*. München: Kösel.

Adler, H.G. 1955. *Theresienstadt. 1941–1945. Das Antlitz einer Zwangsgemeinschaft. Geschichte Soziologie Psychologie*. Tübingen: Mohr.

Adorno, Theodor. 1970. Was bedeutet: Aufarbeitung der Vergangenheit. In *Erziehung zur Mündigkeit. Vorträge und Gespräche mit Hellmut Becker 1959–1969*, Hg. Gerd Kadelbach. Frankfurt/Main: Suhrkamp.

Alternative für Deutschland (AfD). 2017. *Grundsatzprogramm*. https://www.alternativefuer.de/wp-content/uploads/sites/111/2016/03/Leitantrag-Grundsatzprogramm-AfD.pdf. Accessed 19 December 2016.

Angermuller, Johannes, Dominique Maingueneau, and Ruth Wodak, eds. 2014. *The Discourse Studies Reader. Main Currents in Theory and Analysis*. Amsterdam: John Benjamins.

Angress, Werner T. 1978. The German Army's 'Judenzählung' of 1916. Genesis – Consequences – Significance. *Leo Baeck Institute Yearbook* 23: 117–137.

Arendt, Hannah. 1946. Die organisierte Schuld. *Die Wandlung* 1 (3): 333–344.

———. 1948. Konzentrationsläger. *Die Wandlung* 3 (4): 309–329.

W J Dodd, *National Socialism and German Discourse*,
https://doi.org/10.1007/978-3-319-74660-9

Baberadt, Karl Friedrich. 1941. Das unvermeidbare Schmarotzerwort. *Deutsche Presse* 31, Nr. 1 (4. January 1941), p. 16.

Bauer, Gerhard. 1988. *Sprache und Sprachlosigkeit im "Dritten Reich"*. Köln: Bund-Verlag.

Bendt, Jutta, and Karin Schmidgall. 1994. *Ricarda Huch 1864–1947. Eine Ausstellung des Deutschen Literaturarchivs im Schiller-Nationalmuseum Marbach am Neckar 7. Mai–31. Oktober 1994. Ausstellung und Katalog.* Marbacher Kataloge 47. Herausgegeben von Ulrich Ott und Friedrich Pfäfflin. Marbach am Neckar: Deutsche Schillergesellschaft.

Benjamin, Walter. 1936. Das Kunstwerk im Zeitalter seiner technischen Reproduzierbarkeit. In *Gesammelte Schriften*, Unter Mitwirkung von Theodor W. Adorno und Gershom Scholem, Hg. von Rolf Tiedemann und Hermann Schweppenhäuser, Bd. 1/2 (1972), 471–508. Frankfurt/Main: Suhrkamp.

Benz, Wolfgang. 2006. *A Concise History of the Third Reich.* Translated by Thomas Dunlap Berkeley. Los Angeles: University of California Press.

Bergengruen, Werner. 1947. *Zum Geleit.* Pechel 1947, pp. 5–22.

Berger, Stefan. 2004. *Inventing the Nation: Germany.* London: Arnold.

Bergsdorf, Wolfgang. 1978. *Politik und Sprache.* München, Wien: Günter Olzog Verlag.

Bering, Dietz. 1987. *Der Name als Stigma. Antisemistismus im deutschen Alltag 1812–1933.* Stuttgart: Klett-Cotta.

———. 1991. *Kampf um Namen. Bernhard Weiss gegen Joseph Goebbels.* Stuttgart: Klett-Cotta.

Berning, Claudia. 1964. *Vom 'Abstammungsnachweis' zum 'Zuchtwart'. Vokabular des Nationalsozialismus.* Berlin: de Gruyter.

Bernsmeier, Helmut. 1983. Der Deutsche Sprachverein im 'Dritten Reich'. *Muttersprache* 93: 35–58.

Betz, Werner. 1963. Nicht der Sprecher, die Sprache lügt? *Sprache im technischen Zeitalter* 6: 461–464.

Bloch, Ernst. 1938. Der Nazi und das Unsägliche. *Das Wort*, Heft 9 (Oktober), 110–114. Also in: Bloch, *Politische Messungen, Pestzeit, Vormärz.* Gesamtausgabe der Werke, Bd. 11, 1970, pp. 185–193. Frankfurt/Main: Suhrkamp.

Boehlich, Walter. 1955. Über die Sprache. *Merkur* 9: 889–894.

———. 1964. Irrte hier Walter Boehlich? *Frankfurter Hefte* 19: 731–734.

Bohrmann, Hans, and Gabriele Toepser-Ziegert, Hgg. 1984–2001. *NS-Presseanweisungen der Vorkriegszeit.* 7 Bände in 19 Teilen. München: K.G. Saur.

Boveri, Margret. 1965. *Wir lügen alle. Eine Hauptstadtzeitung unter Hitler.* Olten: Freiburg i.B.

Brackmann, Karl-Heinz, and Renate Birkenhauer. 1988. *Nazi-Deutsch. "Selbstverständliche" Begriffe und Schlagwörter aus der Zeit des Nationalsozialismus.* Straelen: Straelener Manuskripte Verlag.

Brecht, Bertolt. 1948. *Writing the Truth: Five Difficulties.* Translated by Richard Winston. *Twice a Year* (New York), Tenth Anniversary Issue.

———. 1988–. *Werke. Große kommentierte Berliner und Frankfurter Ausgabe.* Hg. von Werner Hecht, Jan Knopf, Werner Mittenzwei, and Klaus-Detlev Müller. Berlin, Weimar: Aufbau Verlag. Frankfurt/Main: Suhrkamp.

Brömsel, Sven. 2015. *Exzentrik und Bürgertum. Houston Stewart Chamberlain im Kreis jüdischer Intellektueller.* Berlin: Ripperger & Kremers.

Broszat, Martin. 1986. Zur Sozialgeschichte des deutschen Widerstands. *Vierteljahrshefte für Zeitgeschichte* 34 (3): 293–309.

van den Bruck, Moeller. 1923. *Das Dritte Reich.* Dritte Auflage, bearbeitet von Hans Schwarz. 11. bis 15. Tausend. Hamburg, Berlin, Leipzig: Hanseatische Verlagsanstalt.

von Brück, Max. 1956. *Die Bastion der Sprache.* Hg. Brück et al., 27–30.

von Brück, Max, et al., Hgg. 1956. *Ein Jahrhundert Frankfurter Zeitung. Die Gegenwart.* Sonderheft. Societäts-Druckerei: Frankfurt/Main.

Burleigh, Michael, and Wolfgang Wippermann. 1991. *The Racial State: Germany 1933–1945.* Cambridge: Cambridge University Press.

Busse, Dietrich, Fritz Hermanns, and Wolfgang Teubert, Hgg. 1994. *Begriffsgeschichte und Diskursgeschichte. Methodenfragen und Forschungsergebnisse der historischen Semantik.* Opladen: Westdeutscher Verlag.

Chamberlain, Houston Stewart. 1899. *Die Grundlagen des neunzehnten Jahrhunderts.* München: F. Bruckmann.

———. 1911. *The Foundations of the Nineteenth Century.* London, New York: John Lane.

———. 1915. *Kriegsaufsätze.* München: F. Bruckmann.

Clyne, Michael. 1993. Who Owns the German Language? In *Das unsichtbare Band der Sprache*, ed. John Flood et al., 357–369. Stuttgart: Hans-Dieter Heinz Akademischer Verlag.

Damiano, Carla A. 2005. *Walter Kempowski's "Das Echolot": Sifting and Exposing the Evidence via Montage.* Heidelberg: Universitätsverlag Winter.

Deissler, Dirk. 2004. *Die entnazifizierte Sprache.* Frankfurt/Main: Peter Lang.

Dieckmann, Walther. 1969. *Sprache in der Politik. Einführung in die Pragmatik und Semantik der politischen Sprache.* Heidelberg: Carl Winter.

Dodd, William J. 2003. 'Wir müssen die Kraus'sche 'Fackel' von neuem anzünden'. Zur Entstehung der Rubrik 'Aus dem Wörterbuch des Unmenschen' in der Zeitschrift 'Die Wandlung'. *Jahrbuch der Deutschen Schillergesellschaft* 47: 342–375.

———. 2007. *Jedes Wort wandelt die Welt. Dolf Sternbergers politische Sprachkritik*. Göttingen: Wallstein.

———. 2008. '… dem Kaiser gegeben was des Kaisers ist': Walter Benjamin's Reading of Dolf Sternberger's 'Tempel der Kunst' (1937). In *The Text and Its Context. Studies in Modern German Literature and Society Presented to Ronald Speirs on the Occasion of His 65th Birthday*, ed. Nigel Harris and Joanne Sayner, 63–77. Oxford: Peter Lang.

———., ed. 2013a. *"Der Mensch hat das Wort". Der Sprachdiskurs in der Frankfurter Zeitung 1933–1943*. Berlin, Boston: de Gruyter.

———. 2013b. Dolf Sternberger's *Panorama:* Approaches to a Work of (Inner) Exile in the National Socialist Period. *Modern Language Review* 108 (1): 180–201.

———. 2013c. Gegen 'volkhafte' Sprachauffassungen resistent: Der Sprachkritiker Gerhard Storz. In *Mimesis, Mimikry, Simulatio. Tarnung und Aufdeckung in den Künsten vom 16. bis zum 21. Jahrhundert. Festschrift für Erwin Rotermund zum 80.* Geburtstag, Hg. Hanns-Werner Heister and Bernhard Spies, 47–59. Berlin: Weidler Buchverlag.

———. 2015a. 'Die deutsche Sprache wird die Welt beherrschen': Randbemerkungen zu einem deutschen Sprachdiskurs vor hundert Jahren. *Aptum. Zeitschrift für Sprachkritik und Sprachkultur* 01 (10): 226–239.

———. 2015b. Under Pressure? The Anglicisms Debate in Contemporary Germany as a Barometer of German National Identity Today. *German Politics and Society* 33 (1&2): 58–68.

———. 2017. Darwin's Imperialist Canvas: Dolf Sternberger's *Panorama oder Ansichten vom 19. Jahrhundert* (1938) as Cultural History in the Shadow of National Socialism. In *Biological Discourses. The Language of Science and Literature Around 1900*, Cultural History and Literary Imagination, ed. Robert Craig and Ina Linge, vol. 26, 135–158. Oxford, Bern, Berlin: Peter Lang.

Donahue, Neil H., and Doris Kirchner, eds. 2003. *Flight of Fantasy: New Perspectives on Inner Emigration in German Literature, 1933–1945*. New York: Berghahn.

Dornseiff, Franz. 1934. Sprache und Gesamtkultur. *Geistige Arbeit*, Vol. 1, No. 12, p. 8f. June 20.

Dostojewski, F.M. 1917. *Politische Schriften. Sämtliche Werke I/13. Unter Mitarbeiterschaft Dmitri Merschkowskis*. Herausgegeben von Moeller van den Bruck. Zweite Auflage. München: Piper.

Dühring, Eugen. 1997. *Eugen Dühring on the Jews*. Brighton: Nineteen Eighty Four Press.

Ehlich, Konrad, Hg. 1989. *Sprache im Faschismus*. Frankfurt/Main: Suhrkamp.

———. 1998. 'LTI, LQI…' Von der Unschuld der Sprache und der Schuld der Sprechenden. In *Das 20. Jahrhundert. Sprachgeschichte – Zeitgeschichte*, Hg. Heidrun Kämper and Hartmut Schmidt, 273–303. Berlin, New York: de Gruyter.

Ehrke-Rotermund, Heidrun. 2012. Hitler – ein Massenbetrüger. Bilder als Medium der 'Verdeckten Schreibweise' in Rudolf Pechels Buchbesprechung 'Lob des Scharlatans' (1938). *Jahrbuch der Deutschen Schillergesellschaft* 56: 227–258.

———. 2014. Rudolf Pechel und Wilmont Haacke – zwei Intellektuelle im 'Dritten Reich' oder: Vom 'guten Bekannten' zur Unperson. *Euphorion. Zeitschrift für Literaturgeschichte* 108 (4): 417–448.

Ehrke-Rotermund, Heidrun, and Erwin Rotermund, Hg. 1999. *Zwischenreiche und Gegenwelten. Texte und Vorstudien zur "verdeckten Schreibweise" im "Dritten Reich"*. München: Wilhelm Fink.

Eitz, Thorsten, and Isabelle Engelhardt. 2015. *Diskursgeschichte der Weimarer Republik*. 2 Bde. Hildesheim: Olms Weidmann.

Eitz, Thorsten, and Georg Stötzel. 2007. *Wörterbuch der 'Vergangenheitsbewältigung'. Die NS-Vergangenheit im öffentlichen Sprachgebrauch*. Hildesheim, Zürich, New York: Olms.

———. 2009. *Wörterbuch der 'Vergangenheitsbewältigung'. Die NS-Vergangenheit im öffentlichen Sprachgebrauch*. Band 2. Unter Mitarbeit von Katrin Berentzen und Reinhild Frenking. Hildesheim, Zürich, New York: Olms.

Emonts, Anne Martina. 2012. Unmasking Violence and Domination. Mechtilde Lichnowsky and the 20th Century (Word) Wars. In *Plots of War: Modern Narratives of Conflict*, ed. Isabel Capeloa Gil and Adriana Martins, 87–97. Berlin, Boston: de Gruyter.

Engel, Eduard. 1906. *Geschichte der deutschen Literatur*. 2. Band. Wien, Leipzig: Tempsky und Freytag.

———. 1915. *Ein Tagebuch. Mit Urkunden, Bildnissen, Karten*. Bd. 1: *1914. Vom Ausbruch des Krieges bis zur Einnahme von Antwerpen*. Berlin: Westermann.

———. 1917. *Sprich Deutsch! Ein Buch zur Entwelschung*. 2. Aufl. Leipzig: Hesse & Becker.

———. 1922. *Deutsche Stilkunst*. Dreißigste, umgearbeitete und vermehrte Auflage. 47. bis 57. Tausend. Leipzig, Wien: Hesse & Becker.

———. 1929. *Verdeutschungsbuch. Ein Handweiser zur Entwelschung für Amt, Schule, Haus, Leben*. Fünfte durchgesehene und stark vermehrte Auflage, 41–45. Tausend. Leipzig, Wien: Hesse & Becker.

Fiedler, Mark. 2005. *Sprachkritik am öffentlichen Sprachgebrauch seit 1945: Gesamtüberblick und korpusunterstützte Analyse zum 'Wörterbuch des Unmenschen'*. Tönning: Der andere Verlag.

Field, Geoffrey G. 1981. *Evangelist of Race: The Germanic Vision of Houston Stewart Chamberlain*. New York: Columbia University Press.

Fischer, Torben, and Matthias N. Lorenz, Hg. 2015. *Lexikon der 'Vergangenheitsbewältigung'*. Bielefeld: Transcript.

Fischer-Hupe, Kristine. 2001. *Victor Klemperers "LTI. Notizbuch eines Philologen". Ein Kommentar*. Hildesheim: Olms.

Flanagan, Clare. 2000. *A Study of German Political-Cultural Periodicals from the Years of Allied Occupation, 1945–1949*. Lewiston, NY: E. Mellen Press.

Frei, Norbert, and Johannes Schmitz. 1989. *Journalismus im Dritten Reich*. München: Beck.

Gay, Peter. 1969. *Weimar Culture: The Outsider as Insider*. London: Secker & Warburg.

Gillessen, Günther. 1986. *Auf verlorenem Posten. Die Frankfurter Zeitung im 'Dritten Reich'*. München: Siedler.

Gillham, Nicholas Wright. 2001. *A Life of Sir Francis Galton: From African Exploration to the Birth of Eugenics*. Oxford: Oxford University Press.

Girnth, Heiko. 2015. *Sprache und Sprachverwendung in der Politik. Eine Einführung in die linguistische Analyse öffentlich-politischer Kommunikation*. 2., überarbeitete und erweiterte Auflage. Germanistische Arbeitshefte, Band 39. Berlin, Boston: de Gruyter.

"Glossary of Nazi Germany": Wikipedia. https://en.wikipedia.org/wiki/Glossary_of_Nazi_Germany#U. Accessed 1 October 2017.

Glunk, Rolf. 1966–1971. Erfolg und Misserfolg der nationalsozialistischen Sprachlenkung. *Zeitschrift für deutsche Sprache* 22–27.

Goebbels, Joseph. 1995. Die Tagebücher von Joseph Goebbels. Teil 2. Diktate 1941–1945. Hg. von Elke Fröhlich. München: K. G. Sauer.

Goffman, Erving. 2005. *Interaction Ritual: Essays in Face to Face Behavior*. With a New Introduction by Joel Best. New Brunswick, London: Albine Transactions.

Gołaszweski, Marcin, Magdalena Kardach, and Leonore Krenzlin, Hgg. 2016. *Zwischen Innerer Emigration und Exil. Deutschsprachige Schriftsteller 1933–1945*. Berlin, Boston: de Gruyter.

Goldhagen, Daniel. 1996. *Hitler's Willing Executioners: Ordinary Germans and the Holocaust*. London: Little, Brown & Co.

Grimm, Reinhold. 2003. In the Thicket of Inner Emigration. In *Flight of Fantasy: New Perspectives on Inner Emigration in German Literature,*

1933–1945, ed. Neil H. Donahue and Doris Kirchner, 27–45. New York: Berghahn.

Grüttner, Michael. 2014. *Gebhardt Handbuch der deutschen Geschichte*. 10, völlig neu bearbeitete Auflage, Bd. 19, *Das Dritte Reich 1933–1939*. Stuttgart: Klett-Cotta.

Haag, Anna. 1968. *Das Glück zu leben. Erinnerungen an bewegte Jahre*. Stuttgart: Adolf Bonz.

Haecker, Theodor. 1932. Betrachtungen über Vergil, Vater des Abendlandes. *Der Brenner* 13: 3–31.

———. 1947. *Tag- und Nachtbücher 1939–1945. Mit einem Vorwort*. Herausgegeben von Heinrich Wild. Olten: Summa.

———. 1989. *Tag- und Nachtbücher 1939–1945. Erste vollständige und kommentierte Ausgabe*. Herausgegeben von Hinrich Siefken, Brenner-Studien, Bd. 9. Innsbruck: Haymon Verlag.

Hagemann, Jürgen. 1970. *Die Presselenkung im Dritten Reich*. Bonn: Bouvier.

Häntschel, Hiltrud. 2001. *Irmgard Keun*. Reinbek: Rowohlt.

Hartl, Peter. 1991. *Einführung zur Neuauflage*. Kardorff 1997, pp. 7–31.

Haug, Wolfgang Fritz. 1967. *Der hilflose Antifaschismus*. Frankfurt/Main: Suhrkamp.

———. 1982. Die Sprache des hilflosen Antifaschismus. In *Holzfeuer im hölzernen Ofen. Aufsätze zur politischen Sprachkritik*, Hg. H. J. Heringer, 150–160. Tübingen: Gunter Narr.

Hay, Gerhard, Hartmut Rambaldo, et al., eds. 1995. *Als der Krieg zu Ende war. Literarisch-politische Publizistik 1945–1950. Eine Ausstellung des Deutschen Literaturarchivs im Schiller-Nationalmuseum Marbach a.N.* Marbach am Neckar: Deutsche Schillergesellschaft.

Heiden, Konrad. 1935. *Hitler. Das Zeitalter der Verantwortungslosigkei*t. Band I. Zürich: Europa Verlag.

Heine, Heinrich. 1994. *Historisch-kritische Gesamtausgabe der Werke*, Hg. Manfred Windfuhr, Bd. 5. Hamburg: Hoffmann and Campe.

Heinrichsdorff, Wolf. 1937. *Die liberale Opposition in Deutschland seit dem 30. Januar 1933 (dargestellt an der Entwicklung der "Frankfurter Zeitung". Versuch einer Systematik der politischen Kritik*. Dissertation zur Erlangung der Doktorwürde der Philosophischen Fakultät der Hansischen Universität zu Hamburg.

Henneberg, Nicole. 2003. 'Bohemien, Räuberhauptmann und Sprachforscher'. Der vergessene Wiener Etymologe Adolf Josef Storfer. *Die Horen* 48/4 (212): 61–74.

Hepp, Fred. 1949. *Der geistige Widerstand im Kulturteil der 'Frankfurter Zeitung' gegen die Diktatur des totalen Staates 1933–1943*. Dissertation, Ludwig-Maximilians-Universität München.

Heringer, Hans Jürgen. 1982. Der Streit um die Sprachkritik. Dialog mit Peter von Polenz im Februar 1981. In *Holzfeuer im hölzernen Ofen. Aufsätze zur politischen Sprachkritik*, Hg. H. J. Heringer, 161–175. Tübingen: Gunter Narr.

Heringer, Hans Jürgen, and Rainer Wimmer. 2015. *Sprachritik. Eine Einführung*. Stuttgart: UTB.

Hermanns, Fritz. 1995/2012. Deutsch und Deutschland. Zur Semantik deutscher nationaler Selbstbezeichnungswörter heute. In *Fritz Hermanns: Der Sitz der Sprache im Leben. Beiträge zu einer kulturanalytischen Linguistik*, Hg. Heidrun Kämper, Angelika Linke, and Martin Wengeler, 295–310. Berlin, Boston: de Gruyter.

Hitler, Adolf. 1934. *Mein Kampf. Zwei Bände in einem Band*. Ungekürzte Ausgabe. 97–101. Auflage. München: Franz Eher Nachfolger.

———. 2016. *Mein Kampf. Eine kritische Edition*. Herausgegeben von Christian Hartmann, Thomas Vordermayer, Othmar Plöckinger, Roman Töppel. Unter Mitarbeit von Pascal Trees, Angelika Reizle, Martina Seewald-Mooser. München, Berlin: Im Auftrag des Instituts für Zeitgeschichte München.

Horan, Geraldine. 2003. *Mothers, Warriors, Guardians of the Soul. Female Discourse in National Socialism*. Berlin: de Gruyter.

Horan, Geraldine, Felicity Rash, and Daniel Wildmann, eds. 2013. *English and German Nationalist and Anti-semitic Discourse, 1871–1945*. Bern, Oxford: Peter Lang.

Hung, Jochen. 2016. 'Bad' Politics and 'Good' Culture: New Approaches to the History of the Weimar Republic. *Central European History* 49: 441–453.

Hutton, Christopher. 1999. *Linguistics and the Third Reich: Mother Tongue Fascism, Race and the Science of Language*. London: Routledge.

Jäger, Margret, and Siegfried Jäger. 1999. *Gefährliche Erbschaften. Die schleichende Restauration rechten Denkens*. Berlin: Aufbau Taschenbuch Verlag.

Jancke, Oskar. 1938. *Restlos erledigt? Neue Glossen zur deutschen Sprache*. München: Knorr & Hirth.

Jaspers, Karl. 1946. *Die Schuldfrage*. Heidelberg: Lambert Schneider.

———. 1947. *Von der Wahrheit (Philosophische Logik, erster Band)*. Verlag, München: R. Piper & Co.

Jay, Martin. 1981. Remembering Henry Pachter. *Salmagundi* 52 (53): 24–29.

Jolas, Eugen. 1998. *Man from Babel*. Edited, Annotated and Introduced by Andreas Kramer and Rainer Rumold. New Haven, CT: Yale University Press.

Jung, Matthias. 1995. Amerikanismen, ausländische Wörter, Deutsch in der Welt. Sprachdiskussionen als Bewältigung der Vergangenheit und Gegenwart. In *Kontroverse Begriffe. Geschichte des öffentlichen Sprachgebrauchs in der Bundesrepublik Deutschland*, Hg. Georg Stötzel and Martin Wengeler, 245–283. Berlin, New York: de Gruyter.

Jung, Matthias, Martin Wengeler, and Karin Böke, Hgg. 1997. *Die Sprache des Migrationsdiskurses. Das Reden über "Ausländer" in Medien, Politik und Alltag.* Wiesbaden: Westdeutscher Verlag.

Jünger, Ernst. 1939. *Auf den Marmorklippen*. Hamburg: Hanseatische Verlagsanstalt.

———. 1947. *On the Marble Cliffs*. Translated by Stuart Hood. Norfolk, CT: New Directions.

Junker, Gerhard H., Hg. 2011. *Der Anglizismen-Index. Erste Auflage in Verbindiung mit dem INDEX-Arbeitskreis des Vereins Deutsche Sprache und dem Sprachkreis.* Bern, Paderborn: IFB Verlag Deutsche Sprache GmbH.

Kaes, Anton, Martin Jay, and Edward Dimendberg, eds. 1994. *The Weimar Republic Sourcebook*. Los Angeles: University of California Press.

Kämper, Heidrun. 1996. Zeitgeschichte – Sprachgeschichte. Gedanken bei der Lektüre des Tagebuchs eines Philologen. *Zeitschrift für Germanistische Linguistik* 24: 328–341.

———. 1998. Entnazifizierung—Sprachliche Existenzformen eines ethischen Konzepts. In *Das 20. Jahrhundert. Sprachgeschichte—Zeitgeschichte*, Hg. Heidrun Kämper and Hartmut Schmidt, 304–329. Berlin, New York: de Gruyter.

———. 2000. Sprachgeschichte – Zeitgeschichte. Die Tagebücher Victor Klemperers. *Deutsche Sprache* 28 (1): 25–41.

———. 2005. *Der Schulddiskurs in der frühen Nachkriegszeit. Ein Beitrag zur Geschichte des sprachlichen Umbruchs nach 1945*. Berlin, New York: de Gruyter.

———. 2007. *Opfer – Täter – Nichttäter. Ein Wörterbuch zum Schulddiskurs 1945–1955*. Berlin: de Gruyter.

———. 2011. Telling the Truth: Counter-Discourses in Diaries under Totalitarian Regimes (Nazi Germany and Early GDR). In *Political Languages in the Age of Extremes*, ed. Willibald Steinmetz, 215–241. Oxford: Oxford University Press.

———. 2017. Das Grundsatzprogramm der AfD und seine historischen Parallelen. Eine Perspektive der Politikolinguistik. *Aptum. Zeitschrift für Sprachkritik und Sprachkultur* 01 (17): 16–41. Also in: *Sprachreport* 33 (2): 1–21. Mannheim: Institut für deutsche Sprache.

Kämper, Heidrun, Peter Haslinger, and Thomas Raithel, Hgg. 2014. *Demokratiegeschichte als Zäsurgeschichte: Diskurse der frühen Weimarer Republik*. Berlin: de Gruyter.

Kämper-Jensen, Heidrun. 1993. Spracharbeit im Dienst des NS-Staats 1933 bis 1945. *Zeitschrift für Germanistische Linguistik* 21 (2): 150–183.

von Kardorff, Ursula. 1962. *Berliner Aufzeichnungen aus den Jahren 1942–1945*. Deutsche Buch-Gemeinschaft, Darmstadt: C.A. Koch's Verlag-Nachf. [1962, München, Biederstein Verlag].

———. 1965. *Diary of a Nightmare: Berlin, 1942–1945*. Translated from the German by Ewan Butler. London: R. Hart-Davis.

———. 1997. *Berliner Aufzeichnungen 1942 bis 1945*. Unter Verwendung der Original-Tagebücher neu herausgegeben und kommentiert von Peter Hartl. Ungekürzte Ausgabe, 2. Auflage. München: Deutscher Taschenbuch Verlag.

Kasten, U., and W. Kohlhaase. 1998. *'Mein Leben ist so sündhaft lang': Victor Klemperer—ein Chronist des Jahrhunderts*. Ostdeutscher Rundfunk.

———. 1999. Victor Klemperer—ein Leben in Deutschland. *ARD*.

Kästner, Erich. 2006. *Das blaue Buch. Kriegstagebuch und Roman-Notizen*. Herausgegeben von Ulrich von Bülow und Silke Becker. Aus der Gabelsberger'schen Kurzschrift übertragen von Herbert Tauber (Marbacher Magazin 111/112). Marbach am Neckar: Deutsche Schillergesellschaft.

Keller, R.E. 1978. *The German Language*. London: Faber.

Kempowski, Walter. 1993. *Das Echolot. Ein kollektives Tagebuch. Januar und Februar 1943*. 4 Bände. München: Knaus.

———. 1999. *Das Echolot. Fuga furiosa. Ein kollektives Tagebuch. Winter 1945*. 4 Bände. München: Knaus.

———. 2002. *Das Echolot. Barbarossa '41. Ein kollektives Tagebuch*. München: Knaus.

———. 2005. *Das Echolot. Abgesang 45. Ein kollektives Tagebuch*. München: Knaus.

———. 2015. *Swansong 1945: A Collective Diary of the Last Days of the Third Reich*. Translated by Shaun Whiteside. New York: W.W. Norton.

Keun, Irmgard. 2003. *Nach Mitternacht*. Mit Materialien, ausgewählt von Michael Graef. Stuttgart, Leipzig: Ernst Klett.

Klapper, John. 2015. *Nonconformist Writing in Nazi Germany: The Literature of Inner Emigration*. Rochester, New York: Camden House.

Klein, Josef. 1989. Wortschatz, Wortkampf, Wortfelder. In *Politische Semantik. Beiträge zur politischen Sprachverwendung*, Hg. J. Klein, 3–50. Opladen: Westdeutscher Verlag.

Klemperer, Victor. 1978. *LTI. Notizbuch eines Philologen*. Berlin: Aufbau.

———. 1998a. *Tagebücher 1933–1945*. Herausgegeben von Walter Nowojski unter Mitarbeit von Hedwig Klemperer. Berlin: Aufbau Taschenbuch Verlag.

———. 1998b. *I Shall Bear Witness: The Diaries of Victor Klemperer, 1933–41*. Translated by Martin Chalmers. London: Weidenfeld & Nicolson.

———. 1999. *To the Bitter End: The Diaries of Victor Klemperer, 1942–1945*. Translated by Martin Chalmers. London: Weidenfeld & Nicolson.

———. 2000. *The Language of the Third Reich. LTI: Lingua Tertii Imperii*. Translated by Martin Brady. London: Athlone Press.

———. 2003. *The Lesser Evil: The Diaries of Victor Klemperer, 1945–1959*. Translated by Martin Chalmers. London: Weidenfeld & Nicolson.

———. 2007. *Die Tagebücher (1933–1945). Kommentierte Gesamtausgabe*. Herausgegeben von Walter Nowojski unter Mitarbeit von Christian Löser. Direktmedia (Digitale Bibliothek, CD-Rom Edition).

Knobloch, Clemens. 2005. *Volkhafte Sprachforschung. Studien zum Umbau der Sprachwissenschaft in Deutschland zwischen 1918 und 1945*. Tübingen: Niemeyer.

Koonz, Claudia. 1987. *Mothers in the Fatherland. Women, the Family and Nazi Politics*. New York: St. Martin's Press.

Köpf, Peter. 1995. *Schreiben nach jeder Richtung. Goebbels-Propagandisten in der westdeutschen Nachkriegspresse*. Berlin: Links.

Kottnig, Lothar. 2013. '*Das Phänomen der Revindikation*'. *Metapher und Phrase in der 'Dritten Walpurgisnacht*'. Diplomarbait, Magister der Philosophie, Universität Wien.

———. n.d. Diesmal ohne den Deckmantel. Der sprachliche Befund der *Dritten Walpurgisnacht* zum Nationalsozialismus. http://www.uni-klu.ac.at/germ/downloads/Kottnig.PDF. Accessed 14 October 2015.

Kraus, Karl. 1934. *Warum die Fackel nicht erscheint. Aus: "Die Fackel", Nr. 890–905, Ende Juli 1934*, pp. 1–315. Reprint 2010. Berlin: Wolfgang Hink.

———. 1952. *Dritte Walpurgisnacht*. München: Kösel-Verlag.

———. 1989. *Dritte Walpurgisnacht*. Herausgegeben von Christian Wagenknecht. Frankfurt/Main: Suhrkamp taschenbuch.

———. 2015. *The Last Days of Mankind. The Complete Text*. Translated by Fred Bridgham and Edward Timms. New Haven: Yale University Press.

———. 2016. *The Last Days of Mankind*. Translated by Patrick Healy. Amsterdam: November Editions.

Krauss, Werner. 1946. Macht und Ohnmacht der Wörterbücher. *Die Wandlung* 1 (9): 772–786.

Lämmert, Eberhard, Walter Killy, Karl Otto Conrady, and Peter von Polenz. 1967. *Germanistik—eine deutsche Wissenschaft*. Frankfurt/Main: Suhrkamp.

Lanthaler, Franz, Hanspeter Ortner, Jürgen Schiewe, Richard Schrodt, and Horst Sitta. 2003. Was ist der Gegenstand der Sprachbetrachtung?. *Sprachreport* 2/2003, Mannheim: Institut für Deutsche Sprache, 2–5. ("Bozener Manifest").

Lerchenmüller, Joachim, and Gerd Simon. 1997. *Im Vorfeld des Massenmords. Germanistik und Nachbarfächer im 2. Weltkrieg: eine Übersicht.* Dritte Auflage ed. Tübingen: Gesellschaft für interdisziplinäre Forschung.

Lethmair, Thea. 1956. *Die Frauenbeilage der 'Frankfurter Zeitung'.* Ihre Struktur – ihre geistigen Grundlagen: Dissertation, Ludwig-Maximilians-Universität München.

Ley, Anna. n.d. *Geschichte der deutschen Sektion der Internationalen Frauenliga für Frieden und Freiheit.* wipf.de. Accessed 19 March 2017.

Lichnowsky, Mechtilde. 1946. Worte über Wörter. *Die Wandlung* 1: 521–526.

———. 1948. Werdegang eines Wirrkopfs. *Die Wandlung* 3: 606–615.

———. 1949. *Worte über Wörter.* Wien: Bergland.

———. n.d. *Anmerkungen und Notizen zu Hitlers "Mein Kampf".* Typescript. Deutsches Literaturarchiv. A: Lichnowsky/81.7609/HS007997206.

Lobenstein-Reichmann, Anja. 2005. Sprache und Rasse bei Houston Stewart Chamberlain. In *Brisante Semantik. Neuere Konzepte und Forschungsergebnisse einer kulturwissenschaftlichen Linguistik,* Hg. Dietrich Busse, Thomas Niehr, and Martin Wengeler, 87–208. Tübingen: Niemeyer.

———. 2008. *Houston Stewart Chamberlain: Zur textlichen Konstruktion einer Weltanschauung. Eine sprach-, diskurs- und ideologiegeschichtliche Analyse.* Berlin, New York: de Gruyter.

Maas, Utz. 1984. Als der Geist der Gemeinschaft eine Sprache fand. In *Sprache im Nationalsozialismus.* Opladen: Westdeutscher Verlag.

———. 2015. *Ingeborg Seidel-Slotty.* Updated March 5. Universitätsbibliothek Osnabrück. https://esf.uni-osnabrueck.de/index.php/katalog-m-z/s/427-seidel-slotty-ingeborg. Accessed 30 November 2016.

MacGregor, Neil. 2014. *Germany. Memories of a Nation.* London: Penguin (British Museum, BBC, Allen Lane).

Magub, Roshan. 2017. *Edgar Julius Jung, Right-Wing Enemy of the Nazis. A Political Biography.* Rochester, New York: Camden House.

Mann, Thomas. 1914. Gedanken im Kriege. *Die Neue Rundschau* 25: 1471–1484.

———. 1990. *Gesammelte Werke in dreizehn Bänden.* Frankfurt/Main: Fischer Taschenbuch Verlag.

Marchlewitz, Ingrid. 1999. *Irmgard Keun: Leben und Werk.* Würzburg: Königshausen & Neumann.

Mehring, Marga. 1960. Menschenmaterial. *Zeitschrift für deutsche Wortforschung* 16: 129–143.

Mieder, Wolfgang. 1997. '… as if I Were Master of the Situation'. Proverbial Manipulation in Adolf Hitler's *Mein Kampf*. In *The Politics of Proverbs. From Traditional Wisdom to Proverbial Stereotypes*, ed. Wolfgang Mieder. Madison: University of Wisconsin Press.

Militz, Hans-Manfred. 1998. 'Wejen Ausdrücken': Redewendungen im LTI von Victor Klemperer. *Proverbium* 15: 201–219.

Mitscherlich, Alexander, and Margarete Mitscherlich. 1967. *Die Unfähigkeit zu trauern. Grundlagen kollektiven Verhaltens*. München: R. Piper.

O Dochartaigh, Pól, and Christiane Schönfeld, eds. 2013. *Representing the 'Good German' in Literature and Culture after 1945. Altruism and Moral Ambiguity*. Rochester, NY: Camden House.

Oldfield, Sybil. 1986. German Women in the Resistance to Hitler. In *Women, State and Revolution*, ed. Sian Reynolds. Wheatsheaf: Brighton.

Paechter, Heinz. 1944. *Nazi-Deutsch. A Glossary of Contemporary German Usage*. New York: Frederick Ungar.

Papmehl-Rüttenauer, Isabella. 1937. *Das Wort 'heilig' in der deutschen Dichtersprache von Pyra bis zum jungen Herder*. Weimar: Verlag Hermann Böhlaus Nachf.

Pechel, Rudolf. 1947. *Zwischen den Zeilen: Der Kampf einer Zeitschrift für Freiheit und Recht 1932–1942*. Wiesentheid: Droemersche Verlagsanstalt.

Peukert, Detlev. 1992. *The Weimar Republic: The Crisis of Classical Modernity*. Translated by Richard Deveson. New York: Hill and Wang.

Pfäfflin, Friedrich, and Eva Dambacher. 2001. *"Verehrte Fürstin". Karl Kraus und Mechtilde Lichnowsky. Briefe und Dokumente 1916–1958*. Göttingen: Wallstein.

Pfalzgraf, Falco. 2006. *Neopurismus in Deutschland nach der Wende*. Frankfurt/Main, Berlin, Bern, Bruxelles, New York, Oxford, Wien: Peter Lang.

von Polenz, Peter. 1967. Sprachpurismus und Nationalsozialismus. In *Germanistik—Eine deutsche Wissenschaft*, Hg. Lämmert et al., 111–165. Frankfurt/Main: Suhrkamp.

———. 1988. *Deutsche Satzsemantik*. Zweite, durchgesehene Auflage. Berlin, New York: de Gruyter.

———. 1999. *Deutsche Sprachgeschichte vom Spätmittelalter bis zur Gegenwart*. Bd 3: *19. und 20. Jahrhundert*. Berlin, New York: de Gruyter.

———. 2005. Streit über Sprachkritik in den 1960er Jahren. *Aptum. Zeitschrift für Sprachkritik und Sprachkultur* 02 (05): 97–111.

———. 2007. Geleitwort. *Dodd* 2007: 7–9.

Prümm, Karl. 1982. Antifaschistische Mission ohne Adressaten. Zeitkritik und Prognostik in der Wochenzeitschrift *Deutsche Republik* 1929–1933. In *Weimars Ende. Prognosen und Diagnosen in der deutschen Literatur und politischen Publizistik 1930–1933*, Hg. Thomas Koebner, 103–142. Frankfurt/Main: Suhrkamp.

Rash, Felicity. 2006. *The Language of Violence. Adolf Hitler's 'Mein Kampf'*. New York, Washington: Peter Lang.

———. 2011. German Nationalist and Colonial Discourse: An Introduction. *Patterns of Prejudice* 45 (5): 377–379.

———. 2012. *German Images of the Self and the Other: Nationalist, Colonialist and Anti-semitic Discourse 1871–1918*. Basingstoke: Palgrave Macmillan.

———. 2017. *The Discourse Strategies of Imperialist Writing. The German Colonial Idea and Africa 1848–1945*. London: Routledge.

Reed, T.J. 1996. *Thomas Mann: The Uses of Tradition*. Oxford: Clarendon.

Rehtmeyer, V. 1937. Fremdwort, Deutschheit und Schrifttumsgeschichte. *Muttersprache* 52, Heft 4, Sp. 141–143.

Reifarth, Gert, and Philip Morrissey, eds. 2011. *Aesopic Voices: Re-framing Truth Through Concealed Ways of Presentation in the 20th and 21st Centuries*. Newcastle upon Tyne: Cambridge Scholars.

Reifenberg, Benno. 1964. Einleitung. In *Facsimile Querschnitt durch die Frankfurter Zeitung*, Hg. Ingrid Gräfin Lynar, 6–14. Bern: Scherz Verlag.

Reifferscheidt, Friedrich M. 1939. *Über die Sprache*. Leipzig: Hegner.

Robertson, Ritchie. 1999. *The 'Jewish Question' in German Literature 1749–1939: Emancipation and Its Discontents*. Oxford: Oxford University Press.

Römer, Ruth. 1989. *Sprachwissenschaft und Rassenideologie in Deutschland*. München: Wilhelm Fink.

Rotermund, Erwin. 2011. 'Concealed Writing' (*Verdeckte Schreibweise*) in the 'Third Reich': Forms and Problems of Reception. In *Aesopic Voices. Re-framing Truth Through Concealed Ways of Presentation in the 20th and 21st Centuries*, ed. Gert Reifarth and Philip Morrissey. Newcastle upon Tyne: Cambridge Scholars Publishing.

Rück, Peter. 1993. Die Sprache der Schrift. Zur Geschichte des Frakturverbots von 1941. In *Homo scribens. Perspektiven der Schriftlichkeitsforschung*, Hg. Jürgen Baurmann et al., 231–272. Tübingen: Niemeyer.

Sänger, Fritz. 1975. *Politik der Täuschungen. Missbrauch der Presse im Dritten Reich. Weisungen, Informationen, Notizen 1933–1939*. Wien: Europaverlag.

———. 1977. Zur Geschichte der 'Frankfurter Zeitung'. *Publizistik. Zeitschrift für die Wissenschaft von Presse, Rundfunk, Film, Rhetorik, Öffentlichkeitsarbeit, Werbung und Meinungsbildung* 22: 275–294.

Sauer, Wolfgang Werner. 1989. Der *Duden* im 'Dritten Reich'. In *Sprache im Faschismus*, Hg. Konrad Ehlich, 104–119. Frankfurt/Main: Suhrkamp.

Saunders, Frances Stonor. 1999. *Who Paid the Piper? The CIA and the Cultural Cold War*. London: Granta.

Schaezler, Karl. 1965. Das *Hochland* und der Nationalsozialismus. *Hochland* 75: 221–231.

Schiewe, Jürgen. 2010. Sprachreinheit als Kompensation fehlender nationaler Identität. In *Kommunikation für Europa II. Sprache und Identität*, Hg. Schiewe et al., 25–36. Frankfurt/Main: Peter Lang.

———. 2015. Wilhelm Emanuel Süskinds Stillehre *Vom ABC zum Sprachkunstwerk*. Ein Text (auch) mit verdeckter Schreibweise? *Aptum. Zeitschrift für Sprachkritik und Sprachkultur* 01 (11): 86–96.

Schiewe, Jürgen, and Martin Wengeler. 2005. Einführung der Herausgeber zum ersten Heft. *Aptum. Zeitschrift für Sprachkritik und Sprachkultur* 01 (05): 1–13.

Schiller, Friedrich. 2004. *Werke und Briefe in zwölf Bänden*. Bd. 1: *Sämtliche Gedichte*. Hg. von Georg Kurscheidt. Frankfurt/Main: Suhrkamp.

Schmidt, Hartmut. 1998. 'An mein Volk'. Sprachliche Mittel monarchischer Appelle. In *Sprache und bürgerliche Nation. Beiträge zur deutschen und europäischen Sprachgeschichte des 19. Jahrhunderts*, Hg. Dieter Cherubim et al., 167–196. Berlin, New York: de Gruyter.

Schmidt-Dengler, Wendelin. 2004. Hüben und drüben. Karl Kraus, der Ständestaat und das Deutsche Reich. In *Stachel wider den Zeitgeist. Kabarett, Flüsterwitze, Subversives*, Hg. Robert Kreichbaumer and Oswald Panagl, 113–120. Wien, Köln, Weimar: Böhlau.

Schmitz-Berning, Cornelia. 2000. *Vokabular des Nationalsozialismus*. Berlin, New York: de Gruyter.

Schneider, Wolfgang. 2001. *Frauen unterm Hakenkreuz*. Hamburg: Hoffmann und Campe.

Schöttker, Detlev, and Anja Hübner. 2011. Ernst Jünger, Dolf Sternberger. Briefwechsel 1941–42 und 1973–80. *Sinn und Form* 36 (4): 448–473.

Schulz, Gerhard. 1983. *Die deutsche Literatur zwischen Revolution und Restauration 1806–1830. Geschichte der deutschen Literatur*, Hg. Helmut De Boor and Richard Newald, Bd. VII/2. München: Beck.

Schymura, Yvonne. 2014. *Käthe Kollwitz 1867–2000. Biographie und Rezeptionsgeschichte einer deutschen Künstlerin*. Essen: Klartext.

Seidel, Eugen, and Ingeborg Seidel-Slotty. 1961. *Sprachwandel im Dritten Reich*. Halle: VEB Verlag Sprache und Literatur.

Siefken, Hinrich. 1989. Einleitung. In *Tag- und Nachtbücher 1939–1945*, Hg. Theodor Haecker, 7–17. Innsbruck: Haymon.

———, ed. 1994. *Die "Weiße Rose" und ihre Flugblätter*. Manchester: Manchester University Press.

Simon, Gerd. 1979. *Sprachwissenschaft und politisches Engagement. Zur Problem- und Sozialgeschichte einiger sprachtheoretischer, sprachdidaktischer und sprachpflegerischer Ansätze in der Germanistik des 19. u. 20. Jahrhunderts* (*Pragmalinguisitk* 18). Basel, Weinheim: Beltz.

———. 1982. Zündschnur zum Sprengstoff: Leo Weisgwerbers keltologische Forschungen und seine Tätigkeit als Zensuroffizier in Rennes während des 2. Weltkriegs. *Linguistische Berichte* 79: 30–52.

———. 1985. Sprachwissenschaft im 3. Reich. Ein erster Überblick. In *Politische Sprachwissenschaft*, Hg. Franz Januschek, 375–396. Opladen: Westdeutscher Verlag.

———. 1986. Wissenschaft und Wende 1933. Zum Verhältnis von Wissenschaft und Politik am Beispiel des Sprachwissenschaftlers Georg Schmidt-Rohr. https://homepages.uni-tuebingen.de//gerd.simon/wende1933.pdf. Accessed 1 October 2017.

———. 1989. *Sprachpflege im 'Dritten Reich'*. Hg. Ehlich, pp. 58–86.

———. 2000. *Muttersprache und Menschenverfolgung. Kollektivkritik zwischen Marginalienkult und Gewaltbereitschaft. Homepage Universität Tübingen.* https://homepages.uni-tuebingen.de/gerd.simon/muttersprache.pdf. Accessed 1 October 2017.

Smith, David Gordon. 2008. From 'Anschluss' to 'Zyklon B'. New Dictionary Highlights Words to Avoid. *Der Spiegel Online International*, January 30. http://www.spiegel.de/international/zeitgeist/from-anschluss-to-zyklon-b-new-dictionary-highlights-nazi-words-to-avoid-a-531900.html. Accessed 1 September 2017.

Sösemann, Bernd. 2007. Journalismus im Griff der Diktatur. Die Frankfurter Zeitung in der nationalsozialistischen Pressepolitik. In *"Diener des Staates" oder "Widerstand zwischen den Zeilen"?*, Hg. Christoph Studt, 11–38. LIT: Berlin.

Stange, Erich. 1937. Das Wort und die Wörter. Das Sprachgut der Christenheit in seiner Bedrohung durch die Sprache der Welt. *Pastoralblätter* 78: 1.

Steiner, George. 1969. *Language and Silence: Essays 1958–1966*. Harmondsworth: Penguin.

Stephenson, Jill. 1981. *The Nazi Organisation of Women*. London: Croom Helm.

———. 2001. *Women in Nazi Germany*. Harlow: Longman.

Sternberger, Dolf. 1932. 'Fressendes Gift' bis 'Wiedergeburt'. Wörterbuch der Regierung von Papen in Auszügen. *Deutsche Republik* 6 (2): 1398–1401. July 26.

———. 1938. *Panorama oder Ansichten vom 19. Jahrhundert.* Hamburg: Henry Goverts. Also in: Schriften, V. (1981). Frankfurt/Main: Insel.

———. 1947. Die Vernichtung des Warschauer Ghettos im April und Mai 1943. Auszug aus dem Bericht des verantwortlichen SS- und Polizeiführers Stroop. Mit einer Vorbemerkung von Dolf Sternberger. *Die Wandlung* 2 (6): 524–553.

———. 1977. *Panorama of the Nineteenth Century.* Translated by Joachim Neugroschel. Introduction by Erich Heller. Oxford: Mole Editions, Basil Blackwell.

———. 1987. *Gang zwischen Meistern.* (*Schriften* VIII). Frankfurt/Main: Insel.

———. 1988. *Gut und Böse. Moralische Essais aus drei Zeiten.* (*Schriften* IX). Frankfurt/Main: Insel.

———. 1990. *Verfassungspatriotismus.* (*Schriften* X). Frankfurt/Main: Insel.

———. 1991. *Sprache und Politik, (Schriften XI).* Frankfurt/Main: Insel.

Sternberger, Dolf, Gerhard Storz, and Wilhelm E. Süskind. 1945–1948. Aus dem Wörterbuch des Unmenschen. *Die Wandlung* 1/1–3/3.

———. 1957. *Aus dem Wörterbuch des Unmenschen.* Hamburg: Claassen.

———. 1967. *Aus dem Wörterbuch des Unmenschen.* Hamburg: Claassen.

———. 1986. *Aus dem Wörterbuch des Unmenschen. Nach der erweiterten Ausgabe von 1967.* Frankfurt/Main, Berlin: Ullstein.

Sternheim, Thea. 2002. *Tagebücher 1903–1971.* Herausgegeben und ausgewählt von Thomas Ehrsam und Regula Wyss im Auftrag der Heinrich Enrique Beck-Stiftung. 5 Bde. Göttingen: Wallstein.

Stevenson, Patrick. 2002. *Language and German Disunity: A Sociolinguistic History of East and West Germany, 1945–2000.* Oxford: Oxford University Press.

Stöber, Rudolf. 2010. Presse im Nationalsozialismus. In *Medien im Nationalsozialismus,* Hg. Bernd Heidenreich and Sönke Neitzel, 275–294. Paderborn: Wilhelm Fink/Ferdinand Schöningh.

Storfer, Adolf Josef. 1935. *Wörter und ihre Schicksale.* Zürich: Atlantis Verlag. Reprinted: Verlag Vorwerk 8, Berlin (2005).

Storfer, Adolf. 1937. *Im Dickicht der Sprache.* Wien: Verlag Dr. Rolf Passer. Reprinted: Verlag Vorwerk 8, Berlin (2005).

Storz, Gerhard. 1937. *Laienbrevier über den Umgang mit der Sprache.* Frankfurt/Main: Societäts-Verlag.

———. 1938. *Das Drama Friedrich Schillers.* Frankfurt/Main: Societäts-Verlag.

Stötzel, Georg. 1986. Normierungsversuche und Berufungen auf Normen bei öffentlicher Thematisierung von Sprachverhalten. In *Kontroversen, alte und neue. Akten des VII. Internationalen Germanisten-Kongresses Göttingen 1985*, 86–100. Tübingen: Niemeyer.

———. 1989. Nazi-Verbrechen und öffentliche Sprachsensibilität. *Sprache und Literatur* 20: 32–52.

———. 1995. Der Nazi-Komplex. In *Kontroverse Begriffe. Geschichte des öffentlichen Sprachgebrauchs in der Bundesrepublik Deutschland*, Hg. Georg Stötzel and Martin Wengeler, 355–382. Berlin, New York: de Gruyter.

Stötzel, Georg, and Martin Wengeler, Hgg. 1995. *Kontroverse Begriffe. Geschichte des öffentlichen Sprachgebrauchs in der Bundesrepublik Deutschland*. Berlin, New York: de Gruyter.

Stötzel, Georg, and Thorsten Eitz, Hgg. 2003. *Zeitgeschichtliches Wörterbuch der deutschen Gegenwartssprache: Schlüsselwörter und Orientierungsvokabeln*. Hildesheim: Olms.

Strauss, Leo. 1952. Persecution and the Art of Writing. In *Persecution and the Art of Writing*, ed. L. Strauss, 22–37. Chicago: Chicago University Press.

Strauß, Gerhard, Ulrike Haß, and Gisela Harras. 1989. *Brisante Wörter von Agitation bis Zeitgeist. Ein Lexikon zum öffentlichen Sprachgebrauch (Schriften des Instituts für Deutsche Sprache 2)*. Berlin: de Gruyter.

Studt, Christoph, Hg. 2007. *"Diener des Staates" oder "Widerstand zwischen den Zeilen"?* Schriftenreihe der Forschungsgemeinschaft 20. Juli 1944 e.V., Bd. 8. Berlin: LIT Verlag.

Süskind, Wilhelm E. 1940. *Vom ABC zum Sprachkunstwerk. Eine Sprachlehre für Erwachsene*. Stuttgart: Deutsche Verlags-Anstalt.

Teubert, Wolfgang. 1989. Politische Vexierwörter. In *Politische Semantik. Bedeutungsanalytische und sprachkritische Beiträge zur politischen Sprachverwendung*, Hg. Josef Klein, 51–68. Opladen: Westdeutscher Verlag.

———. 2014. Die Bedeutung von Sprachkritik für die Demokratie. *Aptum. Zeitschrift für Sprachkritik und Sprachkultur* 02 (14): 98–114.

Timms, Edward. 2005. *Karl Kraus. Apocalyptic Satirist. The Post-War Crisis and the Rise of the Swastika*. New Haven, London: Yale University Press.

———. 2015. *Anna Haag and Her Secret Diary of the Second World War. A Democratic German Feminist's Response to the Catastrophe of National Socialism*. Oxford, Berne, Berlin: Peter Lang.

Toepser-Ziegert, Gabriele. 1984. *NS-Presseanweisungen der Vorkriegszeit: eine Einführung in ihre Edition*. Hg. Hans Bohrmann and Gabriele Toepser-Ziegert (1984–2001), Bd. 1. München u.a.: Saur.

———. 2007. Die Existenz der Journalisten unter den Bedingungen der Diktatur. In *"Diener des Staates" oder "Widerstand zwischen den Zeilen"?: die*

Rolle der Presse im "Dritten Reich": (XVIII. Königswinterer Tagung Februar 2005), Hg. Christoph Studt, 75–88. Münster: LIT Verlag Münster.

Tomko, Helena M. 2017. The Reluctant Satirist: Theodor Haecker and the Dizzying Swindle of Nazism. *Oxford German Studies* 46 (1): 42–57.

Topitsch, Ernst. 1960. Über Leerformeln. Zur Pragmatik des Sprachgebrauches in Philosophie und politischer Theorie. In *Probleme der Wissenschaftstheorie. Festschrift für Viktor Kraft*, Hg. Ernst Topitsch, 233–264. Wien: Springer.

Torberg, Friedrich. 1964. Innere und äußere Emigration: Ein imaginärer Dialog. In *PPP: Pamphlete – Parodien – Post Scripta*, Hg. Friedrich Torberg, 53–69. München, Wien: Albert Langen, Georg Müller.

Townson, Michael. 1992. *Mother-Tongue and Fatherland: Language and Politics in German*. Manchester: Manchester University Press.

Tucholsky, Kurt. 1975. *Gesammelte Werke*. Herausgegeben von Mary Gerold-Tucholsky, Fritz J. Raddatz. Reinbek: Rowohlt.

Ullrich, Volker. 1992. Geschönt und darum kaum mehr authentisch. Eine rekonstruierte Neuausgabe der 'Berliner Aufzeichnungen' von Ursula von Kardorff. *Die Zeit*, July 3. http://pdf.zeit.de/1992/28/geschoent-und-darum-kaum-mehr-authentisch. Accessed 20 August 2016.

von Ungern-Sternberg, Jürgen. 1996. *Der Aufruf "An die Kulturwelt!": das Manifest der 93 und die Anfänge der Kriegspropaganda im Ersten Weltkrieg*. Mit einer Dokumentation. Stuttgart: F. Steiner.

Urbach, Karina, and Bernd Buchner. 2004. Prinz Max von Baden und Houston Stewart Chamberlain. Aus dem Briefwechsel 1909–1919. *Vierteljahrshefte für Zeitgeschichte* 52 (1): 121–177.

Voigt, Gerhard. 1967. Zur Sprache des Faschismus. *Das Argument* 9: 154–165.

———. 1974. Bericht vom Ende der 'Sprache des Nationalsozialismus'. *Diskussion Deutsch* 5: 451–456.

Volkov, Shulamit. 1978. Antisemitism as a Cultural Code. Reflections on the History and Historiography of Antisemitism in Imperial Germany. *Leo Baeck Institute Yearbook* 23: 25–46.

Wagner, Frank Dietrich. 1989. *Bertolt Brecht: Kritik des Faschismus*. Opladen: Westdeutscher Verlag.

Waldmüller, Monika. 1988. *Die Wandlung. Eine Monatsschrift*. Marbach am Neckar: Deutsche Schillergesellschaft.

Watt, Roderick. 1998. Victor Klemperer's 'Sprache des Vierten Reiches': LTI = LQI? *German Life and Letters* 51 (3): 360–371.

Weinrich, Harald. 1985. *Wege der Sprachkultur*. Stuttgart: Deutsche Verlags-Anstalt.

Weisgerber, Leo. 1929. *Muttersprache und Geistesbildung*. Göttingen: Vanderhoeck & Ruprecht.

———. 1934a. *Die Stellung der Sprache im Aufbau der Gesamtkultur*, Wörter und Sachen. Vol. 15, 134–224. Heidelberg: Winter.

———. 1934b. *Die Stellung der Sprache im Aufbau der Gesamtkultur*, Wörter und Sachen. Vol. 16, 97–236. Heidelberg: Winter.

———. 1939. *Die volkhaften Kräfte der Muttersprache*. Frankfurt/Main: Diesterweg.

———. 1956. Von den Grenzen des Irrtums und der Verantwortung einer Schriftleitung. *Wirkendes Wort* 6: 158–160.

Wells, C.J. 1985. *German: A Linguistic History to 1945*. Oxford: Clarendon.

Wetherell, Margaret, Stephanie Taylor, and Simeon J. Yates, eds. 2001. *Discourse Theory and Practice. A Reader*. London, Thousand Oaks, New Delhi: Sage.

Williams, Raymond. 1983. *Keywords. A Vocabulary of Culture and Society*. Rev. ed. London: Fontana.

Williams, John, ed. 2011. *Weimar Culture Revisited*. Basingstoke: Palgrave Macmillan.

Wimmer, Rainer. 1982. Überlegungen zu den Aufgaben und Methoden einer linguistisch begründeten Sprachkritik. In *Holzfeuer im hölzernen Ofen. Aufsätze zur politischen Sprachkritik*, Hg. H. J. Heringer, 290–313. Tübingen: Gunter Narr.

Woods, Roger. 1997. *The Conservative Revolution in the Weimar Republic*. Basingstoke: Palgrave Macmillan.

———. 2014. The Referential and the Relational: Victor Klemperer's Diaries in the Nazi Years. *Journal of War & Culture Studies* 7 (4): 336–349.

Zeller, Bernhard, Friederike Brüggemann, and Albrecht Bergold, Hgg. 1983. *Klassiker in finsteren Zeiten, 1933–1945: eine Ausstellung des Deutschen Literaturarchivs im Schiller-Nationalmuseum*. Marbach am Neckar: Deutsche Schillergesellschaft.

Zentner, Christian. 1974. *Adolf Hitlers 'Mein Kampf'. Eine kommentierte Auswahl*. München: Paul List.

Zuckmayer, Carl. 2002. *Geheimreport*. Göttingen: Herausgegeben von Gunther Nickel und Johanna Schrön. Wallstein.

Index[1]

A

Aachener Zeitung, 232
Ackermann, Konrad, 169
Adenauer, Konrad, 255, 257, 259
Adler, Hans Günther, 263
Adler, Jeremy, 284n6
Adorno, Theodor, 174, 256
Aesop, 161, 174
Alker, Ernst, 169
  "Ernte vom Blut und Boden", 169
Alsace/Lorraine, 15, 65, 217–219, 233, 248n4
"Alternative für Deutschland (AfD)", 280–283, 295
Amann, Max, 54
Andres, Stefan, 162, 164
  El Greco malt den Großinquisitor, 162
  Wir sind Utopia, 162
Anecdotes, 123, 124, 132, 135, 136, 142, 148
Antiqua ('Roman') type, 61–63, 214, 215
Anti-semitism, 13, 18, 36n5, 87
Arendt, Hannah, 231
Argumentation strategies, 6, 18, 19, 21, 33, 257
Arndt, Ernst Moritz, 14
Aufbau, 234, 248n7
"Aufruf an die Kulturwelt", 20
Auschwitz, 77, 126, 254

B

Baberadt, Karl Friedrich, 173, 212, 222n8
Baddiel, David, 285n9
Barlach, Ernst, 146, 151n32

[1] Note: Page numbers followed by 'n' refer to notes.

W J Dodd, *National Socialism and German Discourse*,
https://doi.org/10.1007/978-3-319-74660-9

Barth, Karl, 164
Basler, Otto, 57, 58
Batten, Gerard, 275, 284n8
Bauer, Gerhard, 8, 11, 45, 162, 293, 294
Bauhaus architecture, 26
Becher, Johannes, 87
Beck, Ludwig, 136
Bendt, Jutta, 158
Benjamin, Walter, 38n33, 174, 199
Benkard, Ernst, 193, 210
  "Das Ausrufzeichen", 210
Benn, Gottfried, 76, 143, 164
Benn, Hilary, 275
Bergengruen, Werner, 161, 162, 164, 167, 169
Berliner Tageblatt, 76, 136, 143, 182n2, 187, 190
Bermann Fischer, Gottfried, 115
Bernhart, Joseph, 168
  "Hodie", 168
Berning, Cornelia, *see* Schmitz-Berning, Cornelia
Best, Otmar, 138
Betz, Werner, 264, 266
Biermann, Wolf, 259
Binding, Rudolf, 76
Bismarck, Otto von, 15, 169
Bloch, Ernst, 73, 84–88, 92, 96, 98, 107, 108, 124, 143, 148, 163, 174, 292, 293, 297
  "Der Nazi und das Unsägliche", 84, 143, 148
Boehlich, Walter, 121
Bohrmann, Hans, 55, 66n10, 66n12, 66n13, 194
Böke, Karin, 296
Böll, Heinrich, 257
Book reviews, 171, 216
Bormann, Martin, 63
Bourdieu, Pierre, 2
Boveri, Margret, 136, 182n2
'Bozen Manifesto', 3, 268
Brammer, Karl, 53, 66n12
Brandt, Willy, 254, 255, 258, 259
Brecht, Bertolt, vii, 7, 8, 14, 65n4, 73, 84, 87–98, 101, 107, 108, 109n15, 109n16, 110n19, 110n20, 113, 163, 182, 188, 292, 293
  "Fünf Schwierigkeiten beim Schreiben der Wahrheit", 87, 88, 91–95
  Furcht und Elend des Dritten Reichs, 88
  "Maßnahmen gegen die Gewalt", 7
  "Über die Wiederherstellung der Wahrheit", 96–97
Brockdorff, Erika von, 158
Brockmann, Walter, 231
Brooke, Rupert, 19, 36n13
Broszat, Martin, 162, 293
Brumlik, Micha, 253, 278
Brüning, Heinrich, 27
Buber, Martin, 22
Bubis, Ignaz, 279
Buchan, John, 36n13
  The Thirty-Nine Steps, 36–37n13
Büchner, Georg, 87
Bund deutscher Frauen (League of German Women), 27
Busse, Dietrich, 268
Buttmann, Rudolf, 60, 61

C
Cameron, David, 275
Cammens, Minna, 157
Carossa, Hans, 164
Catholic Church, 91, 151n30, 162, 166
Censorship, 15, 47, 54, 71, 126, 165, 168, 218
Cervantes, 259
  Don Quijote, 87
Chagall, Marc, 143, 145
Chamberlain, Houston Stewart, 18, 22, 23, 26, 37n20, 37n21, 37n23, 129, 156, 173, 202
  "Die deutsche Sprache", 22
  Foundations of the Nineteenth Century, 18, 26
  Kriegsaufsätze, 22
Chesney, George Tomkyns, 36n13
  The Battle of Dorking, 36n13
Chomsky, Noam, 65, 264
Clauss, Ludwig, 105
Colonialism, 38n25
Comedian Harmonists, 65
Communist Party (KPD), 47, 158, 259, 272
Concentration camps, 39n36, 39n37, 47, 65, 85, 101, 104, 106, 109n15, 126, 141, 146, 157–159, 162, 163, 167, 259, 261
Confucius, 92
Conrad, Joseph, 36n13
  The Secret Agent, 36n13
'Conservative Revolution', 26, 27, 35, 49, 166, 279, 292

D
Dambacher, Eva, 115
Dante Alighieri, 87
Darré, Walther, 60
Darwin, Charles, 16, 36n9, 174, 195
Das Innere Reich, 165
Das schwarze Korps, 54, 163
Das Wort, 85, 89, 179, 180
Death announcements, 55, 126
Deissler, Dirk, 104, 230–235, 248n8
Denazification, 9, 10, 222, 227–235, 255, 260
Der Brenner, 32, 127
Der Monat, 235, 248n7
Deutsche Akademie für Sprache und Dichtung, 167, 232
*Deutsche Allgemeine Zeitung (*DAZ*)*, 137, 138, 182n2
Deutsche Arbeitsfront (German Labour Front), 52, 249n13
Deutsche Presse, 189, 212
Deutsche Republik, 32, 33
Deutsche Rundschau, 144, 165–167, 234
Deutscher Sprachverein, 57, 59, 172, 278
Deutsches Nachrichtenbüro (DNB), 54
Diaries, 35, 74, 77, 113–115, 122–124, 126–128, 130, 131, 136, 137, 139–143, 145–148, 150n13, 168, 169, 182, 200, 236, 237, 240
Die Auslese, 234
Die Literatur, 165
Die Neue Rundschau, 165
Die neue Weltbühne, 89

Die Wandlung, 231, 232, 234, 241, 243, 246, 248n6
Die Weißen Blätter, 165
Die Weltbühne, 32
Dieckmann, Walther, 6, 268, 281, 296
Dietrich, Otto, 53
Digitales Wörterbuch der deutschen Sprache, 7
DINATAG, 53
Dirks, Walter, 32, 196, 213
Dollfuß, Engelbert, 84
Donahue, Neil, 164
Dornseiff, Franz, 150n8, 241
Dostoevsky, Fyodr Mikhailovich, 38n30
Drews, Wolfgang, 164
Drexler, Anton, 28
Duden dictionary, 46, 57–58, 64
Dühring, Eugen, 16, 36n7, 39n42

E

Eckart, Dietrich, 28
Eckhart, 165
Eggebrecht, Axel, 233
Ehlich, Konrad, 268–270, 294
Ehrke-Rotermund, Heidrun, 164, 166, 167, 248n3
Eichmann, Adolf, 258
Eitz, Thorsten, 38n28, 38n31, 229, 248n1, 248n2, 255, 258, 270, 271, 274, 277, 296
Eliot, T.S., 231
Emonts, Anne Martina, 115
Ender, Emmy, 27
Engel, Eduard, 21–25, 37n21, 37n23, 60, 61, 63, 156, 173, 202, 213, 278
  Deutsche Stilkunst, 23, 38n26
  Entwelschung, 23, 38n26
  Kriegstagebuch, 21
  Sprich Deutsch!, 22, 23, 38n26
Ernst, Max, 143, 145
Esperanto, 217
Eugenics, 36n9
Europäische Revue, 165, 178
'Euthanasia' programme, 151n28, 181, 209
Exile, 1, 4, 7–9, 35, 47, 65, 73, 74, 85, 88, 89, 92, 96, 98, 104, 114, 115, 131, 144, 155, 159–174, 177, 178, 182, 183n11, 189, 190, 192, 199, 212, 219–222, 230, 232, 234, 241, 255, 259, 292, 293

F

'Fahnenwort', 5
Fallada, Hans, 131
Fanal, 32
Feder, Gottfried, 28
Feuchtwanger, Leon, 87
Feuling, Daniel, 168
  "Um ein viel gelesenes Buch", 168
Fichte, Johann Gottlieb, 14, 18, 23
Fiedler, Mark, 276, 277
Filbinger, Hans, 260
Finck, Werner, 164
Fischer-Hupe, Kristine, 236, 237, 239, 240, 249n11
Fischer, Torben, 253
Formalism (linguistic), 264
Foster, Norman, 272
Foucault, Michel, 2, 240
Franck, James, 76
Frank, Anne, 259
Frankfurter Allgemeine Zeitung, 232

Frankfurter Zeitung (FZ), 9, 53, 76, 83, 115, 149n5, 160, 170, 173–175, 177, 182, 182n2, 182n7, 187–222, 232, 241, 242, 247
Franz–Eher–Verlag, 54, 190, 192
Franz Joseph, Kaiser, 19, 37n14
Freisler, Roland, 48, 156, 257
'Fremdwort', 10, 24, 59–62, 172, 208, 213–216, 233, 278
Freud, Sigmund, 165, 172, 255
Frick, Hans, 60, 63
Fritzsche, Hans, 131, 133, 191
Fulda, Ludwig, 22

G

Galton, Francis, 36n9
Geißler, Ewald, 61, 214, 223n10
Geissler, Heiner, 258, 280
Generic reference (THE), 14, 15, 17, 30, 125, 134, 229, 244, 292
George V, King, 37n13
'German (Hitler) Greeting', 158
Germania, 55
Gerth, Hans, 164
Gide, André, 143
Gillessen, Günther, 182n7, 188, 191, 193, 196, 209, 222n1, 222n3
'Gleichschaltung', 10, 46–53, 57, 83, 84, 271, 273
"Glossary of Nazi Germany", 4
Glunk, Rolf, 56, 66n11, 66n13, 179, 180, 268
Gobineau, Arthur de, 17
Goebbels, Joseph, 26, 32, 38n35, 51, 54, 59, 60, 62, 66n9, 76, 77, 105, 131–134, 137, 141, 142, 145, 157, 158, 160, 165, 167, 172, 181, 189–191, 194, 201, 213, 234, 237
Goering, Hermann, 96, 100, 142, 162, 239, 263
Goethe, Johann Wolfgang von, 35n3, 73, 133, 156, 176, 183n9
  Faust, 73, 176
Goffman, Erving, 8, 294
Goldhagen, Daniel, 18
Gothic ('Broken') type, vii, 6, 61–63, 213–216, 230
Graf, Oskar Maria, 87
Graf, Willi, 122, 127, 156
Grafeneck sanatorium, 142
Grammatical solecisms, meaningful, 125, 77
Gramsci, Antonio, 2
Green, Julien, 143
Grice, Paul, 161
Grimm, Reinhold, 160, 161
Grosz, George, 87
Grynszpan, Herschel, 144
Guenther, Hans, 105
Günther, Joachim, 164

H

Haacke, Hans, vii, 93, 272, 284n4
Haag, Albert, 139
Haag, Anna, 114, 122, 139–142, 151n26, 151n27
Habe, Hans, 233, 234
Hadamovski, Eugen, 105
Haecker, Irene, 127

Haecker, Theodor, 32, 49, 74, 114, 122, 127–131, 139, 140, 143, 145, 147, 148, 150n19, 151n20, 151n22, 168–171, 182, 193, 200, 242, 243, 261, 297
  "Das Chaos der Zeit", 168, 170
  Essay on Vergil, 127
  "Tagebuchblätter", 151n20, 169
  Tag- und Nachtbücher, 127, 128
Hallgarten, Constanze, 27
Hamann, Johann Georg, 194
Hamburger Nachrichten, 55
Hänsel, Ludwig, 171
Harden, Maximilian, 22
Harnack, Falk, 156
Harnack, Mildred, 157
Hartl, Peter, 137, 139
Hassel, Ulrich von, 122
Hauptmann, Gerhart, 76
Hausenstein, Wilhelm, 190, 193
Haushofer, Albrecht, 164
Hegele, Max, 141
Heidegger, Martin, 174
  Sein und Zeit, 174
Heiden, Konrad, 144
'Heimat' literature, 101, 169
Heine, Heinrich, 81
Heinemann, Hermann, 258
Heinrichsdorff, Wolf, 194
Henneberg, Nicole, 165, 183n10
Herder, Johann Gottfried, 18, 64, 170, 194, 264
Heringer, Hans Jürgen, 267, 268, 270, 296
Hermann, Liselotte, 157
Hermanns, Fritz, 283
Hess, Rudolf, 96
Heuss, Theodor, 139, 189, 210, 214
Heymann, Lida Gustava, 27, 157
Heym, Stefan, 233
Hindenburg, Paul von, 33–35, 49
Hitler, Adolf, 17, 18, 22, 26–31, 33, 34, 38n34, 39n37, 46, 48, 50, 52, 55, 56, 59, 61, 63, 64, 74–76, 82, 85, 86, 90, 100, 105–107, 114–117, 128, 129, 131, 132, 134, 137, 138, 140–142, 144, 146–148, 149n3, 149n4, 157–159, 162, 168, 170, 180, 181, 187, 197–201, 205, 213, 220, 232, 239, 245, 246, 256, 262, 266, 272, 273, 275–277, 285n9
  Mein Kampf, 17, 28, 29, 38n34, 115, 116, 149n3, 181, 187, 273
Hochhuth, Rolf, 260
Hochland, 74, 127, 128, 151n20, 165, 167–172, 182n8, 216, 223n11
'Hochwertwort', 5
Horan, Geraldine, 38n25, 52
Huber, Kurt, 156
Huch, Ricarda, 76, 158
Hugo, Victor, 87, 167
Humboldt, Wilhelm von, 23, 64, 194, 264
Hutton, Christopher, 36n10, 64

'Imitat', 10, 78, 79, 86, 91, 102, 136, 199, 200, 254
'Inhuman(e) accusative', 265
Internationale Frauenliga für Frieden und Freiheit (IFFF), 27
Ius sanguinis, 285n11
Ius solis, 285n11

J

Jacobson, Alfred, 231
Jaensch, Ernst, 105, 106
Jäger, Margret, 279
Jäger, Siegfried, 279
Jahn, Friedrich Ludwig, 14, 16
Jancke, Oskar, 149n6, 171, 214, 232, 248n8
Sprachdummheiten, 171
Jaspers, Karl
Die Schuldfrage, 229
Von der Wahrheit, 4
Jenninger, Philipp, 254
John Paul II, 258
Johnson, Boris, 275
Jokes, 82, 87, 123, 132, 133, 142, 148
Jolas, Eugene, 231, 234, 235, 248n4
Juncker, Jean-Paul, 275
Jung, Edgar Julius, 26, 48, 49, 55, 108n4, 166, 296
Jung, Matthias, 25, 270, 285n10
Jünger, Ernst, 25–27, 105, 160, 162–164, 194
Auf den Marmorklippen, 162
In Stahlgewittern, 25
Jünger, Friedrich Georg, 131, 164
Juvenal, 87

K

Kafka, Franz, 231
Kallmann, Hans, 210
Kämper, Heidrun, 38n28, 122, 126, 150n18, 228, 229, 240, 255, 270, 280–283, 295
Kant, Immanuel, 215
Kardorff, Ursula von, 114, 115, 122, 136–139, 151n23, 167, 168, 182n2
Kasack, Hermann, 164
Kaschnitz, Luise, 182n2
Kästner, Erich, 114, 122, 131–136
Keller, R.E., 4, 49
Kempowski, Walter, 122, 129, 150n12, 160
Das Echolot, 122
Kerr, Alfred, 137
Kesten, Hermann, 98
Keun, Irmgard, 73, 98–104, 107, 108, 164
Nach Mitternacht, 98, 101, 164
Kierkegaard, Søren, 194
Kiesinger, Kurt-Georg, 260
Kircher, Rudolf, 151n33, 191, 197–199
"Sprache und Stil", 151n33, 197
Kirchner, Dorothy, 164
Kisch, Egon Erwin, 98
Klapper, John, 115, 158, 164, 165
Klausener, Erich, 55
Klein, Josef, 5, 6, 268, 281, 296
Kleist, Heinrich von, 14
Klemperer, Eva, 123, 124, 237
Klemperer, Victor Diaries, 35, 77, 113, 114, 122–127, 137, 147, 150n11, 150n13, 150n15, 150n17, 150n18, 160, 163, 182, 193, 227, 233, 235–238, 240, 242, 244, 247, 249n10, 249n11, 249n12, 269, 279, 281, 293
LTI, 114, 125, 137, 150n11, 236–240, 268, 269, 279, 281
Knobloch, Clemens, 216, 217
Koehler, Wolfgang, 76
Kohl, Helmut, 254, 258, 259, 275
Kolb, Herbert, 264
Kollwitz, Käthe, 27, 158

Koonz, Claudia, 47, 52, 65n2, 182n3
Kottnig, Lothar, 80
Kraus, Fritz, 210
Kraus, Karl, 22, 32, 36n8, 73–88, 92, 98, 104, 107, 108, 108n2, 108n3, 109n6, 109n7, 109n9, 109n10, 115–117, 124, 127, 142, 143, 145, 146, 149n1, 151n30, 171, 182, 188, 193, 200, 210, 212, 241, 265, 292, 293, 297
  Die Fackel, 32, 74, 76, 87
  Die letzten Tage der Menschheit, 85
  Dritte Walpurgisnacht, 73, 74, 76–84, 104, 210
  "Man frage nicht", 74
Krauss, Werner, 164, 231, 233, 234, 241
'Kreisau Circle', 137, 156
Kuckhoff, Adam, 164
Kulturbund zur demokratischen Erneuerung Deutschlands, 234
Küsel, Herbert, 164

L

Language/THE (German) LANGUAGE, 1–9, 21–25, 35, 46, 58, 59, 64, 77, 79, 82, 165, 213, 216, 220, 222, 227, 230–235, 247, 265–269, 278, 294, 296
Langue, 3, 10, 264, 265, 267
Laurent, Fernand, 218, 219
Lawson, Dominic, 274, 275, 284n7
le Fort, Gertrud von, 158, 164
Le Jour, 218, 219
Le Queux, William, 36n13
  The Great War in England in 1897, 36n13
  The Invasion of 1910, 36n13
  Spies of the Kaiser, 36n13
Leaflets, 27, 141, 156–158
'Leerformel', 39n39
Leipelt, Hans Konrad, 156
Lenin, Vladimir Ilich, 92, 95
Lerchenmüller, Joachim, 36n10, 64
Lessing, Theodor, 47, 74
Lexical borrowing, 10, 60
Lexicography, 73, 107
Ley, Robert, 27, 77, 133
Lichnowsky, Karl Max, 115
Lichnowsky, Mechtilde, 84, 114–117, 148, 149n3, 149n5, 233, 234
  "Der Werdegang eines Wirrkopfs", 115
  notes on *Mein Kampf*, 149n3
  "Worte über Wörter", 115
Liebermann, Max, 76, 137
Linfert, Carl, 164
L[ingua] T[ertii] I[mperii], 124
  See also 'LTI'/'LQI'
'Linguistic purism', 59–61, 109n11, 256, 283
Livingstone, Ken, 284n9
Loerke, Oskar, 164, 171
Loesch, Karl Christian von, 144, 145
Lommer, Horst, 233
Lorenz, Matthias N., 253
'LTI'/'LQI', 269
Lübke, Heinrich, 260
Lucretius, 95
Luther, Martin, 63, 169, 170

M

Maas, Utz, 117, 119, 268
Magub, Roshan, 49
Mann, Erika, 27, 157
Mann, Heinrich, 87, 158
Mann, Klaus, 102, 143
Mann, Thomas, 21, 37n16, 71, 72, 89, 141, 155
"Deutsche Ansprache. Ein Appell an die Vernunft", 71
"Gedanken im Kriege", 21
radio broadcasts, 71
Maß und Wort, 89
Matthias, Theodor, 57
Mechtersheimer, Alfred, 258
Melanchthon, Philipp, 87
Merkel, Angela, 275, 281
Mertens, Hanne, 157
Metaphor, 2, 5, 10, 11, 16, 18, 24, 30, 33, 38n34, 50, 80–82, 87, 116, 118, 119, 123, 125, 161, 172, 177, 178, 181, 193, 196, 201, 215, 230, 235, 237, 240, 265, 296
Metonymy ('hinge function'), 196, 201
Metternich, Klemens von, 15, 172
Michalski, Jan, 141
Miller, August, 202
'Mis-speaking', 294
Mitscherlich, Alexander, 255
Mitscherlich, Margarete, 255
Mitterer, Erika, 164
More, Thomas, 92
'Mother-tongue fascism', 46, 64–65
Mühlen, Theodor, 233
Mühsam, Erich, 32, 39n36, 39n37
Müntzer, Thomas, 87
Muth, Carl, 127, 150n19, 167, 169
"Das Reich als Idee und Wirklichkeit—einst und jetzt", 169
Muttersprache, 60, 63, 66n15, 67n17, 67n19, 223n9, 223n10

N

Naumann, Friedrich, 139
'Nazi Complex', 234, 256–283
Nazi legislation, 106
Nebel, Gerhard, 164
Neue Zeit, 234
Neue Zeitung, 234
Neue Züricher Zeitung, 55
Neumeister, Heddy, 182n2
'New Woman', the, 27, 51
Nietzsche, Friedrich, 99, 129, 151n31, 168
'Night of the Long Knives', 26, 48, 55, 108n4, 166, 197
Nominalized style, 79, 104, 118, 119, 177, 210–212, 232, 245
Nordic, 17, 30, 57, 172
Northcliffe, Lord, 36n13
Novalis (Georg Philipp Friedrich von Hardenberg), 170, 194
NSDAP 1920 Party Programme, 28
NS-Frauenschaft, 100
Nuremberg Laws, 48, 102, 103, 194
Nuremberg Tribunals, 229

O

O'Brien, Stephen, 275
Obama, Barack, 39n35
Obituaries, 125, 171

Oldfield, Sybil, 27, 48, 158, 159, 182n3
Orwell, George, 235
Ossietzky, Carl von, 32, 39n36, 163

P

Paechter, Heinz, 73, 104–107, 230, 232
  Nazi-Deutsch, Dictionary of Nazi Terms, 104
Papen, Franz von, 32–35, 49, 55, 76, 81, 108n4, 166, 292
Pariser Tageblatt, 88, 98
Parole, 3, 10, 35, 77, 240, 264, 265, 267, 295
Paulwitz, Thomas, 38n27
Pechel, Rudolf, 26, 144, 162, 164, 166, 167, 181, 233, 234, 248n3
  "Auch die Judenfrage", 166
  "Lob des Scharlatans", 166
  "Nachrichtenpolitik", 167
  "Sibirien", 166
  Zwischen den Zeilen, 167
Penzoldt, Ernst, 164
Pfäfflin, Friedrich, 115
Pflüger, Friedrich, 279
Picasso, Pablo, 143
Planck, Max, 76
Polenz, Peter von, 13–16, 18, 35n2, 36n5, 37n14, 38n35, 39n39, 39n45, 62, 65, 67n16, 81, 108, 109n12, 149n1, 150n10, 182, 256, 261, 264–268, 270, 283, 284n3, 294–296
  Deutsche Satzsemantik, 268
  Deutsche Sprachgeschichte, 268, 283
'Political correctness', 279
Polysemy, ideological, 6, 281
Ponçet, Madame, 146
'Post-truth', 38n35
'Pragmatized' semantics, 5, 295
'Presseanweisungen', 53, 54
'Pressekonferenzen', 53
Probst, Christoph, 156
Propaganda Ministry, 52–54, 61, 131, 133, 134, 136, 138, 167, 168, 174, 179–181, 190, 191, 194, 218
Protocols of the Elders of Zion, 17
Proverbs, 200, 203–206

R

Race, 11, 14, 17, 18, 20, 28, 30, 48, 50–52, 57, 64, 67n19, 78, 103, 105, 106, 119, 121, 140, 142, 171, 194–195, 205
'Racial hygiene', 17, 36n9, 48, 181
Rath, Ernst vom, 144
Rathenau, Walther, 22, 25
Reagan, Ronald, 254, 258
Reck-Malleczewen, Friedrich, 162, 164
  Bockelson, 162
'Red Orchestra', 156, 158
'Reichskulturkammer', 47
'Reichspressekammer', 53
Reichsverband der Deutschen Presse, 53
Reifferscheidt, Friedrich M., 39n38, 165, 169, 171–173, 182n8, 216–217, 221, 223n12, 242, 248n8
  Über die Sprache, 165, 173, 216

Reitsch, Hannah, 51
Religious discourse, 25, 128, 169
Remarque, Erich Maria, 25
Im Westen nichts Neues, 25
Renan, Ernest, 217
'Resistent'/'Resistenz', 11, 123, 148, 159–165, 171, 175–182, 189–222, 248n3, 230, 293
Ridley, Nicholas, 274, 275
Riefenstahl, Leni, 146
Riegel, Hermann, 59
Robertson, Ritchie, 18, 19, 36n5, 36n12, 37n22, 67n19, 292
Röhm, Ernst, 109n18
Römer, Ruth, 36n10, 64
Roosevelt, Theodor, 134
Rosenberg, Alfred
'Amt Rosenberg', 54
Der Mythus des zwanzigsten Jahrhunderts, 26, 168
Rotermund, Erwin, 160, 161, 164, 166, 167
Roth, Josef, 98, 101, 104, 108
Rück, Peter, 62, 63, 214

S

Sänger, Fritz, 53, 66n12, 189–193
Sauer, Wolfgang Werner, 35n1, 57, 58
Saunders, Frances Stonor, 235
Saussure, Ferdinand de, 264, 267
Schaefer, Willi, 50
Schaeffer, Margarete, 157
Schaezler, Karl, 167, 169–173
Scharp, Heinrich, 191
Schiewe, Jürgen, 3, 4, 38n27, 177, 178, 285n10, 292
Schiller, Friedrich, 22, 23, 35n3, 37n24, 87, 156, 175, 182n1
Schillings, Max von, 158
Schimpfsumpf, 130
'Schimpfwort', 5
Schirach, Baldur von, 135
'Schlagwort', 4, 5, 31, 241, 296
Schleicher, Kurt von, 33–35, 55, 144
Schleyer, Johann M., 217
Schlosser, Horst Dieter, 268, 284n5
'Schmähwort', 5
Schmidgall, Karin, 158
Schmidt-Dengler, Wendelin, 79
Schmidt, Hartmut, 37n14, 150n9
Schmidt-Rohr, Georg, 67n19
Schmitz-Berning, Cornelia, 36n10, 38n31, 73, 209, 268, 271, 296
Schmorell, Alexander, 156
Schnabel, Franz, 217, 223n13
Schneider, Reinhold, 52, 164
Schoenberg, Arnold, 26
Scholl, Hans, 127, 137, 156
Scholl, Sophie, 127, 137, 156, 157
Scholtz-Klink, Gertrud, 52, 141
Schopenhauer, Arthur, 77, 194, 195, 210
Schriftleitergesetz, 53, 190
Schröder, Gerhard, 279
Schulze-Boysen, Libertas, 157
Schymura, Yvonne, 158
Seghers, Anna, 157
Seidel, Eugen, 114, 115, 117–122, 137, 150n9, 208, 210, 211, 260, 292
Seidel, Ina, 237
Seidel-Slotty, Ingeborg, 114, 115, 117–122, 137, 208, 210, 211, 260, 292

Shakespeare, William, 73, 87
Macbeth, 73
Siefken, Hinrich, 127, 128, 150n19, 155, 156
Simon, Gerd, 36n10, 64, 65, 67n19
Simon, Heinrich, 190
Simplizissimus, 87
Slogan, 4, 5, 17, 20, 82, 105, 134, 194, 241, 263, 296
Smith, David Gordon, 277, 278, 283
Social Democratic Party (SPD), 158, 258, 259, 272, 279
Spengler, Oswald *Der Untergang des Abendlandes*, 26
'Spiegel Affair', 257
'Sprachlos'/'Sprachlosigkeit', 11, 45, 48, 76, 85, 89, 91, 139, 160, 162, 188, 189, 192, 193, 195, 198, 205–207, 220, 293
Sprachpflegeamt, 57
'Sprachregelungen', 46, 56, 57, 136, 192, 194, 268
'Sprichwort', 203–206
Stein, Ernst, 76
Steiner, George, 266
Stephenson, Jill, 52, 182n3
Sternberger, Dolf, 32–35, 39n38, 39n46, 66n7, 81, 84, 96, 109n8, 115, 151n33, 160, 161, 163, 164, 170, 171, 173–175, 182, 182n7, 188–191, 193, 195–197, 199, 200, 203–205, 207–209, 211, 213, 215–217, 219, 221, 222, 222n6, 223n9, 223n12, 227, 231–233, 235, 237, 240–242, 244, 247, 254, 256, 261–264, 266, 267, 269, 277, 280, 281, 284n3, 293, 294
"Asyl der Wahrheit", 219
"Aus dem Wörterbuch des Unmenschen", 150n11, 227, 231, 234, 240–247, 260–270, 276, 277, 294
"Blick der Liebenden", 66n7, 151n33, 201, 204, 205, 303–304
"Brot kosten Geld", 196
"Das Universalverbum", 211
Der verstandene Tod, 174
"Die neue 'deutsche Normalschrift", 214
"Ein guter Ausdruck", 199, 201
"Ein merkwürdiges Jubiläum", 195, 301–302
"Figuren der Fabel", 174, 191
"Hand-Schrift", 214
"Menschen als Material", 197, 208, 247, 306–307
Panorama oder Ansichten vom 19. Jahrhundert, 174
"Tempel der Kunst", 199
"Über die Nachahmung", 215
"Vademecum zum Gebrauch von Sprichwörtern", 203
"Verschriebene Schreiber", 211
"Wörterbuch der Regierung von Papen in Auszügen", 32
"Zwischen A und B", 200, 204
Sternheim, Carl, 142
Sternheim, Thea, 114, 122, 142–148, 151n29
'Stigmawort', 5, 248n1
Stimmen der Zeit, 165
Stöber, Rudolf, 199
Stone, Shepard, 231
Storfer, Adolf, 165, 172, 173, 176, 183n10, 214

Im Dickicht der Sprache, 165, 172
Wörter und ihre Schicksale, 165
Storz, Gerhard, 150n8, 160, 164, 171–173, 175–177, 182, 183n9, 183n10, 189, 206–208, 211, 213, 214, 222, 223n10, 227, 235, 240–242, 254, 256, 266, 284n3
"Der 'Angeber'", 206, 207, 308–309
"Der Eifer für die Sprache", 214
"Gedankenbahnen in der Sprache", 211
Laienbrevier über den Umgang mit der Sprache, 175–177
"Unbegrenzte Fähigkeiten?", 211, 213
"'volkhaft'/'volklich'/'völkisch'", 207
Stötzel, Georg, 38n31, 229, 233, 248n1, 248n2, 255–260, 268, 270, 271, 274, 276, 277, 294, 296
Strauss, Franz Josef, 257, 270
Strauss, Leo, 161
Streicher, Julius, 17
Structuralism (linguistic), 264, 267
Stuttgart Declaration of Guilt, 228
Süddeutsche Zeitung, 234
Suhr, Otto, 190
Süskind, Wilhelm E., 160, 164, 165, 173, 177–182, 189, 222, 227, 233–235, 240–242, 247, 248n8, 254, 256, 261, 263, 266, 284n3
Vom ABC zum Sprachkunstwerk, 177–181
Swastika comparisons, 82, 127, 145, 146, 169
Swift, Jonathan, 92

T
'T4, Aktion', 151n28
Tacitus, 15
'Tagesparolen', 53, 55, 192
Ten Holder, Clemens, 164
Teubert, Wolfgang, 4, 39n39, 297
Thatcher, Margaret, 274
Theresienstadt, 126, 263
Tillich, Paul, 174
Timms, Edward, 76, 82, 109n10, 122, 136, 139, 141
Toepser-Ziegert, Gabriele, 53, 55, 66n10, 66n11, 66n12, 66n13, 191, 194
Tomko, Helena, 127, 170
'Toothbrush fallacy', 6
Torberg, Friedrich, 183n11
'Totalitarianism', 46, 126
Townson, Michael, 1, 150n10
Treitschke, Heinrich von, 17
Trier, Jost, 64
Trivialization, 257, 259, 280
Tucholsky, Kurt, 32, 33, 39n36, 39n45, 151n33, 248n9

U
Ulbricht, Walter, 259
Ullrich, Volker, 136
Unruh, Walter von, 134
'Unwort', 209, 273

V
van den Bruck, Arthur Moeller, 26, 38n30, 38n31
'Verdeckte Schreibweise', 160, 161, 177
Verein Deutsche Sprache, 278, 285n10

Vergil (Publius Vergilius Maro), 127
Vermes, Timur, 272
Er ist wieder da, 273
Versailles, Treaty of, 14, 26, 58
'Vexierwort', 39n39
Vico, Giambattista, 194
'Volapuk', 217
Völkischer Beobachter, 60, 67n16, 134, 145
Volkov, Shulamit, 18
Voltaire (François-Marie Arouet), 92, 95
von Fallersleben, August, 15, 276
Vossiche Zeitung, 76

W

Wagenknecht, Christian, 76
Wagner, Richard, 17, 18, 22, 23, 86, 129, 170
Walser, Martin, 272, 274
Wannsee conference, 16
Warsaw Ghetto, 72, 132, 231, 254
'Weasel word', 32
Weber, Alfred, 231, 241
Weigel, Helene, 89, 157
Weininger, Otto, 22
Weinrich, Harald, 24
Weisgerber, Leo, 64, 65, 120, 121, 150n8, 208, 260
Die volkhaften Kräfte der Muttersprache, 120
Muttersprache und Geistesbildung, 120
Weiss, Bernhard, 32, 38–39n35
Weiszäcker, Richard von, 254
Weizsäcker, Viktor von, 222n6
Wells, C.J., 4, 49
Wengeler, Martin, 3, 4, 256, 260, 270, 292, 296
'White Rose' group, 127, 156
Wiechert, Ernst, 164
Wilamowitz-Möllendorf, Ulrich von, 171
"Nationale Kultur", 171
Wilhelm II, Kaiser, 19
Williams, Raymond, 4, 38n28, 296
Wimmer, Rainer, 268, 296
Wirth, Joseph, 32

Z

Zentrum Party, 66n6
Zweig, Stefan, 98

Printed by Printforce, the Netherlands